CONTEMPORARY CANADIAN ISSUES

Contemporary Canadian Issues is a partnership between the Bill Graham Centre for Contemporary International History and Dundurn Press to bring together the latest scholarship, from inside and outside academe, on current issues of concern to an informed Canadian general readership. General Editors for the series are John English and Jack Cunningham.

CONTEMPORARY CANADIAN ISSUES

Australia and Canada in Afghanistan

Australia, Canada, and Iraq

BREAKING THE ICE

To Ted,

who encouraged me to return to my law of the sea roots, with many thanks for all your support!

Elizabeth

BREAKING THE ICE

Canada, Sovereignty, and the
Arctic Extended Continental Shelf

ELIZABETH RIDDELL-DIXON

Foreword by John English

bill graham centre | CONTEMPORARY INTERNATIONAL HISTORY

DUNDURN
A J. PATRICK BOYER BOOK
TORONTO

Cover image: CCGS *Louis S. St-Laurent* and USCGC *Healy*. Credit: Jon Biggar, Canadian Hydrographic Services, Fisheries and Oceans Canada.
Printer: Webcom

Library and Archives Canada Cataloguing in Publication

Riddell-Dixon, Elizabeth, 1954-, author
    Breaking the ice : Canada, sovereignty, and the Arctic extended continental shelf / Elizabeth Riddell-Dixon.

(Contemporary Canadian issues)
Includes bibliographical references and index.
Issued in print and electronic formats.

ISBN 978-1-4597-3897-3 (softcover).--ISBN 978-1-4597-3898-0 (PDF).--ISBN 978-1-4597-3899-7 (EPUB)

1. Continental shelf--Arctic regions. 2. Continental shelf--Government policy--Canada. 3. Arctic regions--International status. 4. Canada--Boundaries--Arctic regions. 5. Arctic regions--Boundaries--Canada. 6. Canada--Foreign relations--21st century. I. Title. II. Series: Contemporary Canadian issues

FC191.R53 2017   971.9   C2016-908139-7
                                                   C2016-908140-0

1 2 3 4 5   21   20   19   18   17

Conseil des Arts du Canada   Canada Council for the Arts   Canada

ONTARIO ARTS COUNCIL
CONSEIL DES ARTS DE L'ONTARIO
an Ontario government agency
un organisme du gouvernement de l'Ontario

We acknowledge the support of the **Canada Council for the Arts** and the **Ontario Arts Council** for our publishing program. We also acknowledge the financial support of the **Government of Ontario**, through the **Ontario Book Publishing Tax Credit** and the **Ontario Media Development Corporation**, and the **Government of Canada**.

— *J. Kirk Howard, President*

The publisher is not responsible for websites or their content unless they are owned by the publisher.

Printed and bound in Canada.

VISIT US AT

 dundurn.com | @dundurnpress | dundurnpress |  dundurnpress

Dundurn
3 Church Street, Suite 500
Toronto, Ontario, Canada
M5E 1M2

For Thomas

TABLE OF CONTENTS

List of Diagrams

List of Maps

List of Acronyms and Terms

Area, the	the seabed and its subsoil beyond national jurisdiction
ARTA	Alpha Ridge Test of Appurtenance
AUV	autonomous underwater vehicle
CCGS	Canadian Coast Guard Ship
CCS	Convention on the Continental Shelf
Commission, the	Commission on the Limits of the Continental Shelf
CTD	conductivity, temperature, and depth profiler
ECS	extended continental shelf
GPS	Global Positioning System
LOMROG	Lomonosov Ridge off Greenland
LORITA	Lomonosov Ridge Test of Appurtenance
UNCLOS	United Nations Convention on the Law of the Sea
USCGC	U.S. Coast Guard Cutter

FOREWORD

Breaking the Ice shatters many myths about Canada's stewardship of its vast Arctic lands while celebrating the extraordinary courage and competence of many of its Arctic scientists and diplomats. Elizabeth Riddell-Dixon has written a book of enduring significance for Arctic scholars and scientists, and of considerable importance for students of Canadian international policy. Based on extensive research and interviews, *Breaking the Ice* tells the remarkable story of how Canada responded to the challenge of establishing its Arctic extended continental shelf, a claim that existed because of the United Nations Convention on the Law of the Sea (UNCLOS), whose drafting owed much to the work of Canadian diplomats in the 1970s and early 1980s. *Breaking the Ice* reveals many actions and accomplishments of which Canadians can be proud, but it also exposes expedient chauvinism and political decisions that are embarrassing, if not irresponsible.

Riddell-Dixon vividly describes the work of the Canadian scientists who had the responsibility of discovering where the Canadian claim existed under the rules set out in UNCLOS. Her earlier scholarship, along with that of others, had illuminated the exhausting negotiations of UNCLOS and had pointed out how UNCLOS had established the international legal framework for the Arctic coastal states (the United States, Russia, Canada, Norway, and Denmark, including Greenland). UNCLOS provided a method by which those states could establish their boundaries in an area where charts were few and scientific work was difficult. UNCLOS provided for an extension beyond two hundred nautical miles provided that the Arctic coastal state could establish that the surface below the Arctic sea was in geological terms an extension of its land territory. The concept is complex and Riddell-Dixon provides the detail necessary to understand the foundation of national claims.

The heart of the book is the description of the work of Canadian scientists in tremendously challenging Arctic circumstances. The Canadian Arctic presented the greatest difficulties for the scientists because its thick multiyear ice made work much more demanding than the other principal coastal states faced in establishing their claims in the Arctic Ocean. Riddell-Dixon draws a fascinating portrait of the scientists' work on and below the Arctic ice and gives credits to the talented individuals who gave leadership to the team that accumulated the scientific facts that became the core for the Canadian case. She describes how the Canadians decided to work cooperatively with the Danes and the Americans because their resources were inadequate to carry out the task they faced on their own. Even while the Danes and Canadians quarrelled about who owned Hans Island and the Russians and Canadians bickered about international politics, the scientists quietly accomplished remarkable work together. As Riddell-Dixon illustrates, the Arctic has been marked by astonishing cooperation among the Arctic nations, particularly through the scientific work of the Arctic Council as well as the joint efforts in the delineation of the extended continental shelf.

The Canadian scientists, however, often lacked the cooperation and support of their own government. After a burst of scientific work in the 1970s and 1980s, government support for scientific work and Arctic development fell off drastically after 1989, when the Cold War ended. Conservative and Liberal governments failed to build the ships or provide the aircraft that were essential for research. The CCGS *Louis S. St-Laurent*, Canada's aging but most powerful icebreaker, was not replaced, despite many promises, and Canadian equipment was inadequate for the tasks that the scientists were asked to undertake. The government did develop an autonomous underwater vehicle that assisted the scientific work. It was used in the search for the Sir John Franklin's ships, an enterprise that would far more likely make the front pages than the earnest, dangerous, and often confidential work of the scientists. Riddell-Dixon's admiration for the scientists and her fascination with their work animates many pages of this book. She even describes the "pee pole" and the enormous difficulties in urinating and defecating when it is minus 40°C. And there was always danger in the shifting ice of the Canadian Arctic, and death was narrowly escaped in a few instances.

But the worst shifting went on in Ottawa. Riddell-Dixon excoriates the 2013 decision of Prime Minister Stephen Harper to tell the scientists to go back to their desks and to the Arctic to make sure their scientific analysis of Canada's claim was altered to include the North Pole. Santa Claus must be Canadian even if the scientists and legal experts said he was not. In a raucous response worthy of Don Cherry, many Canadian nationalists praised the decision to stake the claim to the North Pole, but the scientists who had courted Arctic dangers and the diplomats who had negotiated the cooperative approach with the other Arctic states quietly deplored what had happened. The Danes were more direct, and their anger was reflected in their claim, which went far beyond what had been expected. Riddell-Dixon points out that their claim appears to be much stronger and that our nationalist eruption has resulted in the weakening of the excellent cooperation that had marked the Arctic scientific work in the past. She points out that some of the key scientists have retired and the chief scientist on four UNCLOS missions has become a professor at the University of New Hampshire where he is working on the American claim. And our claim itself is more likely to be challenged when it is finally submitted, both because it will include the controversial North Pole and because making a submission after our Danish and Russian neighbours makes the whole process more complicated. Scientific triumph was undermined by partisan ineptitude.

Breaking the Ice deserves the attention of all serious students of Canadian politics and science. The book explains what can be achieved when science and constructive diplomacy coincide and what can be lost when callous political calculation destroys those achievements.

— John English, Director,
Bill Graham Centre for Contemporary International History

PREFACE

This book's title, *Breaking the Ice*, evokes images of icebreakers carving through thick Arctic ice, as depicted on the cover, and of scientific teams drilling through metres of ice to lower their research equipment into frigid waters. It also has symbolic significance: conjuring mental images of telling a story previously untold that needs to be revealed.

In 2007 I returned to my law of the sea roots in response to large numbers of alarmist headlines in the media and in some academic works warning that Arctic countries were engaged in a highly competitive scramble to stake claims for extensions to their continental shelves beyond two hundred nautical miles from shore, and that Canada was lagging behind in this race.[1] Canada and the international seabed (i.e., the area beyond coastal state jurisdiction) was the subject of my Ph.D. thesis, and the majority of my publications in the 1980s through to the mid-1990s examined Canadian foreign policy and international and multilateral law of the sea negotiations.

In 1980 I attended the United Nations Third Conference on the Law of the Sea, where I observed the negotiations and interviewed numerous Canadian and U.N. officials and foreign diplomats. The conference produced the U.N. Convention on the Law of the Sea, which outlines the rules and regulations to govern the world's oceans, including those governing the extended continental shelf regime. From Don Crosby, deputy head of the Canadian delegation and Canada's lead negotiator on continental shelf issues, I first learned of the importance of the Convention's continental shelf provisions for Canada.

Following the conference, my research continued to be largely focused on law of the sea issues, particularly the subsequent eleven years of international and multilateral negotiations to resolve the issues left outstanding at the end of the conference. In 1989 I attended the Preparatory Commission on the International Seabed Authority and International Tribunal for the Law of the Sea in Kingston, Jamaica. The Commission was responsible for translating the terms of the Convention into concrete rules, regulations, and procedures during the period between the signing of the Convention and its entry into force. There again I observed the negotiations and interviewed Canadian and foreign delegates and U.N. officials. Once the Law of the Sea Convention came into force in 1994, my focus shifted from law of the sea issues to the international human rights regime, in general, and women's rights, in particular. Law of the sea issues again came to the fore in 2007, although this time the focus was on the delineation of Canada's Arctic extended continental shelf.

My initial interest was in the political and legal aspects of the delineation process; however, it soon broadened to include a fascination with the science as well. From my first meeting with them at the Bedford Institute of Oceanography in Halifax, Nova Scotia, and in many subsequent conversations, Jacob Verhoef, then director of the Geological Survey of Canada (Department of Natural Resources) and Dick MacDougall, then director of the Law of the Sea Project for the Canadian Hydrographic Service (Department of Fisheries and Oceans), shared their expertise, experiences and stories from the field. They outlined the objectives of the survey missions, described the range of formidable challenges encountered, explained their strategies for overcoming them, and spoke of lessons learned. Although I had no background in the physical sciences, their enthusiasm for the project was contagious. For the many times they discussed the Arctic Extended Continental Shelf Program with me and read and commented on drafts of my articles, my heartfelt thanks! Thanks also go to Stephen Forbes, who subsequently served as chief hydrographer after Dick's retirement, and to Allison Saunders and Louis Simard, then deputy director and director, respectively, of the Continental Shelf Division in the Department of Foreign Affairs, Trade and Development, for their generous assistance with my research for earlier publications on the Arctic extended continental shelf.

Three factors prompted me to move beyond writing journal articles and chapters on the Arctic extended continental shelf to authoring this book. First, the process allowed me to draw together the findings of my previous law of the sea writings and to delve more deeply into various aspects of Canada's Arctic extended continental shelf. Second, learning about the science has been an exciting voyage of discovery, and I wanted to tell other non-scientists about the amazing, ground-breaking research that our scientists have conducted in the Arctic under extremely challenging conditions. Political science and international law journals focus on political and legal analysis but offer little opportunity to expand on the scientific. Third, former prime minister Stephen Harper's implicit criticism of the Canadian scientists and legal experts who worked so hard to prepare Canada's Arctic submission for the Commission on the Limits of the Continental Shelf by the December 2013 deadline was the final catalyst. They were publicly humiliated without being able to tell their side of the story. Their work needs to be celebrated — not castigated! The quality and quantity of data collected and analyzed are in themselves major achievements. The fact that much of this work was done in close collaboration with Canada's Arctic neighbours makes this case a good news story in the realm of Canadian foreign policy.

As part of the research for this book, I again travelled to the Bedford Institute of Oceanography. In May 2015 I spent time there interviewing scientists and technicians involved with the mapping of Canada's Arctic extended continental shelf. A huge debt of gratitude is due to David Mosher, former manager of the UNCLOS Program (Natural Resources Canada), who has helped in numerous ways to bring this project to fruition. He devoted many hours to explaining the science involved in delineating Canada's Arctic extended continental shelf, and to reading and commenting on my three science chapters.

He kindly and most efficiently arranged an amazing — if somewhat daunting — schedule of interviews prior to my arrival at the Bedford Institute: fourteen interviews in two and a half days! Not only did David ensure that I spoke with key people involved in a range of activities related to the Arctic surveys, thereby maximizing the use of my time at the Bedford Institute, but he also brought me a delicious, homemade lobster sandwich for lunch when the interview schedule did not permit a trip to the cafeteria. While I was in Halifax, he took me on a personalized tour of CCGS *Louis S. St-Laurent* — Canada's largest icebreaker — explaining the relevance of the various rooms and equipment needed for the Arctic surveys. He also escorted me through the workshop where the autonomous underwater vehicle used for some of the surveying was being serviced, thereby allowing me to see the equipment first-hand.

While it took months to transcribe all the tapes of the interviews conducted at the Bedford Institute, they contained a gold mine of information. As a result of that trip, what was to be one chapter on the science expanded into three. In fall 2015 I made two trips to the Canada Centre for Inland Waters in Burlington, Ontario, to meet with hydrographers involved with the Arctic extended continental shelf surveys. I am most grateful to all those who gave so generously of their time to share their experiences and insights with me.

Surveying the Arctic continental shelf beyond two hundred nautical miles from shore is hard for the layperson to imagine; hence, the importance of photographs, maps, and diagrams. While individual credits are included with the images in the book, particular thanks are due to Tim Janzen, David Mosher, Patrick Potter, John Shimeld, and Kai Böggild, who shared photographs from their personal collections with me and, in cases where a photograph had been taken by someone else, helped secure permission to include it in this book. James McFarlane, executive vice-president of International Submarine Engineering, was helpful in providing photographs and diagrams of the autonomous underwater vehicle that his company built for the Arctic surveys. A big "thank you" goes to David Mosher, who produced wonderful maps specifically for this publication.

Thanks go to the staff at Dundurn Press, and particularly to my considerate managing editor, Kathryn Lane, for efficiently overseeing and coordinating the production of the book.

Andrew Chater provided valuable research assistance, responding promptly and effectively to requests for information. When answers were not readily available, Andy persevered until they were found. Thanks are also due to Christian Marcussen, senior advisor at the Geological Survey of Denmark and Greenland, for directing me to illuminating resource materials.

I am grateful to colleagues, friends, and family for their support throughout this project. Thanks go to Ted McDorman, an expert in international law, who encouraged me to return to law of the sea research, for his legal expertise, and for his helpful comments on my articles published in *Ocean Development and International Law*. Special thanks go to my friend Ken Ozmon for his generous hospitality during my research trips to Halifax. Not only did he provide delicious meals and gracious accommodation, but he also chauffeured me to and from the Bedford Institute and clipped relevant articles from the local paper. I also wish to thank John English, director of the Bill Graham Centre for Contemporary International History, for his support of this project and for all his mentoring throughout my career. For your ongoing wise counsel and generous assistance, I thank you. Jack Cunningham provided prompt, helpful advice on the publishing process. I am deeply indebted to Martha Grantham for her many contributions to this project, including carefully proofreading chapters, helping to select photographs and diagrams for inclusion, and compiling files for each category of image, and for all the words of encouragement, hugs, and delicious cups of tea that sustained me throughout the process.

To family and friends — most especially Nancy Ruth, Thomas Dixon-McDougall, Gretta Riddell-Dixon, Murray Dixon, Marty and Penny Westmacott, Donna Burton, Penny Brown, and Maruja Jackman — who had the good grace to ask about the project on an ongoing basis, who listened attentively to my progress, and who offered invaluable encouragement and enthusiastic support of my work: my most heartfelt thanks! The book is dedicated to my son, Thomas, a medical geneticist with a profound love of science, in grateful appreciation of all he does to enrich my life.

PROLOGUE

The Arctic has become a hot topic in the media. There are some good news stories, such as the proposal to create the Lancaster Sound National Marine Conservation Area, the discovery of Franklin's ships, and the contributions of the Canadian Rangers to local Arctic communities and Canadian sovereignty. Nonetheless, most Arctic news stories warn of impending doom: increased militarization and potential conflicts among states; competition for natural resources; coastlines eroding as the ice no longer buffers the shore from wave action; the melting of ice roads vital to supplying many northern communities; ships and tankers running aground; melting permafrost causing Arctic airstrips to heave, destabilizing the structural underpinnings of buildings and releasing toxins from previously frozen waste retention ponds into the ground water; polar bears starving; beluga whales under siege as predatory cousins — the orcas — access water previously blocked by ice; and massive cruise ships transiting through a poorly charted and highly fragile environment, thereby evoking fears of humanitarian and ecological disasters.

In contrast to the fearmongering so often reflected in the media, the collaboration among Arctic coastal states in the delineation of their respective extended continental shelves stands out as a particularly good news story. Of course, there are other examples of effective cooperation. In fact, the Arctic has been a forum for considerable cooperation. Over its twenty-year history, the Arctic Council has exemplified constructive collaboration among Arctic countries, Indigenous groups, non-Arctic states, international organizations, and non-governmental organizations to address pressing problems in the region. The Arctic Council is the principal multilateral organization devoted to facilitating cooperation on Arctic issues, especially in the areas of environmental protection and sustainable development, and the only such body in which the participation of Indigenous peoples is enshrined. The Arctic Council has produced many valuable studies, particularly in the areas of environmental protection and sustainable development. Furthermore, several legally binding agreements have been developed to foster multilateral cooperation and to prescribe regulations to safeguard the Arctic and its inhabitants. They include the Agreement on Cooperation and Aeronautical and Maritime Search and Rescue in the Arctic, and the Agreement on Cooperation on Marine Oil Pollution Preparedness and Response in the Arctic. The International Maritime Organization's International Code for Ships Operating in Polar Waters came into force on January 1, 2017.

The Arctic is undergoing fundamental changes as a result of global warming, higher levels of resource exploration and development, and increased interest on the parts of political leaders at the sub-national, national, and international levels. For Canada the two Arctic law of the sea issues generating the greatest publicity are the status of the Northwest Passage and the limits of the extended continental shelf. These issues are frequently conflated; they are in fact quite separate.

The Northwest Passage controversy is centred on the issue of its legal status and the important question: Who can access the Northwest Passage under what conditions? Canada claims that the Northwest Passage comprises its internal waters, while the United States argues that it is an international strait. Under international law, a coastal state has full sovereignty over its internal waters; hence, it has the right to determine who may enter them and under what conditions. The right of transit prevails in international straits. The legal status of the Northwest Passage does not affect Canada's sovereign rights over the living and non-living resources within two hundred nautical miles from shore.

In contrast, the issues pertaining to the extended continental shelf are about control of oil and gas and mineral resources, and not about rights of transit. The water column above the extended continental shelf is designated "high seas," which means that all nations enjoy the freedom of navigation and overflight, as well as the right to fish, conduct scientific research, and lay submarine cables and pipelines in the zone. If the coastal state can demonstrate the continental shelf extends beyond two hundred nautical miles as a natural prolongation of its land territory, it can establish a continental shelf extension on which it has the rights to control the exploration and exploitation of non-living resources.

The delineation of Canada's Arctic extended continental shelf is clearly related to many of the issues mentioned above. Global warming has enhanced access to the Arctic, making it possible for icebreakers to survey previously inaccessible areas. It has increased the prevalence of ice fog as well, which makes flying more hazardous and spot-testing far more difficult. Greater access to Arctic waters encourages interest in offshore oil, gas, and mineral development, as the prospects for exploration and exploitation are more promising. At the same time, concern for the rights and well-being of Indigenous peoples is featuring more prominently in the minds of politicians and the Canadian public.

While the long-term implications — for Arctic inhabitants, in general, and Indigenous people, in particular — of the establishment of an extended continental shelf regime remain to be determined, the issue needs to be addressed. All these developments increase the political and economic salience of the Arctic and are cause for a host of governance concerns at the international, multilateral, national, and sub-national levels. Canada's Arctic extended continental shelf is an issue whose time has come and whose importance will only increase in coming decades.

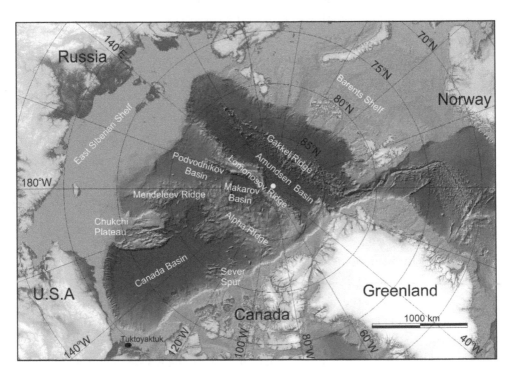

The Arctic Ocean

Canada's Extended Continental Shelf Program's surveys spanned the area from the
Canada Basin through to the Amundsen Basin.

David Mosher, Natural Resources Canada. Map based on data drawn from M. Jakobsson et al., "The
International Bathymetric Chart of the Arctic Ocean (IBCAO)," version 3.0, *Geophysical Research Letters* 39
(2012): doi:10.1029/2012GL052219.

1

INTRODUCTION

For Canada, establishing sovereignty over its continental shelf resources has been a law of the sea priority since the Second World War.[1] Canada has the world's second-largest continental shelf (2,545,259 kilometres), surpassed only by that of the Russian Federation (4,099,812 kilometres),[2] and its seabed is known to contain large quantities of oil, gas, and minerals; hence, there is a strong economic imperative to establish coastal state jurisdiction. The importance accorded to the continental shelf by successive Canadian governments is reflected in speeches, statements, and press releases. For example, in 1946 Thomas Reid, Liberal member of Parliament and subsequently parliamentary assistant to the minister of fisheries, described the 1945 U.S. claim to the continental shelf off its coasts as "one of the most important proclamations made by President Truman."[3] When the First Conference on the Law of the Sea adopted the Convention on the Continental Shelf in 1958, Alvin Hamilton, then minister of northern affairs, declared it to have been "a most significant milestone" — even though questions pertaining to territorial and fishing zones remained unresolved — and the Convention to be of "far-reaching importance to Canada."[4] In 2010, then minister of foreign affairs Lawrence Cannon referred to Canada's submission to the Commission on the Limits of the Continental Shelf as "a priority for our government."[5] Canada assumed the chair of the Arctic Council in May 2013, with a commitment to making resource development a top priority.[6]

Historically, instead of taking unilateral actions, as many coastal states have, Canada has preferred multilateral channels. At the U.N.'s First and again at the Second Conference on the Law of the Sea (1958 and 1960, respectively), the Seabed Committee, and the Third Conference on the Law of the Sea (1973–1982), which produced the U.N. Convention on the Law of the Sea (UNCLOS), Canadian officials were strong advocates for the rights of coastal states and played major roles in defining the rules and regulations governing the continental shelf in a series of important negotiating forums beginning in the late 1950s and continuing into the 1980s. Canada continues to be an active participant in meetings of the states parties to UNCLOS. The rules and regulations governing the world's oceans, which are enshrined in UNCLOS,[7] are highly advantageous to coastal states like Canada. Thus, Canada has incorporated these rights into its own legislation, ratified the Convention, spent over a decade mapping the seabed of its continental shelves and analyzing the resulting data and, in December 2013, filed a submission with the Commission pertaining to its Atlantic extended continental shelf. Canada plans to make a second submission, this time pertaining to its Arctic extended continental shelf.

This book focuses on a new frontier: the delineation of Canada's Arctic extended continental shelf. As historian Shelagh Grant points out, there are several definitions of the Canadian Arctic, including the lands and waters north of one of the following: the tree line, the Arctic Circle, or where the July mean temperature is 10°C.[8] She makes a strong case for choosing the first; however, the area two hundred nautical miles beyond Canada's shoreline meets the criteria for all three definitions. The term *extended continental shelf (ECS)* refers to the area beyond a coastal state's exclusive economic zone, beginning two hundred nautical miles from the straight baselines from which the territorial sea is measured and extending a distance determined by criteria specified in Article 76 of UNCLOS. While the continental margin off Canada's West Coast is narrow, the country has extensive margins off its East Coast and in the Arctic. Canadian scientists estimate that the country's ECS in the Arctic will be three quarters of a million square kilometres.[9]

The book traces the evolution of the ECS regime, discusses Canada's participation in this process, and outlines the key provisions of the regime. It identifies the objectives of the survey missions to map Canada's Arctic ECS, describes the range of formidable challenges encountered, explains the strategies used to overcome them, and highlights the lessons learned. It argues that the process of delineating the ECSs in the Arctic is being conducted in an orderly fashion; there is an international legal regime in place and its rules are being observed by all Arctic coastal states. Furthermore, the process has been characterized by high levels of cooperation and collaboration among federal public servants and, at least prior to December 2013, with our Arctic neighbours as well. The book examines the political, legal, and scientific aspects of Canada's efforts to delineate its Arctic ECS, beginning in the late 1940s and continuing to the autumn of 2016 when the final survey to map Canada's Arctic ECS was completed. It will take several years to analyze the data, interpret them in terms of the provisions outlined in UNCLOS, and draft Canada's submission regarding its Arctic ECS, which the government expects to present to the Commission on the Limits of the Continental Shelf (hereafter the Commission) in 2018.[10] At least a decade will elapse before the Commission has reviewed the submission and made its recommendations. If Canada accepts the recommendations, it will then establish its ECS on the basis of the Commission's findings. Any overlaps between its ECS and those of its neighbours will need to be resolved. So the complex process of establishing Canada's Arctic ECS will be with us for decades to come.

DEFINITION OF TERMS

It is important to note that scientists and lawyers define the continental shelf quite differently. In scientific terms, the continental shelf makes up one part of the continental margin. The latter is a geological formation that includes the continental shelf, continental slope, and continental rise, as depicted in the diagram on the next page.

As Ted McDorman explains,

The continental margin is the physical extension of the landmass of the coastal State with the margin composed of the continental shelf (a platform at relatively shallow depths), the continental slope (the break of the platform towards the deep ocean floor) and the continental rise (the area beyond the slope which merges with the deep ocean floor).[11]

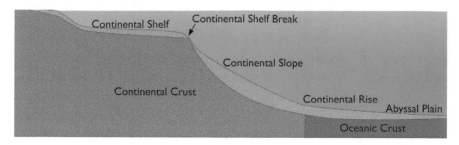

The Continental Margin

Thanks to Thomas Dixon-McDougall for converting my drawing into this electronic diagram.

Thus, in scientific terms, "the continental shelf is the relatively shallow seabed area (100–400 m depth) adjacent to the coast and landward of the continental slope."[12] In juridical (or legal) terms, the continental shelf is a submerged prolongation of a coastal state's land territory that can be narrower or wider than the continental margin or encompass all of the latter. The outer limit of a coastal state's ECS may not exceed the juridical continental shelf. The term *continental shelf* is used in this book in accordance with its juridical definition, while the term *continental margin* refers to the scientific shelf, slope, and rise. Beyond the continental margin lies the deep ocean floor.

The terms *delineation* and *delimitation* are used throughout the book. Delineation refers to the process of precisely defining the outer limits of a country's ECS, in accordance with the provisions set out in UNCLOS. Delimitation refers to the process of establishing a political boundary between the ECSs of two or more states.

In government circles, the delineation of the ECSs off Canada's Atlantic and Arctic coasts is referred to as Canada's ECS Program. In keeping with the focus in this book, the term refers here to the process of preparing Canada's Arctic submission for the Commission. For consistency, imperial measurements taken from articles, field reports, and interviews, except those cited in direct quotations, have been translated to metric equivalents.

A CAVEAT ABOUT RESOURCES

Media articles discussing the continental shelf extensions in the Arctic have frequently referred to the wealth to be derived from resource development. For example, it is frequently stated that the Arctic seabed may contain 25 percent of the world's undiscovered gas and oil reserves.[13] According to the U.S. Geological Survey's estimates, there are "approximately 90 billion barrels of oil, 1,669 trillion cubic feet of natural gas, and 44 billion barrels of natural gas liquids" yet to be discovered in the areas north of the Arctic Circle.[14] The Arctic deposits comprise some 22 percent of the world's undiscovered but technically recoverable hydrocarbon resources, and 84 percent are located offshore.[15] It must be recognized, however, that 95 percent of Arctic deposit resources are found within the exclusive economic zones of Arctic countries,[16] particularly Russia, rather than on the ECS. Furthermore, these oft-cited statistics[17] refer to potential wealth rather than current production.

Most Arctic resources are located on the mainland and within the exclusive economic zone. What resources do exist beyond two hundred nautical miles will be difficult and expensive to develop. Frozen methane (gas hydrates), for instance, can be found on Canada's Arctic ECS, but the technology to develop it is not likely to be available for several decades.[18] Even if all the necessary technology were available, exploring for offshore resources, extracting them, and transporting them to southern markets would be a logistical nightmare involving enormous monetary costs. Oil rigs are very expensive to build, let alone to transport to Arctic waters, and the drilling season lasts only three to four months in the summer. Highly specialized seismic and drilling technologies are required to operate in Arctic waters where icebergs abound, storms are frequent and violent, and powerful currents are prevalent. Operating a floating offshore rig costs between US$260,000 and US$513,000 per day.[19] When accidents occur, expenditures soar. After the tanker *Exxon Valdez* ran aground off Alaska in 1989, spilling 257,000 barrels of oil, Exxon was forced to pay US$2.5 billion for the cleanup.[20] In 2010 it took three months to stop the oil spill in the Gulf of Mexico, where in spite of "thousands of highly skilled workers, scores of specialized vessels and several nearby ports and staging areas, a gusher of unstoppable oil spewed nearly five million barrels of oil for 87 days until it was plugged in a multibillion-dollar effort."[21] Cleaning up the devastation caused by that massive spill continues to this day. An oil spill in Arctic waters would be more catastrophic because of the fragile Arctic ecosystem. It would also be much harder to address because of a myriad of problems: remoteness, ice-clogged channels, winter darkness, high waves that disperse oil and impede the recovery work by skimmers, and ice fog that prevents aircraft from spraying dispersants. Furthermore, oil trapped in or under the ice is less susceptible to bacterial degradation. Global warming causes glaciers to calve, sea ice to become more mobile, and weather to be less predictable and more extreme, all of which increase the risks of damage to rigs and shipping accidents. Since the 2010 Deepwater Horizon spill in the Gulf of Mexico, environmental safeguards have been strengthened for offshore operators, resulting in additional expenses related to emergency response and containment.

Oil and gas from Canada's Arctic ECS cannot compete with more accessible southerly sources, such as the Alberta oil sands and the shale gas deposits in the United States; hence, oil and gas companies have been scaling back on their investments. Between twenty and twenty-five wells were drilled by oil and gas companies in 2002–2003, whereas fewer than five were drilled in 2011–2012.[22] After spending US$7 billion on offshore exploration in the Beaufort and Chukchi Seas, Royal Dutch Shell announced in September 2015 that it would end exploration off Alaska's coast "for the foreseeable future" because the amounts of oil and gas found were inadequate, especially in light of the huge risks and the drop in petroleum prices.[23] In December 2014 Chevron Canada announced that its Arctic drilling plans were being placed on hold "indefinitely" because of "the level of economic uncertainty."[24]

The private sector's dwindling enthusiasm for Arctic exploration was reinforced on December 20, 2016, when President Obama and Prime Minister Trudeau issued a joint statement banning offshore oil and gas development in the Arctic. The president used an obscure provision in his country's 1953 Outer Continental Shelf Lands Act to implement a "permanent" ban on offshore oil and gas drilling in U.S. waters in the Chukchi and Beaufort seas. The prime minister declared a five-year moratorium on granting new licences in Arctic waters, which will be reviewed, considering climate and marine science, at the end of the period. It remains to be seen what will happen when Canada conducts its review and if President Obama's move is challenged in the U.S. courts.

In any case the costs of exploitation are expected to far outweigh the returns; hence, oil and gas exploitation on the Arctic ECS will not be economically viable in the foreseeable future. There are still many resources to develop on Canada's mainland, where the risks and logistical problems are less daunting; thus, there is not much interest in resource development on the islands of the Arctic Archipelago, let alone on the seabed within the exclusive economic zone, and even less interest in resource exploitation on the continental margin beyond two hundred nautical miles.

Nonetheless, land-based deposits are finite, and worldwide demand for oil and gas is expected to rise in the next twenty years. The International Energy Agency estimates that "global oil and gas demand could grow by more than 35% from 2010 to 2035."[25] The Canadian Polar Commission's report points out that "long-term demand for energy, metals and precious gems accompanied by shrinking global reserves will continue to gradually shift competitive advantage to the region's high cost deposits prompting future growth of the North's non-renewable resource sector."[26] Thus, there may come a day when technological innovation and worldwide demand will make such exploitation politically and economically desirable; but there is no immediate pressure for such development. Resources on the continental shelf extensions are not as plentiful, accessible, and economically viable as media coverage would lead us to believe.

INTERDEPARTMENTAL COOPERATION

The names of federal departments frequently change as governments come and go. As well, changes may be accompanied by alterations in the scope of a department's mandate. In the period covered by this book, for example, the department currently referred to as Global Affairs Canada has been called the Department of External Affairs; the Department of External Affairs and International Trade; the Department of Foreign Affairs and International Trade; and the Department of Foreign Affairs, Trade and Development. Natural Resources Canada was previously called the Department of Energy, Mines and Resources. The Department of Fisheries and Oceans was formerly known as the Department of Marine and Fisheries. Throughout the book, the name used is that applicable to the period being discussed.

The preparation of Canada's submission to the Commission delineating its Arctic ECS has been marked by interdepartmental cooperation and collaboration. Three federal departments are centrally involved in the preparation of Canada's submission: the Geological Survey of Canada in the Department of Natural Resources and the Canadian Hydrographic Service in the Department of Fisheries and Oceans, which together are responsible for conducting the scientific research and analysis essential for Canada's submission; and Global Affairs Canada, which writes the legal document. Together scientists and technicians from the first two departments comprise the scientific team for Canada's ECS Program. In light of the costs of obtaining the icebreakers, airplanes, and helicopters necessary for Arctic research, the two departments are doing most of the studies together. Their scientists and technical staff live together for six-week periods in ice camps and on icebreakers and, as discussed in chapter 4, they function extremely well as a team. Their research is symbiotic; hence, their close collaboration is essential in conducting the research and analysis needed to produce cohesive, comprehensive data sets and sound scientific explanations. The director of the UNCLOS Program is always a senior scientist with Natural Resources Canada. For most of Canada's Arctic ECS Program, the position was held by Jacob Verhoef, director of the Geological Survey of Canada. When he retired in 2014, David Mosher continued as manager of the UNCLOS Program. After Mosher left in August 2015 to take up a full professorship at the University of New Hampshire, Mary-Lynn Dickson, a scientist with the Geological Survey of Canada, was named director.

The third departmental member of the team is Global Affairs Canada, whose Continental Shelf Division in the Bureau of Legal Affairs, is coordinating the preparation, presentation, and ultimate defence of the submission. It is responsible for handling the legal aspects, monitoring developments salient to the submission including the actions of other states and developments at the United Nations, managing the negotiations with other countries on the outer limits of the continental shelf ahead of finalizing the submission, and conducting literature reviews so that Canadian officials will understand the knowledge base that will guide the Commission in its deliberations. Monitoring the practice of the Commission is vital to the ultimate success of Canada's submission and involves answering a host of questions. What questions do the commissioners ask? How are data and analysis presented? What trends or themes are emerging in the reviews?

What type of data are deemed necessary to substantiate a point? Answering such questions and analyzing the implications of the answers is rendered difficult both because the issues are diverse and complex and because practice is evolving, which means the authors of Canada's submission are constantly having to adjust to a moving target. The job of the scientists is to collect and analyze the data needed to make the maximum claim possible. It is the job of Global Affairs Canada to decide what the claim should be.

Most of the seismic team and some of the hydrographers working on Canada's Arctic ECS are based at the Bedford Institute of Oceanography in Halifax, Nova Scotia, which facilitates both formal and informal collaboration. For example, Jacob Verhoef and Richard MacDougall, former director, Law of the Sea Project, Canadian Hydrographic Service, Department of Fisheries and Oceans and the lead hydrographer for Canada's Arctic ECS, held formal meetings every Tuesday, but because they worked in the same institution, they conversed almost every day about the project.[27] They consulted with their counterparts in the Department of Foreign Affairs and International Trade by telephone two or three times a week.[28]

The governing structure of the project consists of a federal advisory committee, a steering committee, and a management board that reports to it. The federal advisory committee comprises director generals from a wider cross-section of departments to examine a broad range of law of the sea concerns, including fisheries policies, security, maritime transit, and the continental shelf. It was established to keep government officials in diverse departments both apprised of the activities of other departments and foreign countries and updated on the most recent scientific discoveries. The steering committee, which is responsible for overseeing the entire project, is composed of an assistant deputy minister from each of the three departments (Global Affairs, Fisheries and Oceans, and Natural Resources). Members meet three times a year to discuss issues related to the submission. The management board is responsible for the day-to-day delivery of the program, including the collection and analysis of the scientific data and the preparation of the databases, maps, and reports needed to support the Canadian submission. The board is chaired by the director of the UNCLOS Program and includes the lead hydrographer from Fisheries and Oceans and the legal expert responsible for the submission in Global Affairs. The assistant deputy ministers on the steering committee receive weekly updates prepared by the board's chair with input from the other two board members. As a result, the assistant deputy ministers are familiar with the entire picture and with key decisions.

In preparing the Arctic ECS submission, the three departments worked closely with their counterparts from several other federal departments. The icebreakers and crews used for the ECS surveys were under the jurisdiction of the Canadian Coast Guard. Environment and Climate Change Canada's weather station in Eureka and National Defence Canada's base in Alert (both in Nunavut) were used to stage several missions. The Polar Continental Shelf Program, technically under the auspices of Natural Resources, is not involved in the preparation of Canada's ECS submission. Nonetheless, its logistical support for the ECS missions proved invaluable. For example, well in advance of a survey, the lead scientists for Canada's Arctic ECS Program would request specific numbers of flying hours for the various types of aircraft needed, as well as the pilots and technicians to operate them, and Polar Continental Shelf Program staff would include the request in their budget for the coming year. The contracts were negotiated by the Polar Continental Shelf Program staff, which resulted in major time and energy savings for the senior scientists involved with Canada's ECS Program and facilitated economies of scale. The Polar Continental Shelf's facility in Resolute served as the base for setting up and maintaining the 2010 ice camps. Logistical support also came from Parks Canada. Defence Research and Development Canada of the Department of National Defence had experience using two new technologies used in the ECS surveys: icepicks (seismic instruments deployed from aircraft) and autonomous underwater vehicles to collect bathymetric information beneath the ice. Thus, their deployment in the Arctic involved collaboration between the Department of National Defence and the two departments responsible for mapping the Arctic seabed (Natural Resources, and Fisheries and Oceans). Ice experts from the Canadian Ice Service (a department within Environment and Climate Change Canada) provided invaluable assistance in navigating through the ice.

COOPERATION AMONG ARCTIC COASTAL STATES

Media articles frequently portray relations among Arctic countries in terms of conflict, a zero-sum game, and a race to stake claims, as exemplified by the following headlines: "Arctic Draws International Competition for Oil,"[29] "A New Cold War: Denmark Gets Aggressive, Stakes Huge Claim in Race for the Arctic,"[30] "Iceland Summit Aims to Avert Tensions as Race for Arctic Resources Heats up,"[31] "International Competition Over Arctic Resources Imminent,"[32] "Arctic Resources: The Fight for the Coldest Place on Earth Heats Up,"[33] "Canada Well Behind Russia in Race to Claim Arctic,"[34] "Canada-Russia Arctic War Up for Renewal; Both Countries Talking Aggressively in Battle for Sovereignty,"[35] "Cold Calling: Competition Heats Up for Arctic Resources,"[36] and "Resource Grab Risks Arctic Arms Race, Study Says."[37] Such titles imply a degree of lawlessness and conjure images of a wild frontier.

In contrast to such alarmist headlines, the process of delineating Arctic ECSs has overall been marked by exemplary bilateral and multilateral cooperation among Arctic countries. Collaboration makes good sense in light of the exorbitant costs. In 2007 Denmark and Canada engaged the escort services of the Russian nuclear icebreaker *50 Let Pobedy* (*50 Years of Victory*) at a cost of sixty thousand dollars a day.[38] The limited number of experts able to undertake the work and the logistical difficulties of Arctic surveys provide additional incentives for cooperation. Joint operations reduce the number of data collection missions, which, in turn, lessens the environmental impact of the testing. Working together, officials from cooperating countries can share information and learn from one another, which enhances the quality of the submissions. For example, Canada, the Russian Federation, and Denmark all need to know if the Lomonosov Ridge (underwater mountain range) is continental in origin. Is it an extension of Ellesmere Island? Is it a continuation of Greenland? Is it a prolongation of the Russian Federation's continental shelf? Each country's case will be stronger if they agree on the scientific data, and the Commission's task will be easier if there is consistency in the data submitted and agreement on them. Collaboration helps to legitimize the findings when they are presented to the Commission.

Canadian scientists and technical staff have spent over a decade conducting extensive geological and bathymetric surveys off Canada's East Coast and in the Arctic. While some of this work was done unilaterally, there was also a lot of bilateral collaboration. Canadian and Danish scientists conducted seven joint surveys (2006–2009) in which they collected and analyzed data pertaining to the area north of Greenland and Ellesmere Island. Using the Canadian Coast Guard icebreaker *Louis S. St-Laurent* and the U.S. Coast Guard

icebreaker *Healy*, Canadian and American scientists and technicians conducted surveys together in the Canada Basin and Arctic Ocean (2008–2011).
These collaborative missions are discussed in chapter 5. Such collaborations
resulted in numerous joint publications and joint presentations at scientific
conferences. As the commissioners review the submitted information in light
of accepted scientific knowledge, having the data and analysis accepted by the
international scientific community prior to a submission makes good sense.

In spring 2007 representatives from the departments of Foreign Affairs
and International Trade, Natural Resources, and Fisheries and Oceans met
with officials from the Russian Ministry of Natural Resources and discussed
the possibility of collaboration. In November of that year, Canadian, Danish,
and Russian officials met for three days in Saint Petersburg to discuss scientific and technical matters pertaining to the Arctic continental shelf. Russian
scientists shared some of the charts, maps, and data from their 2001 submission to the Commission.[39] When making a submission, a coastal state must
provide a summary, which includes charts and certain pertinent information, to the U.N. secretary-general, who then is required to make it available to the public. This information is, however, much more limited than
the extensive data, charts, and analysis contained in a state's full submission
to the Commission. Since most of the data, charts, and analyses contained
in a state's submission are confidential, the only way that other states may
discover the details is through consultations with the submitting state. The
sharing of data on the part of Russian scientists, for instance, exemplifies the
high degree of multilateral collaboration in Arctic research and the importance of these meetings. November 2007 also saw Canada and the Russian
Federation issue a joint statement on economic cooperation, which not only
reaffirmed their "commitment to international law, including the orderly and
legally-established process outlined within UNCLOS," but also recognized
"the need for cooperation and collaboration in mapping work in the Arctic
Ocean."[40] Cooperation has not been limited to the Arctic states. Canadian
officials have also benefited from consultations with Australia and New
Zealand, both of which presented substantial justifications for their conclusions, including the detailed criteria for determining the foot of the slope.

At the multilateral meetings in 2008, U.S. scientists were invited to participate as observers. In 2009 representatives of the Canadian, Danish, and
Russian foreign ministries also began to attend the meetings. Participation was
further widened in 2010 to include Norwegian officials; hence the meetings

involved scientists and diplomats from all five Arctic coastal countries. They served as venues in which to share scientific findings as well as opportunities for international legal experts to discuss other issues relevant to submission preparation. In addition to these annual meetings, officials conferred about their respective submissions in other venues, such as the workshop on Arctic margins that was convened in Fairbanks, Alaska, in 2011. While outside the scope of this book, it is worth noting that Canadian officials discussed the ECS in the North Atlantic with their Danish colleagues, as well as the ECS in the areas off Nova Scotia with their U.S. colleagues.

The commitment to peaceful cooperation is not only evident in meetings but has also been formalized. In the 2008 Ilulissat Declaration, Canada, Denmark, Norway, the Russian Federation, and the United States recalled the extensive legal framework that applies to the Arctic Ocean, pledged to strengthen their existing close cooperation in the delineation of their respective Arctic ECS, and committed themselves to the orderly settlement of any possible overlapping claims.[41] They further agreed that the existing international legal regime governing the Arctic Ocean was sufficient and hence there was "no need to develop new comprehensive international legal regime to govern the Arctic Ocean."[42] Seven years later, all eight Arctic countries reaffirmed their "commitment to maintain peace, stability and constructive cooperation in the Arctic" in the 2015 Iqaluit Declaration.[43]

The five Arctic coastal states — Canada, Denmark, Norway, the Russian Federation, and the United States, which is not even a party to UNCLOS — are defining or have defined their ECS in accordance with the norms enshrined in the Convention. Moreover, non-Arctic states, including China, France, Germany, India, Italy, Japan, the Netherlands, the Republic of Korea, Poland, Singapore, Spain, and the United Kingdom, have agreed to respect the sovereignty of Arctic countries, as a condition for being granted observer status at the Arctic Council meetings. This condition includes respecting coastal states' rights as specified in UNCLOS.

CHAPTER OUTLINE

Chapter 2, "The Extended Continental Shelf Regime," is divided into two main parts. The first provides an overview of key developments pertaining to the definition of coastal states' rights on the continental shelf that have occurred since the Second World War and Canada's objectives and role in this evolution. The second part outlines the main components of the legal regime governing the ECS.

Chapter 3, "Scientific Research and the Law of the Sea Convention," examines the various ways in which the bathymetric and seismic data needed for Canada's Arctic submission have been collected. While bathymetric and seismic surveys are the principal sources of data, complementary information is drawn from gravity and magnetic measurements; hence, they, too, are discussed. After exploring the research methodologies, the chapter provides a brief discussion of their relevance to UNCLOS.

Chapter 4, "Ice Camps and Icebreakers: The Human Experience," begins by outlining the generic challenges inherent in conducting Arctic maritime surveys. The importance of physical health and safety and mental health and teamwork are then highlighted. Thereafter attention focuses on the rigours first of setting up and maintaining an ice camp and then of life onboard an icebreaker. It concludes with team members from Canada's ECS Program sharing some of their perceptions of the awe and wonder of the Arctic.

Chapter 5, "The Arctic Extended Continental Shelf Surveys," provides an overview of Canada's scientific missions to survey the Arctic seabed beyond two hundred nautical miles. To put this work in context, it begins by noting the relationship between the surveys and Arctic scientific research done in other venues. Attention is then given to the requirement to do environmental assessments and to the meetings that were held to apprise Indigenous peoples of the ECS surveys. Thereafter a brief overview of each mission is presented. The overviews are not designed to be comprehensive nor do the various missions receive equal treatment. The purpose of the overviews is to provide a flavour of the missions and to trace their evolution — to give an idea of the number and diversity of the missions, the large number of research methodologies employed, the range of challenges faced, and the ingenuity and sheer hard work demonstrated in addressing them. The chapter concludes with a summary of the main scientific findings derived from the missions. It does not attempt to second-guess the contents of Canada's Arctic submission for several reasons. Most of the details pertaining to the scientific findings remain confidential and not in the public domain. Even if such information were in the public domain, I lack the scientific expertise needed to interpret it.

Chapter 6, "Canada's Submission and Other Outstanding Issues," begins by examining the implications of former prime minister Stephen Harper's December 2013 announcement, which stated that Canada's first submission would pertain only to its Atlantic ECS, rather than to its Atlantic and Arctic ECSs, as expected, and that Canadian scientists had been instructed to conduct research in the area of the North Pole so it could be included in Canada's Arctic submission. The chapter's second and third sections deal, respectively, with two outstanding issues that Canada must address: the establishment of the rules and regulations necessary to implement Article 82's obligations regarding revenue sharing for resource exploitation beyond two hundred nautical miles; and the delimitation of maritime boundaries in cases where Canada's Arctic ECS overlaps with those of its neighbours.

The findings of this study are drawn together in chapter 7, "Conclusion." They confirm key tenets found in much of the Canadian foreign policy literature: that multilateralism frequently is the preferred tool to achieve objectives; that the international environment sets the parameters within which Canadian policy-makers must function; and that domestic interests — particularly economic interests — are key determinants of specific foreign policy choices.

A METHODOLOGICAL NOTE

Research for the book was drawn from a variety of primary and secondary sources. The primary sources include government documents, informal newsletters from the field, U.N. documents, and private sector and non-governmental organizations' materials. In addition to the insights drawn from interviews conducted for my previous publications, eighteen individuals who participated in Canada's Arctic ECS Program were interviewed specifically for this book. The interviews were granted on the condition that I would not cite or attribute material to the interviewee without permission. Most of those interviewed agreed to be cited, but some of the information provided by interviewees was given on the basis of nonattribution. A list of most of those interviewed appears at the end of the book.

2

THE EXTENDED CONTINENTAL SHELF REGIME

Interest in the continental shelf can be traced back to the nineteenth century, when coastal states began to claim rights to mine the seabed beyond their three-mile territorial seas.[1] This practice prompted considerable debate over whether the seabed and subsoil of the high seas was *res communis* (owned by the whole community) or *res nullius* (ownerless and hence open to appropriation).[2] Although the League of Nations set up a committee of experts to consider law of the sea matters, it did not adopt legally binding rules and regulations pertaining to the continental shelf. Codification came only after the United Nations convened a law-making conference in 1958. We begin with a historical overview of the evolution of the regime that discusses key developments pertaining to the definition of coastal states' rights on the continental shelf that have occurred since the Second World War and to Canada's objectives and role in this evolution. Thereafter the main components of the legal regime governing the ECS are outlined.

HISTORICAL EVOLUTION OF THE REGIME

Evolution of the Continental Shelf Concept, 1945–1972

By the Second World War, the resource potential of the seabed and subsoil of the continental shelf was widely recognized.[3] Furthermore, technological advances were making exploitation of those resources possible. The first international agreement pertaining to coastal states' rights on the sea-bed beyond the territorial sea was the 1942 Treaty between Great Britain and Ireland and Venezuela Relating to the Submarine Areas of the Gulf of Paria, which dealt with the division of offshore oil fields between Trinidad and Venezuela.[4] In 1945 American president Harry Truman proclaimed "the natural resources of the subsoil and sea bed of the continental shelf beneath the high seas but contiguous to the coasts of the United States ... [to be] subject to its jurisdiction and control."[5] He went on to say that any over-lapping maritime boundaries resulting from this proclamation would be resolved bilaterally according to equitable principles. Previously jurisdiction had been understood in terms of two concepts: a narrow territorial sea of three nautical miles over which the coastal state had sovereignty and beyond which freedom of the high seas prevailed. Truman was the first to clearly assert the rights of coastal states to the resources of the continental shelf.[6] With his proclamation, the modern concept of the continental shelf was born.[7] The U.S. declaration was emulated by many coastal states, although their unilateral claims varied considerably. Latin American countries, for instance, began claiming various degrees of control over distances ranging from twelve to two hundred nautical miles from shore. Although Canada did not resort to such unilateralism, it became a strong and influential advocate of the rights of coastal states in the subsequent law of the sea negotiations.

The increasing number of unilateral claims highlighted the need to codify the law of the sea and prompted the convening of the U.N. First Conference on the Law of the Sea in 1958. The conference adopted four legal instruments, including the Convention on the Continental Shelf, which was adopted on April 29, 1958, and entered force on June 10, 1964. According to Article 1 of the Convention, the continental shelf refers "(a) to the seabed and subsoil of the submarine areas adjacent to the coast but outside the area of the territor-ial sea, to a depth of 200 metres or, beyond that limit, to where the depth of the superjacent waters admits of the exploitation of natural resources of the said areas; (b) to the seabed and subsoil of similar submarine areas adjacent to the coasts of islands."[8] Thus it specified two criteria for determining the outer limits of the continental shelf: depth (in this case, the two-hundred-metre isobath, which is the straight line connecting the parts of the seabed at a depth of two hundred metres) and exploitability. Neighbouring states were responsible for resolving any overlaps in their claims. Canada would have preferred to have a fixed outer limit for the continental shelf rather than the two-hundred-metre isobath criterion, which excluded large parts of Canada's continental margin. Furthermore, it considered the exploitability criterion imprecise; however, it relinquished its original preference in order to facilitate agreement on the Convention.[9] While only fifty-eight states were parties to the treaty, it nevertheless represented a major step forward.

By the time the Convention entered into force in 1964, technology was already facilitating development beyond the two-hundred-metre isobath; hence, exploitability became the key criterion for determining the outer limits. Using exploitability as a key criterion meant that there could be no universal standard for determining outer limits. Instead, the limits varied from place to place depending on the technical prowess of the countries involved and would evolve over time.

The relatively rapid codification of coastal states' rights on the continental shelf beyond the territorial sea was due to several sets of factors.[10] The seabed was known to contain oil and gas vital to the military, which made it a particularly high priority during the Cold War, as well as to national economies. Technological advances made the search for and exploitation of offshore hydrocarbon resources increasingly feasible. Coastal states' rights beyond two hundred nautical miles pertained to the seabed and not to the water column; thus, they did not interfere with freedoms of the high seas, which were cherished by the major maritime powers.

The Convention on the Continental Shelf was superseded by the 1982 U.N. Convention on the Law of the Sea (UNCLOS).[11] States that are parties to the CCS but not to UNCLOS (including Belarus, Cambodia, Colombia, Dominican Republic, Israel, Lesotho, Malawi, Switzerland, the United States, and Venezuela) are still legally bound by the former. Although superseded by UNCLOS, the 1958 convention was nonetheless important because it established coastal states' rights over the continental shelf, and set precedents that were reflected in subsequent legal documents. The decision of the U.N.'s International Court of Justice in the 1969 *North Sea Continental Shelf* cases reflected the 1958 convention's provisions pertaining to "the seaward extent of the shelf; the juridical character of the coastal State's entitlement; the nature of the rights exercisable; the kind of natural resources to which these relate; and the preservation intact of the legal status as high seas of the waters over the shelf," and saw them as having passed into customary international law.[12] These principles were later incorporated into UNCLOS. For example, both conventions give coastal states exclusive sovereignty over the non-living seabed resources of their continental shelves and specify that the exercise of such rights does "not depend on occupation, effective or notional, or on any express proclamation."[13] The superjacent waters remain the high seas.

Canada, which had (and still has) the world's second-largest continental shelf (after the Union of Soviet Socialist Republics, comprising approximately two million square miles (or almost 40 percent of its land territory),[14] became a party to the CCS in 1970. Canada has extensive margins off its East Coast and in the Arctic, much of which lies beyond two hundred nautical miles, so it was not surprising that the Canadian government considered the Convention's criterion for establishing outer limits too restrictive.[15] In the 1960s and early 1970s, the Department of Energy, Mines and Resources used the exploitability criterion extensively in granting exploration licences on the shelf, slope, and rise of Canada's continental margin.[16] Yet in international venues, government officials criticized the exploitability criterion on the grounds that it caused uncertainty, and instead advocated a set boundary for the outer limits.[17] In short, Canada used the existing norms to advance its interest while at the same time working for improvements.

In the late 1960s, pressure for further, substantial international negotiations on the law of the sea was stimulated by rapid developments in marine technology and oceanography, increased concern about pollution, and fear of dwindling resources.[18] There were also concerns about growing numbers of unilateral state claims to increased maritime jurisdiction, including those pertaining to the continental shelf. Clearly the exploitability criterion failed to provide firm, uniform constraints on coastal state jurisdiction. In spite of Cold War tensions, the world's major maritime powers, the United States and Soviet Union, had a shared desire to limit coastal state jurisdiction so as to ensure that the right of innocent passage was unimpeded. Although coastal states, both gave priority to ensuring the freedom of navigation. Since the Second Conference on the Law of the Sea (1960) had failed to resolve any of the outstanding concerns pertaining to coastal state jurisdiction, there were — by the late 1960s — renewed calls to negotiate a body of law pertaining to a broad range of issues.

The main catalyst for convening the Third Conference on the Law of the Sea came on August 17, 1967, when Arvid Pardo, the ambassador from Malta, made a historic declaration to the U.N. General Assembly. In a lengthy and passionate address, Pardo set forth his vision: the seabed beyond national jurisdiction known as "the Area" was to be used for peaceful purposes and its resources developed to benefit all peoples, with special regard for the needs of less developed countries.[19] The deep seabed and its resources, declared Pardo, were the "common heritage of mankind." The scope and newness of Pardo's proposal caught Canada and most other U.N. members by surprise; hence, the Canadian delegation's response focused on the continental shelf, which was its priority and for which Canada already had established policy, and avoided making any concrete commitments regarding the international seabed regime.[20] Pardo's concept of the Area brought to the forefront the need to establish consistent standards for determining the outer limits of coastal state jurisdiction. Ambassador Pardo's phrase "common heritage of mankind" is now frequently replaced by the gender-neutral wording "common heritage of humanity."

In response to Pardo's declaration, the General Assembly formed an ad hoc Committee to Study the Peaceful Uses of the Sea-Bed and the Ocean Floor beyond the Limits of National Jurisdiction (made permanent in 1968) to examine the possibility of establishing an international legal regime to regulate the development of seabed resources beyond national jurisdiction. By 1970 it was widely recognized that the creation of a regime to manage the deep seabed was linked to a wide range of law of the sea issues; hence, in December 1970, the General Assembly recommended that a Third Law of the Sea Conference be convened to negotiate a comprehensive treaty dealing with traditional maritime concerns, such as coastal state jurisdiction and navigational rights, and new issues, including the creation of an International Seabed Authority. Preparatory work for the conference was delegated to the Seabed Committee. Canada managed to secure one of the committee's thirty-five seats, where protecting coastal states' rights on the continental margin remained Canada's top priority.[21]

The Third Conference on the Law of the Sea, 1973–1982

The U.N. Third Conference on the Law of the Sea first met in 1973 to negotiate a comprehensive treaty on the law of the sea. The convention it drafted was seen as a package deal, which meant that states could not register reservations (i.e., they could not pick and choose which provisions to accept and which to reject). Furthermore, it was to be negotiated by consensus, which is an innovative practice still used in U.N. negotiations to this day, whereby an issue is discussed until unanimous — or at least general — agreement is reached.

The Third Conference was the longest and most comprehensive conference the United Nations had convened to that point in its history. On the eve of its opening session, Mitchell Sharp, Canada's secretary of state for external affairs, declared it to be "the most important diplomatic conference ever held under the auspices of the U.N."[22] Although his statement reflected the importance Canada accorded the conference, his perception was not peculiar to Canada.

The Third Conference differed significantly from its predecessors in 1958 and 1960. The number of countries participating greatly exceeded those of its predecessors. While close to ninety states participated at the first two conferences, 158 were represented at the third. Many of the 158 participants were developing states that had come into existence after 1960. Most developing countries had played little, if any, role at the first two conferences. While the principal alignment at the 1958 and 1960 conferences followed East-West divisions, in 1973 the North-South dichotomy dominated (especially in the deep seabed mining negotiations, although alignments varied from committee to committee and according to the issue under consideration). The principal alignment pertaining to the continental shelf pitted coastal states, seeking to expand the areas under their jurisdiction, against the major maritime powers, wanting unhampered freedom of navigation.

The range of issues addressed at the Third Conference was far wider than that considered by previous conferences. In addition to the coastal state jurisdiction and fishing and navigational rights that had been negotiated at the first two conferences, the third also considered such issues as maritime pollution, marine scientific research, and deep seabed mining. Participants at the 1958 and 1960 conferences were preoccupied with the traditional principles that had long governed the law of the sea: state sovereignty and freedom of the high seas. The Third Conference developed new concepts, such as the exclusive economic zone and the common heritage of humanity in order to establish a comprehensive, equitable, and orderly body of law to govern the oceans. The conventions adopted at the First

Conference were, in large part, attempts to codify state practice, whereas the Third Conference worked to create a body of international law for areas where no clear-cut legal norms existed. The Second Conference failed to reach agreements on any legally binding documents.

The Third Conference identified the continental shelf (the definition of its outer limits and the question of whether coastal states would have to share some of the revenues derived from their outer continental shelves) as one of seven "hard core" issues.[23] In light of the breadth of issues addressed, the new concepts being explored, the number of participants, and the diversity of their interests, the Third Conference required nine years of complex negotiations; by contrast, the 1958 and 1960 conferences met for approximately nine weeks and six weeks, respectively.

Canada strongly supported the establishment of the conference and was an active participant throughout its nine years of negotiations. The seabed off Canada's coasts had the potential to supply billions of barrels of oil and gas; thus, from an economic point of view the UNCLOS articles pertaining to the continental shelf were the country's highest priority. For Don Crosby, Canada's senior negotiator in the continental shelf negotiations, the most important objective throughout the law of the sea negotiations was to ensure that any definition of the continental shelf included the outer edge of the continental margin.[24] Canadian officials based their case for coastal state jurisdiction on the Convention on the Continental Shelf and its exploitability criterion; the judgment of the International Court in the 1969 *North Sea Continental Shelf* cases, which affirmed the 1958 convention's definition of the continental shelf; and the large numbers of unilateral claims to coastal state jurisdiction over the continental shelf and their long-standing practice of issuing oil and gas permits on it.[25]

There was early agreement that, in keeping with Pardo's declaration, the international seabed (the Area) would refer to "the sea-bed and ocean floor and subsoil thereof, beyond the limits of national jurisdiction" and that its resources would be developed to benefit humanity as a whole, giving special consideration to the needs and interests of the South.[26] The question remained: how far did coastal state jurisdiction extend and hence where did the Area begin?

The conference's first major breakthrough in establishing coastal state jurisdiction over the continental shelf came in 1976, when consensus was reached on the concept of an exclusive economic zone extending beyond the territorial sea to a distance two hundred nautical miles from shore. Its acceptance represented a compromise between coastal states seeking to maximize their jurisdiction and the major maritime powers wanting as few restrictions as possible on their navigational rights. The exclusive economic zone is the area extending from the outer edge of the territorial sea up to "200 nautical miles from the baselines from which the breadth of the territorial sea is measured."[27] The territorial sea, contiguous zone (which stretches twelve nautical miles beyond the territorial sea), and exclusive economic zone are all measured from baselines drawn along the coast. Within the exclusive economic zone, the coastal state exercises sovereign rights to explore, exploit, conserve, and manage the living and non-living resources in the water column and seabed.[28] In deference to the wishes of the major maritime powers, the freedom of the high seas prevails in the exclusive economic zone; hence, all states enjoy freedom of navigation and overflight, as well as the right to lay submarine cables and pipelines.[29] A coastal state may interfere with the freedom of navigation only if a vessel's actions threaten its rights pertaining to the living and non-living resources of the exclusive economic zone.

Agreement on the exclusive economic zone settled the question of coastal state jurisdiction within two hundred nautical miles from shore; however, questions pertaining to the delineation of the continental shelf beyond that point were not resolved for another three years. Here the struggle was between the "margineers" (wide-margin states, like Canada), on the one hand, and countries, particularly members of the Group of 77, that were either landlocked or had narrow margins, on the other. The latter wanted the international seabed to be as large as possible, since they expected to derive revenues from mineral exploitation in the Area to fuel their economic development. The countries seeking to restrict coastal state jurisdiction were numerous, making up almost one third of the delegations, while there were "a mere handful" of margineers.[30] Since decision-making during the conference was by consensus, having such a large bloc of opposition was serious. Of the margineers, relatively few had experts on their delegations capable of engaging in the highly complex discussions of geology and geophysics. Yet the delegations with this competence had the advantage of having in their midst the most knowledgeable experts at the conference. Such was the case with the Canadian delegation. Don Crosby, alternate deputy head of delegation, was a brilliant geologist with extensive experience and expertise pertaining to the continental shelf and its natural resources. Through hard work and persuasive arguments, he and other experts succeeded in securing a definition of the continental shelf that well reflected the interests of the margineers. UNCLOS defines the continental shelf as a submerged, natural prolongation of the coastal state's land territory.[31] The concept of natural prolongation had been introduced in the 1969 *North Sea Continental Shelf* case (*Denmark and the Netherlands v. Germany*).[32] When such prolongations extend beyond two hundred nautical miles they belong to the coastal state up to a distance of three hundred fifty nautical miles from the baselines or one hundred nautical miles measured from the 2,500-metre isobath (a line connecting the parts of the seabed that lie at a depth of 2,500 metres).[33] On its ECS (i.e., its continental shelf beyond the exclusive economic zone), the coastal state has sovereign rights to explore and exploit the non-living resources and sedimentary species of the seabed and subsoil.[34] The details of these provisions are discussed in greater depth later in the chapter's section entitled "The Legal Regime."

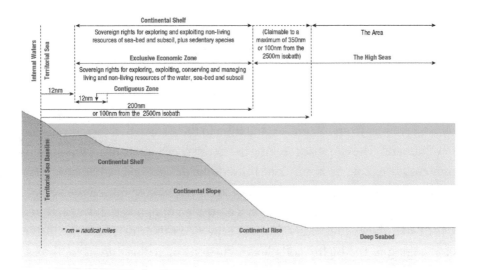

Maritime Ocean Zones
Fisheries and Oceans Canada.

Clearly, the provisions are highly advantageous to a wide-margin country like Canada, whose ECSs in the Atlantic and Arctic Oceans total "approximately 1.75 million square kilometres — equivalent in area to the three Prairie provinces."[35] Of the 1.75 million square kilometres, approximately three quarters of a million square kilometres are in the Arctic.[36] Section 17 of Canada's 1996 Oceans Act defines the continental shelf in conformity with the norms enshrined in UNCLOS.[37]

In 1981 the Republican administration of U.S. president Ronald Reagan announced that it would conduct a review of all the provisions in UNCLOS, much to the consternation of the vast majority of the world's countries, which had worked long and hard over the preceding eight years of the U.N. Conference on the Law of the Sea to negotiate a comprehensive treaty. The conference was left marking time for a year, while the United States conducted its review. The Reagan administration then announced that it was rejecting UNCLOS on the grounds that its provisions, particularly those pertaining to the development of the international seabed (the Area beyond national jurisdiction), were not consistent with its capitalist, free enterprise values. Ironically, most of the Reagan administration's key objections were to provisions that had been proposed by the former Republican secretary of state, Henry Kissinger, in 1976, in order to secure concessions from the Group of 77 to safeguard the United States' interests as a potential deep seabed mining country.

The U.N. Third Conference on the Law of the Sea held twelve sessions, for a total of ninety-five weeks of formal negotiations. The resulting convention consists of 436 articles (320 in the main text and 116 in its nine annexes). In 1982, after more than nine years of complex negotiations, delegates to the conference voted to accept UNCLOS. Given the number and diversity of the states involved, as well as the range of issues covered by this treaty, the approval was a notable accomplishment. Yet there was disappointment that the conference had not been able to reach consensus on a law of the sea convention and had instead been forced to call a vote. Four countries (including the United States) voted against the treaty and seventeen abstained. The United States and several other Western industrialized countries refused to accept the treaty because Part XI (the provisions for the international seabed regime) was seen to discriminate against private enterprises and to give too much discretionary power to the International Seabed Authority.

Post-Conference Developments

Reaching a compromise agreement on the regime for the Area took an additional eleven years of negotiations, held in two forums: the Preparatory Commission on the International Seabed Authority and the International Tribunal for the Law of the Sea (1983–1994); and the U.N. secretary-general's consultations (1990–1994).[38] The North-South polarization, with the Group of 77 on one side and developed deep seabed mining states on the other, prevented the Preparatory Commission from realizing its central objective: to reach consensus on an international seabed regime before UNCLOS became law. The real breakthrough on the deep seabed mining issues was achieved not in the Preparatory Commission, but in informal consultations organized by U.N. secretary-general Javier Pérez de Cuéllar, and subsequently carried on by his successor, Boutros Boutros-Ghali. In 1990, Pérez de Cuéllar invited a select group of thirty countries (including the United States — a key potential deep seabed mining state that had not signed UNCLOS and hence was not entitled to membership in the Preparatory Commission — Canada, and several other developed deep seabed mining states, as well as some of the more moderate members of the Group of 77) to discuss amending the deep seabed mining provisions, in the hope of clearing the principal roadblock to securing universal acceptance of the Convention before it entered into force. In June 1994 the consultative group succeeded in resolving the impasse by revising those elements of Part XI that were considered objectionable by the industrialized states. There were clear winners and losers in this process. Members of the Group of 77 made the greatest concessions. The 1982 Law of the Sea Convention was the first international treaty to embody provisions to advance the developing countries' cherished goal of creating the New International Economic Order (a global economic system more reflective of their interests with more favourable terms of trade and greater development assistance). In the secretary-general's negotiations, the United States and other industrialized, potential seabed mining countries had the strongest bargaining position. If they withheld their support for the Convention (and with it the promise of financial and technological resources), the international seabed regime would not be viable. Thus the developing countries agreed to amend the provisions to make them more palatable to the industrialized states. The

Draft Resolution and Draft Agreement Relating to the Implementation of Part XI of the United Nations Convention on the Law of the Sea, negotiated by the secretary-general's consultative group, was adopted by the U.N. General Assembly on July 28, 1994.[39] Thus the major impediment to ratification of UNCLOS was removed prior to its entry into force on November 16, 1994.

Canada, like most developed countries, was slow to ratify for fear the international seabed regime would place heavy financial burdens on it.[40] Nonetheless, by 2004, four of the five coastal Arctic states (Canada, Denmark, Norway, and the Russian Federation) had become parties to UNCLOS; hence, they are legally bound by it. In chronological order, their ratification dates were as follows: Norway, June 24, 1996; the Russian Federation, March 12, 1997; Canada, November 7, 2003; and, Denmark, November 16, 2004. The United States is not a party, in spite of repeated requests to the U.S. Senate by the Obama administration, as well as by the Clinton and Bush administrations before it, for accession. For example, in her speech to the U.S. Congress prior to being appointed secretary of state, Hillary Clinton declared accession to UNCLOS to be a priority for the Obama administration.[41] Successive U.S. administrations have argued that the UNCLOS provisions pertaining to freedom of navigation and coastal state jurisdiction have passed into customary international law. As such, Washington considers the provisions for the ECS as part of international law and acknowledges that the "rules for defining the ECS are based in international law, specifically Article 76 of the Convention on the Law of the Sea."[42] Canada also considered the sovereign rights of coastal states over the non-living resources of the continental margin to be enshrined in customary international law.[43]

The Convention outlined compromise provisions and many of the details were left to be resolved later. Since the Convention entered into force in 1994, its provisions have been clarified and elaborated upon by the states parties to UNCLOS and by the Commission on the Limits of the Continental Shelf. For example, the states parties have on several occasions amended the deadlines for making submissions. The convention requires states to make their submission within ten years of ratification or accession.[44] In response to concerns raised by developing countries that they lacked the resources to comply with the original timeline, the states parties decided in 2001 that countries that had become parties to the Convention before 1999 would have until 2009 to file their submissions.[45] At their 2008 meeting, the states parties realized that many countries would not make the 2009 timeline, so they agreed that such states could fulfill their obligations by filing preliminary information indicating that they intend to make a submission, the status of the preparatory work, and when they expect to submit.[46] During its first five years of operation, the Commission focused on formulating rules for the application of the Convention's articles. On September 12, 1997, the Commission adopted its Rules of Procedure, which were subsequently revised and expanded.[47] The resultant hundreds of pages of documentation attest to the complexity of the topic.

Article 76, which specifies the criteria for claiming an ECS, is less than one page long; hence, several documents have been written to interpret and elaborate upon its provisions. In 1999 the Commission unanimously adopted a set of scientific and technical guidelines to aid states in preparing their submissions and the Commission in reviewing them.[48] As the provisions in Article 76 and Annex II were open to various interpretations, clarification was required. For each of the key concepts identified in Article 76 (e.g., the enabling and constraining formulae, the foot of the slope, the 2,500-metre isobath, sediment thickness, and sea floor highs), the guidelines discuss the potential problems in interpreting the text and present acceptable ways of implementing them. The use of various types of research methodologies referred to in Article 76 and Annex II are also clarified. Four months after adopting the guidelines, the Commission produced a series of flow charts to further assist states by outlining each step in the process of delineating their continental shelves and indicating the options at each stage.[49] In 2006 the Commission produced a training manual to provide additional guidance to states planning to make submissions.[50] It has also established a Committee on the Provision of Scientific and Technical Advice to Coastal States, and it offers periodic training courses to assist countries in the preparation of their submissions.

From the point of view of establishing role models, it is unfortunate that the details of the submissions already reviewed by the Commission and the specifics of its recommendations are not in the public domain. "In essence, the deliberations of the CLCS do not form a body of public jurisprudence that can be consulted by coastal states searching for guidance from past decisions."[51] As a result, the details of a submission can only be gleaned on an ad hoc basis through discussion with officials from the countries involved. Since 2005 the executive summaries of each submission and the Commission's recommendations pertaining to it have been posted on the Commission's website.[52] This information is an important resource as the precedents set in the course of the submission/review process provide guidance to states making later submissions. For example, in reviewing Australia's submission pertaining to the Tasmanian Sea, the Commission indicated that if a saddle (underwater trench between the land mass and the shelf) is significantly shallower than the deep ocean floor, there is a geomorphological connection.[53] The recommendation is relevant to Canada as there is a saddle between the Canadian archipelagic islands and the Lomonosov Ridge.

In keeping with U.N. General Assembly Resolution 57/141,[54] states parties to UNCLOS have contributed advice, expertise, technical information, and accounts of their practical experience to a directory to aid countries preparing submissions.[55] Furthermore, several experts have sought to identify trends and precedents from the executive summaries of the submissions and the Commission's recommendations that are in the public domain.[56]

In addition to the clarifications and elaborations emanating from the meetings of the states parties and the Commission, the UNCLOS provisions are being interpreted and reinforced by international judicial bodies. For example, a coastal state's inherent right to an ECS was reaffirmed by the International Court of Justice in the 1969 *North Sea Continental Shelf* cases and by the International Tribunal for the Law of the Sea in the 2012 *Bay of Bengal* case.[57]

THE LEGAL REGIME

The international regime to delineate the outer limits of the continental shelf beyond two hundred nautical miles and the rights and responsibilities of coastal states in this area are specified in Part VI (Articles 76 to 85) and Annex II of UNCLOS. As Ted McDorman points out, the key legal components of the continental shelf regime were laid out in the 1958 Convention on the Continental Shelf and later largely repeated in UNCLOS.[58] There were, however, several important differences. UNCLOS was much more precise in outlining the criteria for delineating the ECS and the rules and regulations of the continental shelf regime, and it provided for the Commission to oversee the process which had not been envisaged in the 1958 convention.[59] These provisions have been further clarified by the states parties to UNCLOS and by the Commission.

According to UNCLOS, a country's continental shelf "comprises the sea-bed and subsoil of the submarine areas that extend beyond its territorial sea throughout the natural prolongation of its land territory to the outer edge of the continental margin, or to a distance of 200 nautical miles from the baselines from which the breadth of the territorial sea is measured where the outer edge of the continental margin does not extend up to that distance."[60] *Prolongation* means that there must be unbroken continuity "from the shoreline to the outer edge of the continental margin."[61] On its continental shelf, the coastal state has sovereign rights to explore and exploit "the mineral and other non-living resources of the sea-bed and subsoil together with living organisms belonging to sedentary species."[62] As was the case with the Convention on the Continental Shelf, the water column above the ECS is classified as "high seas," meaning that all states enjoy freedom of navigation and overflight, and the right to fish, conduct scientific research, construct artificial islands and other legal installations, and lay submarine cables and pipelines.[63]

Responsibility for defining its continental shelf rests with the coastal state, which must conduct scientific research to determine if its continental shelf extends beyond two hundred nautical miles and, if so, the limits of its outer edge. UNCLOS outlines both enabling criteria and constraints. The process of determining whether or not the natural prolongation of a coastal state's submerged land territory actually extends beyond two hundred nautical miles is called the test of appurtenance. For this purpose, a coastal state may use either the distance or the depth enabling formulae, both of which require the same first step: identifying the foot of the continental slope. Article 76 specifies that "in the absence of evidence to the contrary, the foot of the continental slope shall be determined as the point of maximum change in the gradient at its base."[64] Thus it provides two sets of criteria for defining the foot of the slope: "in the absence of evidence to the contrary" and "the point of maximum change in the gradient," without assigning priority to either. The *Scientific and Technical Guidelines of the Commission on the Limits of the Continental Shelf* resolves this ambiguity by defining "the point of maximum change in the gradient" as the "general rule" and "the absence of evidence to the contrary" as the "exception."[65] Even if the coastal state is presenting evidence to the contrary in its submission, it must also include "the results of applying the rule of maximum change in the gradient."[66] As a general rule, the foot of the slope is the point at which the slope becomes very gentle and transitions to the deep sea floor (i.e., less than one-degree change).[67] It is "the point of inflection where you're going from a very high gradient to a very low gradient."[68] Yet evidence to the contrary is to be taken seriously. In addition to the bathymetric and geomorphological evidence required to satisfy the general rule, the coastal state must also provide all necessary geological and geophysical evidence, and the Commission is obligated to examine all such material.[69]

Measuring from the foot of the continental slope, the coastal state may use either enabling formula. The thickness criterion allows the coastal state to measure seawards from the foot of the slope until the sediment thickness is equal to 1 percent of the distance travelled;[70] thus, "if you have 1 km of sediment in depth you can go out 100 km from your margin."[71] The distance formula involves determining an outer limit point at a distance not exceeding sixty nautical miles from the foot of the slope.[72]

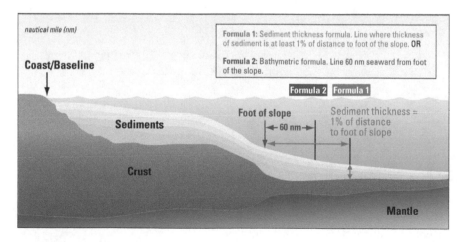

Extended Continental Shelf Formula Lines
United States Extended Continental Shelf Project.

The sediment thickness criterion is often referred to as the Gardiner formula or the Irish formula in recognition of the fact that it was first proposed by the Irish geologist Piers R. R. Gardiner. The criterion was included "to ensure that a coastal State secured jurisdiction over all the hydrocarbon resources that might possibly exist in the offshore areas adjacent to it."[73] The distance criterion is frequently called the Hedberg formula, after the American geologist, Hollis D. Hedberg, who first proposed it.

If the above-mentioned enabling criteria show that the continental shelf extends beyond two hundred nautical miles, it is then necessary to establish the outer limit. To limit unchecked incursions into the international seabed area, UNCLOS imposes constraints on the area of the continental shelf over which the sovereign rights of the coastal state apply. Again it provides coastal states with two options: the outer limits "shall not exceed 350 nm from the baselines from which the breadth of the territorial sea is measured" or extend beyond "100 nautical miles from the 2,500 metre isobath."[74]

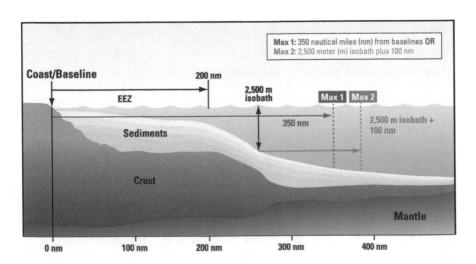

Extended Continental Shelf Constraint Lines

United States Extended Continental Shelf Project.

Unlike the 1958 Convention on the Continental Shelf, Article 76 of UNCLOS provides concrete constraints. When the 2,500-metre isobath is more than 250 nautical miles seaward of the baselines, it makes sense to use it and measure out a further one hundred nautical miles. Canada, like other countries, will use the combinations of enabling and constraint criteria that maximize the area of its continental shelf.

After gathering and analyzing the scientific data and relating the findings to the legal requirements of the ECS regime, the coastal state makes a submission to the Commission.[75] The mandate, membership, and decision-making procedures for the Commission are outlined in Annex II of UNCLOS. Canada was active at the Third Conference on the Law of the Sea in establishing the norms pertaining to the Commission. In fact, the Canadian delegation presented the first detailed proposal regarding the body.[76] Its nine articles provided a framework for subsequent negotiations, and some of the specifics, such as the expertise required of commissioners, were incorporated into the Convention. As Canada proposed, the Commission has two key roles: (a) to review the material submitted and make recommendations pertaining to the delineation of a state's ECS; and (b) to respond to coastal states' requests for advice.[77] Nonetheless, Canada would have preferred further limits on the Commission's authority.

In practice, the Commission has focused on the first role. UNCLOS does not explain "the scope and nature of the advice or how it could be provided" and states tend to request advice of individual commissioners rather than the Commission as a whole.[78] UNCLOS stipulates that the "limits of the shelf established by a coastal State on the basis of these [the Commission's] recommendations shall be final and binding."[79] Canada had suggested that the coastal state "take into account" the Commission's recommendations when establishing its ECS rather than having to set its limits "on the basis" of the recommendations; however, it accepted increased restrictions on its autonomy in order to secure agreement on the extension.[80] Even with the Convention's stronger wording, it is clear that the coastal state — not the Commission — establishes the outer limits of the continental shelf. Thus the submission to the Commission is only one part — albeit an important part — of a longer process to delineate Canada's ECS.

Every five years, states parties to UNCLOS elect the twenty-one members of the Commission. The commissioners are chosen for their expertise in geology, geophysics, or hydrography, while ensuring due regard for the U.N. rules on geographic representation.[81] At least three members are to "be elected from each geographic region."[82] In practice, this requirement translates into "five members from the African States; five members from the Asia-Pacific States; three members from the Eastern European States; four members from the Latin American and Caribbean States; three members from the Western European and other States; and the remaining one member from among the African States, the Asia-Pacific States and the Western European and other States."[83]

Commissioners may stand for re-election. Commission members are expected to act independently and to be impartial; hence, they are not involved in the review of their own countries' submissions. Nonetheless, there are advantages to having a national on the Commission. The member can have input into the interpretation and application of the Commission's guidelines, which build on the provisions in UNCLOS. He or she can also provide useful guidance on Commission procedures and precedents.

There are also disadvantages to membership. A state that nominates its national expert for membership is expected to pay the costs of that person attending the meetings in New York, which is a deterrent, especially for poor countries. Several Commission chairs have noted problems with the attendance records of some commissioners, which have been blamed on a lack of funding to attend sessions.[84]

A voluntary trust fund was established to assist developing countries in meeting the financial obligations of having a national on the Commission. For instance, to defray the expenses of participating at the thirty-eighth session (July 20–September 4, 2015), $170,000 in trust funds was divided among eight commissioners, while $146,000 helped seven members attend the thirty-ninth session (October 19–December 4, 2015).[85]

Donations to the fund are voluntary and to date the amounts generated have been insufficient to cover the full costs incurred by participants from developing countries. Furthermore, as the number and length of the sessions has increased, costs have risen. The issues of medical, dental, and travel insurance for the commissioners and the state's responsibility to finance the participation of its national are routinely brought up by the chairs of the Commission in their sessional reports.

In addition to the financial costs, sending an expert to New York can mean one less person to work on the submission. Who, if anyone, can be spared? Is the information gleaned through membership going to be relevant in several decades when the Commission finally gets around to reviewing your country's submission?

The election process is highly political. Canada nominated Richard Haworth, a geophysicist formerly with Natural Resources Canada, in the 2012 election, and he served his first term from 2012 to 2017. Canada is part of the "Western Europe and Others" category, which has three seats on the Commission and the opportunity to compete, along with Africa and Asia, for a floating seat. Within the group, competition is stiff, as it includes Australia, France, Ireland, New Zealand, Norway, Spain, Portugal, and the United Kingdom, all of which have made submissions (it will also include the United States if and when it accedes to UNCLOS).

The commissioners review the coastal state's submission, assess the extent to which it has defined its ECS in conformity with existing international legal norms, and make recommendations to the state regarding the establishment of the outer limits of its continental shelf.[86] The reviews are conducted by subcommissions composed of seven members each.[87] After conducting an in-depth examination of the material in a submission and holding consultations with the submitting state, the subcommission presents its written recommendations to the Commission for approval. Following the precedent set during the United Nations Conference on the Law of the Sea, "the Commission, its subcommissions and subsidiary bodies shall make every effort to reach agreement on substantive matters by way of consensus and there shall be no voting on such matters until all efforts to achieve consensus have been exhausted."[88] When votes are taken on matters of substance, which include the recommendations pertaining to submissions, an affirmative vote by at least two-thirds of the commissioners present and voting is required.[89] Once approved, the written recommendations are forwarded to the submitting state.

In cases where the coastal state disagrees with the Commission's recommendations, the former must present a new or revised submission to the Commission within a reasonable period of time.[90] The process of submission, review, and resubmission could conceivably go on for years and has been described as "a narrowing down 'ping-pong' procedure" that should ultimately result in the coastal state and the Commission being in agreement over the former's ECS.[91]

The Commission is an evolving body. Over time its interactions with states parties have increased and it has become more transparent. To aid states in preparing their submissions and commissioners in conducting the reviews, the Commission has published guidelines and manuals, run training courses, and developed procedures and templates for performing the evaluations, which are important for consistency and fairness. Having a group of experts to verify the documentation provided by coastal states is needed for two reasons: the criteria outlined in Article 76 are scientifically and technically complex; and oversight is needed to safeguard against coastal states extending their jurisdiction into the international seabed area, which is the common heritage of humanity.[92] As Anna Cavnar points out, the Commission does more than verify the technical and scientific accuracy of the data and analysis in a submission: "It is responsible for interpreting article 76's legal and technical provisions, assessing the state's interpretation against its own, determining how to reconcile differences, ensuring the state's technical and scientific data support the reconciled understanding, and recommending to the state that it either establish the proposed boundaries or amend them."[93] The Commission serves as the legitimator in the ECS delineation process: "Where a coastal State and the Commission are generally in accord with the location of an outer limit this will provide great legitimacy to that boundary and make challenges of the boundary more difficult. A coastal State outer limit not in accord with Commission recommendations will be less legitimate and more open to challenge by other States or perhaps even the International Seabed Authority."[94] Adhering to the process outlined in UNCLOS is essential in determining both the outer limit of a state's continental shelf extension (i.e., the full extent of the seabed where the state has the right to explore and exploit resources) and the degree to which the international community considers a country's ECS to be legitimate. In most cases, submitting states treat the Commission "as a body whose opinion (recommendations) matters and, as [a] result, as a body which needs to be satisfied."[95]

UNCLOS is clear that the coastal state does not have to exercise sovereignty over the continental shelf in order to enjoy its rights: "The Rights of the coastal State over the continental shelf do not depend on occupation, effective or notional, or on any express proclamation."[96] These rights are exclusive; if a coastal state does not explore or exploit the resources of its ECS, no other state may engage in such activities without the former's express consent.[97] Thus, Russia planting a flag on the Arctic seabed beneath the North Pole in August 2007 was a symbolic gesture that had no legal ramifications for any Arctic country, including Canada. Delineating the outer limits of the continental shelf is not governed by the "use it or lose it" maxim as former prime minister Stephen Harper incorrectly asserted in 2007: "Canada has a choice when it comes to defending our sovereignty over the Arctic. We either use it or lose it."[98] A state's continental shelf either meets the UNCLOS criteria for an ECS or it does not. Furthermore, as the International Tribunal for the Law of the Sea affirmed in the 2012 *Bay of Bengal* case, the coastal state has these rights whether or not it has made a submission to the Commission, received the latter's recommendations, and established the outer boundaries of its ECS based on the recommendations.[99] Most coastal states do not have continental shelves that meet the criteria for an extension and those, like Canada, that do are indeed fortunate.

The provisions in UNCLOS pertaining to the ECS represent a compromise, agreed to at the Third United Nations Conference on the Law of the Sea, between ECS states and countries, particularly the members of the Group of 77, that wanted the international seabed to be as large as possible. Coastal states with ECS are required to make monetary payments or contributions in kind through the International Seabed Authority for distribution to all states parties to UNCLOS with respect to the exploitation of non-living seabed resources beyond two hundred nautical miles.[100] This obligation is examined in greater depth in chapter 6.

The international regime specifies timelines for making submissions, although the requirements have evolved over time. Countries, like the Russian Federation and Norway, that ratified or acceded to UNCLOS prior to 1999 had until 2009 to make their submissions, while states, such as Canada and Denmark, that became parties after 1999 had ten years from the time of ratification or accession. Having ratified on November 7, 2003, and become a party to UNCLOS on December 7, 2003, Canada had to present its documentation to the Commission by December 6, 2013. As a party to UNCLOS, Canada is entitled not only to make a submission to the Commission but also to participate in the ongoing work of the states parties to further develop the rules, regulations, and procedures for the Commission; however, by the time Canada had ratified UNCLOS, a good deal of this work had already been completed.

As mentioned earlier, the fifth Arctic coastal state, the United States, has not acceded to UNCLOS. Republican opposition, which dates back over three decades, remains the principal obstacle. Following the 2014 midterm elections, Republicans outnumbered Democrats in the U.S. Senate by a margin of fifty-four to forty-four, and there was insufficient support to carry a vote in favour of accession. Yet as increasing numbers of coastal countries make their submissions to the Commission, pressure continues to build within the United States for accession so that it, too, can present a submission and thereby begin the process of gaining international recognition of its ECS. In the meantime, the United States is conducting research on the continental shelf beyond two hundred nautical miles in accordance with the UNCLOS provisions.

Considerable academic attention has been paid to the question of whether states that are not party to UNCLOS may make a submission to the Commission. The general conclusion is that they are not entitled to do so under either UNCLOS or customary international law.[101]

The major problem confronting the Commission is its workload.[102] Demands on the commissioners' time began slowly, with the Russian Federation being the first to make a submission in December 2001 and no further submissions arriving until May 2004. The initial turnaround was fairly quick, with the Commission providing Russia with its recommendations in June 2002. Between December 2001 and December 2008, the Commission received sixteen submissions and reviewed five.[103] Not surprisingly, a large number of submissions (thirty-five) arrived in 2009, the deadline for countries that had become parties to UNCLOS prior to 1999. By the end of 2011, the Commission had received fifty-nine submissions and reviewed fourteen. As of October 2016, the Commission had received eighty-two full, partial, or revised submissions, had reviewed twenty-six, and was in the process of reviewing another thirteen. It is estimated that some eighty-five coastal states may ultimately make submissions to the Commission.[104]

While the Commission has shown some improvement in the pace of its work in recent years, it will be years before most of the countries on the submission list receive their recommendations. This situation leaves coastal states with a dilemma: either to keep their submission teams together for years until their submission is considered, or to show up to defend submissions with new teams less familiar with the data.

To be fair, the commissioners have faced some major challenges. They are charting new ground in conducting the reviews. When the ECS provisions were being negotiated, knowledge of the seabed was far less advanced than it is today; hence, the drafters could not have foreseen the technological complexity of implementing the legal requirements.[105] In addition, the Commission's workload proved to be heavier than expected, with more states making submissions than was envisaged when UNCLOS was negotiated. In 2007 it was estimated that the Commission could expect as many as sixty-five submissions, "almost double the number of submissions forecast at the time of the drafting of the Convention."[106] By 2015 eighty-two submissions (including five resubmissions) had been received and, given the number of notices of preliminary information and the fact that some countries with the potential to establish their ECS have not yet become parties to UNCLOS, more are expected. Furthermore, some of the submissions were enormous. Coastal states must submit eight copies of the main body documents and two copies of the supporting documents. Australia's submission was approximately thirty-four thousand pages and weighed about six hundred kilograms. Most submissions are much smaller. Canada's submission pertaining to its Atlantic ECS comprised about 2,500 pages of text. Reviewing these lengthy documents is a huge job.

The backlog has prompted some procedural changes. Between 1997 and 2012, the Commission generally held two short sessions per year. Until 2004 the majority of sessions only lasted five days. The trend to longer meetings became noticeable in 2005, when two nineteen-day sessions were convened, and thereafter to the end of 2012, most sessions were between three and five weeks in duration. In 2013 the Commission began convening three sessions of about seven weeks each per year, with four weeks annually being devoted to plenary business.[107] So far this change has not significantly reduced the backlog. At its thirty-seventh session in April 2015, "the Commission recognized that the increase in the number of weeks of work had not yet translated into a proportional increase in the number of recommendations approved."[108] Time is not the only factor affecting progress in conducting reviews; how quickly states respond to the commissioners' requests for further information is a factor, as is the volume and complexity of the additional data that are provided.[109]

In addition to the substantial increases in meeting time, other procedural changes have been made. Four new subcommissions were created in 2012, bringing from three to six the number of subcommissions able to actively review submissions, which represented a doubling of capacity.[110] Prior to this change, the rules had stipulated that "unless the Commission decides otherwise, only three subcommissions shall function simultaneously while considering submissions."[111] By 2015, nine subcommissions were meeting concurrently, which has "decreased the projected waiting period for submissions in the queue."[112] As the overall number of commissioners has not increased, memberships in subcommissions overlap. While originally the subcommissions examined only one submission at a time, that has changed to allow for multiple reviews; for instance, commissioners can review one submission while waiting for responses on another.

There have been repeated calls to provide the Commission with more resources. For example, Canada, the United States, and fifteen other countries sponsored a nonbinding resolution in the U.N. General Assembly in December 2007 that reaffirmed the importance of the Commission's work, encouraged states to make their submissions on time, and emphasized the need to provide the Commission with the resources necessary to function effectively.[113] The adoption of this resolution formally acknowledged the need to support the Commission and to act in conformity with the UNCLOS. The issue of workload, as well as the Commission's resources, has been discussed at the annual June meetings of the states parties to UNCLOS,[114] but overall little concrete action has been taken to address the problem. There is no requirement in UNCLOS for assessed contributions to pay for the Commission, and the question of who should pay for additional resources, if they are provided, is contentious. Developed states parties, which currently fund over 50 percent of the United Nations' budget, do not want to incur further financial obligations, especially when most are facing serious budgetary restraints domestically. Landlocked states and states whose continental shelves do not extend beyond two hundred nautical miles do not want to pay for a process that is of no direct benefit to them. In addition to the question of who should pay, there is the question of whether greater resources, in particular more experts devoting longer periods of time to reviewing the submissions, will in fact significantly improve the Commission's functioning.

Although the Commission now meets twenty-one weeks a year, membership is still a part-time job. There are anomalies among the members: some are consultants; some are on government payrolls; their rates of remuneration differ depending on the country of origin; some get benefits while others do not; some are highly competent professionals while others are less effective; and some do not receive funding from their country to attend the Commission meetings. If membership on the Commission became a full-time job, would states be willing to pay the added expenses? Would highly qualified professionals be willing to sit full-time? If those best qualified were not willing to give up their current jobs, would the full-time requirement result in less qualified people being the only ones willing to serve? Would a funded, full-time Commission attract political appointees lacking the necessary professional qualifications where the countries in a geographic area decide in advance not to offer more candidates than the seats available to their region? The problem of inadequate resources to address the backlog of work does involve questions of increased funding, but it is more complicated than just asking for more money. The more politically sensitive issue of whether more resources will result in greater efficiency and better quality and quantity of work must be addressed.

CONCLUSION

The past seven decades have seen the codification and implementation of an international ECS regime. UNCLOS includes checks and balances and reflects trade-offs. The rights of the two major negotiating blocs in the continental shelf negotiations — the coastal states and the major maritime powers — were each respected. Coastal state jurisdiction was greatly expanded, yet other countries enjoy freedom of navigation in the water column and airspace of both the exclusive economic zone and the ECS. Coastal states that meet the prescribed geomorphological and geological criteria have ECSs. The Commission provides scientific checks on coastal states' submissions, and ECS countries have to make payments or contributions in kind as compensation for having extended their jurisdiction beyond two hundred nautical miles into the common heritage of humanity. While a coastal state has sovereign rights to the non-living resources and sedimentary organisms on or under its ocean floor, it also has responsibilities. It is required to "adopt laws and regulations to prevent, reduce and control pollution of the marine environment" resulting from seabed activities within its jurisdiction.[115] States may lay cables and pipelines on another country's ECS; however, the coastal state must consent to the pipeline's route, and its right to establish the conditions for laying cables or pipelines in areas under its jurisdiction must be respected.[116] Although the Canadian government has been issuing licences for hydrocarbon exploration beyond two hundred nautical miles off its East Coast since the early 1960s, it has yet to create a comprehensive oil spill response capability for this area.[117]

Canadian officials were strong advocates for the rights of coastal states and played major roles in defining the rules and regulations governing the continental shelf in a series of important negotiating forums beginning in the late 1950s and continuing to this day. While asserting the rights of coastal states, Canada also recognized that its interests would best be protected by legally binding international instruments; hence, compromises were made to secure this objective. The resulting rules and regulations governing the world's oceans, which are enshrined in UNCLOS, are highly advantageous to coastal states like Canada. Thus, Canada has incorporated these rights into its own legislation, spent over a decade mapping the seabed of its continental shelves and analyzing the resulting data, and filed its submission pertaining to the Atlantic ECS with the Commission in December 2013. As discussed in chapter 6, Canada plans to make a second submission, which will address its Arctic ECS. The UNCLOS provisions are revisited in chapter 3 in relation to the research methodologies used to delineate Canada's ECS.

3

SCIENTIFIC RESEARCH AND THE LAW OF THE SEA CONVENTION

As discussed in chapter 2, responsibility for defining its ECS rests with the coastal state, which must conduct scientific research to determine if its continental shelf extends beyond two hundred nautical miles, and, if so, the limits of its outer edge. Scientists and technicians from the Geological Survey of Canada and the Canadian Hydrographic Service are working as a team to conduct the scientific research and analysis needed for Canada's Arctic ECS submission.[1] The undertaking requires "a knowledge of the regional geological framework coupled with the measurement, analysis, and interpretation of three parameters: the shape of the seabed, the depth of water, and the thickness of the underlying sedimentary material."[2] Article 76 of UNCLOS provides enabling criteria (formulae for establishing the extent of the continental margin beyond two hundred nautical miles) and constraining formulae (to define the outer limits of the continental shelf). To determine if these criteria are met involves mapping the ECS, using bathymetry and seismic reflection profiling as the principal sources of data. Bathymetry involves measuring water depths and mapping the morphology (shape) of the ocean floor. This information is essential in determining the foot of the slope of the continental shelf and the 2,500-metre isobath. Seismic techniques are used to penetrate the layers of the ocean bed to measure sediment thickness, and the sound velocity of the rock structures to determine if the rocks are of the same composition as the continental shelf adjacent to Canada's coastline.

This chapter examines the various ways of conducting bathymetric and seismic research in an Arctic context. Thereafter attention is given to gravity and magnetic measurements, which provide information to complement the data derived from bathymetric and seismic techniques. Canada's Arctic ECS Program's field experience in conducting these various types of research and the scientific findings resulting from this work are examined in chapter 5. Following its discussion of research methodologies, this chapter provides a brief discussion of the relevance of bathymetry and seismology to UNCLOS.

BATHYMETRY

The International Bathymetric Chart of the Arctic Ocean and the General Bathymetric Chart of the Ocean provide the information necessary both for desktop studies and for planning field operations. These databases comprise largely low-resolution data contributed from many sources. Their base maps are important in determining where ECSs are feasible and where the best survey areas are likely to be.

In conducting Arctic bathymetric surveys, Canadian scientific and technical staff use a variety of methodologies depending on the conditions, the resources available, and the type of data for which they are looking. These methodologies involve the use of single-beam and multibeam echo sounders. Profile lines can be charted using icebreakers and autonomous underwater vehicles, while spot tests can be conducted on ice floes and from a helicopter hovering above an open lead. Each method has its advantages and limitations.

Single-beam and multibeam echo sounding systems include transducers that both send sound waves and record their return. They convert electrical impulses (voltages) to vibrations in a plate on the hull of the ship. These vibrations create pressure waves in the water column that propagate to the sea floor. The pressure waves reflect off the sea floor and return toward the sea surface. The transducer then vibrates as a result of these returning pressure waves and converts the vibrations back into electrical impulses (voltages). In a single-beam system, the transducer (or array of transducers) is generally one component that sends and receives the sound, whereas in a multibeam system, it usually has two parts: an array of transmitters and a separate array of receivers.

A single-beam echo sounder sends out a cone of sound. Like a flashlight beam, the cone is narrower at the point of emission and wider as it moves away from that point. The deeper the water, the wider the radius of the cone on the ocean floor. The first — and only the first — sound wave (echo) to return is recorded. Normally the beam that has least far to travel is the one that will be first to return and thus to be recorded. The single beam receives a single sound wave in response to each acoustic emission. The time to travel down to the sea floor and return is measured. This time measurement is converted to depth by multiplying the travel time by the velocity that sound travels in water (and dividing by two, since the sound travels down and back). Sound velocity in water varies with temperature, density (salinity), and pressure, so these measurements may be made to derive velocity. For each acoustic emission, one point of depth is recorded. A cone of sound is sent out at regular intervals and the process is repeated as the ship moves forward to create a profile of the shape of the sea floor. When breaking ice, interference noise is introduced into the water column and ice scraping along the transducer blocks sound emission and reception, so measuring even single-beam soundings from an icebreaker is not a trivial matter; often, it is impossible.

The multibeam echo sounder transmits hundreds of beams of sound through the water column in a fan shape and records the echoes of the returning waves to map the ocean floor and model it in three-dimensional detail. The process is then repeated over and over again along the line to generate a swath of soundings of the sea floor. The sound waves returning from the outer beams of the swath are travelling farther and take longer to return than do those going straight down under the ship. In open water, the width of each swath is generally four to seven times the water depth, and swaths are taken with overlapping sweeps so that all the sea floor is surveyed.

In the High Arctic with its heavy ice conditions, it is often not possible to have overlapping profile lines and the aforementioned noise interference generally limits the number of successful return echoes. Swath width is frequently limited to one to three times water depth, and line spacing is generally broad. Special survey techniques have been adopted to survey in ice as a result of these limitations, including following a lead icebreaker ("Follow the Leader"), stopping the ice breaker and tilting the fan of beams fore and aft (the "Hokey-Pokey"), spinning the ship in place (the "Pirouette"), and the "Leap-frog" (steam ahead a swath width and turn the ship perpendicular to the line to swath along the line instead of perpendicular to it).

Both the single-beam and multibeam echo sounders measure the time difference between the emission of the sound and its return to determine distance. The deeper the water column, the longer it will take a sound wave to return. Single-beam surveying provides a continuous track of individual points; although in ice, it may not be continuous because of noise and ice interference. A multibeam sonar produces a multitude of points along a beam of the track. The redundancy obtained with a multibeam system makes it ideal for acquisition of data while breaking ice. The redundancy limits the impact of noise interference on coverage and allows averaging over a specified area to improve accuracy (gridding).

Helicopter spot sounding.

Don Glencross © Her Majesty the Queen in Right of Canada, as represented by the Minister of National Defence, 2010.

During icebreaker missions, the ship moves along the survey line collecting multibeam soundings; however, there may be spots off the plan line that the hydrographers want to check, so in terms of cost, time and efficiency, it may make more sense to fly the helicopter to the area where spot tests are needed, rather than diverting the icebreaker on additional trajectories, which would add a lot to the distances it has to cover. If there are areas of open water, the helicopter hovers while a single-beam transducer is lowered on the cargo hook into open water, where it sends out a sound wave and records the returning echo.

Alternatively, the helicopter can land on the sea ice so that the echo sounder transducer can be placed directly on the ice surface, with the aid of a bonding agent, such as an edible oil product. The depth measurement is taken through the ice, so the value must later be adjusted to account for the thickness of the ice. The ship is usually going slowly enough to launch the helicopter, make the side trip, and get back before it has gone too far along its plan line. Spot tests from hovering helicopters offer the hydrographers an opportunity to collect extra data without interfering with the course set for the main bathymetric and seismic work; however, their importance should not be overstated. The spacing between the spot soundings means that they cannot be used to identify either the contour at 2,500 metres or the foot of the slope. If the spot checks identify a previously unknown feature of interest, the chief scientist may decide to chart a new course for the ship.

Historically, spot soundings taken on the ice have provided the principal source of bathymetric data in parts of the Arctic, particularly along the Canadian margin, where thick, multiyear ice prevented access by icebreakers. Such surveys usually involve the laborious tasks of setting up ice camps, which are discussed in chapter 4, as well as helicopter flights out to each individual test location to place the equipment. A helicopter lands at predetermined sites every one and a half to twenty kilometres along selected profiles, the transducer is placed directly on the ice, and the sound waves it emits penetrate both ice and water and echo off the seabed. The spacing of the tests depends on the gradient and complexity of the ocean floor, with denser measurements needed near the foot of the slope.[3]

Transducer on the ice.

Tim Janzen, Fisheries and Oceans Canada.

Placing transducers is heavy work, as each weighs ten to sixteen kilograms. When the helicopter lands, the hydrographer must dig through the snow cover to place the transducer directly on the ice to ensure accurate readings.[4] Snow or air under the transducer, or air bubbles in new ice, impede the flow of acoustic energy. Deep snow must be cleared before the quality of the ice can be assessed. If the ice proves to be too rough and/or too full of bubbles to accurately transmit the sound waves, then the site will have to be abandoned and the work of clearing will have been in vain. When sites are deemed conducive to surveying, a bond is created by pouring a thin layer of edible oil on the ice before placing the transducer. As Tim Janzen, hydrographer in charge of the 2010 Borden Island ice camp explained, the "oil we used was Petro Canada EP320. It is petroleum based, but biodegradable, eco-friendly, and edible, but not tasty. It is the kind of product used in machines for food manufacturing, where the oil may enter the food stream in small quantities."[5] When activated, the transducer sends a sound wave down through the ice and water column to the bottom, and the returning echo is recorded on a graph to show the water depth. The equipment is then returned to the helicopter, which subsequently flies to the next spot and the process is repeated. Under ideal conditions, the entire spot sounding procedure takes between five and ten minutes at each location;[6] however, the time needed for taking off, landing, and travelling between test sites must also be factored into the equation.

As parts of the Arctic are impossible to access by icebreakers or from ice camps, Canadians pioneered the use of autonomous underwater vehicles to extend the bathymetric survey lines. An autonomous underwater vehicle (AUV) is a long, cylindrical, unmanned vessel equipped with a high-resolution, multibeam bathymetric system that may also carry a single-beam transducer. The onboard sensor package can be customized, based on the data needed and the weight restrictions of the AUV for a particular mission. In theory, an AUV offers significant advantages over traditional survey methods, particularly in terms of being able to access areas where poor ice would be difficult to sound through or where it is unsafe to

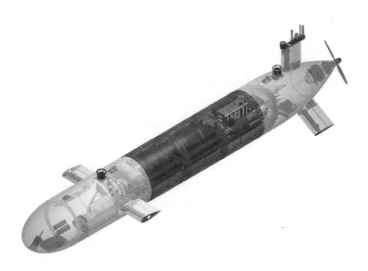

International Submarine Engineering Explorer AUV.

International Submarine Engineering, B.C., Canada.

land or for humans to walk. It is programmed to follow a pattern under the ice and close to the sea floor, collecting bathymetric data, and to come back to a certain point, where the recorded data can be retrieved and the AUV recharged. It has an operational limit of 48 hours, which translates into a range of about four hundred kilometres, and can be launched anywhere that there is open water or where a hole in the ice has been created. Once under the ice, it is unaffected by surface conditions and it takes continuous measurements as it cruises along a pre-programmed flight path, acquiring data as a surface vessel in open water might do.

Experimenting with AUVs to collect data was a joint venture involving three federal departments. Canada's Department of Fisheries and Oceans provided the field trials and the Departments of Natural Resources and National Defence each paid for one of the AUVs. It was agreed that the two AUVs would be available to all three partners as needed, but that one would belong to Natural Resources Canada while the Department of National Defence retains proprietorship of the other. As discussed in chapter 5, an AUV was deployed to collect bathymetric data on two occasions during Canada's Arctic ECS Program: once from an ice camp and once from an icebreaker. That the voyages took place under ice and the AUV was able to conduct a survey and return to the ice camp or icebreaker, respectively, while collecting multibeam data, meant it was a big success. The AUVs designed and built for Canada's ECS mission are unique in several aspects: they are constructed in modules so they can be transported by Twin Otter fixed-wing aircraft to ice camps; they are built to travel to depths of five thousand metres; and they contain a homing system so they can find their way back to a moving ice camp or ship in the ice.

Far from being autonomous, as the name implies, operating an AUV requires a great deal of human effort. When launched from an ice camp, it needs to be transported in pieces, assembled on location, and then disassembled at the end of the mission before being shipped back. Those designed for the ECS surveying are seven metres in length and weigh 1,800 kilograms;[7] thus, they are heavy and awkward to move. To place them in the water involves cutting a long, deep trench through ice that is generally two to three metres thick to accommodate the length of the AUV. This task is no small undertaking. A hot-water drill is used to cut the hole; however, it cannot operate in high winds, when the risks of scalding would be severe.

All this work requires personnel, who must be fed and housed. The Borden Island ice camp that was set up for the AUV deployment in 2010 was the largest of all Canada's ECS Program's ice camps.

Deployment from an icebreaker requires lowering the AUV over the side of the icebreaker without having it hit the ship, thereby damaging its sensitive instruments. Once in the water, the AUV needs to be calibrated, and it takes many hours to complete a helical pattern down into the water column and back up. This procedure is fairly easy to do in an ice camp on shore-fast ice, where one can take whatever time is needed to get the job done. In contrast, the ice pack around an icebreaker is constantly in motion, which means the calibration process is easily disrupted; thus time is of the essence. Although two AUVs were built specifically for Canada's Arctic ECS Program, only one has ever been deployed at a time, in large part because their deployment requires very specialized expertise and such experts are in short supply. Within the Canadian government, the expertise resides in Defence Research Development Canada (Department of National Defence); however, staff from International Submarine Engineering, the company that made the AUVs, has been involved with each deployment.

Getting an AUV to navigate back to the hole in the ice or to the open water around the icebreaker so it can be recharged or taken out is a major challenge. A ship or an aircraft uses a Global Positioning System (GPS) to stay in contact with the satellites and hence to determine its precise location. Under the ice, the AUV has no access to the satellites and must rely on a different means of tracking its positions, using Doppler sonar and inertial measurement systems; however, without being able to pop up to the surface to check its positioning, the AUV may stray off course. How can one predetermine if and when and where the ice floe with the trench may drift? Will the open water that existed around the icebreakers at the time the AUV was launched still be open when it returns, or will the ship be surrounded by a sea of ice? What techniques will facilitate the retrieval of data and the recharging of the AUV under the ice without removing it from the water? These and other challenges have been faced in the deployments discussed in chapter 5. Experience shows that the advances in AUV technology are amazing; however, considerable work remains to be done before they are the solution to the challenges of Arctic bathymetric surveying.

With multibeam and single-beam echo sounders gathering data from icebreakers, hovering helicopters, AUVs, and spot tests on ice, the hydrographers have a range of tools in their toolbox. There is no set hierarchy among them; it is a case of using the right tool for the task at hand. A single-beam or multibeam echo sounder mounted on an icebreaker offers several advantages over spot tests conducted from ice camps: the deployment is far less labour-intensive; and, while spot soundings may be kilometres apart, it produces continuous profiles. Nonetheless, spot soundings on ice allow scientists to survey in areas that would otherwise be inaccessible. If one is trying to locate large ocean features (e.g., mountain ranges), it is effective to use the multibeam echo sounder on a ship, to collect swaths five, ten, or fifteen kilometres wide — down through the water column — to map them. If one wants a more detailed look at a feature, an AUV skimming over it will have a narrower swath and hence produce higher resolution data. If the AUV is down at three thousand metres and only one hundred metres above the sea floor, it will only get a 650-kilometre-wide swath. So it is getting a high-resolution, detailed picture of a relatively narrow area. The denser the bathymetric data, the more detail you have about the shape of the sea floor; hence, helicopter spot-testing is less useful than the continuous profile derived from deploying a transducer on an icebreaker. Yet spot soundings from a helicopter are an efficient way of gathering additional data without diverting the ship from its planned course.

As mentioned above, it is critical to know the velocity of sound in the water column in order to convert the travel time of the sound waves to depth. Sound velocity in water is a function of the density of the water, which in turn is a function of temperature and salinity. In an ocean basin, these properties change both vertically and horizontally. In order to know the sound velocity through the water column, either this property is measured directly with a sound velocity profiler or it is calculated from temperature and salinity data, which are recorded with a conductivity, temperature, and depth profiler (CTD).

A sound velocity profiler measures the time of flight of a sound wave between a transducer and a receiver. It consists of a mini-transducer that sends an acoustic wave across the small gap to a receiving plate and measures the time it takes the pulse to make the trip. Since the distance between the mini-transducer and the reflecting plate are known, the speed of sound through each water sample can be calculated. A sound velocity profiler is mounted on the hull of the ship that constantly monitors and records the speed of sound of the surface water. Occasionally, a sound velocity profiler is deployed to the full depth of the ocean to record the vertical water velocity structure. The CTD contains three sensors: one to measure conductivity (e.g., the amount of salt); a thermometer to measure temperature; and a pressure sensor to measure water depth. A common method for measuring conductivity, temperature, and depth is with an expendable probe, or, more typically for hydrographic surveying, an expendable bathythermograph probe, which simply measures temperature and depth. There is a well-established empirical relationship between temperature and acoustic velocity in seawater. The expendable probes are small torpedo-shaped instruments with very thin copper threads attached. The thread spools out as the probe sinks through the water column, transmitting the signal back to the surface where it is recorded and inputted into the survey software. These probes are released from the stern as the ship is underway, thus saving time.

In icebreaking operations, there is generally open water behind the stern of the vessel within which the probe can be launched. Ice rapidly moves into the ship's track, however, and the ice will break the thin copper thread. It is generally considered a successful deployment if the probe reaches 250 metres below the sea surface. This depth is not ideal but most of the variability in the ocean structure in the Arctic Ocean occurs within these surface waters.

For multibeam bathymetric operations, an inertial motion unit is required to measure the ship's pitch (movement from bow to stern), heave (movement up and down in the waves), roll (movement side to side), and heading (direction the ship is actually moving). It is necessary to record the motion of the vessel on all axes in order to position the data from the returning sound waves accurately. For example, if the ship rolls just as the sound wave is emitted, the latter may go out at a more horizontal angle rather than going straight down. The inertial motion unit records all the facts about the ship's motion relative to one another so the system knows exactly in which direction the pulse is going or from where it is received at any given instant. The critical fact is that the position of every sound pulse's impact on the sea floor (i.e., its point of reflection) must be known accurately, which requires pinpointing its location using the x axis to measure longitude (east-west), the y axis to depict latitude (north-south) and the z axis to measure elevation (water depth). Each sounding must be accurately located in geographic space; otherwise, the data are useless. In multibeam sounding, each emission consists of hundreds of beams or pulses spread out in a fan shape, and each of these beams must be tracked and its position on the sea floor calculated using the position and attitude information about the ship and the water velocity structure. The number of calculations for every sound emission is immense.

SEISMIC REFLECTION AND REFRACTION DATA

Seismic surveys penetrate the layers of the ocean bed to measure sediment thicknesses and their sound velocities. Seismic measurements are taken in time (i.e., the time it takes for a sound wave to travel down into the seabed and return), which must then be converted to depth (thickness). Just as in measuring the velocity of sound in water, knowing the velocity of sound in sediment is necessary to make this conversion from time of travel of the acoustic echoes to thickness of sediment. Velocity structure of the underlying bedrock also helps to determine the type of rocks. Continental rocks, for example, can be distinguished from oceanic rocks, and in some cases this is important in establishing natural components of a continental margin in the context of UNCLOS Article 76.

Thus, reflection and refraction seismology are needed for Canada's Arctic ECS Program. Both involve making a noise, either by the discharge of compressed air from an airgun or detonating a dynamite charge, and listening for the returning sound waves. The airgun or dynamite makes a sound (i.e., a pressure wave under water) that is sensed by the hydrophones or geophones. Both are sensitive microphones. Hydrophones are used in the water, while geophones are placed on land or on ice. In reflection seismology, the sound travels down into the earth and reflects off the various layers under the ocean floor, where there is an impedance change (i.e., a change in velocity and/or density). Each time there is a velocity-density change, a reflection (echo) is sent back. It provides a picture of the configuration of the layers in two-way time — the time it took for the wave to travel down and come back up. This information is needed to determine sediment thickness.

In the case of refraction seismology, a velocity change causes the sound waves to bend (refract along a layer) and to echo back at a later point. Velocity can be determined from the time and distance a wave spends within a particular layer. As a result, each wave provides velocity information about the layers through which it has travelled.

While reflection and refraction seismology use the same sound source, the waves return to different locations. In reflection seismology, the receiver is close to the sound source and the separation between the two is fixed. The travel path of the acoustic wave is near vertical. In marine refraction seismology, the sound source and receiver progressively separate with each successive "shot" of the sound source. For land or on-ice refraction surveying, there is one shot and many receivers with increasing distance from the source (i.e., on-ice refraction profiling).

The thick multiyear ice off the Canadian Arctic Island Archipelago makes it impossible for even icebreakers to survey, so work was also conducted from the surface of the ice. For Canada it was particularly important to study the areas where Lomonosov Ridge and Alpha Ridge adjoin the Canada continental margin to determine natural prolongation and natural components of the margin. Refraction data were acquired at spots on the ice along profile lines and reflection data were acquired at camps on the drifting ice. Ice operations can take place only in late winter, when daylight begins to return to the north, and early spring before the ice becomes unstable because of melting. That means that these operations take place in cold weather (typically between minus 20°C and minus 40°C).

When conducting refraction seismic surveys on ice, the sound waves need to penetrate a long way (e.g., greater than forty kilometres beneath the seabed), so a large sound source (i.e., dynamite) is required. A total of eleven charges located twenty kilometres apart are needed for each two-hundred-kilometre seismic line. Between the shots, 115 to 150 seismic-recording instruments are set out on the ice, one and a half to two kilometres apart. Dynamite charges suspended one hundred metres below the ice are set off in sequence, and the echoes from the various layers of sediment and rock beneath the seabed are received at each instrument.

The process is labour-intensive, involving multiple steps and numerous helicopters. Although the exact organization of the work teams varied somewhat from year to year, the overall process remained the same. The survey line was chosen and the sites of the dynamite charges and the recording equipment along that line were determined. An Arctic ice expert determined where the ice was strong enough to land a helicopter, yet thin enough to facilitate drilling holes down into the ocean. The location of each site was recorded using GPS readings and visually marked using black garbage bags filled with snow, so subsequent teams could find them. In addition, a satellite beacon was left to continuously relay its position to the base of operations.

Auger to drill four metres through the ice to lower the dynamite into the ocean.
Lloyd Litwin, Geophysics Technician, University of Saskatchewan.

The next set of tasks required not only skill but also considerable strength. Using a power auger, a twenty-five-centimetre hole was drilled through ice three to four metres thick.[8] The dynamite was lowered through the holes in the ice, one hundred metres into the ocean below. For the sound energy to travel the length of the entire line, the larger shots (i.e., 350 kilograms) were placed at each end, while the charges in the middle were considerably smaller (i.e., 175 kilograms) as they were only going half the distance in each direction.[9] For reasons of safety and efficiency, a blaster (a licensed expert in the use of dynamite, who are not that plentiful today) connected the dynamite charge to the detonator. Unfortunately, much of this fine work can only be done with bare hands in frigid cold.

Prior to detonating the explosions, recording instruments had to be set out to register the returning sound waves. Placing the seismic instruments on the ice poses several logistical complications. Before they are even taken out, there is the challenge of how to warm them and their batteries up to the desired 20°C, when frigid external temperatures make it difficult to raise the temperature in the workroom sufficiently to warm the equipment.[10] Then there is the problem of how to keep them warm enough to operate between the time of deployment, the firing of the charges, and the recovery of the instruments. Battery life is finite and they are not designed to operate effectively when cooled below minus 20°C.[11] If the weather turns bad, the instruments could be left out for a week or more, as was the case with the 2006 Lomonosov Ridge Test of Appurtenance (LORITA) mission when the weather turned nasty shortly after the recording boxes had been set out, and the science staff worried that the batteries would die before they had even set off the charges.[12] Fortunately such was not the case.

In 2006, the first year surveying, ECS Program director Jacob Verhoef had to justify to government auditors the purchase of 150 picnic coolers and gel packs; a necessary expense, he explained, to keep his equipment *warm*. Contrary to usual assumptions about coolers being used to keep food and beverages cold, in this case the coolers kept the seismic recorders relatively warm while being transported and when sitting on the ice. The story illustrates how Arctic research faces its own unique challenges that require "thinking outside the box" to devise creative and innovative solutions. After the 2006 experience, new seismic-recording boxes were specially designed. Not only did the new boxes provide necessary insulation, the design had a unique

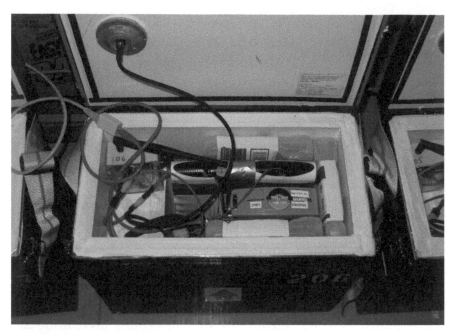

Insulated boxes with seismic equipment.

Ron Verrall, Geological Survey of Canada. Thanks to Jennifer Verrall, Ron's widow, for granting permission to use his photograph.

feature that reduced the amount of frigid air flooding into the box whenever the lid was opened. Before being shipped to the Arctic, the new boxes were tested in freezers to ensure the batteries inside could survive up to ten days on the ice.[13] It was essential to ensure that the equipment was functioning effectively before spending all the time, energy and resources to deploy it.

When the helicopter landed at each site, the installers had to carry the seismic-recording box (weight: twenty-three kilograms) containing the geophone, recorders, computer hardware and the batteries, to the designated spot. They then dug through the snow to place the geophone directly on the ice, because snow reduces the sound penetration. Wires connect the geophone to the instruments in the recording box. Setting out the recording equipment usually takes a full day.[14]

Once all the instruments had been set out, the dynamite was detonated in a timed sequence.

Setting off the charge. The explosion visible is the detonator cord. The main charge is one hundred metres below the ice.

Thomas Funck, Senior Research Scientist, Geological Survey of Denmark and Greenland.

A length of a primacord [detonating cord] connects the explosives with the surface. An electrical detonator cap is attached to the primacord above the water, and a long extension wire is taken off a safe distance to a "blasting box." This box puts out a fairly large current at an exactly known time. The current sets off the detonator cap, and the cap ignites the primacord. The detonation runs along the primacord at a rate of 6 km per second, so it takes only a few milliseconds for the detonation to get down to the main explosives and set them off.[15]

The system is well designed. When the dynamite is detonated, the sound waves go off in all directions. Some go straight down, while others go up, hit the ice, and are reflected back down, so most of the energy is directed downward.[16]

The blaster and his/her team had to be on the ice to set off the dynamite. "The ice is too thick to break up with the explosion but you certainly feel it. The ice rises about fifteen centimetres. I just about fell over the first time it happened. It is an odd feeling when the ground heaves up."[17] When the detonator cord goes off, it makes a lot of smoke, which smells like exploding firecrackers. Those experienced know not to breath in the smoke as it contains nitroglycerine, which opens up blood vessels and causes wicked headaches.[18]

Finally, after all the charges had been exploded, the helicopter(s) returned to each site so the instruments could be recovered and the garbage bags emptied of snow. Retrieving the instruments was frequently hampered by impediments to flying (e.g., ice fog and blowing snow), shifting ice, and drifting snow that hid the instruments and their markers. Once retrieved, the recording boxes were taken back to the ice camp by helicopter, from where they and the seismologists were flown by cargo plane to the base of operations (e.g., Eureka or Alert). Once at the base, the equipment was warmed up, the data downloaded, the memory cleared, and the batteries recharged so they were ready for the next deployment.[19]

The procedures described above are required for each and every site. All these steps were repeated ten or eleven times over the length of every survey line, each of which spanned several hundred kilometres. Given the limited carrying capacity of the helicopters (e.g., a maximum of eleven instrument boxes at a time),[20] the distances travelled, and the time needed for each task, putting out and retrieving 150 instrument boxes is a lengthy process. Using several helicopters at once helped to speed up the process but it required careful coordination. Each helicopter team had a specific time at which each of its dynamite charges could be detonated to avoid simultaneous explosions from different sites confusing the data recorders.[21] With three helicopters flying in relatively close proximity along a single profile line, coordination was also essential for safety reasons.

Seismic work was not only done on remote ice floes; it was also conducted in the ice camps — particularly the remote cache camps — although not using dynamite. Instead a small airgun, placed in the water below the ice, sent out sound waves that were reflected back from the geological layers under the ocean floor and recorded on hydrophones suspended under the ice.[22] To lower the airgun into the ocean, a one-metre-square hole had to be cut in ice. They used a chainsaw until water began to seep into the hole and then switched to a gas auger. As Mike Gorveatt, with his vast experience in Arctic logistics, explained, "As you near the bottom with the drill, you can feel it starting to go faster and you pull back so you are ready for the smash when it breaks through into the ocean." It is very heavy work, which takes two people — one holding each side of the auger — two or three days to complete. The airgun is then lowered down the hole, where it hangs one and a half metres below the ice. A tent is pitched over the hole to protect the compressor and the electronics. Smaller holes are drilled in a big circle around the airgun, and the hydrophones are lowered into the ocean. The more accurately and evenly they are spaced, the better the information collected. The hydrophones were hardwired to recording devices in the heated tents. Both hard copies and electronic copies of the information recorded were sent out on the supply planes to the science staff at the main camp, who checked that the collection was proceeding as needed and conveyed further instructions, such as directions to change the depth of the airgun or alter the filter settings, on the daily radio call.

As the ice floes on which the remote camps were built drifted, the airgun kept firing and the returning waves were recorded over a considerable distance, along an albeit erratic course. As the airgun was small, the waves it produced were not able to penetrate a long way below the ocean floor; however, they did produce shallow, high-resolution reflection data. In contrast, refraction seismology requires a much more powerful energy source, such as dynamite or a large airgun, and it produces a much deeper but much coarser resolution record. The smaller airguns were useful in areas where the data on sediment thickness were required. Furthermore, the reflection seismology done on the remote ice camps benefited from a quiet environment in which much more of the returning signal was audible than was the case in noisier venues, such as an icebreaker. Here was another example of taking every opportunity to collect additional data.

To extend the seismic lines into inaccessible areas, the science staff experimented with icepicks. This method of surveying involves the same procedures for setting the dynamite charges as that used when conducting research from the ice camps; however, the retrieval process is different. The icepicks contain geophones that transmit data to recording devices on an aircraft.

> Because of the Aurora's long-range capability, these geophones can be placed much farther out than our helicopters can reach. The plane will drop a dozen, or so, in a line covering maybe twenty kilometres, and each of the icepicks will radio its signal back to

the Aurora. The aircraft will stay in the neighbourhood recording these signals until all shots [dynamite charges] have been fired. At least two such lines will be covered.[23]

An icepick contains a seismic receiver and a transmitter. After being dropped from a long-range Aurora airplane, the icepick parachutes down, penetrates through the snow, and lodges in the ice below. These instruments are dropped roughly four kilometres apart. After dropping all the icepicks needed for a profile, the Aurora flies to a higher altitude so it can record the data broadcast from transmitters on the icepicks. The dynamite is detonated, and the sound waves detected by the icepicks are recorded on equipment in the airplane. Whereas it takes days to transport 150 seismic recorders by helicopter and to place each by hand, the Aurora can distribute sixteen icepicks in five minutes, and it can record data from multiple instruments at the same time. Furthermore, the Aurora aircraft can cover a wider territory.

Yet there are challenges inherent in using icepicks. Timing is critical, as the plane can stay in the air only for a limited period. Thus, setting the dynamite charge, placing the icepicks, moving the airplane to a higher elevation, and deploying the charge must all be carefully coordinated. The Aurora aircraft requires a team of seventeen to keep it operational, as well as a hanger and a paved runway, neither of which is found in the Canadian Arctic islands; hence, once the dynamite charge is set, the airplane must be called from Thule, Greenland. Dropping the instruments is a tricky operation, which can involve flying at a height of only 150 metres and at a speed of 480 kilometres an hour, in an environment where visibility is frequently limited. The icepicks are considered biodegradable; hence, they are not retrieved. The technology is particularly useful when there are very short weather windows; however, significant coordination is required and, with a large aircraft and crew, standby time in the Arctic is expensive. Nonetheless, the operations are far less labour-intensive and time-consuming than setting up and surveying from an ice camp.

All the surveys conducted on ice and from aircraft comprised spot tests. In contrast, icebreakers permitted the collection of continuous lines of seismic reflection and refraction data. In marine seismic surveying, an airgun or airgun array towed behind the vessel is used as the sound source, rather than dynamite. An airgun is a pneumatic device that releases pressurized air within the water, and the subsequent expanding bubble makes the pressure wave.

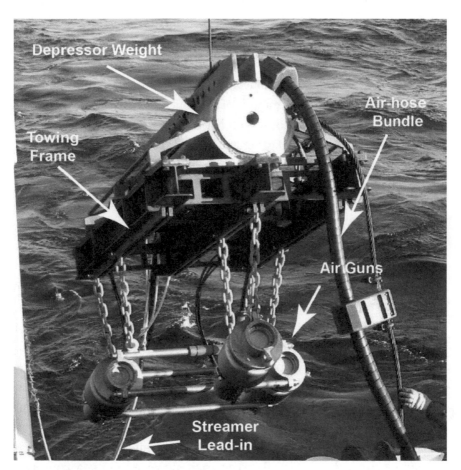

Airgun array.

Deborah R. Hutchinson, United States Geological Survey.

The receiver is an array of hydrophones configured in a long garden, hose-like streamer. A hydrophone is a small ceramic piezoelectric cell that senses a pressure wave and converts it to a voltage (similar to a transducer, discussed above). The streamer is towed horizontally behind the vessel near the sea surface and can be as long as twelve kilometres and consist of thousands of hydrophones, in some industry applications.

In the Arctic Ocean, modifications to seismic equipment and techniques are necessary because of the heavy ice. The airgun array and receiver are towed nearly twelve metres below the ice surface to protect them from the thickest ice. The source array is towed vertically off the stern of the vessel to protect it from ice impact. It consists of three airguns arranged on a sled made of steel I-beams. To ensure that the sled rides below the ice, it carries a weight made of an empty bomb left over from the Second World War that was filled with lead. Another example of ingenuity in using existing materials to solve a problem! The airgun sets off blasts of compressed air every ten to twenty seconds and the sound generated penetrates down through the layers below the ocean floor. Because the source has to be kept close to the ship, the ship and its occupants bear the brunt of the sound against the ship's hull.

The airguns have to be held apart to keep them from beating one another to pieces each time a shot occurs.[24] A double rail welded to the top of that bombshell serves as the towing point. The "umbilical cord" shields the six electrical lines (two per gun), six electrical signal lines (two per gun) and three air lines (one per gun). The compressors that supply the air to the airguns must be warmed for at least twenty minutes prior to deployment so their fluids are brought up to a temperature at which they can function efficiently. Antifreeze is injected into the airlines to prevent freeze-up in the lines, and the guns and lines on the ship are wrapped with heating wire.

The hydrophone streamer comprises four sections: a deck cable that stays on the ship; stretch sections that expand in length when the streamer gets caught in ice; anti-vibration sections, which accommodate the vibrations as the streamer is towed through the water; and the active sections containing the hydrophones. Between each active section is a converter that takes the analogue signal picked up on hydrophones, and converts it to a digital signal that is transmitted back to the laboratory on the ship.

The complete streamer consists of seven pieces, two digitizers, and two repeaters (amplifiers). Each piece, digitizer, and repeater is joined with threaded connectors consisting of fifty-four pins and O-ring seals — twenty-two connections in all. It is precise and painstaking work to splice all of the sections together, on the deck of the ship in freezing temperatures. Clearly, the units were designed for "down south" working conditions, but this effort is absolutely necessary. The streamer sustains tremendous pulling forces, and any water egress or faulty connection means no data and a lot of wasted effort in deployment, recovery, and ship time. The streamer is filled with food-grade silicone, so in the event of a leak, no environmental damage is done. Most of the time, small cedar floats are used to keep the streamer horizontal by preventing its tail end from sinking. The opportunity cost of using the floats is that they are prone to getting caught in the ice.

The receiver (hydrophone streamer) was kept short (less than three hundred metres) to minimize risk of damage and allow for rapid deployment and recovery. Novel deployment techniques had to be implemented. For example, the end of the streamer was weighted to deploy vertically in order to avoid entanglement in ice. When first tried, the weight was tied on and a small parachute was attached, so when the ship started moving, the parachute opened under water and pulled the weight off the streamer, allowing the streamer to come to a horizontal attitude. More sophisticated techniques were later used, which included acoustically releasing the weight after deployment.

Once the streamer is deployed, the airgun sled is put in the water. The guns are not fired until an "all clear" signal is announced by the mammal observers (individuals tasked with protecting animals within a range of one thousand metres of the survey vessel). If any mammal (except the human beings on the ship) is observed within one thousand metres of the

Coiling streamer on deck.

Don Glencross © Her Majesty the Queen in Right of Canada, as represented by the Minister of National Defence, 2010.

vessel at any time during the survey, then the seismic operations are ceased. Once there is a go-ahead, the guns are ramped up slowly. Although there is little likelihood of marine mammals in any of the survey areas of the High Arctic Ocean, the cautionary principle is followed and ramping up the signal provides an opportunity for animals to escape.

Retrieving the equipment is a trickier operation that can be done only in open water with the vessel stopped or nearly stopped. It is helpful, therefore, to find what is known as a polynya or lead (open water surrounded by sea ice). An A-frame is used to lower the airgun sled over the stern of the ship into the water and to haul it out again. The seismic sled comes out of the water covered in salt water, which can freeze quickly, leaving the deck treacherously icy and the airgun frozen solid. Large chunks of ice sometimes come out with the sled, and care must be taken not to be underneath when they fall to the deck. While it would be much easier to use a winch to pay out and haul in the streamer, these tasks must be done by hand so one can feel if the streamer is getting snagged on the ice and, if so, to quickly give it slack so it is not ripped apart. One person hauls the streamer in, while others coil it in a figure-eight configuration on the deck. In spite of all the care taken, streamers do get stuck in the ice. Borden Chapman, chief technologist for the 2007, 2008, 2009, 2010, and 2011 ECS surveys using CCGS *Louis S. St-Laurent,* and consulting engineer for the 2014, 2015, and 2016 voyages, recalled that

> one day the streamer got wrapped around ice floes on both the port and starboard sides. As it was under tension, there was a good chance that it would snap and flip back, seriously hurting someone, so I was prepared to cut it with the fire axe. The ship's captain and chief officer decided to attempt a rescue and spent two hours maneuvering the vessel back and forth, twisted it one way and then the other to push the ice away, and they managed to free the streamer. We tested it and it was fine. We were running out of spare parts, so they saved the program with their phenomenal handling of the ship.[25]

In the interviews with members of Canada's ECS Program's team, the captain and crew of CCGS *Louis S. St-Laurent* were frequently complimented for their superb handling of the ship. Reflection data are also derived from a sub-bottom profiler (a high-frequency, 3.5 kilohertz seismic sounder), attached to the vessel's hull. It images from the sea floor to twenty to one hundred metres below the sea floor. Its operation is identical to a bathymetric sounder but at slightly higher power and lower frequency. In southern operations, the transducer is typically on a ram that protrudes below the ship, making good coupling with the surrounding water. This configuration is not possible with icebreakers, as something protruding would not last long. The transducer, therefore, is in a liquid-filled chest inside the hull of the vessel, and the transducer plates are against the hull of the ship. Unfortunately, the three-centimetre-thick steel hull absorbs a lot of the acoustic energy.

Launching sonobuoy.

Don Glencross © Her Majesty the Queen in Right of Canada, as represented by the Minister of National Defence, 2010.

In marine survey operations in open water conditions, seismic refraction data are acquired with airguns for the sound source, and the sound receivers are ocean bottom seismometers. These instruments sit on the sea floor and record the sound waves as the ship approaches and passes over them. After the experiment, they rise to the sea surface and are recovered and the data are extracted. In ice-covered seas, of course, this technique is not possible as the rising instruments are trapped beneath the ice. Expendable sonobuoys are used as the receivers. This technology was adopted from naval submarine warfare operations.

The sonobuoys are cylindrical in shape, with hydrophones suspended underneath to sense the returning sound waves and a surface float containing a radio transmitter to convey the data to the icebreaker. They are usually tossed off the stern of the icebreaker or sometimes thrown out of a helicopter. They are activated by salt water, so once tossed into the ocean, they sink, deploy a float with an antenna attached, and deploy a hydrophone to listen for the seismic sound waves. It is always rewarding to toss one in and see that the antenna deployed. In the Arctic, there is typically a layer of fresh water on the surface. Freezing seawater rejects salt, thus sea ice is fresher than surrounding seawater. When the ice melts, it is also fresher than the surrounding seawater and, because of its lower density and colder temperature, floats on the surface. Sometimes the sonobuoy is never activated because it does not encounter salt water.

As the icebreaker moves away from the deployment position, the sound from the airguns of the ship travels laterally through deeper and deeper layers before returning to the hydrophones on the sonobuoy, where it is converted to voltage, which is then transmitted back to the ship using a radio signal. As it is not possible to go back to retrieve the sonobuoys in the Arctic, they are expendable and sink to the bottom of the ocean eight hours after deployment. A number of factors can cause the signal to be lost before eight hours have elapsed: the moving sea ice can crush the transmitting antenna, the ice can snip off the hydrophone dangling in the water below the sonobuoy to hear the sound signal, or the radio signal may become too weak to transmit over larger distances.[26] As the data they collect are only valuable when the distance between the ship and the sonobuoy is changing (increasing or decreasing), they are not deployed when the ship is stopped or likely to become stuck in the ice.[27]

While bathymetry reveals water depth and the typography of the ocean floor, seismic techniques show what underlies it. As such, they are the principal sources of data for Canada's Arctic ECS Program. Nonetheless, other complementary sources of information were also collected and analyzed.

COMPLEMENTARY SOURCES OF DATA

Gravity and magnetic studies supplied complementary data for Canada's ECS submission and are most useful on larger, regional scales. Gravity surveys measure the Earth's gravitational field (i.e., the pull of the Earth). The gravitational pull varies with one's position on the globe and with the density of the underlying rock. For example, a sedimentary rock is less dense and hence has a lower gravity measurement than does a denser igneous rock. There are global gravity anomaly models, which provide measurements for different types of rocks in different parts of the world and with which the data from the Canadian Arctic can be compared. Magnetic surveys measure the Earth's magnetic field, which, like the gravitational field, is affected by the underlying bedrock. Different types of rocks have different magnetic properties. Magnetic surveys are useful in identifying the rocks underlying the seabed as well as providing an indication of its geologic history. The *Scientific and Technical Guidelines of the Commission on the Limits of the Continental Shelf* specify that "in areas with ice cover or very deep basements, modelling of a combination of a heterogeneous gravity and a magnetic data set may be a valuable supplement to a sparse seismic database used in the mapping of the top of the basement."[28]

Gravity surveys are conducted from an icebreaker, from an aircraft, or on ice. On ice, the process is laborious as the gravimeter is sensitive and must be placed directly on solid ice, which often requires digging through mounds of snow before a suitable location is found. Gravity surveys were rarely done from the ice camps because they are expensive and do not cover enough ground to warrant the cost. Onboard an airplane or an icebreaker, the gravimeter sits in one location and records as the aircraft or ship moves along. In contrast to the labour-intensive work of placing seismic and bathymetric instruments on the ice or deploying the seismic sled and streamer from an icebreaker, the gravimeter mounted on the ship or airplane requires only minimal supervision, and it provides a constant stream of information to help to fill in the knowledge gaps. Gravity measurements can map differences from the gravitational field of the Earth (the "Earth field").[29] These differences are minute, so the measurements must be precise. All aspects of the ship's or aircraft's motion must be corrected, even the speed and direction of the ship motion. If the ship travels in the direction of the spin of the Earth, it has a different gravity measurement than if it travels against the direction of the spin of the Earth. (If you want to lose weight, measure yourself while travelling quickly in an easterly direction (i.e., with the spin of the Earth). CCGS *Louis S. St-Laurent* did not have its own gravimeter so one had to be leased for each of the ECS surveys.

Magnetic surveys are conducted from an aircraft. Magnetometers do not work when mounted on an icebreaker where they would be surrounded by lots of steel shielding them from the Earth's magnetic field. In warmer climates, a magnetometer can be towed behind a ship, but that is not practical in the Arctic.

DATA PROCESSING

All the raw data collected during the ECS surveys require processing. Experts are needed to take the data in the various formats in which they have been collected and create databases, converting the information into geographic information systems software, from which maps, charts and figures can be derived.[30]

The process begins in the field where the raw data are initially assessed to ensure that the science staff are getting the information required for the submission.[31] Once they are back at their offices in the south, it is too late to find out that the data were defective or inadequate. While still in the field, there is the possibility of redoing a portion of a survey because of a data gap or if the data quality is insufficient. The hydrographers operate the multibeam system twenty-four hours a day, and stored data are verified and processed.[32] Data collected from the ice camps are taken back to the base of operations where they are downloaded and run through software packages to assess their quantity and quality.

The noise of an icebreaker ploughing through the ice produces a lot of extraneous noise that is problematic for both bathymetric and seismic systems, which are listening for returning acoustic signals. "The worst thing is chunks of ice hitting a metal hull right next to a listening device."[33] The data from the transducers, hydrophones, and geophones need to be cleaned, which means removing all the extraneous noise. All the incoming data need to be recorded and then processed using data acquisition and processing systems on the ship or in the field laboratory. Other relevant information, including the time, date, location, water temperature and salinity, and navigational data, must all be factored into the calculations. These tasks demand in-depth knowledge of data processing systems, dexterity in using them, and many long hours of work.

Seismic data require a lot of processing as the recorders provide raw data measured in time, while Article 76 of UNCLOS has a sediment thickness component that must be expressed in metres — not time. Towing the airgun and streamer 11.5 metres below the surface restricts the frequency content of the incoming data, which means that more processing is needed than is the case when the equipment is towed behind a ship in open water, but probably the biggest factor is the ship's variable speed. When breaking ice, or even following a lead icebreaker, it is not possible to proceed at a constant speed. In fact, the ship may be stuck in ice for an extended period. When the ship slows or stops, the hydrophone streamer sinks and when the ship picks up speed, it floats to become horizontal in the water. In southern operations, devices called "birds" are used on the streamer to maintain a constant attitude. These birds would not survive in the ice. This constant change in depth and, in fact, variable depth along the streamer, complicates the processing immensely. Depths at various points along the streamer are continuously recorded to assist in the processing.

Bathymetric data, particularly multibeam bathymetric data, undergo significant processing in real time. A significant amount of editing is required post-acquisition to remove noise — especially in icebreaker operations. The *Scientific and Technical Guidelines* specify that "the location of the point of maximum change in the gradient at the base of the continental slope will be conducted by means of the mathematical analyses of two-dimensional profiles, three-dimensional bathymetric models and preferably both. Methods based on a purely visual perception of bathymetric data will not be accepted by the Commission."[34] As a result, expertise in the use of the appropriate software packages as well as in understanding beam patterns is essential. Being able to spot anomalies or potential errors is in large part a matter of experience. If, for instance, the inertial motion unit is showing a large degree of roll that is not being felt by those onboard, the experienced operator will spot a potential problem that warrants investigation.

Although the navigational data for the icebreaker missions need less processing than do those derived from seismology or bathymetry, calculations are still required to ensure that the information about the ship's speed, direction, and heading are accurate.[35] Each day, the navigational data from the day before are downloaded and run through a software package to create a point and a line file. The information is plotted on the geographic information systems' maps of the area by using a computer, to show the distances and routes covered each day.

BATHYMETRIC AND SEISMIC DATA AND THE ECS REGIME

Relating the scientific research to the UNCLOS regime is complicated by several factors. First, UNCLOS frequently uses "scientific terms in a legal context, which at times departs significantly from accepted scientific definitions and terminology."[36] The contrast between the legal and scientific definitions of the continental shelf (discussed in chapter 1) provides a graphic example of this point.

Second, many key terms are left undefined. For example, no criteria are provided in Article 76 to distinguish oceanic crust from continental crust, although the distinction is the most important scientific criterion for distinguishing the continent from the ocean floor.[37] Likewise, ocean ridges, submarine ridges, and submarine elevations are not defined, although the terms are highly significant in determining a coastal state's entitlement regarding an ECS. The term "ridge" is common in the names of undersea features, recognizing any morphologically elevated and typically elongated structure, irrespective of its genetic origins.

Third, the *Scientific and Technical Guidelines* are effective in outlining key problems in interpreting the UNCLOS provisions but often fail to provide definitive answers desired by scientists. For example, the *Guidelines* point out the Convention's failure to define sea floor highs without rectifying the deficiency by providing definitions of their own.

To recap from chapter 2, UNCLOS provides enabling formulae to determine if the continental shelf beyond two hundred nautical miles is indeed a prolongation of the land mass and constraint formulae to delineate the outer limits of the continental shelf. The test of appurtenance is the process of determining whether there is natural prolongation of a state's land territory beyond two hundred nautical miles. According to the enabling formulae, the coastal state may use either the sediment thickness formula (establishing outer limit points where "the thickness of the sedimentary rocks is at least 1 per cent of the shortest distance from such point to the foot of the continental slope"); or the distance formula (sixty nautical miles seaward from the foot of the slope).[38] Both formulae require the same first step: determining the foot of the slope. The foot of the slope position is determined from a bathymetric profile that shows the maximum change in gradient. When one sees schematic diagrams of the seabed, this task seems fairly straightforward; but the geology is never easy. Slope is almost never a simple morphological feature (i.e., never a sloped line that changes to a horizontal line). Hence, defining the foot of the slope is a complex process, especially in areas like the Canada Basin where there is a very gradual change in slope in some regions. As a result, it is hard to define the foot of the slope based on the requirements specified in UNCLOS.

Article 76 defines the foot of the continental slope as the point of maximum change in the gradient at its base. According to the *Scientific and Technical Guidelines*, the base of the continental slope is "a region where the lower part of the slope merges into the top of the continental rise, or into the top of the deep ocean floor where a continental rise does not exist."[39] A combination of seismic and bathymetric information is needed in the process of identifying the base of the slope zone and determining the foot of the continental slope within that zone.

Seismic information about geological processes, such as submarine landslides, which can only occur on a slope and not on the deep ocean floor, is used to define a base of the slope zone. Thereafter bathymetric profiles through that base of slope zone are used to identify the maximum change of the gradient in that zone. In cases where the foot of the slope cannot be located, the "evidence to the contrary" provision of Article 76 may have to be used, which means marshalling geological evidence to indicate where the continental crust ends and oceanic crust commences. This distinction is never straight forward either, and often only determined based on seismic reflection and refraction information. Once the foot of the slope is established, seismic reflection provides the data about sediment thickness.

If the criteria needed to pass the test of appurtenance are met, the coastal state may then use either of two constraint formulae to establish the outer limit: the distance criterion (i.e., a maximum of 350 nautical miles from the baselines) or the depth criterion (i.e., one hundred nautical miles from the 2,500-metre isobath).[40] The primary sources of evidence for the latter are single-beam and multibeam echo sounding measurements, although "bathymetric information derived from seismic reflection and interferometric side-scan sonar measurements may be considered as the primary source in a submission for the purpose of delineating the 2,500-metre isobath in special cases such as in ice-covered areas."[41] The provisions exemplify the ways in which the *Guidelines* assist states in the preparation of their submissions by establishing hierarchies among the research methodologies, while at the same time showing flexibility in recognition of the enormous diversity found in real environments.

The distance measurements are calculated by the Canadian Hydrographic Service, which is responsible for establishing Canada's baselines, from which the country's territorial sea and other maritime zones are measured. They provide the distance measurements for the UNCLOS enabling and constraining formula (e.g., sixty nautical miles from the foot of the slope, 350 nautical miles from the baselines, and one hundred nautical miles from the 2,500-metre isobath). The officials doing the work are not the same people working on Canada's Arctic ECS Program; such delineation work is done by staff in Ottawa. The hydrographers involved with the ECS surveys were primarily based in Burlington, Ontario.

The Lomonosov and Alpha Ridges are sea floor highs; thus the legal provisions for such features are very important to the delineation of Canada's ECS. Article 76 of UNCLOS mentions three types of sea floor highs: oceanic ridges of the deep ocean floor, submarine ridges, and submarine elevations.[42] The provisions for these features are among the most contentious in the ECS regime. As Ron Macnab, an internationally recognized marine geophysicist, points out, the terms are not defined in either

UNCLOS or the *Scientific and Technical Guidelines*, which relegate sea floor highs to the role similar to that played by wild cards in a poker game and leave the coastal state facing much uncertainty: a "coastal state might base its entire argument on the understanding that a particular ridge or elevation formed an integral part of its continental margin, only to have the CLCS [Commission] disallow that interpretation and thereby force a costly and time-consuming reassessment."[43] The Commission shies away from concrete definitions; instead advising that ridges must "be examined on a case-by-case basis."[44] Macnab points out that this provision "implies a recognition by the Commission that there are no single criteria for determining which ridges may be classified as submerged prolongations, and which may not."[45] When the state and the Commission have differing interpretations of whether a feature qualifies as a ridge or a submarine elevation, Article 76 and Annex II of UNCLOS appear to give preference to the Commission's position.[46]

Oceanic ridges of the deep ocean floor lack geomorphological continuity with the land territory (i.e., their origin, evolution, and configuration differ from that found on land). As such, they cannot be considered part of the continental margin.[47] Submarine ridges and submarine elevations have geomorphological continuity with a state's land territory; hence, they are considered submerged natural prolongations of the land mass and may be used to build a case for an ECS. In the case of submarine ridges, "the outer limit of the continental shelf shall not exceed 350 nm [nautical miles] from the baselines from which the breadth of the territorial sea is measured."[48] Submarine elevations have not only morphological continuity but also geological continuity with the land territory. As such, they confer greater legal entitlement, allowing the coastal state to use either of the constraint formulae: 350 nautical miles from the baselines or the one hundred nautical miles from the 2,500-metre isobath.[49]

While the legal entitlements are clear, neither UNCLOS nor the *Guidelines* provide definitions for the sea floor highs or distinctions based on crustal types, without which it is hard to distinguish submarine ridges from submarine elevations.[50] The Commission accords importance to the processes by which continental margins form and continents evolve; hence, its recognition of submarine elevations is premised primarily on the following criteria:

(a) In the active margins, a natural process by which a continent grows is the accretion of sediments and crustal material of oceanic, island arc or continental origin onto the continental margin. Therefore, any crustal fragment or sedimentary wedge that is accreted to the continental margin should be regarded as a natural component of that continental margin.

(b) In the passive margins, the natural process by which a continent breaks up prior to the separation by sea floor spreading involves thinning, extension and rifting of the continental crust and extensive intrusion of magma into and through that crust. This process adds to the growth of the continents. Therefore, sea floor highs that are formed by this breakup process should be regarded as natural components of the continental margin where such highs constitute an integral part of the prolongation of the land mass.[51]

Refraction seismology is needed to supply information about the structure and composition under the ocean floor to ascertain if it is consistent with that found on shore. Distinguishing among oceanic ridges, submarine ridges, and submarine elevations is a complex process, requiring in-depth understanding of the morphology, geological origins, tectonic evolution, and crustal characteristics of the seabed.

CONCLUSION

Bathymetry and reflection and refraction seismology are essential to establishing that the seabed beyond two hundred nautical miles is indeed a prolongation of a coastal state's land territory and to delineating the outer limits of an ECS. Gravity and magnetic measurements can be used to complement these primary sources. The practical application of the research methodologies examined in this chapter and strategies for overcoming the many challenges to conducting surveys beyond two hundred nautical miles from shore in the High Arctic are explored in the subsequent two chapters. Chapter 4 focuses on the human experience of living on the ice and in an icebreaker for long (generally six-week) periods, while chapter 5 provides an overview of Canada's ECS Program's missions and their findings.

4

ICE CAMPS AND ICEBREAKERS: THE HUMAN EXPERIENCE

Living in an ice camp or on an icebreaker presents many difficulties to test the human body and spirit. The chapter begins by outlining the generic challenges inherent in conducting Arctic maritime surveys. The importance of physical health and safety, mental health, and teamwork are then highlighted. Thereafter attention focuses on the rigours first of setting up and maintaining an ice camp and then of life onboard an icebreaker. The chapter concludes with members of the UNCLOS team sharing some of their perceptions of the awe and wonder of the Arctic.

THE CHALLENGES OF MAPPING THE ARCTIC SEABED

In conducting their research, Canadian scientists have grappled with a series of formidable challenges: the size and remoteness of the survey area, physical oceanography, weather, ice conditions, short seasons, the logistics of ensuring that all the necessary equipment is on hand, the limited pool of scientists and technical support people with Arctic expertise, and the need for advance planning.

Area Is Vast and Remote

The area to be mapped is vast, stretching a thousand kilometres from east to west. Moreover, the profiles need to be charted more than eight hundred kilometres out from the coast. In accordance with Article 76 of UNCLOS, the outer limits of the continental shelf will be defined by

Remoteness: aerial view of Borden Island ice camp.

Michael Black, Multidisciplinary Hydrographer, Fisheries and Oceans Canada.

straight lines joining points no more than sixty nautical miles apart. In theory, profiles need to be taken at least every sixty nautical miles to establish these points. To compensate for unavoidable diversions, such as those occurring when an icebreaker needs to go around large, impenetrable ice floes — problems not addressed in UNCLOS — Canadian scientists planned their Arctic profiles to be fifty nautical miles apart.[1]

Remoteness makes it difficult, time-consuming, and expensive to get to the Arctic. For example, the 2015 UNCLOS survey cost twenty million dollars.[2] The Canadian Forces Station at Alert and the Environment Canada weather station at Eureka, both of which were used to stage some of the UNCLOS missions, are 4,161 kilometres and 3,874 kilometres respectively from Ottawa.[3] There are ice-covered areas in the northern Arctic Ocean where surface vessels have never been able to penetrate, let alone conduct survey work. Thus the surveying for Canada's ECS submission charted new ground, forcing project teams to confront challenges never before tackled. The vastness of the Arctic is hard to imagine, as exemplified by Tim Janzen's account of searching for fuel caches.

Since helicopters cannot carry sufficient fuel to fly to the designated survey areas, do the work and then fly back to the main camp, fuel is stored at designated caches. Ice floes drift so it is essential to be able to find them. In the early years of the UNCLOS ice camps, before GPS was available, we used to mark the caches with huge orange flags over three metres long that would whip in the wind. You would think there would be no way to miss the fuel drums, which are either rusted red or bright blue, beside a gigantic, orange flag, but once [you are] up in the air, they disappear from view. You may take the aircraft down a few hundred metres to search, and spot a tiny speck in the distance, which you decide to check. Ten minutes later you may be close enough to see some orange.[4]

With distances that great, even large, colourful fuel drums accompanied by a huge, bright orange flag are tough to spot. A single person in a green snowsuit would be impossible to find unless he/she had a mirror or something to create an anomaly on the horizon.[5]

Physical Oceanography

Physical oceanography works against scientists seeking to conduct surveys north of Canada's land territory. As David Mosher explained, "The Beaufort Gyre circulates the ice in a clockwise fashion, piling up the ice against the Canadian Archipelago margin. In the area we need to work, ice is the thickest, hardest, oldest, and under pressure as a result. Massive shear zones along the margin make it impossible to access by icebreaker or to set up ice camps."[6] As a result, the ice in the Canadian Archipelago actually becomes denser and more impenetrable as the summer progresses.[7]

Weather

In contrast to the 1980s, when scientific missions in the Arctic enjoyed fabulous flying weather and aircraft could fly every day for forty or fifty days straight without a single bad weather day, the UNCLOS Project encountered many weather problems, especially along the margin of the Arctic Archipelago.[8] Dense ice fog makes flying helicopters and airplanes extremely hazardous. It is likely to occur when frigid air and a cold land mass meet open, warmer water. In particular, ice fog seriously curtails the use of helicopters, which are essential when working both from ice camps and from icebreakers. With limited visibility, the pilot cannot distinguish between sky and land/ice. As David Mosher explained, "If you are travelling in a helicopter and visibility becomes poor, the pilot has to land and you can be stuck there for minutes, hours or even days until the visibility improves. You always travel with a sleeping bag and a toothbrush!"[9] Ice fog is a serious impediment to data collection when the latter requires the helicopters to land a number of times an hour, day after day. Freezing fog poses another challenge to the helicopters. As the moisture freezes, the helicopter blades get heavier and heavier and torque increases to the point when the helicopter falls out of the air. Needless to say, the pilots do not fly under such conditions.

Bitterly cold temperatures also present problems for the scientific teams and their equipment. Patrick Potter, a mathematical geophysicist with Geological Survey of Canada, said that when he stepped out of the aircraft on his first trip to an ice camp it took only ten seconds in the biting wind for his nose to freeze, although he was clad in a parka, fur hat, and goggles.[10] He still feels the legacy of that injury each time it is cold and windy.[11] While preoccupied doing a demanding task, Mike Gorveatt, an Arctic logistics specialist with Natural Resources Canada, failed to notice that his hat had slipped off his ears, leaving them to freeze.[12] In the wind, it only takes about fifteen seconds for bare hands to start to freeze at minus 30°C,[13] yet there are jobs, such as connecting the wires to the detonator when doing seismic surveys on the ice, that can only be done with bare hands, even when the temperature is minus 35°C or colder.

Below minus 40°C, machinery ceases to function properly, and flexible equipment, such as fan belts, hoses, and fuel lines for camp stoves, break like glass. If you use regular lubricant, instead of cold weather grease, wheels will not turn because the lubricant freezes. Some of the diesel delivered to the 2010 Borden ice camp was the wrong grade and, being too viscous, did not flow properly into the tent heaters — a serious concern in frigid temperatures.[14] The problem was solved by thinning the diesel with other fuel,[15] a relatively easy task in southerly climes but more formidable in the Arctic. "All you want to do is pump a few litres of fuel from one drum to another, but the hose is frozen and twisted and might break off if you try to straighten it, the diaphragm of the pump is so stiff that it creaks and groans with each stroke, threatening to tear like last time, and it takes all your strength to hold the pump still, and then the plastic pick-up pipe snaps off and falls into the drum."[16] Large quantities of snow mean extra work clearing runways. When surveys are conducted from ice floes, bathymetric and seismic recorders and gravimeters must be placed directly on the ice, not in snowdrifts, thus requiring the scientist to dig through the snow before placing a sensitive instrument. On numerous occasions, the retrieval of sensitive instruments was delayed and made very difficult by the onset of bad weather. Often instruments would be covered in deep snow and/or on drifting ice floes. As a result, instruments were exposed to the elements sometimes for periods of a week to ten days, and a few were never found.[17]

Weather presents challenges to those onboard ship. In open water, high winds and billowing seas can take a toll on members of the science team who are prone to seasickness. Weather also affects the equipment. Gravity readings, in particular, require corrections to compensate for the sudden, random nature of the noise introduced by breaking through the ice.[18]

Climatic conditions exert a huge, pervasive influence, yet they are hard to predict.[19] For example, in 2008 the ice left Resolute around July 13 but it was back again by July 28. In 2008, the ice north of Yukon and Alaska was very thick, while in 2007 it was minimal. In the summer of 2007, the Russian side of the Arctic Ocean was virtually clear of ice and the ice conditions were light in the Canada Basin. Canada was able to take advantage of these conditions and collect a significant amount of high-quality bathymetric and seismic data near the Beaufort Sea by using its most powerful icebreaker, CCGS *Louis S. St-Laurent*. In contrast, weather conditions in 2007 posed serious challenges along the Arctic margin, where the ice actually became denser as the summer progressed, which made travel through it impossible in August and September. This pattern is typical as a result of the Beaufort Gyre, discussed earlier in the chapter. In the winter of 2007, the Nares Strait between Ellesmere Island and Greenland did not freeze over near Alert; frigid air meeting warmer water caused ice fog that reduced visibility, resulting in the loss of 90 percent of the workdays, which seriously compromised progress that year. The previous year, bad weather caused by unusually warm temperatures in April resulted in the loss of 60 percent to 70 percent of the workdays in the eastern Arctic. Such erratic developments make planning difficult.

Ice

Fractured ice in winter and thick ridges of multiyear ice in summer impede data collection. Arctic winds and currents push multiyear sea ice against the islands of the Canadian Arctic Archipelago causing huge build-ups of thick compressed ice. As Paola Travaglini, chief hydrographer on the 2014 mission, recalled,

> Many times the ice in the area in which we had wanted to collect data was too thick and the icebreaker could not get through, so Dave [Mosher, chief scientist] and I would determine the next best option. Sometimes such decisions had to be made at three o'clock in the morning because the original route was impassable. In choosing a new survey line, we considered what data already existed, what data required validation, and where the gaps were as well as what was feasible given the ice conditions. These are very strategic decisions when one has such limited survey time.[20]

Once the decision was made, it would be communicated to the ship's captain on the bridge and logistical arrangements would be changed to the requirements of the new plans. Huge build-ups of thick, compressed ice poses severe challenges to Arctic researchers, who must respond with flexibility and ingenuity.

Ice with pressure ridges.

Kai Böggild, Natural Resources Canada.

In addition to impeding transit, multiyear ice has the consistency of concrete so it poses a hazard to vessels' hulls and propellers as well as to scientific equipment. Ice or air under the ship interferes with the acoustic signals used for bathymetric surveys and impacts the ability to measure the bottom accurately. The force of even a small, bedroom-sized chunk of ice getting between the vessel and the tow cable can throw the almost 2,300-kilogram seismic airgun and streamer out of the ocean and into the large ice blocks rolling in the vessel's wake.[21]

It is not uncommon for cracks to develop in the ice on which a camp is situated. Ruth Jackson, chief scientist for the 2007 LORITA and 2008 Alpha Ridge Test of Appurtenance (ARTA) ice camps and for the 2007 and 2008 missions on CCGS *Louis S. St-Laurent*, recounted, "I've been in camps where the ice has split open a kilometre wide, right through the centre of our camp, right through the centre of our hydrohole [hole cut in the ice]. Our electrical lines were pulled out. It took us several weeks to re-establish things."[22] Furthermore, if one happens to fall into a crack "it is darn hard to get out, with mukluks and mittens on."[23] During the 2006 LORITA mission, bad weather necessitated the evacuation of a remote cache camp using a Twin Otter aircraft; however, a helicopter had to be left there on the ice and for ten days it was not certain whether they would be able to retrieve it.[24] In April 2009 the ice breaking up around the cache camp caused the emergency evacuation of the personnel stationed there.

Even more dangerous than cracks are pressure ridges that cause the ice to buckle, tipping a camp and its inhabitants into the sea.[25] As such occurrences can happen quite quickly, one needs to be vigilant in looking for warning signs. Water levels in the hydrohole could start to fluctuate, or ice, which has been drifting steadily eastward, could suddenly begin drifting westward, where it would collide or push into other ice floes.[26] To facilitate rapid evacuation, helicopter pilots at some remote camps in the 1970s and early 1980s slept with their helicopter batteries under their beds to avoid spending hours warming up the batteries before takeoff.[27] The threats of ice cracking or buckling are familiar hazards, but with climate change the ice has become much more unstable and the dangers greater.[28]

Unstable ice conditions also impede locating explosives and seismic instruments that were deployed on the ice prior to the onset of bad weather. In spring 2007, the ice floe containing a fuel cache moved eighty kilometres in three days during a storm, thereby presenting further challenges to operations.[29]

Helicopter and Twin Otter pilots flying to remote locations have to be able to read the ice so they can find places to land that are sufficiently flat, smooth, stable, and thick. It is a highly specialized skill and mistakes can be fatal.

Short Seasons

The combination of ice fog, winter darkness, and thick ice results in narrow time frames during which research can be conducted. As the sun does not come up until the end of February, the spring program cannot begin before mid-March and it needs to be completed by the end of April or first week of May, as warmer temperatures bring snow, ice fog, and cracking ice.[30] Surveys using icebreakers are conducted when the sea ice is thinnest; thus, they usually begin in mid-August and run to the end of September. By mid-September, temperatures are again frigid, the sea is freezing over, and the days rapidly become shorter.[31] Navigation in darkness poses serious hazards in the High Arctic. "An icebreaker can work in lighter ice conditions in the dark, but it is exceptionally difficult in heavy ice conditions as visibility is limited to the distance of the ship's flood lights. Pressure ridging and large multiyear ice floes cannot be seen until you're already into them."[32] The ice is thinnest in mid-September; however, the days are getting shorter so August to mid-September is the best compromise. There are still twelve hours of daylight in late September, but that quickly diminishes to only nine hours by October 10.[33] These factors severely limit the hours available to work.

Logistics of Providing Necessary Equipment

The logistics required for Arctic data collection are complex and complicated. One needs to bring everything that will be needed and to take it back when the research project is completed. For an ice camp, all the heavy equipment and supplies have to be shipped up the preceding summer, during the short window of opportunity when they can be sent as far north as possible by sea. In summer 2008, for instance, four cargo containers and close to two thousand drums of jet and diesel fuel left Montreal on the icebreaker CCGS *Terry Fox* for Eureka, from where they were ultimately flown 560 kilometres to the principal 2009 ice camp.[34] For the 2010 ice

Runway at ice camp off Borden Island.
Michael Black, Multidisciplinary Hydrographer, Fisheries and Oceans Canada.

camp off Borden Island, equipment and supplies were shipped by sea to Resolute, from where they had to be flown to the camp. Needless to say, the cost of these shipments is huge; however, the cost of not shipping in advance and later having to fly heavy or bulky equipment all the way from the south is exorbitant.

It is, however, not possible to ship heavy freight by sea to the most northerly locations. Canadian Forces Station Alert, which served as the staging point for several UNCLOS missions, is a case in point. "Alert's fuel and other bulk supplies are ocean-freighted into Thule, Greenland, and are transported by military Hercules over the relatively short hop (680 km) from Thule to Alert. This air haulage takes place two or three times per year, and the operations, which are called 'Boxtop,' involve several 'Hercs' all flying 24 hours per day for a frenetic two weeks or so."[35] Clearly long lead times and careful planning are essential to ensure all necessary equipment is transported to Alert during this short window of opportunity.

The bathymetric and seismic surveys conducted on ice required the use of both helicopters and Twin Otter (DeHavilland DHC-6) airplanes, each of which helped to compensate for the limitations in the other.[36] A Twin Otter airplane can travel much faster and carry much heavier loads than a helicopter. It is a utility aircraft capable of taking off and landing in relatively short distances; however, unlike a helicopter it still requires a flat landing surface. Arctic ice is often rough and broken or covered in deep snow. Although helicopters cannot land on badly broken ice, they require relatively little and less exacting landing space than the Twin Otter, so they are much better suited to laying out the survey lines. Twin Otter aircraft are vital in transporting fuel and explosives to designated cache sites, from which the helicopter can be resupplied.

When an ice camp is being set up, initial supplies and personnel are sent out in a Twin Otter aircraft on skis. A large runway must be cleared to permit landing the bigger cargo planes, such as a Buffalo or a DC-3, that are needed to transport the large quantities of fuel required by the helicopters and other aircraft, the equipment necessary for the seismic and bathymetric surveys, and all the provisions for the camp. In terms of speed and efficiency, the Buffalo airplane offers significant advantages over the Twin Otter in transporting fuel and freight: "The Otter will burn about three and a half barrels of fuel in delivering six barrels to the ice camp. The Buffalo, on the other hand, will use about seven barrels of fuel while it delivers 46. And the delivery times are about the same. The efficiencies of scale are obvious."[37] The Buffalo is also more efficient than the DC-3. "While the DC-3 burns 10 barrels of fuel to deliver 17 [barrels], the Buffalo can deliver 40 drums to the Ward Hunt Island camp and burn 10."[38]

Travelling with barrels of fuel can be physically uncomfortable and psychologically troubling. One must be careful to ensure that the barrels do not roll into someone's leg or toes, and sometimes the barrels take so much room that the only place for one's feet is on top of the barrels.[39] Being in an airplane loaded with fuel can cause uneasiness; hence, the hydrographers' guide provides some reassurance: "while flying in a Twin Otter with fuel drums it is normal to hear an uncomfortable popping sound during take-off. This is just the drums de-pressurizing."[40]

Canada does not have many icebreakers, let alone those with heavy-duty capacity; hence, surveys were planned around the availability of CCGS *Louis S. St-Laurent*. If something breaks, the chances of getting a replacement from the south before the six-week window of opportunity closes are pretty slim, especially in summer when an icebreaker is a week or more outside helicopter range. In August 2007 the new compressor broke after only four days of use. If it had not been for the chief technician and his team, who managed to

Twin Otter carrying passengers and fuel drums.

Tim Janzen, Fisheries and Oceans Canada.

make replacement parts, that year's survey would have been aborted. On the same voyage, the steel beam needed for towing the seismic equipment broke in the ice. The following year, not only was the beam replaced by one twice as strong, but CCGS *Louis S. St-Laurent* carried four spares. It was also equipped with not one but two sleds on which the seismic airguns were mounted and behind which the recording devices were towed. Lost equipment and breakage can be costly in terms of money but, most seriously, they can result in the loss of time, which is irreplaceable and especially critical when one has such limited periods for conducting the research.

Scarcity of Expertise

One of the most serious challenges to the UNCLOS research has been finding sufficient numbers of scientists with expertise in Arctic research.[41] From 1958 until the early 1990s, Canadian hydrographers conducted springtime Arctic surveys each year; thus they had experience working on the ice and putting up ice camps. This pattern stopped in 1989 when funding was cut to the point where expensive, systematic Arctic surveys could no longer be mounted and the focus moved to what were considered to be higher priorities in the south. This trend resulted in a general reduction in Arctic scientific work. For some seventeen years, little bathymetric or seismic work was done in the Arctic; hence, those hired during that period had little opportunity to gain Arctic experience. In recognition of this lost expertise, Ronald Verrall wrote a comprehensive manual full of practical advice for living and conducting scientific research in the Arctic, to which scientific teams doing Arctic research still refer.[42] Most of those who actively engaged in Arctic research prior to the early 1990s are now retired. The seventeen-year hiatus saw the pool of Arctic experts dwindle, and those remaining often put in long hours and spent significant periods away from home. In addition to the loss of human capital, much of the equipment needed for Arctic missions — both the scientific instruments and the camping equipment — sat unused for years before the warehouses were cleaned out. A major reason for running joint surveys with Denmark was the need to pool scarce resources — not just money, although that was critical — but also expertise and equipment.

In the mid-1990s, Canada was a world leader in the production of desktop studies analyzing existing data and in the publishing of maps, such as the bathymetric charts. Sadly Canada's prowess in producing Arctic desktop studies dwindled in the years immediately prior to its ratification of UNCLOS in 2003, because of a lack of government funding. As a result, there was little fresh data to analyze. When significant funding for Arctic ECS surveys was announced in 2004, it was necessary to acquire new equipment and to rebuild the expertise.

While Arctic research is tough for all, it presents particular challenges for the chief scientist, which can make it harder to find a candidate willing to serve. One of the main burdens is the legal liability.[43] In 2003 Canada's criminal code was amended as a result of the Westray Mine disaster of 1992 and the public inquiry that followed. Paragraph 217.1 reads, "Every one who undertakes, or has the authority, to direct how another person does work or performs a task is under a legal duty to take reasonable steps to prevent bodily harm to that person, or any other person, arising from that work or task."[44] This legal liability is daunting in light of the many dangers and challenges inherent in surveying in the most remote parts of the Arctic. Months before each Arctic mission begins, the chief scientist organizes meetings for the team members to explain the objectives and various aspects of the programs, how they all fit together, the survey plans, and the work they will be doing. A chief scientist can distribute safety manuals and hold safety briefings, but there are decisions affecting a mission that are well beyond the chief's control. Ruth Jackson, who spent her career working as a scientist in the Arctic and who served as chief scientist on four UNCLOS surveys, said, "I may request additional personnel and write a specification for that job but not be included in the hiring process; thus I may not meet the new person until they arrive at the survey site. That was the case with two blasters — supposedly people with licences to use explosives — who arrived at the ice camp having previously loaded charges, but never having actually detonated any."[45] By the time the surveys are underway in remote regions, it is too late to start a new hiring process. Yet were the blasters to injure themselves or others, the chief scientist could be held personally responsible under Article 217.1 of the criminal code.

The number of workers is always limited on a survey, and it is imperative to capitalize on good weather to move the agenda ahead. The chief scientist must allocate personnel resources so as to maximize efficiency, while minimizing the risks to personnel and equipment. The two considerations are not always compatible, as Ruth Jackson explained: "If the qualified blasters are deployed elsewhere, is it acceptable to ask somebody who is not trained in explosives to move boxes of dynamite? The task is relatively safe, but if there were an accident, how would the chief scientist fair in court?"[46] These are tough decisions that add to the stress of the job.

Even without detonating the dynamite, there are risks. The helicopters delivering explosive charges for the seismic survey lines carried several hundred kilograms of dynamite on each run, which can be very unsettling for passengers onboard.[47] The flights were non-smoking; however, travelling with cargoes of dynamite or fuel gives a whole new meaning to the phrase "smoking is not good for you."[48] Drifting ice poses other hazards, as one has no control over the movement of an ice floe under which a large load of dynamite is suspended. "The dynamite charges needed for the seismic survey were set out under the ice at the top of the Nares Strait. If the ice ridge there had broken, the explosives would have been carried down the strait by the gyre [current moving in a circular motion] and into the shipping lanes. The explosives were ready to detonate with their primer cords attached and the gyre can travel two hundred kilometres in a day."[49] Fortunately, the ice ridge did not break, the explosives were not carried into the shipping lanes, and no ships were blown up; but the risk was there.

There are risks inherent in helicopter travel, even when not carrying combustible or explosive cargoes. In 2012 a helicopter on a routine ice reconnaissance operation from CCGS *Amundsen* crashed north of Banks Island, killing a leading sea ice researcher as well as the ship's commanding officer and the helicopter pilot.[50] According to David Mosher, "assigning someone to conduct helicopter operations is daunting and the chief scientist is personally liable. As a result, I did all of the helicopter drops of sonobuoys myself."[51]

Another important area that may be beyond the control of the chief scientist is the acquisition of large pieces of equipment. In Canada, such purchases are coordinated through the Department of Public Works, which sends out the specifications, and companies bid on the contracts. Public Works chooses the equipment, which is often delivered directly to the icebreaker or survey base. The compressor for the 2007 voyage of CCGS *Louis S. St-Laurent* exemplifies the kind of problems that can result from this practice.

> Compressors produce high-pressure air that feeds the airguns, and they can be 2,500 psi, which can be lethal. The first night we ran them, the high-pressure ends blew out. Now, at that point, I [as chief scientist] faced a dilemma: should I say this survey cannot be done because it is unsafe and abort the mission or should I ask the chief technician and the ship's engineer to attempt reparations? Those are the types of decisions you are forced to make.[52]

Ruth Jackson decided to continue the mission and the chief technician, ship's engineer and their respective crews did an amazing job of rebuilding the equipment, not just once but many times.

Scheduling the work shifts is complicated and must be handled with sensitivity. For the chief scientist, the most important consideration when assigning people to work teams is compatibility.[53] No one wants to work the graveyard shift (i.e., midnight to 8 a.m.).[54] Some work eight-hour shifts and get paid for overtime. Others are hired to work twelve hours straight for twelve hours of pay. Thus, after eight hours of work, some are receiving overtime and others are not; however, compensation was not raised as a serious issue by the team members interviewed.

The chief scientist's day is spent overseeing operations — ensuring that the equipment is functioning well and that the data are being recorded properly — allocating resources, dealing with questions and concerns, and finding the right person to address problems or fix broken equipment as needed.[55] The chief scientist works out navigational strategies with the ship's captain to best maximize the quality and quantity of data collected. If ice conditions preclude continuing on the preselected path, what will be the new route? The chief scientist also decides if it is necessary to go back to a particular spot to do further testing, to stop for four hours to do the CTD rosette cast, and to deploy or retrieve seismic equipment. Consultations with the ship's captain ensure that the right members of the crew are available at the right time to do the work that needs doing. In an ice camp, duties include monitoring weather reports, which play a critical role in determining work plans, and monitoring the drifting ice floes on which remote camps and fuel caches are located. A helicopter has a very limited range so it is essential to know where the fuel is when it is needed.

Lone helicopter.
David Mosher, Natural Resources Canada.

Having a capable chief scientist is essential, but it is also vital to have a good chief technician, who can direct the technical team efficiently to resolve mechanical problems as soon as possible and who works well with the ship's crew to ensure that the equipment is moved and deployed safely.[56] The technical team works shifts. In most cases, each shift is sufficiently well staffed that it is not necessary to get them out of bed during their designated rest periods; however, the chief technician is expected to get up to oversee the handling of all emergencies with the equipment, which means being on call twenty-four seven.[57] If, for example, the seismic streamer is damaged during a voyage, the spare parts are used to build another system but in the course of the reconstruction process, the technical team and its leader could be on deck for eleven or twelve hours.[58] "You never go to bed expecting that you will necessarily get a full night's sleep and when you do, you smile."[59] When asked to recall some humorous stories from his voyages, Borden Chapman replied, "There were so many frustrating moments, especially in the first couple of years, and we were always under a lot of pressure to keep the equipment running. Six weeks of twelve-hour plus days. There were not many humorous moments!"[60]

The dearth of those with Arctic expertise is exemplified by the fact that most of the technicians whom Borden Chapman, chief technician on CCGS *Louis S. St-Laurent* for most of the UNCLOS surveys, engaged were retirees from the Bedford Institute of Oceanography with years of experience dealing with machinery and equipment in Arctic contexts.[61] In spite of being retired himself by that point, Chapman was asked to come back in 2014 when it was clear that further UNCLOS surveys were scheduled and experienced technicians were in short supply. He served again as consulting engineer on the 2015 and 2016 UNCLOS missions.

Need for Advanced Planning

In light of the formidable challenges any project team confronts, advanced planning is essential. Arctic research programs require a lot of forethought, extensive preparations, and considerable flexibility in adjusting to changing weather and ice conditions and other new circumstances. Jacob Verhoef, former director of the Geological Survey of Canada, said that they had "a five-year plan that changes every month."[62] While the objectives for conducting the research remain firm, the specific logistics must be adapted to the realities encountered in the field. For example, the location of a base camp may need to be moved if the ice breaks up or open water causes ice fogs to descend. Weather and ice conditions can change quickly. Scientists are provided with satellite images prior to departure and they have at least a rough idea of what the ice is going to be like; until they are there, however, it is impossible to know how bad it is or could be.[63]

PHYSICAL HEALTH AND SAFETY

Participants on an Arctic mission need to be physically and mentally healthy. If someone becomes seriously ill or is badly injured in an accident, help is a long way off. Field work is strenuous; all participants are required to have a medical examination prior to the mission. Safety manuals and other useful information are distributed, and each participant is outfitted with the requisite clothing (parkas, boots, hats, hand protection, etc.) and safety equipment. If it does not fit well, it will not protect properly and it may actually pose threats to one's well-being. To facilitate dressing properly for the conditions, the Canadian Hydrographic Service suggests using the acronym COLD: "keep your clothes clean, avoid overheating, make sure your garments are loose-fitting to ensure that your blood circulation is not constricted, and stay dry."[64] Wearing three or four layers is seen as the best way to follow the COLD prescription.[65]

Prior to a mission personnel receive training in safety procedures, emergency survival skills in a marine environment, wilderness first aid, and the use of firearms.[66] There are many hazards to avoid (e.g., frostbite, spinning helicopter blades, Twin Otter propellers, and problems with wild-life), and the proper use of safety equipment, such as life jackets, lifeboats and survival suits, must be mastered. Knowing how to operate machinery properly in an Arctic context is essential. How does one Ski-Doo on rough ice without being thrown off? How does one drill holes in the ice without getting wet feet, having the drill break through the ice and disappear into the ocean, or having the drill freeze before it can be disassembled?

On its earlier UNCLOS missions, CCGS *Louis S. St-Laurent* had a nurse onboard; however, as it travelled increasingly farther north and farther from land, it was necessary to have a doctor as well as a nurse. In 2010 a team member required a medical evacuation from the ship, which meant spending seven days in transit to get the person back to a point where he could be airlifted to medical care and they could resume their surveying.[67] Travelling at one hundred kilometres per hour, helicopters only have two hours of flying time, so a total of two hundred kilometres is a maximum.[68] Clearly, missions to the High Arctic exceeded that limit by a considerable margin. In such remote areas, accidents and illness can be life-threatening as well as costing a great deal of time and money. "If you are at the North Pole, no one can fly in to get you. An airplane cannot land and a helicopter would run out of fuel long before it got there."[69]

While not quite at the North Pole, the ice camps were too far from help to take unnecessary risks. There are many potential dangers when living in an ice camp: polar bears, walking or driving a Ski-Doo over the brow of a hill and becoming disoriented in the sea of whiteness and unable to find one's way back to camp. As a result, team members are advised to "ensure that you are within visual and hailing range of at least one other person when working in the field."[70] The camp manager is responsible for the safety of the team; however, all members are required to have taken at least a basic first aid course and preferably the advanced version.[71] There are strict protocols in place whether one is at an established base, like the Eureka weather station or the Canadian Forces base at Alert, or in a remote ice camp, that require anyone leaving the camp to tell the person in charge when, where, and with whom they are going; when they plan to be back; and what equipment they are taking (e.g., radio, GPS).[72] As camp manager for Project Cornerstone's remote ice camp in 2010, Mike Gorveatt required those leaving camp to call in every half hour. In turn, Mike was expected to contact Tim Janzen, manager of the main camp, on a daily basis both for safety reasons and because Tim was directing the research program. The arrangement sounds logical and straightforward in theory, but it proved to be much more complicated in real life. The communications systems between the remote camp and the main camp did not always function well. On days when communication between the two camps proved impossible, messages were relayed via the Polar Continental Shelf Program's base six hundred kilometres away in Resolute.[73] Ironically, although the distances were greater, communications seemed to work better between the remote camp and Resolute than with the main camp. The well-being of those in the remote camp was monitored: "If you missed one call, they stayed on alert and if you missed the second one, they sent a plane."[74] The staff at Resolute monitored the ice by satellite and the pilots of the supply planes circled around the camps before landing or after taking off to assess the ice conditions and, if problems were spotted, they reported them to the camp manager, who would decide on the necessary course of action.[75] The nursing station in Resolute was the closest medical facility for the 2010 ice camps, but the nearest doctor was in Iqaluit. Project Cornerstone's remote ice camp was a four-hour flight to the main camp, and from there it was a further seven hours by air to reach a nurse.[76]

Unexpected and potentially life-threatening situations can confront even those most experienced. During a seismic refraction survey, a helicopter deposited Ruth Jackson, Mike Gorveatt, and Jay Ardai on an ice floe so they could set out the seismic-recording equipment.[77] They needed to coordinate with another team working on the same line but they were unable to make contact from the ground, so the pilot launched his helicopter in the hope of facilitating better communications. At altitude, the pilot could no longer see the team on the ground. They could see him flying in search patterns but they were unable to attract his attention. They burned boxes to create smoke signals, but the only smoke generated was white, which did not show up against the Arctic snow and ice. With fuel running low and no success finding the three members of the science team, the helicopter pilot called for a Twin Otter, which can travel farther and faster, to be sent out to search. The Twin Otter pilot knew approximately where they were, so he flew around in the general area. When he circled out of the sun, they flashed their mirrors at his eyes and he spotted them. The helicopter pilot was directed to the correct spot to collect them. Fortunately they were only stranded for two or three hours — albeit in the biting cold — and they had excellent survival skills, so all three were fine. As Mike Gorveatt recalled, that "little mirror could have saved our lives that day. That is how fast things can happen." The next morning he arrived at the helicopter carrying a large coil of rope and threatened to tie himself to the helicopter skids so the pilot could not leave them on the ice again. Clearly a sense of humour helps in such circumstances!

It is not uncommon for helicopters and other aircraft to develop engine problems. In April 2009 on a helicopter trip back from a day of fieldwork when team members were still 150 kilometres from the main camp, the warning light suddenly came on indicating engine failure.[78] The pilot managed to land safely, and, after a forty-minute wait in frigid conditions, a second helicopter rescued the team.[79] The same month, three men were stranded overnight at the cache camp when the hydraulics of their Twin Otter aircraft malfunctioned. Suddenly a two-person camp had to accommodate five people.[80]

MENTAL HEALTH AND TEAMWORK

Everyone interviewed for this book stressed the importance of sound mental health and effective teamwork. People in an ice camp or on an icebreaker are part of a very small community, in which all members depend on one another for their mutual well-being. "You can achieve almost anything, if everyone is working as a team."[81] On the other hand, the community cannot survive well if people are unhappy. If two people are not getting along, their conflict has to be resolved. Bad relations tend to escalate and to breed an atmosphere of negativity. Sonya Dehler, chief scientist for the 2015 ECS Mission and subdivision head, Geological Survey of Canada, commented, "You can't let it escalate to the point where it involves other people and starts to jeopardize the mission. It is the job of the chief scientist to deal with interpersonal conflicts. What is the issue and what can be done about it?"[82] Personal animosities, while rare, must be addressed and not be allowed to fester.

With experienced people who have worked together for a long time, these types of issues do not tend to arise. It is more likely to occur with new people or when someone is worried about something extraneous, like problems at home, that can carry over into interactions with others.[83] Leaving home for significant periods of time presents challenges for many. Primary caregivers have to find someone to care for their children, elderly parents, or infirmed relatives for the whole six-week period, before they can even set off on an icebreaker voyage or to a remote ice camp. Leaving family and friends behind for six weeks can be stressful. Participants need to be reconciled in advance to the fact that they will, to a large extent, be out of contact with those left at home. There are no cellular telephones, no Wi-Fi, and no Facebook. Loved ones will be missed and there may be concerns about their well-being, yet one cannot call home every day.

Then there are personalities that are just not suited to life either on an icebreaker or in an ice camp, where egos must be put aside and one must help with a variety of tasks, as the need arises. "People who are not good team players are weeded out quickly. Word goes around that you don't want that man or that woman, so they don't get invited back, although you may be stuck with them for the one mission."[84] Overall there are relatively few personnel problems as most chosen to go on the missions, and certainly those who are invited to participate on more than one, have strong track records of being collegial, hard-working, flexible, and good team players with positive attitudes, who are willing to pitch in whenever the need arises.[85]

Happiness is very important when a group of people is living together in close quarters, isolated from the outside world, so those in charge have to make sure everything is well run. After a warm place to sleep, food is the next most important thing for good morale.[86] "Meals are your time to step away from work, to take a break and relax, to sit down with co-workers that you may not see on a regular basis, to talk about work or life, to share experiences, or to tell a funny story. It is an important social time and it revolves around the food. If the food is terrible, you only eat what you have to and get out as fast as possible which seriously detracts from the enjoyment of an important social event."[87] On the other hand, good meals are something to which one looks forward. They can also be opportunities for team members to come together to coordinate their work. At the ice camps and on the icebreakers, the days were punctuated by three main events: breakfast, lunch, and dinner.

For the ice camps, food orders were placed by radio and the provisions were sent out by plane. "Sometimes you even got some fresh veggies; however, you had to know when they were coming so you could have a cooler waiting to put them in to transport them inside. At minus 40°C, they would freeze outside in short order. The cooler kept them warm."[88] While the range of options may have been limited, the residents of the ice camps did have some choice in the groceries that arrived. In this endeavour, as in all aspects of the mission, teamwork was essential. "There was no standing on ceremony. Everyone would go and help the person whose task was the highest priority. When a plane was coming in, everyone went out to clear the runway."[89]

While teamwork is vital, there is nonetheless a chain of command both in the ice camps and on the icebreakers. Each morning in the ice camps, the team members gathered to share views and concerns. This information was vital to creating task-related priorities; for instance, what expertise and resources were required where and whether personnel needed to be transported between the camps. If people had to be transported, the camp manager would reschedule aircraft to accommodate the need, depending on availability of aircraft, weather conditions, and so on.

The coast guard ships are run on a "military chain of command" model, which makes sense when one is navigating through such inhospitable conditions and running so much complex machinery. The Canadian Coast Guard is a civilian organization, whereas "the U.S. Coast Guard is a military force, and the *Healy* is designed as such, with few portholes, steel decking and bulkheads and fewer creature comforts than the *Louis*."[90] The ship's captain is responsible for handling emergency situations onboard. As Ruth Jackson recalled, "If Borden [the chief technician] decides that the airguns need to be pulled out of water at 3 a.m., he cannot go directly to the bridge. Instead he must get me [the chief scientist] up and I must go to the bridge to say they need to come out."[91]

Arctic surveying is still a male-dominated field. For example, of the twenty-one science staff members on CCGS *Louis S. St-Laurent* in 2014, only three were women; for the 2015 mission, the number of female members of the science staff increased to five; and in 2016, six of the twenty-four science staff members were women, so the numbers increased slowly but steadily over the final three years of surveying. Three women (Ruth Jackson, Sonya Dehler, and Mary-Lynn Dickson) have served as chief scientist on the UNCLOS missions in the Arctic, with Jackson holding the position four times. As in most workplaces, there are some inappropriate, sexist comments, yet none of the women interviewed complained of serious sexual harassment. They are strong women who are not afraid to speak their minds and who would not suffer sexism in silence. Jackson and Charlotte Keen led expeditions themselves and participated in decades of scientific studies; both internationally recognized scientists, they are credited with paving the way for the women who followed.[92]

ICE CAMPS

Travelling in the far north is an adventure in itself. Flights are frequently delayed, sometimes for days at a time. In 2008, for instance, the flight from Edmonton, Alberta, to the Eureka weather station in Nunavut (the site from which that year's ice camp was established), was delayed several times and then required a refuelling stop in Resolute.[93] Upon arrival at the weather station, the equipment was unloaded but "in the cold and the wind and the confusion of unloading all the 'big' freight, the personal baggage had been forgotten" and had to be flown back from Resolute the following day.[94] Thus, personal items like toothbrushes and pajamas were missing in action the first night.

Using an established settlement, like the Eureka weather station or the Canadian Forces Station in Alert, offers the advantages of existing, permanent structures and facilities and a much greater level of comfort than that found in an ice camp; however, it also necessitates adapting to the rules of the place. The regime at the military base at Alert was not always well suited to the needs of the scientists. For example, dinner was served daily from five to six, with no possibility of getting food served thereafter, whereas the scientists did not get back from their field work before seven and frequently they were later; thus, they depended on their colleagues putting aside food for their return.[95]

Ice camps were used for UNCLOS surveys in the springs of 2006, 2008, 2009, and 2010. Working from ice camps poses many challenges and requires a great deal of forethought and preparation. First, a site must be chosen. It is not easy to find pieces of ice that not only are long enough and sufficiently flat and smooth to accommodate a camp and a runway for the cargo planes, but also are located in an area in which the scientists want to conduct surveys. The ice selected must be unlikely to develop cracks or break apart, so it can safely hold a camp and a runway. The ice under the principal Alpha Ridge Test of Appurtenance (ARTA) camp was five and a half to six metres thick.[96] The choice of location must be made by someone with expertise in Arctic ice, who is able to judge its age and thickness. Richard MacDougall, former director of the Law of the Sea Project for the Canadian Hydrographic Service, spent two days in the summer of 2008 flying across the islands along the edge of the Arctic Ocean, covering as much as 1,600 kilometres a day cramped in a Twin Otter (DeHavilland

DHC-6) aircraft, to find suitable sites for future base camps.[97] In spite of the extensive search, only a few suitable sites were found. Before a location is finalized, an auger is used to drill down through the ice to determine its thickness.[98] Holes are drilled at intervals around the perimeter of the airstrip and they are retested about once a month.[99] To ensure safety, the process is repeated as the weather warms.

Ideally an ice camp would be located in the centre of the survey area; however, it is rare to find a sufficiently large, flat, smooth, stable piece of ice in the desired location. As a result, all the main ice camps had to be located quite some distance from the survey lines. For example, the 2009 camp off Ward Hunt Island was 160 kilometres from the start of the survey area and some 480 kilometres from its outer edge.

Once the site is chosen, arrangements must be made with the closest settlement to secure a base (e.g., Alert, Eureka, or Resolute) to which supplies can be sent, at which accommodation can be provided, and from which personnel and equipment can be flown to establish the ice camp. Erecting an ice camp is a herculean undertaking that was generally done by

Auger boring through ice to test depth.

Tim Janzen, Fisheries and Oceans Canada.

personnel from the Canadian Hydrographic Service. At times, it was done by outside contractors working to the chief scientist's specifications. In either case, everything needed — the insulated tents, wood for tent floors, mattresses and bedding, kitchen equipment, food, toilet(s), shower(s), plumbing tools and hardware, electrical wiring, generators, diesel stoves to heat the tents and for cooking, snow-melting equipment to get water, tools for the workshop, communications equipment, and fuel for the aircraft, generators, heaters, and stoves — had to be transported first to base (e.g., Alert, Eureka, or Resolute) and from there hundreds of kilometres to the principal ice camp. Planning what equipment will be needed is a huge job but so is keeping track of all the equipment as it is shipped first to the staging base and then to the ice camp. At the end of a mission, all this equipment (as well as the garbage) has to be packed and shipped out so that the ice is left pristine. As noted in a field report, "Establishing and removing this infrastructure often occupies more time than conducting the survey work. It is also the most labour-intensive part of the season, exposing personnel to manual labour in the cold and the frustration of dealing with equipment

Erecting tent at Ward Hunt ice camp.
Tim Janzen, Fisheries and Oceans Canada.

that won't move, plastic parts that shatter like glass and hoses and belts that break rather than bend at forty below."[100] In some cases, they not only took out their own garbage and equipment but also cleaned up messes left decades earlier. In 2009 the airplanes that brought out the equipment, personnel and supplies to the ice camp frequently returned to Eureka with fuel drums — some full, some empty and some filled with garbage — and other trash that had been left at the Parks Canada site on Ward Hunt Island in the 1950s.[101] Throughout the spring ice camps, the temperatures ranged from minus 50°C to minus 30°C, which is tough on people and equipment.

Until a runway is built, only small planes on skis, such as the Twin Otter, which has limited carrying capacity, can access the ice camp. A smooth ice runway has to be built to accommodate cargo planes, such as a Buffalo or a DC-3. In 2006 the arduous process was begun by hand, as they shovelled the hard-packed snow off a 244-metre-long strip of ice.[102] The resulting runway permitted a Skyvan (a plane capable of taking off and landing in a short space) to bring in a small Bobcat, which was used to clear the rest of the 900 to 1,200-metre runway needed to land the larger cargo planes.[103] While a huge improvement over shovelling by hand, the Bobcat itself had trouble moving the hard-packed snow.[104] The overall process was similar in each subsequent year, requiring crews working in shifts twenty-four hours per day. As noted in a 2009 field report,

> The runway needs to be 120 feet wide, which is too wide for the snow blower to blow the snow to the edge of the runway in one pass. The procedure is to start in the centre and blow towards the edges and re-blow until the edge is reached. The snow is so dense that only 2–3 feet can be cut off in each pass — so it is a slow process but the end result is a runway that can take planes on wheels and no huge banks on the sides — to catch snow the next time it blows.[105]

That year it took over two weeks to prepare a runway one thousand metres long and forty metres wide.[106] Yet the hard work was not always rewarded. In 2008 they never managed to clear a large enough runway to land a Buffalo aircraft, so they had to make do with Twin Otters and the Skyvan.

Transporting the Bobcat to an ice camp and then unloading it is quite a procedure.[107] As a safety feature, the Bobcat is built so that it cannot operate

Ramp for Bobcat.

Tim Janzen, Fisheries and Oceans Canada.

without its cab in place; however, with the cab attached, the Bobcat was too large to fit in any of the cargo planes used. The design had to be adapted so the cab could be removed and the Bobcat operated by a remote control when the cab was off. It took three days to build a wooden ramp strong and stable enough to hold the weight of the Bobcat as it was driven off the aircraft. Even so, it was tricky to manoeuvre it out of the aircraft and down the ramp and, at the end of the mission, to reverse the operation. The Bobcat was needed to maintain the runway, load and unload the cargo from the aircraft, move heavy equipment, and clear the snow from the camp.

The area of habitation has to be carefully planned.[108] A section of clean snow upwind from the tents and the soot from their chimneys has to be marked off, so people do not walk through their source of drinking water. At the opposite end of the camp, downwind from the tents, latrines are erected. In between, tents for preparing and eating food, sleeping, and working have to be set up.

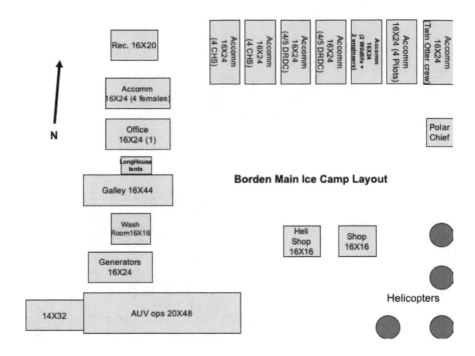

Rec. 16X20

Accomm 16X24 (4 females)

Office 16X24 (1)

LongHouse tents

Galley 16X44

Wash Room16X16

Generators 16X24

14X32   AUV ops 20X48

N

Accomm 16X24 (4 CHS)

Accomm 16X24 (4 CHS)

Accomm 16X24 (4/5 DRDC)

Accomm 16X24 (4/5 DRDC)

Accomm 16X24 (2 Wildlife + 2 engineers)

Accomm 16X24 (4 Pilots)

Accomm 16X24 (Twin Otter crew)

Polar Chief

Borden Main Ice Camp Layout

Heli Shop 16X16

Shop 16X16

Helicopters

Layout of Ice Camp off Borden Island
Tim Janzen, Fisheries and Oceans Canada.

Ice camp off Borden Island.

Michael Black, Multidisciplinary Hydrographer, Canadian Hydrographic Service, Fisheries and Oceans Canada.

Human waste is a huge problem in an ice camp, and the larger the camp, the more challenging the logistics.[109] Right at the beginning, a pee pole is erected so that all the urination occurs at the one spot and a large patch of yellow snow is not discovered two months later by someone digging snow to put in the snow-melting equipment to create drinking water. Thereafter the latrine is built. Urine is collected in large garbage cans (ideally ones with tight-fitting lids). Every day the garbage cans full of liquid urine are carefully lifted onto a Ski-Doo trailer and pulled far enough from camp to be dumped. During the trip, someone has to hold the can so it does not tip over en route; however, accidents have been known to happen. Propane toilets are now used to collect and burn fecal material. When the toilet reaches fullness, urine and grey water from the kitchen are added, the mixture is stirred, then the chamber is sealed and the propane burner is ignited. The liquids evaporate and the remaining solids burn to ash, which is then packed into drums and flown south for disposal. In the larger camps, the camp maintenance person generally does this task and gets "dirty pay" (i.e., a higher rate of pay for the period during which he or she is doing this unsavoury work).

Elimination is a challenge at the individual level, as well. "When one wakes in the wee hours of morning (pun intended) to the beckoning call of nature, at minus 40°C, it is always an internal power struggle: do I try to wait until morning; go through the ritual of dressing for the elements which can take some time, taking a firearm in case of bears, and then undressing again; or risk going as is, with all speed?"[110] It is not an easy decision to make when none of the options is particularly appealing. Various strategies have been used to try to increase the comfort level, including "carving toilet seats from Styrofoam and keeping them with you in your tent."[111] Pranks were known to happen. On occasion, a Styrofoam toilet seat was taken from someone's tent, lowered deep into the ocean where the pressure squeezes the air out so it came back as a teeny-weeny toilet seat.[112]

Other solid waste, such as kitchen garbage, is burned in incinerators, located away from the habitation area. They are created by cutting holes in the top of forty-five gallon drums to which jet turbines have been attached to force air into the barrels to make the flames burn at extremely high temperatures. As a result, solid waste is reduced by a considerable amount, and what is shipped south is largely ash.

Incinerator.

Tim Janzen, Fisheries and Oceans Canada.

Ice camps rely on diesel to run the heaters, generators and other equipment, that are all so essential to life and the success of the mission. In addition to the cost and logistical problems of transporting the diesel, it poses other challenges. "It does not matter whether the generators are up-wind or down-wind, the water you drink tastes like diesel fuel. Everything smells like diesel."[113] Even the camp inhabitants, themselves, smell like diesel.[114]

The number of people living in the principal ice camps increased over time. In 2006, the first year of ECS surveying, most stayed at the Alert military base and only three were stationed at the ice camp, while in 2008 and 2009 some 30 people, including scientists, pilots, technical staff, helicopter engineers, camp cooks, and mammal observers, lived in the ice camps. By 2010 the number had grown to over 40. With time, the quantity and sophistication of the equipment likewise increased. In 2006 there were three helicopters and two Twin Otters at the ice camp, whereas in 2009 five helicopters, two cargo planes (a Buffalo and a DC-3), and two Twin

Otter aircraft were required for the project. When the UNCLOS surveys began, survey sites were marked with garbage bags filled with snow. A few years later, GPS equipment was also used. As sites for the main ice camps were located considerable distances from the survey areas, refuelling camps were set up in closer proximity to the test sites, both for safety and for logistical efficiency. They served as refuges in bad weather, caches both for fuel for the helicopters and for equipment for the survey teams, and sources of weather information. Several of these remote camps also conducted reflection seismic data acquisition using an airgun and hydrophones suspended below the ice, as described in chapter 3. The camps were operated by a skeleton crew of two when they were just caches or three when they were also conducting seismic work. Although setting up a two- or three-person camp is a much smaller undertaking than establishing a large one, many of the same tasks are still necessary, such as setting up the tents, cooking facilities, snow-melting equipment, generators, electrical wiring, sanitation, and fuel depot, and providing for the care of aircraft and other equipment. Life in the remote camps was rougher and tougher than that at the larger camps.[115] For example, "snow blew in around the bottom of the tents, and it could be 38°C degrees at seven feet and minus 20°C by your feet, because there was no way to move the air around. Your forehead would be sweating and your feet would be cold."[116] The bigger camps had electricity so they had fans to move the air around in the tents; however, they had to be careful not to let the floors get too warm or the ice underneath them would have started to melt, making the floors uneven. The larger ice camps had a cook, whereas those at the remote camps cooked their own meals. One person looked after everything during the day to keep the camp running, while the other two worked twelve-hour shifts (midnight to noon and noon to midnight) managing the seismic reflection work. Those working the shifts shared a tent because they were never there at the same time. Good interpersonal skills and a willingness to be a team player are essential when there are only two or three people living and working together in isolation from the rest of the world.

Additional fuel and supplies were left at unmanned caches along the survey profiles. Again, ice floes had to be located that were long, smooth, and thick enough to land a Twin Otter aircraft. "To determine whether a piece of ice is of suitable length to act as a runway, they fly low over the prospective strip, time the length it takes to travel over it and then land."[117] Twin Otter aircraft on skis transported fuel and supplies to the refuelling camps and caches. Ski-Doos were used to transport fuel, food, and other supplies from the runway to the camp.

The camps were on sea ice and sea ice moves. At the beginning of the 2006 spring mission, the ice camp drifted westward at a steady pace of almost five kilometres a day.[118] Thus it was critical to erect beacons so the camp's location could be tracked by GPS. Ensuring good communication between an established centre (e.g., Alert, Eureka, or Resolute) and teams out on the ice is essential for three reasons: (1) to get help in an emergency; (2) to provide weather reports for the pilots; and (3) to coordinate the work.[119] Contact also facilitated the placing of food orders.

Each year there were problems trying to get equipment designed in the south to function properly in the harsh northern conditions. As noted in a 2009 field report,

> There is a new Kubota Tractor with an ill-fitting snow blower, the same rental Honda generator we had problems with last year and despite asking the outfitter to service the generator it still has the same dead battery as when we returned it in May, two new Herman Nelson heaters that have summer wheel bearing grease which means wheels do not turn at 40 below, and three new Yanmar generators that all are running poorly and backfiring.[120]

Efforts were made to address as many of these problems as possible before the equipment was sent from the base to the field.

The tasks of daily living that we tend to take for granted in the south can be arduous, time-consuming, and frustrating endeavours at an ice camp. Each year there were difficulties installing a functional shower. In 2008, for instance, they had to battle a series of problems with the "fancy," "high-tech" water heaters for the shower and finally resorted to heating buckets of water on the stove.[121] Doing one's laundry at the ice camp was described as "hard work," involving a ten-step process:

1. Fill large garbage can with white snow
2. Haul full garbage can back to your tent

3. Transfer snow into large aluminum pot
4. Melt snow over stove; top up with snow as required
5. Four hours later, you might have enough water (preferably warm)
6. Fill two plastic bins with water
7. Steal dish soap from the galley tent, give one bin a few squirts
8. Wash laundry in one bin, rinse in the other, then wring out
9. When water is black in both bins, it is probably a good idea to save the remaining unwashed laundry for another day when your laundry washing enthusiasm is significantly higher than it is at this point.
10. Hang up your wet laundry wherever you can in your tent, and pray it will be dry before you need it. Endure abuse about your choice of underwear.[122]

Icebreakers have laundry facilities and working showers; however, they present their own challenges as discussed below.

ICEBREAKERS

According to David Mosher, chief scientist on four UNCLOS missions, the chief scientist's worst job onboard an icebreaker is allocating rooms.[123] The lower decks are the noisiest; hence their cabins are the least desirable. In assigning cabins, many factors must be considered: seniority; union rules (e.g., a union requirement for one category of worker might be a single room); shifts; need (one worker might be deemed to be doing higher-priority work than another and hence needs better rest); and gender.[124] Coast Guard captains, for instance, might want to assign the best rooms to their officers and crew, whereas the chief scientist might prefer the scientists and technicians to be as rested as possible so the objectives for which the icebreaker was hired are realized.[125] Given all the equipment problems encountered over the years with the seismic gear on CCGS *Louis S. St-Laurent*, it was imperative that the chief technician, in particular, have a quiet place to sleep.[126] When it is not possible to give each team member a single room, efforts are made to pair people of the same sex who have

CCGS *Louis S. St-Laurent.*

Kai Böggild, Natural Resources Canada.

opposite shifts or at least partially different shifts so people have at least several hours a day to themselves.[127]

To start the 2007, 2008, 2009, 2010, and 2011 voyages, the scientists and technicians flew to Kugluktuk in western Nunavut, from where they were transported four at a time to the flight deck of CCGS *Louis S. St-Laurent*, which was anchored off shore. As there were no wharfs in the Canadian Arctic to accommodate large ships, luggage and food were also transported to the vessel by helicopter. CCGS *Louis S. St-Laurent* has a wide hull with a relatively shallow draft, good for moving through ice but not so ideal in billowing waves. Hence, anyone at all prone to seasickness had a tough time in open water and, obviously, there was no turning around and going home because someone felt queasy. On its 2014 mission, CCGS *Louis S. St-Laurent* sailed from St. John's, Newfoundland, to the Eurasian Basin, most of which was in rough open water. For the 2015 and 2016 missions, the scientists and technicians boarded at Tromsø, Norway, thereby both avoiding an uncomfortably bumpy voyage and saving precious time.

Until 2014 CCGS *Louis S. St-Laurent* carried one helicopter; however, an accident on one of the coast guard ships caused a change in policy, and since then it has been equipped with two helicopters. They are needed to provide aerial surveillance to aid with navigation through the ice, to transport personnel to and from the ship when necessary, to provide medical evacuations over short distances, to conduct bathymetric spot tests, and, on occasion, to deploy sonobuoys. It was used about fifteen times on the 2014 mission, which is not frequent; however, when the need arises it is crucial.[128]

Meals on CCGS *Louis S. St-Laurent* were served at set times three times a day. One-hour maximum each for breakfast, lunch, and dinner. The galley was accommodating of preferences and allergies, and they would put aside meals that could be heated in the microwave at a later time.[129] After dinner each evening, a meeting was held in the boardroom to discuss what was accomplished that day and what was planned for the following day. The scientists would report their findings and their colleagues from the diverse disciplines had the opportunity to comment and ask questions, which not only kept everyone apprised of the progress being made in individual disciplines but also showed the interrelationship among the various types of work being done. At times, individual scientists were asked to lecture on their respective areas of expertise. Having the right mindset for an Arctic voyage is as important as physical health. As Walli Rainey, a marine geoscience technologist with the Geological Survey of Canada, commented, the "*Louis* appears to be a very large ship when you get on but a very small ship by the end of a six-week mission. During this period, some 120 people are living and working together in the same confined space, seeing each other day in and day out, and after six weeks, you have heard all the good stories."[130] Finding a quiet time for oneself could be a challenge. It could be hardest on members of the science staff working in confined spaces, such as the seismic laboratory on the aft section of the ship, where those who maintained and deployed the seismic equipment monitored its functioning (e.g., making sure the airgun fired properly and that the compressed air flowed steadily to the airgun). It was often stressful work, especially when the equipment was not functioning well. To make matters worse, the confined space could quickly overheat and become stuffy.[131]

Seismic lab on CCGS *Louis S. St-Laurent*.

David Mosher, Natural Resources Canada.

In more southerly climes, coast guard crews usually work shifts of twenty-eight days on and then twenty-eight days off, which means voyages of four rather than six weeks in duration. In northern waters, however, rotations are forty-two days because of the vast distances that need to be covered.

Many team members find the isolation from family and friends difficult. Today there are Iridium satellite phones onboard, but the service is very expensive so its use is kept to a minimum.[132] An email server works through the satellite phones, so one can send simple emails (no pictures, just text). The messages are accumulated and then sent out as a batch at the end of the day. Likewise, incoming emails come in as a batch once a day.

After living in close proximity to others for six weeks, it can take some days to reintegrate back into one's home life. Family and friends need to respect the fact that their returning loved one may not be instantly ready to resume a daily routine. They may need time to be alone, to catch up on sleep, and to readjust their sleep patterns.

For some, the work shifts are so strenuous that sleep comes easily. Others have their sleep disturbed by the twenty-four hours of daylight, even when they are exhausted. A simple solution is to get some aluminum foil from the kitchen and put it over the window to block the light: "A little bit of duct tape and a little bit of tin foil does the trick. You have to be versatile."[133] The midnight sun can present other challenges. As Hans Böggild recalled, "Several times I got so engrossed writing the blogs for the trip that I failed to notice the time passing and suddenly realized that it was four in the morning."[134] Because it was so bright, there were no external, visual clues that it was time for bed. With only two and a half hours until breakfast and then a full day of activities, it was a short night.

The ship had some amenities to help with what leisure time there was, including an extensive movie and book collection, a piano, a large screen television, several lounges, and exercise equipment. The vending machines dispensing candy and chips were located in close proximity to the exercise machines, so anyone sneaking in for a snack was in full view of sweating exercisers, and vice versa. As there are many decks and many steep staircases on CCGS *Louis S. St-Laurent*, most people got a fair bit of exercise in the course of a day, even without using the equipment. The galley, located on a lower deck, required crew and science staff to climb down several sets of steep stairs.

There was no designated social director, but people organized activities (e.g., card games, Saturday night bingo, competitions, variety shows, movies and popcorn in the lounge, and musical evenings). Those with instruments had impromptu jam sessions. There were ceremonies for momentous occasions, such as crossing the Arctic Circle, when certificates were given to those making their first transit, and arriving at the North Pole, when again certificates were distributed. When the 2014 mission reached the North Pole, CCGS *Louis S. St-Laurent* sounded its horn, the loudspeaker on CCGS *Terry Fox* played Stan Rogers's "Northwest Passage," and the gangplanks on both ships were lowered allowing those onboard to leave the ships for the first time in three weeks.[135] On the ice, two teams squared off for a game of hockey; some teed-off with golf balls; some played ice floe soccer; and many had their picture taken with Santa.[136] Everyone onboard participated in the so-called Ice Bucket Challenge that became a global phenomenon. A charity event to raise money for ALS (amyotrophic lateral sclerosis) research, it involved pouring buckets of ice water over one's head.[137] Similar celebrations were held when the 2015 and 2016 voyages reached the North Pole.

One imagines the beautiful, white expanse of the Arctic to be a very quiet environment but life on an icebreaker is a very noisy experience, with the frequent yet irregular bangs of the vessel hitting the ice, the airguns going off, the engines roaring, the compressors hissing and booming, and the bubbler deploying, sending out a stream of bubbles to lubricate the ice so it flows more easily along the sides of the ship as the blade under the bow cuts through the ice.[138] "If you are below deck and the ship is breaking ice, it sounds like you are in the belly of a snow plow. It is a very loud, low rumbling sound and you hear the ice scraping the sides of the ship as you move through it."[139] "The constant loud noise is hard to get used to. It is like being in a semi-continuous earthquake."[140] The lower the deck, the higher the decibel level; thus, upper deck cabins were most desirable. Anyone able to get off the icebreaker for even a few hours during a cruise would comment on the peace of being on an ice floe. The contrast between that quiet and the noise onboard was described as "breathtaking."[141] Yet such reprieves were rare.

The ride is not only noisy but it can also be jarring.

> When the ship hits a big, solid ice pan, you can be thrown off your seat. In 2010 the *Louis* hit an ice pan in the wrong spot (slightly off to the side rather than head-on) and instead of breaking the ice, the ship road up the ice before sliding off and sending everything flying. All our equipment, including our computers, needs to be tied down. Otherwise you go back to your cabin and everything that was on the desk is on the floor.[142]

There was always motion and often turbulence; thus, the pre-cruise briefing included instructions to "always keep a hand free for the rail."[143] "It is impossible to describe the physical jarring as the ship breaks through the thick ice. It would shake your fillings out. It is that intense!"[144] A particularly unpleasant experience of turbulence was described as follows: "One day, we hit a very deep piece of ice and the ship went over on a forty-five degree angle. For an eternity of seconds, it felt like the ship was tipping over."[145] As one never knew when the next jolt would come, care was exercised all the time — when moving about the ship, working, eating meals, resting, and bathing. Several tips were offered for avoiding falls in the shower. "You can lean against the shower wall to stay upright, or you can take a wide stance with loose knees so that you're ready to shift your weight at all times. Now there's something you never think about when you're showering at home."[146] Breaking through ice felt like being in a collision, at times powerful enough to throw you from your bunk.[147] When turbulence was expected, an announcement was made over the loudspeaker; however, not all encounters with tough ice could be anticipated.

The captain and crew of CCGS *Louis S. St-Laurent* worked in concert with the scientists to maximize the quality and quantity of data collected. "It was an amazing example of teamwork."[148] There was also a high level of cooperation between the respective crews, and the scientific and technical teams on USCGC *Healy* and CCGS *Louis S. St-Laurent*. Rather than jockeying to be admiral, they all worked as a wonderful team.[149] When one ship got stuck, the other would come to the rescue. CCGS *Louis S. St-Laurent* was most likely to get trapped in the ice, as it could not travel at full speed (let alone reverse) while towing the seismic gear. Sometimes USCGC *Healy* would have to reopen the channel in front of the Canadian icebreaker. Other times, USCGC *Healy* would come around and carve a path on each side of CCGS *Louis S. St-Laurent*, thereby relieving the ice pressure. When there were technical problems, technicians from the two countries cooperated to find answers. Likewise, scientists collaborated to obtain the best possible research outcomes. At times, Canadian hydrographers participated in the scientific work on USCGC *Healy* and American scientists did likewise on CCGS *Louis S. St-Laurent*, which provided good opportunities for sharing of expertise, experience, and ideas.

CONCLUSION

Living and working on an icebreaker or in an ice camp presents many challenges: lengthy absences from home; long, tough workdays; the frustrations of equipment failures; physical danger; and demands on one's emotional reserves. Yet in spite of these challenges, all those interviewed spoke about the Arctic with reverence and awe, as reflected in their comments below: "To have the opportunity to go places where no human has ever been … to be one of the first people to actually see what's beneath the sea floor in an unexplored area … it's just thrilling."[150] "You're literally surrounded by white. You can get mesmerized watching the ice go by. As the *Louis* breaks through,

Awe of the Arctic.

Dwight Reimer, Natural Resources Canada.

these very, very large pieces of ice slowly flip, showing every colour of blue you can imagine and as they close in behind the ship, you think, Wow!"[151] "Sometimes the ice is loose, like an asteroid field with little blocks of ice floating by, and sometimes you are breaking through a seemingly unending field of pack ice. It is fascinating to watch."[152] "Everywhere you look is a white expanse. The vastness makes you feel pretty darn small."[153] "In our urban world, we sometimes feel divorced from the natural environment. In the Arctic, you were constantly reminded that the world is much bigger than the one we have created. It is very inspiring!"[154] "It's hard to describe the sense of peace and rugged beauty.... It's magical to be out there on the ice."[155] "When you are out on the deck of the *Louis* looking at that much white, that much ice, that much space, and that much distance, then the vastness of where you are hits home."[156] "The shades of blue, the white, the horizon where the sea and the ice and the sky all meet, it's breathtaking, absolutely breathtaking."[157] "From high up in the helicopter, the environment around the icebreaker appears so vast. The earth looks a bit like the moon because it is light with various hues of blue emanating from the different types of ice and you feel as the early astronauts must have felt when they looked back at earth from space: Wow! Our earth is a planet spinning in space."[158]

Arctic sunset.

Tim Janzen, Fisheries and Oceans Canada.

In addition to the physical beauty, the majesty, and the grandeur of the scenery, being in the Arctic as part of an isolated, mini-community offers other rewards. "You get to know your colleagues so much better than you would in an office situation."[159] "To be around the various scientists and technicians was inspiring because they had so much expertise, experience, and depth of perception about what is going on in the natural environment. There was never a moment that I did not feel I was learning something."[160]

For most I interviewed, being on a ship or in an ice camp meant that one got to know all kinds of people with different backgrounds, people one might not meet otherwise. In some cases, lasting friendships were made. "A remote camp is the best place you can be because there are no email and no phones. You are in contact with the outside world twice per day by radio. The group makes its decisions and sets its work schedule without outside interference or criticism."[161] "In spite of not liking the cold, I love what I do! It is very rewarding."[162] "Working in a remote ice camp makes you think back to our pioneer ancestors who had to survive in an age before gasoline engines and electricity, by making use of whatever was available on location and by using a fulcrum or a block and tackle to do the heavy lifting. That is what you are in the Arctic — a pioneer. I love it!"[163]

Expressions of a deep passion for the work they did was typical of every member of the science team I interviewed, and that passion and deep commitment comes through in the field reports, too. The scientists who do the UNCLOS work and the technical crews who support them are dedicated to the project and they take great pride in the quality of their work.

5

THE ARCTIC EXTENDED
CONTINENTAL SHELF SURVEYS

With dense fog, bone chilling temperatures, and ice (often too thick to navigate through even with a powerful icebreaker or too rough to land a helicopter or airplane on), Arctic research is not for the faint-hearted. Yet in spite of the challenges described in chapters 3 and 4, Canada's UNCLOS team has made enormous strides in mapping the Arctic seabed beyond two hundred nautical miles — an area about which little was previously known.

This chapter's main objective is to provide overviews of the UNCLOS scientific missions to survey the Arctic seabed beyond two hundred nautical miles.[1] To put this work in context, it begins by noting the relationship between the UNCLOS surveys and the Arctic scientific research done in other venues, the requirement to do environmental assessments, and the need to apprise Indigenous peoples of the UNCLOS surveys. Thereafter a brief overview of each mission is presented. The overviews are not designed to be comprehensive, nor do the various missions receive equal treatment. When the methodology used for a survey is similar to that discussed in previous missions, there is no need to repeat the details. Thus, for instance, the first icebreaker missions receive more detailed examination than do the subsequent ones, since it was during the former that most of the pioneering with techniques, methodologies, and the development of equipment occurred. Refinements were made thereafter and they continue to be made, but overall the learning curve was steepest in the first few years of surveying. Later experiments with new technologies, such as AUVs and icepicks, likewise receive more extensive treatment. Blogs and unofficial newsletters from the field were written for some missions and not others; thus there are not equal amounts of information available about the everyday experiences and trials of their respective participants. As a result, the discussions of the missions vary in terms of length and level of detail. This fact in no way undermines the central objective for including the overviews, which is to provide a flavour of the UNCLOS missions and to trace their evolution — to provide an idea of the number and diversity of the missions, the large number of research methodologies employed, the range of challenges faced and the ingenuity and sheer hard work demonstrated in addressing them. The chapter concludes with the main scientific findings derived from the missions.

PAST AND CONCURRENT STUDIES

The UNCLOS surveys did not occur in a vacuum. A coastal state's rights to the adjacent continental shelf were recognized in the 1958 Convention on the Continental Shelf and then clarified in UNCLOS. Thus, Canada's need to establish its ECS was recognized decades before it ratified UNCLOS, although the surveying process intensified after 2003. While this chapter focuses on the mapping missions conducted specifically for Canada's Arctic ECS Program in the post-ratification period, scientific data for Canada's Arctic submission are also drawn from previous and concurrent studies. The preliminary indication of the size of Canada's ECS off its East and Arctic Coasts was drawn from a desktop study done in 1994[2] and these estimates appeared on the Department of Foreign Affairs, Trade and Development's website prior to the change of government in the fall of 2015. According to the site, "Canada's extended continental shelf in the Atlantic and the Arctic Oceans will be sizeable: approximately 1.7 million square kilometres — equivalent in area to the three Prairie provinces."[3] While the desktop study provided a starting point, the quantity and quality of data on which it was based was insufficient to support Canada's Arctic submission.[4]

The Polar Continental Shelf Program was established in 1958. Managed by Natural Resources Canada, it "provides Canadian and international scientists and research teams with cost-effective logistics and consulting and support services."[5] Canada's Arctic ECS Program's success in collecting large quantities of high-quality data would not have been possible without the logistical support provided by the Polar Continental Shelf Program.

Other Arctic research projects provided important data and valuable experience for several individuals who subsequently became prominent figures in Canada's Arctic ECS Program. In the late 1970s and 1980s, the Canadian government funded several important, multidisciplinary scientific programs based on large ice floes on the Canadian polar margin. Key examples were the 1979 Lomonosov Ridge Experiment, the 1983 Canadian Expedition to Study the Alpha Ridge, and Hobson's Choice Ice Island (1984–1991). During the spring of 1979, the Lomonosov Ridge Experiment ice station drifted across the entire Lomonosov Ridge collecting data pertaining to its crustal structure and morphology, marine geology, and physical and chemical oceanography. It served as an excellent example of interdisciplinary and Canada-U.S. cooperation. The Canadian Expedition to Study the Alpha Ridge, which ran from March to May 1983, again involved cooperation among Canadian and American scientists, who collected bathymetric, seismic, and gravimetric data pertaining to the Alpha Ridge. When its ice floe started to melt, a more permanent facility was sought. Hobson's Choice Ice Island was a huge iceberg, three kilometres wide, seven kilometres long, and fifty metres thick, that calved off the Ward Hunt Ice Shelf north of Ellesmere Island.[6] Discovered by the Polar Continental Shelf Program in 1984, it was named after its then director, George Hobson. Here the Canadian government built a science facility, which got bigger and better over the decade during which it functioned, gathering geological core samples from the ocean floor as well as ice core samples. It was a good idea to use an iceberg drifting in the circulating currents of the Arctic Ocean instead of setting up a series of ice camps in different parts of the Arctic margin or chartering an icebreaker. Ruth Jackson and David Mosher established the camp in 1985. Ruth Jackson, who also spent time on the Canadian Expedition to Study the Alpha Ridge, went on to become chief scientist on two of the icebreaker missions and two of the ice camps for the Canada's ECS Program. David Mosher occupied the Ice Island for the entire field season of 1985 and for a number of field seasons thereafter. He became chief scientist of four of the ECS icebreaker missions to the Arctic and manager of UNCLOS

Program. Gary Sonnichsen, current manager of the UNCLOS Program, also served several summers on the Ice Island. Unfortunately, Hobson's Choice Ice Island drifted along the Canadian Arctic Archipelago but never drifted into the Beaufort Gyre of the greater part of the Canada Basin. It was abandoned in 1989 and broke apart in 1991 when a storm blew it into shallow channels north of Resolute. Nonetheless, the experience gained and the research undertaken at Hobson's Choice Ice Island — as well as by the Canadian Expedition to Study the Alpha Ridge — left important legacies for Canada's Arctic ECS Program.

In 1998 the Swedes leased CCGS *Louis S. St-Laurent* on a program called Tundra, to conduct scientific surveys in and among the Arctic Islands. Jane Eert, a physical oceanographer with Fisheries and Oceans, and Mosher led the geological sampling. The mission was their first experience working on CCGS *Louis S. St-Laurent*. Eert subsequently participated in each of the UNCLOS voyages onboard CCGS *Louis S. St-Laurent*.

The Geological Survey of Canada and Germany's Bundesanstalt für Geowissenschaften und Rohstoffe (Federal Institute for Geosciences and Natural Resources) have been doing collaborative scientific work in the Arctic since 1997. In 2001 German Federal Institute for Geosciences and Natural Resources charted CCGS *Louis S. St-Laurent,* and invited geologists from Natural Resources Canada to participate in a study that examined the rocks under Nares Strait, which flows between Greenland and Ellesmere Island from Baffin Bay in the south to the Lincoln Sea in the north. The mission established the baseline geological framework between Canada and Greenland.[7] As such it was valuable background for several who later served as senior scientists for Canada's Arctic ECS Program, including Ruth Jackson and Gordon Oakey, a research scientist with the Geological Survey of Canada. Through his participation on the mission, Borden Chapman, who served as the chief technician on CCGS *Louis S. St-Laurent* for most of the UNCLOS surveys, gained knowledge of — and experience with — the icebreaker's capacity and existing equipment. From that expedition, it was clear that the equipment would require significant modifications for the UNCLOS surveys.[8]

In 2008 Canadian scientists again collaborated in a project organized by the German Federal Institute for Geosciences and Natural Resources.[9] As the field camp was on the northern coast of Ellesmere Island, and thus on Canadian territory, Gordon Oakey (Department of Natural Resources) made all the logistical arrangements (technical field support, equipment, and fuel shipments) for the camp. Germany sent a large group of field geologists to do rock sampling, looking at faults and folds, to determine the basic geological mapping on the area. The camp also served as a base from which to do magnetic mapping by helicopter. This mission was important to establishing the geological framework and geophysical signature of north Ellesmere Island and its offshore areas, which served as a baseline with which to compare the data collected beyond two hundred nautical miles for Canada's Arctic ECS Program.

ENVIRONMENTAL ASSESSMENTS AND RELATIONS WITH INDIGENOUS PEOPLES

In accordance with government procedures, an environmental assessment was done on the impact of the seismic and bathymetric surveys. In the assessments, they had to say how much noise would be produced (higher sound levels triggered a more rigorous assessment); however, even the seismic work using dynamite was usually well below the trigger levels.[10] As part of this process, meetings were held with territorial governments and local communities. For each survey, the scientists prepared a lengthy report (between 300 and 350 pages) on its short- and long-term impact on birds, mammals, fish, and wildlife,[11] which were reviewed by senior departmental administrators.

The governments of Yukon, the Northwest Territories, and Nunavut were not directly involved with Canada's Arctic ECS Program as the research was being done beyond two hundred nautical miles from shore. Nonetheless, they were kept apprised of its objectives and overall work plans.

Oil, gas, and mining operations have the potential to cause severe environmental damage and irreparable harm to the economic and cultural well-being of Indigenous peoples, who have for centuries depended on marine mammals, sea birds, and fish for food, clothing, and tools. These creatures also have cultural significance for the Indigenous peoples of the north. Increased traffic to and from offshore oil and gas operations may disrupt the traditional migration and breeding patterns of marine mammals, sea birds, and fish. Oil slicks can kill them. The noises from seismic blasts and drilling can drive away these valuable, living resources, and invasive species may enter Arctic waters on the hulls of ships and in the ballast water they carry.

The requirement to consult with Indigenous peoples is stipulated in numerous articles of the United Nations Declaration on the Rights of Indigenous Peoples, A Circumpolar Inuit Declaration on Sovereignty in the Arctic, and A Circumpolar Inuit Declaration on Resource Development Principles in Inuit Nunaat. Although not legally binding, all these documents confirm that resource development must involve Indigenous participation in governance matters affecting their communities and must significantly safeguard and improve their economic, social, and cultural well-being.

Canada is required by law to consult with Indigenous peoples when projects are likely to affect their well-being, as outlined in Section 35 of Canada's Constitution Act of 1982 and the Nunavut Land Claims Agreement. Indigenous and Northern Affairs Canada stipulates guiding principles for Indigenous consultation and accommodation and steps to govern their implementation. Furthermore, the Supreme Court of Canada has established some important legal precedents pertaining to the need to consult. Through a series of judgments (*Haida Nation v. British Columbia* (2004), *Taku River Tlingit First Nation v. British Columbia* (2004), *Mikisew Cree First Nation v. Canada* (2005), and *Beckman v. Little Salmon/Carmacks First Nation* (2010)), the Court has affirmed the Crown's responsibility to consult with Indigenous peoples when proposed actions will affect the latter's interests. The rules vary from territory to territory.

The UNCLOS surveys were conducted far beyond the jurisdiction of territorial governments and Indigenous governance bodies, and at great distances from any Indigenous settlements. The North Pole area, which has been the subject of considerable research, is located thousands of kilometres from the nearest Indigenous community, and all the UNCLOS surveys were a long way north of traditional hunting grounds. Nonetheless, meetings were held with Indigenous communities to inform them of the process and to explain the need for the UNCLOS surveys and their objectives.

Ruth Jackson and/or Kevin DesRoches met about once a year with all five coastal communities in the western Arctic. Some sessions were held in conjunction with consultations arranged for other scientific endeavours, which represented a considerable cost and time saving both for the government and the Indigenous communities. The sessions were often convened to coincide with meetings of local hunter and trapper associations.[12] For example, beginning in 2009, the Inuvialuit Game Council allocated a day of its meeting to hear presentations by the federal scientists and to discuss Canada's Arctic ECS Program with them. From the federal government's point of view, the meetings were expensive: pilots and aircraft had to be hired for five days at a time to facilitate a day-trip to each of the communities in the western Arctic, the cost of accommodation in Inuvik; and the time of the scientists who participated in the briefings; however, when the expenses were divided among ten or twelve programs, they were more affordable.[13] The sessions were generally held in the winter, when Indigenous hunters and trappers were most likely to be in their communities rather than out on the land.[14] Since the runways in many communities are dirt strips and pilots prefer to land and take-off when there is light, there was a relatively narrow window of opportunity (i.e., 10 a.m. to 2 p.m.) in which to hold the meetings.[15] Officials from the various federal government departments and programs represented made presentations explaining their respective research programs, which were followed by questions from the community members and general discussion.[16] In the eastern Arctic, the visits focused on Grise Fjord, Canada's most northern community. Information sharing was also done by teleconferencing and when the scientists and Indigenous leaders met in other venues, such as conferences or meetings pertaining to other matters. As the Inuit are a maritime people, fish and marine animals are vital to their health and economic, social, and cultural well-being. Not surprisingly, their principal concern was the impact that the deployment of the airgun on CCGS *Louis S. St-Laurent* would have on wildlife.[17]

Like any travel to the Arctic, flights are costly and delays are common. Bad weather grounded Ruth Jackson for a week in Resolute when she was en route to conduct a briefing in Grise Fjord.[18] Logistical problems were not uncommon. One may arrive at the building where the meeting is to be held to find the door locked, leaving one standing outside in the dark at minus 40°C, or the tables and chairs are upstairs and the meeting room is downstairs, or the projector has not been set up in advance, thus delaying the presentation.[19]

In the western Arctic, government scientists received permission from the Inuvialuit to conduct five years of study on the condition that they carry local mammal observers on their ships. Finding people to do the job is not always easy, as many Indigenous people cannot or do not wish to leave their communities for long periods. When the airgun was being deployed, the three (or, in the early missions, four) observers worked shifts so the entire twenty-four-hour day was covered.[20] The environmental assessment dictates that the airguns must not be fired within one kilometre of a mammal. When a mammal was spotted, the observer communicated the information to the ship's officer on the bridge who, in turn, called the science staff in the seismic laboratory to shut down the airgun.[21] The airgun could not be redeployed until the mammal was no longer within the one-kilometre radius of the ship. A small shelter with large windows was erected on the deck of CCGS Louis S. St-Laurent to provide the mammal observers with some relief from the harsh elements.

Although mammals are relatively rare in the completely ice-covered, northerly regions beyond two hundred nautical miles from shore, mammal observers were also employed in the ice camps. When an animal or its tracks were spotted, the mammal observers went out on Ski-Doos to assess the situation and determined a course of action, thus ensuring the well-being of both the animals and the people. Polar bears, wolves, foxes, Arctic hare, and seals were occasionally seen by ice camp residents, while those on the icebreaker missions sometimes saw polar bears and seals in the survey areas and, when transiting through channels en route to the survey areas, walrus and whales.[22]

In addition to fulfilling their wildlife responsibilities, some of these monitors proved to be very effective in fixing machinery and, in the course of participating in the research programs, some learned new trades, such as operating a Bobcat for subsequent years' ice camps. A mammal observer on CCGS Louis S. St-Laurent in 2007 returned the following year as an airgun technician, and he was also employed as an airgun technician, on southern programs.

The monitors taught the scientists and technicians valuable lessons about how and what to look for when searching for wildlife. For instance, polar bear tracks can be seen but there are other clues to their possible presence, such as seeing foxes or ravens or their tracks in the area, as these creatures often follow bears, scavenging on the latter's kills.[23] The mammal observers, who were drawn from Arctic Indigenous communities, also had valuable experience assessing ice conditions and keeping equipment functioning in temperatures between minus 30°C and minus 40°C. For example, "they brought their own spark plugs, indicating (politely) that the ones in the skidoos were not appropriate for that kind of cold."[24] Nelson Ruben, who served as a mammal observer on numerous UNCLOS missions, was a skilled, self-taught mechanic with years of experience repairing snowmobiles and other vehicles in his hometown.[25] He provided valuable assistance with the airguns, welding, and other mechanical tasks.[26]

On the final day of the 2008 ARTA mission, during the team's three hour wait for their flight home, a wildlife monitor, Tom Kiguktak, showed the southerners how to build an igloo.[27] Under his direction, they cut the ice blocks with handsaws, while Tom constructed the igloo, explaining the mechanics of the task as he proceeded. As Patrick Potter commented, it was "a parting gift" and "a memory I'll treasure forever."

THE UNCLOS SURVEYS, 2006–2016

The discussion of the first six years of the survey missions (2006–2011) is divided into two categories: "Research Offshore in the Deep Water of the Arctic Ocean" and "Research Along the Canadian Margin," based on their geographic location north of Canada's continental land territory.

> In the western arctic, in the Canada Basin, the sediment thickness was the key factor and to determine this, seismic surveys were required. Since ice conditions in the western arctic generally allow the use of heavy icebreakers to collect scientific data … a data collection program was designed utilizing these vessels. In the eastern arctic where heavy ice conditions generally occur, especially in the region north of Ellesmere Island, icebreaker use is often difficult if not impossible.… As a consequence, offshore ice camps were constructed in this region to use as base camps from which data were collected using helicopters, fixed-wing aircraft, and autonomous underwater vehicles.[28]

Although the programs in each region involved seismic and bathymetric research, the methodologies for conducting them varied considerably, largely because the ice challenges in the two regions are different. Of the whole Arctic region, Canada's Arctic margin has the toughest ice conditions, with lots of thick, multiyear ice. Thus, missions along the Canadian Arctic margin used diverse research strategies (ice camps, icebreakers, and icepicks), whereas ice conditions further offshore in the

Arctic Ocean permitted icebreakers to access much of the Canada Basin and Arctic Ocean. The ever-changing conditions necessitated flexibility and ingenuity in the choice of research strategies.

The surveys conducted after the prime minister's December 2013 announcement, saying that Canadian scientists had to do further research to support a claim to the North Pole, expanded the study area for Canadian scientists. Fragile ice conditions that have continued to deteriorate over the last decade now make occupying ice camps extremely dangerous. Use of icebreakers for this extended program was the only alternative. The 2014, 2015, and 2016 surveys all traversed the Arctic Ocean from the Amundsen Basin to the Canada Basin.

Even before the UNCLOS surveys began, desktop studies had provided indications as to which of the formulae outlined in UNCLOS would maximize Canada's ECS in different parts of the Arctic.

> In general, the sediment thickness formula (Gardiner line) and the 350 M [nautical miles] from the Territorial Sea baselines constraint formula will maximize the continental shelf in the western Arctic. Determining that Alpha and Lomonosov Ridges are natural prolongations of the continental shelf and form submarine elevations is key to planning data collection in this area using the 2500 metre depth contour combined with the 350 M [nautical miles] as constraint formula. Sparse seismic data in the Amundsen Basin north of Greenland indicate that the sediment thickness formula will be used in this area.[29]

As the features and geological histories of the areas being studied varied significantly, the foci of the missions were tailored to address these differences. It was known before the UNCLOS surveys began that the sediment thickness of the Alpha Ridge was thin; hence, sediment thickness was not the focus in that area. Instead, research over both the Alpha and Lomonosov Ridges concentrated on the structures of the features. In contrast, determining sediment thickness was the primary objective in the Canada Basin and Amundsen Basin.

Funds to begin the scientific surveys required for Canada's submission to the Commission were allocated in the 2004 budget, which "announced $69 million over ten years for the collection of bathymetric and seismic data. The

2008 budget announced an additional $40 million to cover increased data collection and logistics costs as well as legal costs for submission preparation."[30] In August 2014, the Treasury Board announced that $170.6 million had been allocated for the period from 2004 to 2021.[31] The surveys began in the spring of 2006.

The table below was adapted from the list on the Global Affairs Canada website, which does not provide specific dates. The precise dates in this table are taken from formal field reports compiled by the chief scientist after the mission. Unfortunately, formal field reports do not exist for all the surveys. In some cases, newsletters are available; however, it is still difficult to pinpoint the precise timeframe of a mission as the starting and finishing dates depend on what one is measuring. Does the mission start when work to build the ice camp begins? When both the main and the cache camps are operational? When the scientists first arrive? When the seismic surveying begins? When the bathymetric surveying begins? Or when the author of the newsletter arrives and starts recording events? Does an icebreaker mission begin when the ship leaves Halifax? When the scientific team goes onboard? Or when it reaches the start of the survey area? In light of these difficulties, for some surveys, the months during which they took place — rather than the specific dates on which they began and ended — are provided.

Year	Dates	Mission
2006	March 23–May 6	Joint Canada-Denmark Lomonosov Ridge Test of Appurtenance survey (LORITA)
2007	March	Bathymetric survey conducted from Alert
	August 14–September 16	Participation in Joint Danish-Swedish Lomonosov Ridge off Greenland survey (LOMROG I)
	August 30–October 11	Canadian Survey using CCGS *Louis S. St-Laurent*
2008	March 22–April 30	Alpha Ridge Test of Appurtenance (ARTA) survey
	April	Testing icepicks

Year	Dates	Mission
2008	August 22–October 2	First Joint Canada-U.S. survey using CCGS *Louis S. St-Laurent* and USCGC *Healy*
2009	March 1–April 30	Joint Canada-Denmark survey from ice camp off Ward Hunt Island
	March 17–May 15	Joint Canada-Denmark aerogravity survey (LOMGRAV)
	March 21–April 10	Project Cornerstone I (testing logistics for AUV)
	July 31–September 10	Participation in Joint Danish-Swedish Lomonosov Ridge off Greenland survey (LOMROG II)
	August 6–September 17	Second Joint Canada-U.S. survey using CCGS *Louis S. St-Laurent* and USCGC *Healy*
2010	February 21–May 29	Ice camp off Borden Island (including Project Cornerstone II)
	August 4–September 15	Third Joint Canada-U.S. survey using CCGS *Louis S. St-Laurent* and USCGC *Healy*
2011	August 18–September 29	Fourth Joint Canada-U.S. survey using CCGS *Louis S. St-Laurent* and USCGC *Healy*
2014	August 9–September 17	Survey using CCGS *Louis S. St-Laurent* and CCGS *Terry Fox*
2015	August 7–September 17	Survey using CCGS *Louis S. St-Laurent* and CCGS *Terry Fox*
2016	August 11–September 18	Survey using CCGS *Louis S. St-Laurent* and Swedish icebreaker *Oden*

Research Along the Canadian Arctic Margin

Research along the Canadian margin of the Arctic focused on mapping the Lomonosov and Alpha Ridges — submarine mountain ranges — and the Amundsen Basin, to determine if they constitute natural prolongations of Canada's submerged land territory. Much of this work was done as joint ventures between the Geological Survey of Denmark and Greenland, on one hand, and the Geological Survey of Canada (Department of Natural Resources) and the Canadian Hydrographic Service (Department of

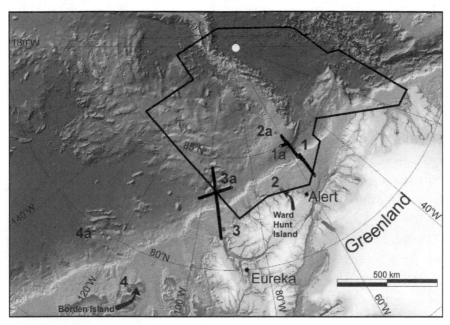

Ice Camp Locations

Red dots represent ice camps:

1	LORITA main camp	1a	LORITA remote camp (seismic reflection)
2	Ward Hunt main camp	2a	Ward Hunt remote camp (and fuel cache)
3	ARTA main camp	3a	ARTA remote camp
4	Cornerstone (AUV) main camp	4a	Cornerstone remote camp

Thick black lines are the seismic refraction lines from LORITA and ARTA.
The black polygon represents the area flown for the LOMGRAV survey, during which aeromagnetic and aerogravity data were recorded.The yellow dot indicates the North Pole.

David Mosher, Natural Resources Canada.

Fisheries and Oceans), on the other. A memorandum of understanding was signed between the Geological Survey of Canada and the Geological Survey of Denmark and Greenland in June 2005. The initial plans involved conducting research from both icebreakers and ice camps. As time went on, they also experimented with new technologies (such as icepicks and AUVs), to provide further data to support the principal seismic and bathymetric surveys conducted from icebreakers and ice camps.

2006

Lomonosov Ridge Test of Appurtenance (LORITA) Survey

In spring 2006, Canadian and Danish scientists began their collaborative Lomonosov Ridge Test of Appurtenance (LORITA) project to collect data north of Greenland and Ellesmere Island to determine if the Lomonosov Ridge constitutes a natural prolongation of Canada's and Greenland's submerged land territory.[32] As such, seismic refraction surveys were the priority.[33] The Lomonosov Ridge is an underwater mountain range that runs 1,800 kilometres from north of Greenland and Ellesmere Island to Siberia and divides the Arctic Ocean into two major basins: the Eurasia and the Amerasia Basins. Most of the scientists and their equipment were based at the Canadian Forces Station in Alert, which is located on the northeastern tip of Ellesmere Island, the most northerly large island in Canada's Arctic Archipelago. Yet Alert was too far from the survey lines to allow direct commuting.

> The distance from Alert to the north end of the shot line is about 240 nautical miles, or nearly 450 km. In order to get helicopters out that far, the weather has to be flyable the whole way. An additional concern is that of fuel. The helicopters cannot carry enough fuel to get out to the ice camp and back. This means that at some point en route to the ice camp they pass the point of no return. If they run into bad fog past that point they are in trouble.[34]

The solution was to establish two camps: a main ice camp on the frozen Arctic Ocean about 250 kilometres north of Alert (where the seismic refraction work was conducted), and a remote camp to serve as a cache for fuel, explosives, and other equipment. The three people stationed at the remote camp kept it operating twenty-four hours per day: taking care of the equipment, preparing for the surveys, and reporting on local weather conditions (a valuable assist to the pilots). They also conducted seismic reflection research using the small airgun suspended below their ice floe. The three helicopters needed to take the survey crews out to the profile lines and one pilot were based at the ice camp, while two Twin Otter aircraft were used to ferry most of the personnel and their equipment from Alert to the ice camp on daily basis.[35]

Preparing helicopters to deploy seismometers on the pack ice.
John Shimeld, Geophysicist, Natural Resources Canada.

The bad weather and difficult ice conditions that plagued so much of the work along the Canadian margin were particularly challenging in 2006 and they were evident from the beginning of the mission. The first news-letter from the field stated, "Mother Nature is not co-operating" and went on to talk about ice fog, high winds, seriously broken ice, delayed helicop-ters, and the need to relocate their ice camp thirty nautical miles north of the originally planned site.[36] A series of gales over a period of about two weeks prompted concern that they might have to evacuate the camp "because the pack ice was moving rapidly, many leads were opening in our area of operations, and increasing levels of fog from the newly exposed unfrozen ocean were at times preventing the helicopters from flying."[37]

As John Shimeld, geophysicist and scientist for numerous ice camps and icebreaker missions, and seismic lead for the 2016 Canada-Sweden Polar Expedition explained,

Sea fog is highly variable and it can close in rapidly, making it impossible for pilots to see the horizon and the snow-covered ice on which they need to land. On one flight, the helicopter pilot was forced to make an impromptu landing on the ice while there was still just sufficient visibility to do so. We waited on our lonely float-ing island for the fog to clear, and I won't deny that we shared a little

Leads in the pack ice near the LORITA ice camp.
John Shimeld, Geophysicist, Natural Resources Canada.

trepidation since the prospect of camping out in the helicopter for any length of time wasn't particularly cheery. Luckily the fog cleared within about twenty minutes, and the pilot flew us safely back to Alert where a warm supper awaited.[38]

Ice is not stationary; hence, nor was the ice camp.

Under normal weather conditions, the ice in the Lincoln Sea is under compression and the whole pack tends to drift slowly back-and-forth in response to high pressure air cells moving across the region — it's as though the icepack breathes. The speed of this movement rarely exceeds a tenth of a kilometre per hour, but during gales the ice camp travelled westward at more than a kilometre per hour. Tracking the movement of individual floes was essential for the overall safety of the team, and for the success of the field program. In one three-day period, during which the helicopters were grounded due to poor weather, the seismic recorders drifted several tens of kilometres from their deployment locations. If we hadn't eventually been able to find them, there would be no records from the seismic experiment and we would not have learned a thing about the geology of the Lomonosov Ridge![39]

A beacon was set up at the ice camp so its location could be tracked by GPS from Alert.[40]

In the course of the thirty-one-day mission, the helicopters had only been "able to fly five full days and five partial days."[41] Bad weather resulted in the loss of "65–70% of the planned survey days."[42] Yet, in spite of the challenges, the 2006 LORITA project achieved its main objectives: collecting seismic refraction data "along a 440 km-long north-south profile and a 110 km long profile along the bathymetric trough."[43] While little bathymetric data were acquired during the mission, the seismic data were of high quality.[44]

In addition to the strides made in seismic data collection, some valuable lessons were learned as the result of having to deal with the atrocious weather conditions.[45] For example, it was evident that insulated boxes had to be specially designed to protect the recording equipment and its batteries, even when they had to be left out on the ice for a week or more. Visually marking the sites with the recording boxes with snow-filled garbage bags was insufficient as a snowfall could quickly bury them. GPS readings had to be taken at each site. Both changes were implemented before ice camps were again used in 2008.

2007

Surveying the Lomonosov Ridge was again the focus in 2007. In addition to conducting bathymetric surveys from Alert, Canadian scientists participated in the Lomonosov off Greenland mission, which was organized by the Swedish International Polar Year project.

Bathymetric Survey Conducted from Alert

In March 2007, hydrographers from Fisheries and Oceans Canada headed north with three objectives: most importantly, complete the bathymetric surveys, which they had been unable to do during the 2006 LORITA mission; second, create bathymetric profiles every fifty nautical miles between the Lomonosov Ridge and Ellesmere Island; and, third, collect the bathymetric evidence needed to identify the foot of the slope and the 2,500-metre isobath on the Lomonosov Ridge's eastern and western slopes.[46] Unfortunately, terrible weather conditions (even worse than in 2006) prevented the realization of these objectives.

> The ice for 100 M [nautical miles] off the shore north of Alert was continually in motion, emptying ice through Nares Strait between Ellesmere Island and Greenland.... It was difficult to find ice flows [*sic*] 300 metres in length for twin otters to land with fuel caches. In one three-day period a fuel cache drifted 50M. The open water caused summer-like flying conditions of ice crystals and ice fog despite normal winter temperatures and over 95% of the time was lost. Little of the bathymetric objective was achieved.[47]

Even the best-laid plans cannot overcome bad weather and treacherous ice conditions.

Lomonosov Ridge off Greenland (LOMROG I) Survey

The LOMROG I survey was a joint Swedish-Danish venture. Canada participated in the portion of the cruise that sought to collect data around the Lomonosov Ridge. The project chartered the world's most powerful icebreaker, the Russian *50 Let Pobedy*, to carve a path in the ice, and the Swedish icebreaker, *Oden*, to follow with the scientific equipment. The Russian *50 Let Pobedy* is a 75,000 horsepower, nuclear icebreaker.[48] The mission encountered severe conditions with no open water and "multiyear ice, three-five metres thick with pressure ridges to six metres."[49] *Oden* had trouble following, partly because its bow was wider than the track of *50 Let Pobedy*, and partly because of the need to move slowly with the seismic equipment.[50] *Oden* experienced difficulty collecting good bathymetric and particularly seismic data in the jumbled ice left by *50 Let Pobedy*. The airgun and streamer were towed twenty metres below the surface. As *Oden* applied power to continue its forward motion, the airgun and streamer rose to the surface and became trapped among huge pieces of ice in the ship's track. By the time the escort contract with *50 Let Pobedy* was fulfilled, only twenty kilometres of seismic line had been run on the Lomonosov Ridge and a significant amount of Danish gear had been damaged or lost. When the seismic gear was not in the water, *Oden* was able to acquire more bathymetric data by breaking the ice and then performing pirouettes (360-degree turns). After encountering multiyear ice three to five metres thick and under compression, the Lomonosov portion of the mission was aborted and *Oden* moved to less severe ice conditions east of Greenland where it could work unescorted. Nonetheless, participation in LOMROG I enabled Canadian officials to test the feasibility of using icebreakers to collect data along the Arctic margin without having to finance the whole mission. Since most of the Canadian portion of the survey had to be aborted, not having to pay the full costs was indeed a benefit. As a result of their bad experience in 2007, the scientists planned to conduct the following spring's surveys from ice camps.

2008

The principal mission in the spring of 2008 was the ARTA survey. Overlapping with its final weeks, icepicks (a new technology for collecting seismic data) were tested.

Alpha Ridge Test of Appurtenance (ARTA) Survey

In the spring of 2008, Canadian scientists and technicians conducted seismic and bathymetric surveys needed for the test of appurtenance on the Alpha Ridge, which lies north of the mouth of Nansen Sound, the inlet between Axel Heiberg and Ellesmere Islands.[51] Operations were initially based at the Eureka weather station on Ellesmere Island, from where they commuted to establish ice camps closer to the areas to be surveyed. Eureka could not be used as the staging ground for daily survey operations as it was located some 180 kilometres from the start of the survey lines, which then extended north for hundreds of kilometres; thus commuting from the weather station would have meant an additional 360 kilometres of flying each day.[52] Having a base closer to the survey area was essential.

Setting up the principal camp was the first priority, but the task was time-consuming, labour-intensive, and made all the more difficult by variable weather that at times brought high winds, poor visibility, and temperatures of minus 50°C.[53] It was located on a smooth piece of ice some 1,830 metres long, ten kilometres northeast of the entrance to Nansen Sound.[54]

ARTA camp.

Ruth Jackson, Natural Resources Canada.

Being only about five kilometres from shore and on permanent ice that was largely surrounded by land, it remained stationary. Such was not the case with the smaller camp, which was located far from shore and which at one point was drifting at a rate of three hundred metres per hour.[55] This remote camp, with its staff of three, was located almost one hundred kilometres north of the principal camp. Its staff gathered seismic reflection data and the camp also served as a cache for fuel and explosives. Because of the bitter cold, their Ski-Doo was housed in the cook tent overnight so they could start it in the morning. "The sleep tents were too small and the Ski-Doo was critical to our work; however, having a Ski-Doo in the galley tent made midnight snacking an adventure."[56]

Much of the equipment had been sitting in Resolute for a couple of months in minus 40°C and minus 50°C temperatures before being flown to Eureka for the 2008 mission. After being brought into a warehouse at the weather station, it took five days to warm it up. As Patrick Potter recalled, "The warehouse, itself, was about 15°C but when the instruments, which were like blocks of ice, were brought in, they cooled down the room. So it took a long time to warm everything up. The first week at Eureka was spent warming, sorting and testing the equipment, and waiting for the outside temperature to reach minus 40°C. If it is colder than that, the helicopter pilots will not fly because fuel turns to gel which does not flow."[57] Before full-scale seismic surveying began, chief scientist Ruth Jackson arranged for a trial run along a short line, with only three dynamite charges and thirty recording instruments.[58] In sequence, the blasters were flown out in helicopters to set the charges, the instrument people placed the recording instruments, the charges were detonated, and the equipment was retrieved. Doing a small-scale survey had many advantages. Some team members had done this type of work before, while it was new to others. The trial familiarized everyone with the procedures, tested the equipment, and identified any problems; hence, it was important for safety, comfort levels, and efficiency. Furthermore, the test survey was conducted along a line from which data were wanted so it moved the overall agenda ahead.

Like all the UNCLOS surveys, the ARTA mission faced serious challenges. They never managed to clear a large enough runway to land a bigger cargo plane, such as the Buffalo, which meant the Skyvan and Twin Otter aircraft had to carry all the supplies. Given their much smaller carrying capacity, fuel shortages were constant problems. To carry the same amount of fuel as the Buffalo could have transported in one load would take the Twin Otter seven and a half trips.[59] The problem was compounded the further out one had to travel. For example, for the Twin Otter to deliver six drums of fuel to the main camp and the remote camp, took three and a half and seven drums, respectively; whereas it required nine and a half drums of fuel to carry only five drums to the outer seismic refraction line.[60] Some of the Primacords broke or malfunctioned causing failed or only partial detonations.[61] Initially, the cooks at the main camp were housed with the food, which posed a safety hazard since that tent would have been a key target for a hungry polar bear; hence, a separate tent had to be found and erected. The camp's Iridium satellite telephone would not work inside the tent so Jackson had to get fully dressed in polar gear and stand outside in frigid conditions to make the daily calls to the remote camp at 8:15 a.m. and 8:15 p.m.[62] The remote camp drifted almost twenty-seven kilometres during the survey period.[63] Although it was collecting excellent data, it had to be vacated earlier than planned because of unstable ice.[64]

Galley tent.

Tim Janzen, Fisheries and Oceans Canada.

In addition to the major challenges, there were more minor annoyances. The flight that carried Jackson, John Shimeld, and Patrick Potter to Eureka left again before their personal luggage had been unloaded so, like those similarly inconvenienced at the start of the LORITA project, they had to spend the first night without their personal belongings.

Mother Nature was much more cooperative in 2008 than she had been in 2006. It was very cold with temperatures ranging from minus 52°C to minus 30°C; however, cold air is generally associated with the clear skies needed for flying.[65] The ARTA project not only succeeded in surveying the three main seismic lines that had been planned, but the quality of resulting data were deemed to be "great."[66] In addition to the test line, bathymetric and seismic reflection and refraction data were collected along the principal 350-kilometre profile as well as on a 174-kilometre cross line.[67] The quantity and high quality of data collected was a tribute to the design and testing that the equipment had undergone on site and over the preceding years, as well as to the hard work and dedication of the team.

Experimenting with Icepicks

Overlapping with the final week of the ARTA project, an experiment was run to test a new technology — icepicks dropped from an Aurora aircraft — to extend the seismic survey lines farther north in the Arctic Ocean. Icepicks are cylinder-shaped instruments, equipped with geophones that transmit data to recording devices on an aircraft. They come equipped with a parachute on the top to keep them upright as they descend and a spike at the bottom to stick in the ice. Explosions still had to be set off under the ice, but there was no need to set out the recording equipment by hand. The project was a cooperative venture between the Geological Survey of Canada (Natural Resources Canada) and Defence Research and Development Canada (Department of National Defence). The latter had experience using icepicks as listening devices to monitor submarines in the Arctic and it cooperated in the test of their utility in conducting seismic surveys during the spring of 2008.

As the project was far less labour-intensive than the traditional seismic methodology (fewer holes had to be drilled and there was no need to set out and subsequently collect the recording boxes), only a small team was needed to conduct the experiment.[68] There were setbacks, including fog that delayed flying, some mechanical problems with the Aurora aircraft, and explosions that fired at the wrong times.[69] Most of the icepicks reached their desired targets, although some fell on rough ice and failed to stick, thus losing contact with the ice, and a few went straight through thin ice and disappeared into the ocean.[70] As Richard MacDougall commented, "The quality of the contact between the ice-pick and the ice and the uncertainty of the geographic position of each ice-pick meant the data were significantly less accurate than those obtained from the receivers that were hand placed and in good contact with the ice."[71] Although the data collected using the icepicks were of lower quality than those gathered using the traditional methods, they nonetheless confirmed that the structural model obtained for the Alpha Ridge extended beyond the area covered by the traditional seismic recorders.[72]

2009

In the spring of 2009, Canadian scientists and technicians participated in four UNCLOS studies. Two were joint ventures with their Danish colleagues: bathymetric and seismic surveys conducted from an ice camp off Ward Hunt Island; and an airborne geophysical survey over the Alpha and Lomonosov Ridges and the Amundsen Basin. Canadian scientists also participated in the second phase of the LOMROG survey that was a joint venture between Denmark and Sweden. A separate mission, Project Cornerstone, tested the feasibility of using an AUV in the Arctic environment.

Joint Canada-Denmark Ice Camp off Ward Hunt Island

The principal objective of the 2009 ice camp was to continue the process of collecting the bathymetric data required to determine the foot of slope, the 2,500-metre isobath, and the shape of the seabed on the Lomonosov Ridge and between the continental land mass and the Alpha and Lomonosov Ridges.[73] The ice shelf north of Ward Hunt Island was selected as the site for the camp as it was the piece of ice closest to the survey area that was sufficiently large and flat to accommodate a base camp and runway. Ward Hunt Island is just north of Ellesmere Island and the Canadian land closest to the North Pole.

Ward Hunt camp: the main drag.

Tim Janzen, Fisheries and Oceans Canada.

The Eureka weather station again served as the base for setting up the camps. All the equipment and personnel had to be transported first to Eureka and from there to the principal ice camp. There were some pre-existing emergency shelters near the shore of Ward Hunt Island, constructed by Parks Canada to serve as bases from which to stage exploratory trips to the North Pole, which provided some refuge for those first sent out to establish the principal ice camp.[74] Throughout the 2009 spring mission temperatures remained in the minus 30°C and minus 40°C range.

Once the principal camp was largely established, a site for the refuelling camp had to be found. After flying in the vicinity of the survey area, a promising site over the Lomonosov Ridge was found 270 kilometres north of the main camp and five hundred kilometres from the North Pole.[75] Once again, it was essential to have a transmitter at the cache camp, as the ice on which it was placed drifted at a rate of 1.4 kilometres a day.[76] A month of work preparing the ice camps and the equipment was needed before the scientific research could begin in earnest.

The mission faced a range of challenges, including an emergency evacuation of the remote ice camp when the ice started to break up.[77] Although data collection was impeded in some areas by ice conditions, the mission successfully conducted 763 bathymetric spot soundings over some 1,100 line-kilometres.[78] (A line-kilometre is a linear measure; however, a line may not be straight, so one is measuring the distance along the line and not the distance achieved in one direction.)

Airborne Geophysical Survey (LOMGRAV)

Overlapping with the period of the Ward Hunt camp was a complementary airborne geophysical survey designed to expand the area covered and to provide supporting data for the primary finding of the ground research. It was conducted jointly by the Danish National Space Institute and the Geodetic Survey Division (Natural Resources Canada). An airplane specially equipped with gravimeters, magnetometers, and several GPS receivers collected gravity and magnetic measurements on a systematic grid over the Alpha and Lomonosov Ridges and Amundsen Basin. The measurements from the Lomonosov Ridge and Amundsen Basin were needed by both countries, while those for the Alpha Ridge were considered — at least at that point in history — to be relevant only to Canada's submission.

The 2009 aerogravity and aeromagnetic survey collected gravity and magnetic data using airplanes that flew over the area to be surveyed. This was done in order to determine if there was continuity between its findings and the data collected in the 2008 joint German-Canadian study that had established the geological framework and geological signature of north Ellesmere Island and its immediate offshore.[79] It was also designed to link the data from two magnetic studies commissioned by Natural Resources Canada between 1986 and 2003: one over the Lincoln Sea and one in the Axel Heiberg Island area.[80]

Between March 17 and May 15, 2009, the long-range airplane operated out of the airports at Alert, Eureka, and Station Nord, Greenland. Although gravity and magnetic readings had been done from both ships and ice floes in the course of Canada's Arctic ECS Program, the best coverage came from the airborne geophysical surveys.[81] The airplanes provided good quality and constant readings with a dense grid of coverage. As a result of its dense survey lines, the mission proved to be a tremendous source of gravity and magnetic information.[82] Furthermore, they covered a much larger area and flew over regions inaccessible by ship or helicopter. Gordon Oakey, an expert in plate tectonics and gravity and magnetic modelling, who had participated in the 2008 joint survey with Germany, brought together and analyzed the various data sets to create a tectonic framework for the High Arctic north of Ellesmere Island and Greenland. Canada now has continuous onshore and offshore mapping all the way from the Lincoln Sea to the west of Axel Heiberg Island.[83]

Joint Danish-Swedish Survey LOMROG II (Lomonosov Ridge off Greenland)

In spring 2009 Canadian scientists also participated in the second phase of the Danish-Swedish Lomonosov Ridge off Greenland (LOMROG II) survey, paying for five days of the Swedish icebreaker *Oden*'s time.[84] For Canada and Denmark, the main objective of the voyage was collecting seismic, bathymetric, and gravimetric data in the Amundsen Basin and along the Lomonosov Ridge.[85] Unlike the LOMROG I mission in 2007, which used *50 Let Pobedy* and *Oden*, the LOMROG II survey only had use of *Oden*. Although the ice conditions were described as "severe," the ice was not under compression so they were able to cross the Lomonosov Ridge six times, gathering multibeam bathymetric data and gravity measurements.[86] Between the bathymetric lines gathered by the ship's transducer, spot tests were done by helicopter along eleven profiles.[87] Collecting the seismic data was more challenging but by making two sweeps to carve a channel through the ice before deploying the seismic equipment, they succeeded in gathering 380 kilometres of reflection seismic data and refraction data from thirty sonobuoys.[88]

Project Cornerstone I

Toward the end of March 2009 — overlapping with the Ward Hunt camp — a new project began: Project Cornerstone. Its mandate was to work out the logistics of using an AUV to do ECS mapping prior to its first scheduled deployment in 2010. The venture involved personnel from Natural Resources Canada, the Canadian Hydrographic Services, Defence Research Development Canada, International Submarine Engineering Incorporated (the company that subsequently built two AUVs to assist with Canada's UNCLOS mapping), and St. John's Memorial University in Newfoundland. As International Submarine Engineering had not completed work on the AUVs ordered for the 2010 deployment, the 2009 project used an Explorer AUV on loan from Memorial University.

The project was based at the Canadian Forces Station in Alert, from which two ice camps were established. The larger of the two was situated on "a lovely large smooth pan about 2.7 kilometres in length and about 1 m thick," in Dumbell Bay.[89] A smaller camp was located two kilometres north of Cape Belknap, which is on the northern tip of Ellesmere Island. As both camps were located in relatively close proximity to Alert, the team stayed at the base and travelled out to the camps by Ski-Doo each day.

At the main camp, a steam drill was used to cut a trench through two metres of ice, through which the AUV could be lowered into the ocean. The hole was then covered with a heated tent. While the AUV used for the tests in 2009 was smaller than those being built for the 2010 deployment, it was still 4.5 metres long, and weighed 670 kilograms:[90] hence, drilling the hole, removing all the ice, and assembling the AUV were major undertakings. The AUV was transported to the tent in sections and a portable crane was erected to assist with reassembly and then with lowering it into the water. In spite of leaving two stoves on in the tent, ice still formed overnight in the hole, which had to be scooped out and carried away in the morning.[91]

Research at the smaller camp focused on testing the acoustic equipment so vital to the navigation and retrieval of the AUV. Once launched, the AUV cannot be reprogrammed. Instead it has to navigate under the ice along pre-determined survey lines to its destination, which could be on a moving ice floe. As a single battery charge is only sufficient to cover about four hundred kilometres, the AUV needs to know where to find the recharging station.

As was the case with all the Arctic scientific missions, there were equipment problems, largely resulting from the cold temperatures and periods of foggy weather; and gasoline supplies ran short, which curtailed the number of Ski-Doo trips to the northern camp toward the end of the project. Nonetheless, the field trials were successful. The large launching hole was drilled and maintained throughout the operation, the AUV was assembled and lowered into the water, and the cradle containing the connector needed to lower the vehicle, to download data, and to recharge the AUV's battery was deployed. Furthermore, tests were conducted to assess the efficacy of two acoustic navigational systems. The Long Range Acoustic Bearing System "helps direct the AUV when it is a long distance from the recovery hole."[92] Based on the 2009 tests and methodological refinements made in the field, it was concluded that the system would provide continuous contact between the AUV and the recharging station, even when they were over one hundred kilometres apart: the "AUV, upon hearing the signal, will know which direction to swim in order to get to the recovery hole."[93] The Short-Range Localization System operates when the AUV is within ten kilometres of the recovery hole: a "modem on the AUV will communicate acoustically with a number of other modems hanging from the ice. It will measure its distance from each of the stationary modems and, since it knows their locations, it will be able to calculate its own position."[94] Testing these navigational systems was a vital precursor to the 2010 AUV deployment. They enabled the science staff to predict that the AUV would successfully reach its destinations, using its sophisticated navigational system that constantly recorded its depth and location and made adjustments when needed, with the aid of the short-range acoustic instruments and longer range acoustic beacons indicating the location of the recovery holes. Project Cornerstone also provided a useful training ground for those new to Arctic field research as it was conducted from an established base, yet involved work on the ice.[95] As such it was a good introduction to some of the skills that would be needed in the 2010 ice camp, whose location was much more remote and at which conditions were much tougher. As the AUV was never released to travel in the Arctic Ocean, the testing of an actual launch, deployment on a survey grid, and recovery was left for the following year's mission, which was run from an ice camp near Borden Island.

Research Offshore in the Deep Water of the Arctic Ocean

In the offshore regions of the Arctic Ocean, Canadian scientists and technicians conducted bathymetric surveys to measure water depth and the contours of the ocean floor, and seismic research to ascertain sediment thickness and the composition of the layers beneath the ocean floor. The Mackenzie River empties enormous amounts of sediments into the Beaufort Sea. These deposits extend for hundreds of miles out from shore, into the Canada Basin, which is part of the Arctic Ocean. Using icebreakers, five major surveys were conducted in the offshore regions of the Arctic Ocean between 2007 and 2011. The first was undertaken unilaterally by Canada, while the subsequent four were done jointly with the United States. In addition, in 2010 an ice camp located just south of Borden Island was the site of Canada's Arctic ECS Program's first launching of an AUV. The following year, an AUV was deployed from an icebreaker.

Perennial ice cover severely restricts access to the Canada Basin; hence, it is "the least studied ocean basin in the World."[96] Prior to 2007, when the ECS missions began, there were few seismic or bathymetric lines in the Canada Basin; thus there was a serious gap in the knowledge for Canada's ECS submission. Clearly, further bathymetric and seismic surveys were needed. While polar environments always present challenges, UNCLOS research in the offshore regions of the Arctic was aided by relatively good weather and lighter ice conditions than those experienced along the Canadian Arctic margin. Again the program required much planning so that alternative strategies were available if ice conditions delayed (or advanced) the schedule or prevented following preordained profile lines.

2007

Canadian Survey Using CCGS Louis S. St-Laurent

At the end of August, Canada's most powerful icebreaker, CCGS *Louis S. St-Laurent,* set off for the country's first UNCLOS mission offshore in the deep water of the Arctic Ocean. The six-week mission surveyed the southern portion of the Canada Basin.[97]

Through his participation in the 2001 German study of the Nares Strait and then during a prototype mission in 2006 on CCGS *Louis S. St-Laurent,* Borden Chapman, chief technician for most of the UNCLOS icebreaker missions, had seen that the seismic equipment would require serious alterations before the Canadian icebreaker could be sent out on its 2007 venture.[98] In particular, the seismic gear had to withstand the harsh conditions, including the threats posed by huge chunks of churning ice in the wake of the icebreaker and the problems of recording returning sound waves with all the extraneous noise caused by the loud engines, the breaking ice, and the ship's bubbler system. In open water, the seismic source array and streamer are towed behind the vessel; however, in the Arctic both need to be submerged deep below the churning ice. Since it is not practical to cut a hole in the hull of an icebreaker to lower the equipment down through the centre of the ship, "a heavy depressor, called 'the airgun sled,' was constructed to suspend the airguns and streamer immediately below the stern of the vessel. At a fixed tow depth of 11.5 metres, the sled and streamer were just below the keel of the vessel and most of the sea ice."[99]

Yet in spite of this redesigning, the mission faced a myriad of technical problems, the most serious of which involved the landing and retrieving of the seismic equipment and functioning of the compressor. That first year a small crane on the quarterdeck was used to lift the 2,300 kilogram sled over the stern into the water and then to retrieve it. The procedure was dangerous as the weight swung over the heads of the crew on deck with the crane at its maximum capacity.[100]

In 2007 CCGS *Louis S. St-Laurent* travelled alone; hence, it had to carry the seismic gear and break ice. The seismic gear had to be taken out of the water not only for repairs but also whenever the icebreaker had to back up to ram the ice in its path.

CCGS *Louis S. St-Laurent* is driven though the sea by three large propellers; port and starboard propellers located on the outer side of the hull and a centre prop positioned just forward of the ship's rudder. During seismic acquisition, the centre propeller was "turned off," which eliminated the propeller's wake that caused noise in the streamer and potential damage to the airgun sled. However, with the loss of the centre propeller's thrust across the face of the rudder, vessel steering became difficult. To keep the vessel on a true course required constant adjustment of the revolutions to the two outer propellers, and over compensation of rudder movement. This added greatly to the duties of both the vessel's Officer of the Watch and the Quartermaster on the bridge. Without the centre propeller, not only was steerage affected, but about 40% of the vessel's icebreaking power was lost.[101]

Icebreakers rely on momentum, generated by bulk and speed, to break the ice, while the seismic streamers must be towed at no more than four knots for two reasons.[102] First, the hydrophones cannot get good readings when the ship is moving quickly. Second, the risk of damage to the streamer increases at higher speeds. Yet a speed of three or four knots does not create enough momentum to break the heavier ice. Force equals mass times acceleration, thus with little of the latter, there is insufficient force.

When deployed, the seismic equipment was directly below the stern, and in close proximity to the propellers, so the vessel could not go astern without the risk of the gear getting tangled with the ship's rudder or propellers.[103] Thus, each time the ship got stuck, the seismic gear had to be taken out of the water before CCGS *Louis S. St-Laurent* could deploy its central propeller and its full 27,000 horsepower to back up before ramming ahead into the ice.[104] In the first four years of surveying, eight days was the longest period during which they were able to sail without pulling the seismic gear out of the water and they were proud of this accomplishment.[105] When eight days of continuous deployment in a six-week survey are cause for rejoicing, the extent of the challenges is evident!

The supply of high-pressure air to the airguns caused no end of problems. The acquisition procedures for government purchases resulted in a less expensive model being selected. The result was a lot of stress, frustration, and lost time. As Borden Chapman recalled, "We had problems with every piece of pipe, every hose, and every electrical connection. To keep that compressor going kept us working full time."[106] While managers sitting in their warm offices in the south may raise concerns about paying overtime, such issues are of little relevance to the chief scientist when his/her technical team are struggling on the deck under miserable conditions (e.g., enduring howling winds and freezing temperatures and handling ice-cold metal) to repair equipment without which the mission may have to be aborted.[107]

There were also problems with the high-pressure hoses and lines supplying the compressed air to the airgun sled from the compressor.

> To fire properly, the airguns are charged with approximately 2,500 pounds per square inch of warm compressed air. When the airgun "fires," the air is released into the sea. But as the air pressure drops, so does the air temperature inside the gun and associated hoses (Pascal's Ideal Gas Law). The result of the sudden pressure/ temperature drop causes the moisture in the airgun and hoses to accumulate. In very cold Arctic waters, the buildup of moisture eventually leads to airgun freeze-up. An airgun, which was normally 12" in diameter, all of a sudden increased in size to 24" because it was completely encased in ice. The guns would simply stop firing.[108]

Canada's Arctic ECS Program initially recommended the purchase of a hydrophone array and logging system costing several million dollars. As Borden Chapman recalled, "This array was developed for military applications and was tested and proven to be extremely durable. The desired array was capable of withstanding Arctic conditions; however, a less expensive model was purchased, costing in the area of $250,000, which had never been developed or tested for use in Arctic ice conditions."[109] As was the case with the compressor, the cheaper model caused a myriad of problems. As the streamer was lowered into the frigid water, the mechanical connections loosened, allowing seawater to seep into the internal electrical connections. Over time, the technicians became increasingly adept at dealing with this problem but they were never able to completely overcome the initial design flaw.

Sadly, the troubles did not end there, as Borden Chapman explained:

> The 300-metre seismic streamer, which was supposed to remain parallel to the sea surface, sagged when the icebreaker slowed down and sank to a vertical state each time the ship stopped. Thus, the tail end of the streamer would sink to a depth of 300 metres. Because the streamer was only built to withstand maximum water pressures to a

depth of 200 metres, the signal quality would deteriorate. Repeated stops and streamer "dives" resulted in internal streamer components failing. Adding floats or "birds" to control the streamer attitude caused it to snag in the ice. A bio-degradable silicone was added to improve streamer buoyancy.[110]

Even with these additions, John Shimeld, who was in charge of data processing, constantly had to do complex post-acquisition processing to compensate for the fluctuations in pressure depths as the streamer rose and sank.

In light of all the technical problems, it was amazing that Chapman and his team were able to successfully build and rebuild the equipment and to keep it functioning during the voyage. Most members of the technical team were retirees of Nova Scotia's Bedford Institute of Oceanography, whose expertise and mechanical skills were invaluable. Many of these retirees were hired for subsequent UNCLOS missions. Although Borden retired in 2011, he agreed to come back and assist with the 2014, 2015, and 2016 missions. The hiring of retirees speaks highly of their credentials, but it also illustrates the dearth of such experts currently working full-time in the government departments. The weather cooperated and the mission succeeded in collecting "2987 km of seismic reflection profiles perpendicular to the margin and along a line 350 nm from the coast" and 7,783 kilometres of bathymetric data from the transducers onboard.[111] This bathymetry was augmented with 180 spot soundings taken from a helicopter hovering over open water, while a transducer slung beneath the aircraft was lowered into the water.[112]

The final report made a series of recommendations to assist subsequent surveys.[113] Generally the ice was denser the further north they travelled, which led to the conclusion that two icebreakers working in tandem would be needed for the subsequent years' studies in the more northerly regions. A further recommendation suggested starting the 2008 mission in mid-August (two weeks earlier) when the ice was likely to be less dense and the hours of daylight greater. The report stressed the need to carry spare parts and to work out problems encountered when equipment was deployed in sub-zero temperatures.

Although equipment problems did occur in subsequent years, overall the advice was heeded. Two icebreakers were used for three weeks of the 2008 survey, and the mission did start a week earlier. In between its spring activities in the Gulf of Saint Lawrence and the 2008 UNCLOS survey, CCGS *Louis S. St-Laurent* was refitted with innovations specially designed to overcome problems encountered on the previous summer's voyage.[114] Chapman and his technical team collaborated with a Halifax, Nova Scotia, company, Lengkeek Vessel Engineering, to design and build an A-frame to lift the seismic sled in and out of the water from the stern deck. To address the problem of the hydrophone streamer sinking each time the ship slowed or stopped, biodegradable oil under pressure was pumped into the tubing that encased it to provide additional buoyancy in the colder Arctic waters. The anticipated water temperature and towing depth were used to calculate the amount of pressure needed for the streamer to tow horizontally.

All the technical problems encountered in 2007 made clear the need to have a second, duplicate system ready at all times to provide 100 percent redundancy. Additional airguns and an additional hydrophone array (streamer) and compressor were purchased. At the same time, a second tow sled was constructed. The original airgun sled used in 2007 was modified and strengthened for the 2008 season. Having duplicate seismic systems onboard resulted in minimal down time for the program. If an airgun sled and streamer failed, the second system could be deployed and the survey continued. Gear recovery and redeploy times were reduced to twenty to thirty minutes, minimizing time lost to the survey.

The compressors were re-plumbed and their controls re-engineered. Computerized monitoring systems were added to each machine. With two compressors, one could be in use while the other was being repaired. Heated enclosures were constructed for each compressor, keeping the machines warm, which meant that either machine could be started and brought online quickly, without normal warm up times. And yet these enclosures had to be exceptionally well ventilated because of the high volumes of air required to cool the diesel engines, even in the Arctic. On several occasions, the compressor's cooling fans failed because of inadequate air supply inside the compressor enclosures. Once this issue was addressed no subsequent fan failures occurred.

The high-pressure hoses and air lines from the compressors to the airgun sleds were wrapped with heat tape and insulation. Small amounts of biodegradable antifreeze were regularly injected into the air supply lines. This kept the air supply from the compressor to the quarterdeck at approximately 5°C eliminating the airgun "freeze-ups" experienced the previous year. Further, on the quarterdeck, a large, heated manifold cabinet was built to house all the high-pressure air shut-off and air dump valves. All these measures cured the 2007 icing problems.

2008

First Joint Canada-U.S. Survey Using CCGS *Louis S. St-Laurent* and USCGC *Healy*

Prior to this collaborative expedition, U.S. scientists had for several years been collecting bathymetric data on the slope of the Arctic continental shelf, including work on the Chukchi Cap and Northwind Ridge; hence, they already had a significant database. On August 22, CCGS *Louis S. St-Laurent* departed from Kugluktuk in western Nunavut to begin the 2008 survey. It spent two weeks conducting research alone before meeting up with USCGC *Healy* on September 9 for the first Canada-U.S. ECS mission.[115] The main objectives of the mission were to collect seismic data needed to determine sediment thickness and bathymetric information necessary to identify the foot of the slope.[116] By combining forces, they planned to access the areas where the ice was densest. They agreed to develop one data set and to interpret it jointly.

CCGS *Louis S. St-Laurent* and USCGC *Healy*.

Jon Biggar, Canadian Hydrographic Services, Fisheries and Oceans Canada.

In most cases, the United States' newest and most technologically advanced icebreaker, USCGC *Healy*, went ahead to break the ice, and CCGS *Louis S. St-Laurent* followed with the seismic equipment.

Unlike CCGS *Louis S. St-Laurent*, which only had a single-beam echo sounder, USCGC *Healy* had a multibeam transducer mounted in its hull. While USCGC *Healy* deployed its multibeam sonar technology, CCGS *Louis S. St-Laurent* continued to run its single-beam transducer as well as its sub-bottom profiler to maximize the data collected. The latter also towed the seismic airgun and streamer containing hydrophones. This survey methodology was used on all the joint Canada-U.S. ECS missions conducted from icebreakers.

Using two icebreakers offered important advantages not available to single-vessel expeditions: versatility, expediency, and greater safety for the ships and their equipment.

Single-ship operations with towed gear in the Arctic are limited to operating in light to moderate ice cover where the ship can avoid backing and ramming to move through the ice field. For the single-ship work in 2007, the track lines were rarely straight because of the need to seek open-water leads or areas with new ice where the need to back and ram through ice was minimized. Although 3000 kilometres of data were collected, the straight-line distance covered was much less. Using two ships increased safety and efficiency in these polar operations and made possible the collection of data along straighter paths in areas where surveying otherwise would have been impossible.[117]

Because scientific missions conducted north of the latitude 75° north can expect heavy ice conditions, such missions require two icebreakers: one to carve a path through the ice and a second equipped with the seismic instruments to follow.

In areas where seismic data were required, USCGC *Healy* led because the seismic equipment was more vulnerable to ice damage, and in this way a much better quality of seismic data was acquired. In areas where the shape of the sea floor (bathymetry) was the more important type of data, the ships reversed order and the Canadian icebreaker led, again to improve the data quality. It is worth noting, "there were occasions when it was impractical for either ship to lead because of the high likelihood of getting stuck. In these situations, the ships ran side by side so that the path broken by each relieved the ice pressure to allow the other to make forward progress. During such times, the seismic system was on deck until reaching lighter ice conditions when normal two-ship operations could resume."[118] For both seismic and bathymetric data collection, it is preferable not to be breaking ice because of the extraneous noise it creates; thus, when bathymetric research was the priority, CCGS *Louis S. St-Laurent* went first.[119] USCGC *Healy* generally led in the Canada Basin, where collecting seismic data pertaining to sediment thickness was the priority, whereas on the Alpha Ridge, the focus was on determining the foot of the slope position and the 2,500-metre isobath, so collecting bathymetric and sub-bottom profiler information was the priority.[120] Of course, it would be ideal to have the highest quality seismic and bathymetric data, but when you get into such difficult ice conditions, one frequently has to choose which will be the priority.[121]

Working alone, CCGS *Louis S. St-Laurent* gathered 1,300 kilometres of seismic data and with USCGC *Healy* a further 1,500 kilometres was collected.[122] USCGC *Healy* recorded 5,500 line-kilometres of bathymetry, which was augmented by 158 spot soundings taken from the helicopter.[123] The ice conditions allowed the 2008 survey to proceed further north than originally expected; hence the plans for 2009 were adjusted to reflect this success.

2009

Second Joint Canada-U.S. Survey

In early August Canadian and U.S. scientists embarked on a second joint surveying mission, employing similar research strategies to extend the survey lines in the Canada Basin.[124]

> The principal objective was to acquire multichannel seismic reflection and refraction data along positions that serve to establish sediment thicknesses along Canadian and U.S. western Arctic continental margins. Secondary objectives included bathymetric sounding at specific locations along this margin to validate bathymetric data acquired by other means (e.g., satellite altimetry [gravity testing]) in order to establish baseline information such as the 2500 m contour position.[125]

The ships encountered heavy ice over the Alpha Ridge, and the lead ice-breaker could travel only one nautical mile per hour. On average, the icebreakers burn thirty-three thousand to thirty-four thousand litres of diesel per day, however, near the Alpha Ridge, where the ice was very thick, the lead icebreaker burned eighty thousand to ninety thousand litres of diesel per day, averaging two metres travelled for every litre consumed.[126] Needless to say, such activity is extremely costly and impossible to sustain over long distances because conventionally powered ships cannot carry sufficient fuel. Yet overall, weather and ice conditions cooperated and the mission was deemed "a tremendous success," during which "4069 line-km of high quality multichannel seismic reflection data were acquired, in addition to seismic refraction data recorded from 51 sonobuoys deployments. 8355 line-km of single beam bathymetry were achieved, in addition to 177 helicopter spot soundings."[127] The ships were able to go all the way up to 84° north and they collected 50 percent to 60 percent more data than planned.[128] In addition, the multibeam sonar on USCGC *Healy* made an exciting discovery: a 2,650-metre-high seamount where the previous charts had shown only a contour line.[129] Together the Americans and Canadians agreed to name it Savaqatigiik Seamount, "which means 'Collaboration Sea Mount' in the Inupiaq language of Alaska."[130]

2010

Two missions were undertaken in 2010. In the spring, Canada's UNCLOS team achieved the first Arctic deployment of an AUV from an ice camp. Later that summer, they conducted the third joint survey with their U.S. counterparts, using CCGS *Louis S. St-Laurent* and USCGC *Healy*.

Ice Camp off Borden Island (Project Cornerstone II)

The camp was on an ice floe located south of Borden Island 650 kilometres northwest of Resolute.[131] There were more than forty people participating in two separate sets of activities: collecting bathymetric data using helicopter spot soundings and deploying an AUV.[132] The former had limited success because bad weather and ice fog curtailed the use of helicopters, and "there was only one day of unobstructed flying weather during the entire month of April."[133] In contrast, the AUV deployment was considered "a resounding success."[134] The experiment was done in close collaboration with Defence Research and Development Canada (the research arm of the Department of National Defence) and the private company International Submarine Engineering Limited. The technology has been used routinely in more southerly climes and Defence Research and Development Canada had experience using AUVs in the Arctic to lay fibre optic cables under ice; however, 2010 marked the first test of an AUV's effectiveness in conducting bathymetric surveys in polar conditions.

Finding a suitable location for the camp involved finding not only a large, flat, stable piece of ice two to three metres thick, but also one under which the water depth was fifty to one hundred metres to allow the AUV to do the manoeuvres needed for its calibration.[135] Setting up first the camps and then the docking stations at the base camp and at a remote camp 350 kilometres offshore was impeded by bad weather and unstable ice conditions.[136] Delays in any part of the setup of the camp jeopardized time available for science since weather conditions normally deteriorate in May; time lost is time lost for good. To lower the 7.4-metre-long AUV into the water, and subsequently retrieve it, required drilling a large (eight metres by three metres) hole through two to three metres of ice.[137] There were delays because the hot-water drill used to cut through the ice cannot operate in the high winds that were common. It required three days of work to remove thirty tons of ice to get the AUV into the water.[138] Once the large trench was cut at the base camp and a smaller hole (for recharging the battery) was dug at the remote camp, the holes were sheltered under heated tents. As the AUV sensors are easily damaged by frigid temperatures, its sections had to be transported quickly between the aircraft on which it arrived and the heated tent.[139]

The offshore ice was in constant motion, however, and as a result the original remote camp drifted out of the AUV's range while the base camp was being readied for the AUV launching; thus, it was necessary to relocate the remote camp.[140]

The objective of its first voyage was "to survey an unseen stretch of seabed called the Sever Spur, a deep sea formation around 339 kms long that lies under the ice of the Canada Basin."[141] It took three days for the AUV to travel from the base camp to the remote camp, a distance of four hundred kilometres.[142] As the remote camp drifted some twenty kilometres over the three days and it was not possible to communicate with the AUV during its

The AUV in sections on rails ready for assembly.

Tim Janzen, Fisheries and Oceans Canada.

journeys, this navigational feat was a major accomplishment.[143] Although enormous amounts of work had been done previously to ensure its readiness, waiting for the AUV to reach its destination caused much nail biting. After the data were downloaded and its battery was recharged, the AUV was sent out on its return voyage. Downloading the data at the remote camp was a precaution, which in this case proved unnecessary as the AUV made it safely back to the main camp where all the data were downloaded.

On both journeys, the AUV cruised along some 100 metres above the ocean floor, collecting single-beam bathymetric data.[144] The tests demonstrated that the AUV "could operate under the ice to 5000 m water depth, acquire bathymetric data and return to a location that is unknown prior to mission programming."[145] At the same time, it was clear that the navigational system would require further fine-tuning as the positions were significantly out; thus requiring extra processing of the data to correct for errors.[146] Nevertheless, the tests showed the AUV to have appreciable

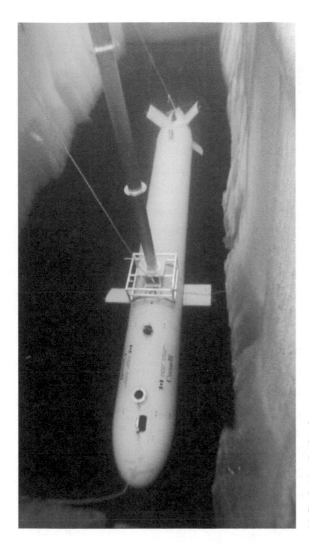

The AUV being lowered through the thick sea ice at the ice camp in 2010.

Don Glencross © Her Majesty the Queen in Right of Canada, as represented by the Minister of National Defence, 2010.

advantages over the helicopter spot soundings. With the latter, one has to land or hover to get a data point along the profile, which is time-consuming, is impossible in bad weather, and results in one data point every two to five kilometres. The AUV allows its operator to move along the same kind of profile, getting one data point every fifty metres, and the result is a much more accurate profile.[147] It was the first successful deployment of an UNCLOS AUV. The following year, it was again deployed, this time using an icebreaker as the launching pad and a multibeam sonar for the acquisition of bathymetric data.

Third Joint Canada-U.S. Survey

On August 4, 2010, CCGS *Louis S. St-Laurent* set off from Kugluktuk to join USCGC *Healy*. The mission's main objectives were to complement their previously acquired information on sediment thickness by collecting seismic reflection and refraction data, and to take bathymetric soundings along the Arctic continental margins of Canada and the United States.[148] The voyage encountered a series of problems.[149] Heavy fog reduced visibility and made it all the more vital to maintain good communications both between the Canadian and U.S. icebreakers and between the chief scientist who was overseeing the data collection and the captain on the bridge of CCGS *Louis S. St-Laurent*. A leak in the streamer required removing it from the water at 2 a.m. Several survey days were lost while a propeller shaft was repaired, and then a full week was lost when a medical emergency forced them to travel back to Tuktoyaktuk "from 82 degrees north all the way through the heaviest ice to 70 degrees."[150] In spite of the setbacks, data collection was impressive: "3673 line-km of high quality multichannel seismic reflection data were acquired in addition to seismic refraction data recorded from 34 sonobuoy deployments. 9500 line-km of single beam bathymetry data were obtained plus 61 helicopter spot soundings. In collaboration with the United States Coast Guard Cutter *Healy*, similar amounts of multibeam bathymetric and chirp subbottom profiler data were acquired."[151] They travelled more than ten thousand kilometres, achieving their objectives in the southern portion of the Canada Basin and realizing most in the northern section.[152]

2011

Fourth Joint Canada-U.S. Survey

On August 18 CCGS *Louis S. St-Laurent* again set sail from Kugluktuk on what was then expected to be its final UNCLOS survey. The main objectives of this fourth joint venture with USCGC *Healy* "were to acquire multichannel seismic reflection, refraction and bathymetric data along positions that serve to establish sediment thicknesses, structural and morphologic criteria along Canadian and U.S. western Arctic continental margins."[153] USCGC *Healy* and CCGS *Louis S. St-Laurent* were able to advance more expeditiously than expected in the early stages of the survey because of light ice conditions; however, they encountered increasingly heavy ice as they moved into the more northerly regions, especially the Sever Spur area, which slowed progress.[154]

The UNCLOS team not only collected seismic data using the hydrophone streamer and sonobuoys but also acquired bathymetric data using an AUV as well as transducers mounted on the ships. In addition to the Project Cornerstone tests of the AUVs in 2009 and 2010, CCGS *Louis S. St-Laurent* did a cruise off Newfoundland in April 2011 to get those involved with the AUV deployment comfortable using the vessel, to get the ship's crew acquainted with the equipment and its requirements, and to work out the logistics of launching an AUV from an icebreaker.[155] The AUV was launched from the Canadian icebreaker in the northeastern part of the route (e.g., over the Sever Spur) where the ice was too thick for the ships to penetrate.[156] This region was the most difficult part of the mapping. Once a pool of open water was found, the ship's crane lowered the AUV over the side of CCGS *Louis S. St-Laurent*, using ropes fore and aft to ensure it remained parallel to the vessel.

Launching an AUV from CCGS *Louis S. St-Laurent*.

Don Glencross © Her Majesty the Queen in Right of Canada, as represented by the Minister of National Defence, 2010.

It is a tricky procedure, as the AUV is more than seven metres long; if it swings it could hit the side of the boat and damage its electronics.[157] Once in the water, the slip hook was released and the AUV deployed. The AUV carried a multibeam transducer; thus it was able to acquire a six-hundred-metre-wide swath of bathymetric data along its track, sounding the sea floor more than once per metre along and across track.

After the technical problems incurred on its first deployment had been addressed, the AUV succeeded in collecting good quality multibeam bathymetric data on its second mission, travelling 110 kilometres, including under the very heavy ice conditions in the Sever Spur region.[158] During its deployment, CCGS *Louis S. St-Laurent* drifted approximately ten kilometres; however, the AUV returned within a few metres of the ship.[159]

Retrieving an AUV from the water.

Don Glencross © Her Majesty the Queen in Right of Canada, as represented by the Minister of National Defence, 2010.

The ship's captain skilfully manoeuvred CCGS *Louis S. St-Laurent* to break the ice around the AUV, enabling the latter to be retrieved without damage. Waiting for the AUV to reach its destination and then return to the ship was stressful. "You put a two-million-dollar piece of equipment in the water and send it out for two hundred miles and expect it to come home. The technology is amazing!"[160] It was the first time that an AUV had been successfully deployed and recovered in ice from an icebreaker in the High Arctic.

An equipment failure on the CCGS *Louis S. St-Laurent*, which could not be remedied at sea, ended the seismic survey somewhat prematurely.

> Prior to the voyage, the centre propeller had been removed as part of the vessel's annual refit. When the propeller was reinstalled the seizing bolts were not tightened enough. As a result, the propeller loosened on the shaft and subsequently was sliding back and forth as the ship moved ahead or astern. Fortunately, the ship's chief officer and the chief technician noticed a "strange thumping noise" while deploying the seismic gear on the quarterdeck. A small ROV (remote operated vehicle), piloted by DRDC [Defence Research and Development Canada] personnel, was deployed and the vessel's chief engineer immediately identified the problem. Had the centre propeller not been taken out of service, it might have fallen off the end of the shaft into the ocean or done damage to the shaft itself. The USCGC *Healy* escorted the Canadian icebreaker back to open water, as the latter's ability to steer and break ice was compromised as a result of the loss of use of the centre shaft. When the CCGS *Louis S. St-Laurent* reached Cambridge Bay, divers took the propeller off the shaft, which was an engineering feat in itself and secured it onboard the vessel.[161]

Saving the centre propeller avoided the major expense that would have been incurred in replacing it.

In spite of these problems,

> 1437 line-km of high quality multichannel seismic reflection data were acquired in addition to seismic refraction data recorded from 21 sonobuoy deployments. 7848 line-km of single beam bathymetry, subbottom profiler and shipborne gravity data were obtained

from the *Louis S. St-Laurent* over the course of the entire mission, plus 75 helicopter spot soundings. 110 km of bathymetric data were acquired by the AUV and in excess of 4500 line-km of multibeam bathymetric data were acquired from the USCGC *Healy*.[162]

The data derived from the AUV showed "a clear maximum change in gradient at the base of the outermost ridge and the position of this break is able to be precisely determined."[163] In other words, the AUV data identified the foot of the slope.

Prior to 2007, when the UNCLOS surveys in the deep water of the Arctic Ocean began, Canada had only three thousand kilometres of seismic reflection data. After the five years of UNCLOS missions, they had acquired "over 15000 km of bathymetry, sub-bottom profiles, and 16-channel seismic reflection data" over the Alpha Ridge and the Canada Basin and refraction data to define the velocity structure of the sedimentary layers in the region.[164]

Survey Tracks, 2007–2011

Red lines are CCGS *Louis S. St-Laurent*'s survey tracks, 2007–2011.
Black lines are the seismic refraction lines from ARTA and LORITA.
Yellow dot is the North Pole.

David Mosher, Natural Resources Canada.

By the end of the 2011 mission, Canadian scientists were optimistic that they had the bathymetric and seismic data needed for Canada's submission, which left two years to complete the analysis and write the submission.[165]

Instead of presenting Canada's Arctic submission to the Commission in December 2013, the prime minister announced that further survey-ing was needed to allow Canada to claim the North Pole. Between the announcement and the end of the 2015 mission, some fifty million dol-lars was allocated to facilitate this work. The figure is calculated from two government documents outlining the money allocated to Canada's Arctic ECS Program, for both the Atlantic and the Arctic submissions. The Treasury Board announced in August 2014 that $170.6 million had been allocated for the period from 2004 to 2021.[166] Eight months earlier, the total budget for the period from 2004 to 2017 was said to be $117 mil-lion.[167] Therefore $53.6 million was allocated after December 2013. While some of this money was used to maintain the databases for the Atlantic submission, most was needed for the subsequent Arctic ECS research. The post-December 2013 missions are discussed below.

Post-December 2013 Missions

At the end of the 2011 survey it was assumed that the UNCLOS research was complete; hence, the equipment was put away or allocated to other projects. The short timeline between announcing the 2014 mission and CCGS *Louis S. St-Laurent* setting sail in August of that year meant a scramble to resurrect and service the UNCLOS equipment. Denmark had collected bathymet-ric data and seismic reflection around the North Pole but, especially after the Canadian prime minister's announcement, it was unwilling to share it or to sell it to Canada.[168] Mapping the area around the North Pole and the Lomonosov Ridge and identifying the foot of the slope positions necessi-tated having a high-resolution multibeam sonar.[169] In the icebreaker mis-sions run from 2008 to 2011, the multibeam echo sounder on USCGC *Healy* had provided multibeam data for both countries; however, since Canada was going to conduct several years of surveys alone, it needed its own mult-ibeam equipment. Early in 2014, the Canadian government authorized a seven-million-dollar upgrade on CCGS *Louis S. St-Laurent*, which included the purchase of a multibeam transducer.[170] Installing this equipment was a massive undertaking. To generate a "swath" of beams requires two arrays

The transmit array with the installation of the forty-eight modules, and all associated cabling is almost complete. The transmit array is installed longitudinally, along the vessel's keel.

Tracey Clarke, Senior Naval Architect, courtesy Canadian Coast Guard, Fisheries and Oceans Canada.

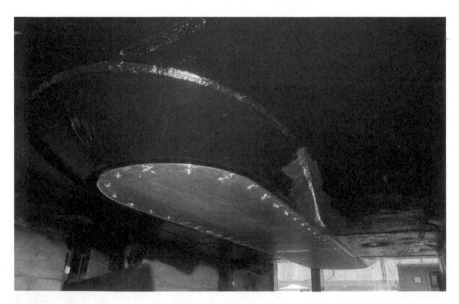

The titanium window is installed to protect the receive array. The receive array itself includes eight individual transducer modules. It is installed aft of, and at ninety degrees to, the transmit array.

Tracey Clarke, Senior Naval Architect, courtesy Canadian Coast Guard, Fisheries and Oceans Canada.

perpendicular to one another (a *transmit* array and a *receive* array). Thus, the installation necessitated cutting two holes in the icebreaker's hull, "one approximately 9 by 1.5 by 0.5 metres and the other approximately 4.5 by 1.0 by 0.5 metres, structurally integrating custom recesses, installing the sounder arrays into those recesses behind protective windows, and integrating multiple additional parts of the system throughout the ship."[171]

Scott Youngblut, engineering project supervisor, data acquisition, Canadian Hydrographic Service, Department of Fisheries and Oceans, commented, "Imagine seeing a 120-metre icebreaker sitting on blocks of wood with a huge hole being cut in its hull. Imagine someone working under that enormous ship, cutting the hole or tightening a bolt."[172] The full ocean-depth ice-strengthened sonar (EM 122) they installed is the largest multibeam model in the world, although Canada is not unique in owning one.[173] Prior to 2014, Canada had never had one that large to do deep ocean surveying.[174] A smaller sonar had been mounted on another Canadian icebreaker; however, as Youngblut remarked, "This was a bigger sonar on a larger ship, done on a much shorter timeline." Paola Travaglini, chief hydrographer on the 2014 voyage, concurred: "To have a system ordered, installed, tested and operational in about six months was a miracle."[175]

Prior to the 2014 mission, the hydrographers and technicians from the Bedford Institute of Oceanography ran quite a few tests in the Atlantic Ocean to ensure the equipment was working properly and to determine the kind of data they could acquire.[176] Given the tight timeline, it was not certain that there would even be a 2014 mission. It was not just a question of equipment; it was the challenge of finding the personnel needed at such short notice. Borden Chapman was brought out of retirement for three months to help Desmond Manning, a marine geoscience technologist with Geological Survey of Canada, who had taken over as chief technician and was working long and hard to get the equipment ready, and both provided technical support on the 2014 survey.

From a scientific point of view, the acquisition of the EM 122 sonar for Canada's Arctic ECS Program had valuable spinoffs for Canada's scientific research more generally as it enhanced the country's capacity to conduct bathymetric surveys in the Arctic. "Now we have our own data, collected on our ship using our own system, which makes us more independent and allows Canada to operate in the Arctic alone without necessarily needing to partner with other countries."[177]

2014

Canadian Survey Using CCGS *Louis S. St-Laurent* and CCGS *Terry Fox*

In early August 2014, CCGS *Terry Fox* and CCGS *Louis S. St-Laurent* set off from St. John's, Newfoundland, to collect seismic and bathymetric data in the Amundsen Basin east of the Lomonosov Ridge and around the North Pole. Finding the foot of the slope was the focus of the 2014 mission so multibeam bathymetric and sub-bottom profiler data were the priorities. While a lot of bathymetry had been collected in the Arctic Ocean using the continuous feeds from the multibeam and single-beam sonar technologies onboard the icebreakers, the previous spot-testing along the Arctic margin had produced a lot less data and they did not comprise unbroken lines.[178] The mission's other objectives included collecting seismic reflection and refraction data to determine sediment thickness in the Amundsen and Canada Basins, and to assist in identifying foot of the slope zones and in establishing the geological relationship of the Lomonosov Ridge and the surrounding basins.[179]

Canadian icebreakers CCGS *Terry Fox* and CCGS *Louis S. St-Laurent*.

David Mosher, Natural Resources Canada.

Severe ice conditions caused a multitude of problems for the mission generally and, most especially, for its seismic program. The ice was thick and under pressure. Several sonobuoys deployed off the stern of the ship were crushed by the ice.[180] The initial plans were for CCGS *Terry Fox* to act as the lead icebreaker and open a "path through the ice," while CCGS *Louis S. St-Laurent* followed, collecting both seismic and bathymetric multibeam sonar data.[181]

The arrangement was problematic on several scores. CCGS *Terry Fox* was about six and a half metres narrower than CCGS *Louis S. St-Laurent*; the lead opened by the former was not wide enough to allow the latter to pass through without having to do ice-breaking of its own. In addition, CCGS *Terry Fox* did not have sufficient weight to break through heavy multiyear ice, which meant either that it could not get through the ice or that it rode up onto the ice, causing it to deflect off course. The latter resulted in a curved lead that was difficult for the wider CCGS *Louis S. St-Laurent* to navigate as it had trouble making the sharp turns of the lead opened by CCGS *Terry Fox*. The situation was further complicated because CCGS *Louis S. St-Laurent* could not use its central propeller when the seismic gear was

Streamer in the ice "Yikes!"

David Mosher, Natural Resources Canada.

deployed, which limited its power and its ability to steer. To get through the ice and to control steerage, CCGS *Louis S. St-Laurent* had to increase revolutions to its port or starboard propellers while the centre propeller was out of commission. Any use of the centre propeller could result in damage to the hydrophone streamer. On several occasions, CCGS *Louis S. St-Laurent* had to "rev" its propellers to get through the ice, which resulted in damage to the hydrophone streamer.[182]

Leaks in the streamer were common and caused equipment failure. On separate occasions, the revving propellers and churning ice caused the hydrophone streamer and the umbilical cables to the air guns to become wound around the seismic sled.[183] In each case, a careful untangling was required to avoid destroying the equipment.

To help overcome problems caused by heavy ice conditions and the relative sizes of the two Canadian icebreakers, a new plan was devised. CCGS *Louis S. St-Laurent*, which was bigger and more powerful, travelled down the survey line for several kilometres breaking the ice, then turned and came back on the same line breaking ice along the same path. CCGS *Terry Fox* followed, further breaking up the ice. On the third pass, CCGS *Terry Fox* went ahead and CCGS *Louis S. St-Laurent* deployed the seismic gear. While this new modus vivendi was a significant improvement over the original plan, it was far from perfect. "Even with this solution, the *Fox* would have to frequently return to assist the *Louis* and line patterns were rarely straight."[184] The icebreakers frequently encountered one pressure ridge after another and, on at least one occasion, spent a whole day to go around a single ice floe.[185] Breakage, leaks, and equipment failures continued. The need to go over the same path three times resulted in heavy fuel consumption, which caused significant delays (e.g., ten hours) when CCGS *Terry Fox* had to be refuelled from the larger tanks on CCGS *Louis S. St-Laurent*.[186] According to CCGS *Louis S. St-Laurent* Commanding Officer Anthony Potts, CCGS *Louis S. St-Laurent* usually burnt thirty tons of fuel a day when travelling through ice; however, the consumption rate was 50 percent higher in the severe ice conditions encountered on the 2014 mission.[187] With the tough ice conditions and fuel running low, David Mosher, chief scientist, and Potts decided with regret that the mission would have to abandon the survey plans for the area of heaviest ice in the region of the Lomonosov Ridge and head for the Canada Basin.[188]

Even so, the surveying was not without challenges. Ice conditions were relatively light as they crossed the Podvodnikov Basin and Mendeleev Ridge, but became very thick as they approached the Canada margin, which made progress slow and again resulted in damaged equipment.[189] For example, on September 13 the streamer was thrown to the surface in the churning ice and water behind the ship and became snagged on the ice, which resulted in its floats being ripped off and the acoustic release at its end being torn off and lost.[190]

In light of the challenges faced, particularly by the seismic program, it was fortunate that the mission's primary objectives were the collection of multibeam and sub-bottom profiler data. Although they traversed the area of the Arctic with the thickest ice, they were unable to use the AUVs, which had already been allocated to the search for Franklin's ships. Nonetheless, in the course of the mission, they acquired "8355 line-km of multibeam bathymetric and coincident subbottom profiler data."[191] The seismic program fared much less well. With thick, compressed ice under pressure, it was often too risky to tow the seismic sled and streamer, and when deployed there were frequent leaks and damage to the equipment. As a result, only "746 line-km of high quality multichannel seismic reflection data were acquired, in addition to seismic refraction data recorded from 13 Sonobuoys."[192] The contrast between the 746-line-kilometres of seismic reflection data collected in 2014 and the over 15,000 line-kilometres acquired in the four previous missions testifies to the severity of the ice conditions encountered in 2014.

2015

Canadian Survey Using CCGS *Louis S. St-Laurent* and CCGS *Terry Fox*
The primary objective for the 2015 survey was similar to that for the 2014 mission: collect multibeam bathymetric and sub-bottom profiler data in the areas around the Lomonosov Ridge and in the Amundsen Basin in the vicinity of the North Pole.[193] As such, the 2015 mission focused on an area with very thick and very old multiyear ice.[194] In spite of these conditions, the other important objective was to acquire seismic reflection and refraction data "along strategically placed profile lines to obtain information on sediment thickness, velocity and the nature of the crust."[195]

This time CCGS *Louis S. St-Laurent* and CCGS *Terry Fox* picked up fresh crews and the scientific and technical personnel in Tromsø, Norway, rather than having them all set off from St. John's.[196] Tromsø was a good choice for two reasons. First, although there are points in Canada closer to the North Pole than Tromsø, one cannot provision from them. Tromsø is closer to the North Pole than any Canadian port, so it was a good place to re-provision the icebreakers with fuel, food and other supplies. It is the most northerly, deepwater port serviced by commercial airlines, and it is also en route to the Eurasia Basin. Second, flying the scientists and technicians to Tromsø, rather than sending them on the sea voyage, saved staff time.

In the thick ice, they again used the technique employed the previous year to circumvent the problems that resulted when the wider-hulled CCGS *Louis S. St-Laurent* tried to follow the narrower, less powerful CCGS *Terry Fox*. CCGS *Louis S. St-Laurent* broke the ice travelling down a line some thirty-two kilometres long, turned, and came back on the same line breaking ice along the same track. The exact length of the run varied depending on where they were. The ice pressure was such that if they went farther than thirty-two kilometres, the line was completely closed in by the time they got back to the starting point. CCGS *Terry Fox* followed, further breaking up the ice. On first pass, CCGS *Louis S. St-Laurent* rode up on the ice, using its own weight to break it, and the broken ice tended to fold under the ship. On the second pass, the icebreaker was primarily pushing the broken ice out of the way to the side. Yet even with two ships travelling up the line and back, the ice was under such pressure that it was still closing in behind the ship. On the first pass, the breaking ice caused a lot of extraneous noise in the multibeam data, which showed the water column but the quality was not great. On the second pass coming back, they collected good data because they had already broken the line once. As they were going through two metres of ice under massive amounts of pressure, the second run was very much needed. On the third pass, CCGS *Terry Fox* went ahead and CCGS *Louis S. St-Laurent* deployed the seismic gear. The third run produced the best bathymetric data and the only seismic data. If they had only been collecting bathymetric data, the first two passes would have sufficed; although the second pass was definitely needed to get good quality multibeam data.

The 2014 mission had shown once again that there are areas of really thick, multiyear ice, which even Canada's largest icebreaker cannot access, so the initial plans for the 2015 mission included the use of an AUV to conduct bathymetric surveys under the impenetrable ice, mapping particular features of interest and then returning to the ship.[197] Although CCGS *Louis S. St-Laurent* carried an AUV it was not used to collect data because of procurement delays, which resulted in the sensors required to position it under the ice and to collect the necessary data not being delivered prior to the ship's departure from Halifax. Since its success and return to the ship could not be guaranteed, it was not deployed on any extended research voyages under the ice. On the final stage of the voyage, after the mapping was completed and the ships were heading toward their final destination, Kugluktuk, they did three days of testing the AUV, near Banks Island in the Canada Basin, during which it was deployed for three separate trials, all within the acoustic range of the ship.

During the six-week voyage a "total of 9053 line-km of multibeam bathymetric and coincident subbottom profiler data were acquired," and "[d]etailed multibeam bathymetric data were obtained along-track in the Amundsen Basin and also targeted three proposed foot-of-slope points and the 2500 m isobath on the flank of Lomonosov Ridge."[198]

Unlike the multibeam bathymetric sonar and sub-bottom profiler that ran continuously while the ship was moving, the seismic operations were severely limited by ice conditions, particularly in the Amundsen Basin.[199] As a result, the acquisition of seismic data focused on the area around the Lomonosov Ridge.[200] "Two survey lines provided sediment thickness information near the outer constraint line towards the Gakkel Ridge, and eight seismic lines were run onto the slope of the Lomonosov Ridge."[201] The 2015 mission acquired "527 line-km of high quality multichannel seismic reflection data," and of the forty-four sonobuoys deployed, "17 recorded good quality seismic refraction data suitable for velocity modelling."[202] The auxiliary programs were successful: "Good cooperation among the various onboard science teams allowed for the collection of chemical and physical oceanographic samples throughout the survey areas and along transit routes."[203]

2016

Joint Canadian-Swedish Survey Using CCGS *Louis S. St-Laurent* and Swedish Icebreaker *Oden*

As had been the case with previous missions, extensive planning and preparations were required for the final UNCLOS survey. The need was all the more pressing as this mission was the last opportunity to collect data for Canada's Arctic ECS submission. Weekly planning meetings for the 2016 mission began soon after the 2015 survey ended.[204] Members of the science team devised a survey plan and back-up plans should ice conditions prevent areas from being surveyed, and reviewed previously collected data, newly published scientific results, and recommendations that had been issued by the Commission. Two science-planning workshops were held at the Bedford Institute of Oceanography in Dartmouth, Nova Scotia, and another took place in Helsingborg, Sweden.

On July 22, 2016, CCGS *Louis S. St-Laurent* departed Halifax en route to Tromsø, Norway. Most of the scientific team boarded at Tromsø, although a few scientists from the Canadian Hydrographic Service travelled with the ship during its transit, mapping the North Atlantic for use by other programs. In Tromsø, after a crew change, refuelling, and provisioning, CCGS *Louis S. St-Laurent* proceeded to its August 11 rendezvous with *Oden*, Sweden's largest icebreaker, off the Norwegian island of Svalbard, where equipment was tested before starting the transit to the survey area in the Amundsen Basin. In the subsequent six-week period, data were collected in areas of the Amundsen Basin, Lomonosov Ridge, Marvin Spur, Alpha Ridge, and Canada Basin.

As with earlier ECS missions, the 2016 survey was led by scientists from the Geological Survey of Canada and the Canadian Hydrographic Service; Canada's scientific team was drawn from these departments as well as from Environment and Climate Change Canada. The 2016 voyage marked the first time that a representative from Global Affairs Canada had participated on an UNCLOS survey.

The primary objectives of the 2016 survey were geophysical data acquisition from the Amundsen Basin in the eastern Arctic Ocean to the Canada Basin in the western Arctic Ocean, and the collection of rock samples. The secondary objective was an innovative large offset, wide-angle seismic refraction experiment to investigate deep crustal structure, a first in the Arctic Ocean, involving collaboration between scientists from the Geological Survey of Canada and the Geological Survey of Denmark and Greenland. Both *Oden* and CCGS *Louis S. St-Laurent* had multibeam sonar systems, and bathymetric mapping was undertaken continuously during the survey. It proved valuable in obtaining foot-of-slope profiles to delineate the outer limits of the extended shelf and, in support of dredging operations, in identifying steep rock faces where the probability of successfully collecting rocks was highest. The third objective was to undertake five days of geophysical data collection for the U.S. ECS Program in the Canada Basin. In return, USCGC *Healy* would dredge rock samples for Canada's UNCLOS Program from the eastern side of the Canada Basin. Thus, there were three components to the 2016 mission: a Canada-Sweden joint survey; unilateral data collection in the Canada Basin; and a quid pro quo data sharing arrangement with the United States.

From August 11 to September 2, Canadian and Swedish scientists collaborated on a joint survey. Unlike previous icebreaker surveys where Canada had only a single science team, the 2016 survey had science parties on both vessels, making coordination more complex and time-consuming, but it was worth the extra effort. Twenty-four members of Canada's science team sailed on CCGS *Louis S. St-Laurent*, collecting seismic and bathymetric data, using the methods described earlier in the chapter. Four Canadians (two from the Geological Survey of Canada and two from the Canadian Hydrographic Service) worked on *Oden*. In addition to the experienced Swedish and Danish scientists on *Oden*, there was a program to train early-career scientists who undertook research on a variety of topics concerning dredge samples, water column imaging, geophysical mapping, sediment core samples, physical oceanography, trace gas biogeochemistry, meteorology, ice management, and heavy metal concentrations in water, air, ice, and snow.

To coordinate Canada's data collection between the two vessels, Mary-Lynn Dickson, chief scientist, and Gary Sonnichsen, Canada's project manager on *Oden,* communicated multiple times a day, beginning with a 6:30 a.m. call, and using cell phones, the ships' radios, emails, and a file-sharing system on which they could each post and access documents.

Geophysical and bathymetric mapping were conducted from CCGS *Louis S. St-Laurent* and, as during previous surveys, an ancillary oceanography program of seawater sampling and physical oceanographic profiles of the water column was supported. *Oden's* primary role was to provide icebreaking support to CCGS *Louis S. St-Laurent*, and for most of the survey the former was the lead vessel with CCGS *Louis S. St-Laurent* following behind. During some of the transits CCGS *Louis S. St-Laurent* took the lead to give personnel on *Oden* some respite from the jarring motion and noise that accompany breaking ice.

On September 2, the two icebreakers parted company and *Oden* began its trip back to Svalbard, while CCGS *Louis S. St-Laurent* carried on alone with its UNCLOS surveying. They encountered some tough ice in the northern Canada Basin; but it was mostly free of ice or covered with loose ice so they were able to tow the streamer. They recovered the seismic gear and streamer for the final time on September 11, and reached Kugluktuk, their final destination, on September 18 — one day ahead of schedule.

Although CCGS *Louis S. St-Laurent* and USCGS *Healy* worked independently in 2016, there was cooperation between Canada and the United States in terms of data sharing. During the unilateral portion of its voyage, CCGS *Louis S. St-Laurent* conducted five days of data collection for the U.S. ECS Program. In turn, U.S. scientists on USCGS *Healy* collected rock samples for Canada's Arctic ECS submission.

While thick multiyear ice had seriously impeded progress in 2014 and 2015, the 2016 mission encountered less daunting ice conditions. Furthermore, *Oden* was better suited to the task at hand than CCGS *Terry Fox*, which was not designed to carve channels through the thick, multiyear ice found north of Canada's Arctic Archipelago. *Oden* was more powerful than CCGS *Terry Fox,* and it had a wider hull than either CCGS *Louis S. St-Laurent* or CCGS *Terry Fox.* Being seven metres wider than CCGS *Louis S. St-Laurent, Oden* carved a wide track for the former to follow. The combination of light ice conditions and large areas of open water ponds and leads, the use of two powerful icebreakers, and the assistance of an ice observer from the Canadian Ice Service, who each day at 5 a.m. downloaded ice imagery from which she found the leads and determined the best routes through the ice, allowed the science teams to cover the survey area and acquire high rates of data collection. The 2016 survey acquired more geophysical data in the first week than had been collected over six weeks during the 2015 survey in the same area. Overall, the geophysical data acquisition in 2016 was double that of 2014 and 2015 surveys combined.

Favourable ice conditions were a blessing in terms of the quantity and quality of data collected, but it meant that the team had to work harder because the gear was in the water all the time and the data streams were ongoing, which meant constant monitoring of the equipment and the incoming data. They worked twelve-hour shifts for forty-seven days.

While the 2016 mission benefited from much better ice conditions that its predecessors, there were nonetheless some major challenges. Fortunately, the team included Borden Chapman and his crew of technicians, who were hired on contract for the mission, as well as Desmond Manning as Natural Resources Canada's chief technician; thus those most experienced with the UNCLOS survey equipment were on hand to deal with the emergencies. Many of the crew of CCGS *Louis S. St-Laurent* had participated on the 2014 survey, and their skills were needed almost immediately for a successful engine repair in Tromsø. The repair delayed CCGS *Louis S. St-Laurent*'s departure by two days but, without them, the icebreaker's departure would have been delayed by at least a week. Challenging conditions were encountered on the southern portion of Alpha Ridge, toward the Canadian Archipelago, which forced both ships to turn back but not before a spare hydrophone streamer had been lost in the heavy ice. The first streamer, had been lost earlier on the voyage, when high winds pushed the ship into the streamer, causing it to be destroyed in the ship's propeller. The technical crew again saved the day, using spare parts to build a new streamer, which lasted for the rest of the cruise.

While specific numbers for the line-kilometres of data acquired were not available at the time of writing this book, the 2016 survey met all of its objectives and was a very successful scientific collaboration between Canada, Sweden, Denmark, and the United States. It accomplished a remarkable feat: a single-season, geophysical transect from the Amundsen Basin, across the Lomonosov Ridge, Marvin Spur, Alpha Ridge, and Nautilus Spur, and into the Canada Basin. Several large offset, wide-angle refraction experiments were successfully completed, which yielded incredibly detailed images of deep crustal structure below the Arctic Ocean. For the first time rock and sediment core samples were acquired by the Canadian UNCLOS Program, which are expected to yield valuable scientific knowledge about the geology and history of the Arctic Ocean. Geophysical mapping for the United States was completed in the Canada Basin, and the United States successfully recovered rock samples for Canada. On the transit back to Sweden, *Oden* collected geophysical and bathymetric data that will support Canada's submission to the Commission. Canada now has the data necessary for its revised Arctic submission.

SCIENTIFIC FINDINGS

In spite of operating in some of the world's most difficult and challenging conditions, Canada's UNCLOS team is to be commended for the large quantities of high-quality data they collected and analyzed. There was a steep learning curve, and the quality of the data improved greatly over the years as a result both of technical innovations and extensive improvements to the equipment and operating systems. For instance, they had three thousand kilometres of seismic data pertaining to the offshore deep water of the Arctic Ocean prior to the UNCLOS surveys.[205] The bathymetric data were likewise scarce, consisting for the most part of spot soundings through the ice, which were insufficient for accurately identifying either the foot of the slope or the 2,500-metre isobath.[206] Between 2008 and 2011, the joint Canada-U.S. missions added "15,481 line-km of seismic-reflection data, 171 seismic-refraction profiles and about 38,000 line-km of multibeam sonar, gravity and subbottom profiler data."[207] As Jacob Verhoef commented, "it's not a small addition to the knowledge, it's a quantum jump!"[208] Gordon Oakey explained that

> prior to Canada's Arctic Extended Continental Shelf Program, we had thirty years of scientific literature based on hypotheses with little data to back them up. The Arctic Ocean is the last large piece of real estate on the planet where we do not understand the first order geological problems. Prior to the UNCLOS surveys, we did not even have puzzle pieces because the data was so scarce. The UNCLOS data provides some of the pieces of the puzzle. From a scientific point of view, it is a brilliant piece of work![209]

Canada's submission to the Commission will be much more convincing if a series of strong arguments can be marshalled to back up its various claims. For example, using the 2,500-metre contour, Canada could claim large portions of the Alpha Ridge and the Lomonosov Ridge;[210] however, the surveys were not limited to bathymetry. The aeromagnetic research was designed to help determine if the Alpha Ridge has continental — as opposed to oceanic — affinities, which Canada hopes will be the case. Seismic research has shown the Lomonosov Ridge to be a prolongation

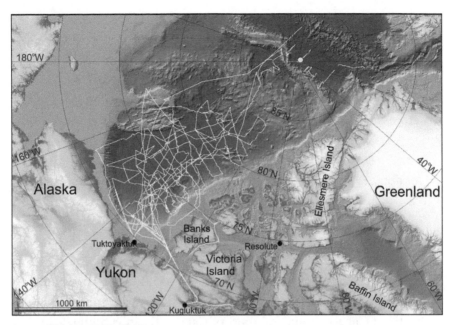

Survey Tracks, 2007–2015

Yellow lines are CCGS *Louis S. St-Laurent*'s survey tracks, 2007–2015. Yellow dot is the North Pole.

David Mosher, Natural Resources Canada.

of the North American and Russian continental margins. In short, the more strong arguments one can make drawing on a variety of scientific data, the better.

Canada Basin

Bathymetry showed the Canada Basin to be relatively flat and deep. For example, the eastern Canada Basin is around 3,800 metres deep. As such, the 2,500-metre isobath is of limited use. Fortunately, there are large amounts of sediment in the basin so the sediment formula along with the 350-nautical-mile constraint can be used.

Before Canada's Arctic ECS Program conducted its seismic reflection data in the Canada Basin, nobody knew how much sediment was there. The sediments are thinnest at the northern end, where they pinch out against the Alpha Ridge, and ten to twelve kilometres thick in the south.[211] Using the foot of slope plus 1 percent of the sediment thickness enabling formula, ten kilometres of sediment would result in an extension of one thousand kilometres.[212] Of course, the constraint formulae would set outer limits; however, the 1 percent sediment rule moves Canada's ECS a long way off shore.[213]

The seismic refraction surveys provided information on the velocity structure of the crust within the Canada Basin and to the outer Alpha Ridge.[214] As Gordon Oakey commented,

> for decades prior to the UNCLOS surveys, it had been assumed that Canada Basin was an oceanic basin which meant that it was basaltic oceanic crust formed at a spreading ridge system, like the North Atlantic spreading ridge; therefore, that it was oceanic crust rather than continental shelf. It was a total surprise to find that it was not a giant oceanic basin, as was published in 1979. Instead, we found that there is only a very small region of oceanic crust in the very centre of Canada Basin and most of Canada Basin is thinned continental crust. It is a paradigm shift in terms of understanding the tectonic framework and the development of the whole Arctic.[215]

In addition to the highly valuable data on sediment thickness and the composition of the Canada Basin's crust, the research has provided a wealth of information about how the Canada Basin was formed, which will strengthen Canada's submission by providing a context in which to situate its arguments. A geological description of its history and tectonics supports the other claims for a prolongation of continent land mass.[216]

Alpha Ridge

Although the extensive information collected for the Canada Basin provides a framework for understanding the tectonic environment in which the Alpha Ridge formed, much remains to be learned about the latter. The Alpha Ridge is a large igneous province (volcanic plateau).[217] What is not known is whether this large igneous province formed within continental crust or oceanic crust or whether it formed during the opening of the Canada Basin or afterwards.[218] "We have a pretty good understanding of the fundamental crustal structure of Canada Basin but the Alpha Ridge is a completely different crustal structure. While the former has six to eight kilometres of crust, the latter has over twenty-five kilometres of crust."[219] The large volcanic edifice masks a lot of the underlying geology so it is very hard to tell what underlies the Alpha Ridge. Bathymetric surveys identified a bathymetric saddle north of Ellesmere Island, separating the Alpha and Lomonosov Ridges from the continental land mass; hence, seismic research was required to determine the crustal structure of different geological layers of the ridges so they could be compared with the velocity structure on the adjacent continental shelf to ascertain if they are continuous.

The Alpha Ridge is morphologically contiguous with the Lomonosov Ridge, but it remains to be determined if the two ridges are geologically continuous. An examination of the Commission's reviews of submissions shows that the

> classification of seafloor highs is determined on the basis of the geological characteristics of the features in addition to their already proven morphological continuity with the landmass of the coastal state. In this approach, the CLCS [Commission] makes an assessment as to what extent a seafloor high is geologically associated or continuous with the landmass of the coastal state, and to what extent it is geologically different to the surrounding deep ocean floor. This assessment is made solely on the basis of geological and geophysical evidence.[220]

The data from the gravity and magnetic surveys compose an important part of building an argument for continuity with the land mass. If the ridges are geologically contiguous as well as morphologically contiguous, Canada can argue that the Alpha Ridge is an integral part of the continent.

The ARTA refraction line showed that the Alpha Ridge is an intrinsic part of the continental margin of Ellesmere Island, while the magnetic data showed that the volcanics associated with the Alpha Ridge are actually exposed onshore on Ellesmere Island (i.e., the volcanic rocks on northern Ellesmere Island are part of the large igneous province).[221] Demonstrating that the volcanics are an integral part of the margin is an important consideration for determining continuity with the offshore.[222]

The Alpha Ridge has the highest magnetic anomalies of any feature in any ocean, and no distinctive pattern had been observed in the data before

Canada's ECS Program collected data in that region.[223] The gravity signature and particularly the very high magnetic signatures, which show radiating dykes that radiate back to the Canadian Arctic islands indicate the Alpha Ridge's contiguous nature with Ellesmere Island.[224] If Canada can argue that the Alpha Ridge is geologically contiguous with the Lomonosov Ridge, and thus an integral part of the continent, a claim beyond 350 nautical miles may be made. Denmark/Greenland's 2014 submission pertaining to its continental shelf north of Greenland classified the Alpha Ridge as "[m]orphologically continuous with the land mass of Greenland" but concluded that there was not enough data to warrant classifying it as a submarine elevation "that is a natural component of the Northern Continental Margin of Greenland."[225] In its revised submission relating to the Arctic Ocean, the Russian Federation asserted that both the Mendeleev-Alpha Rise and Lomonosov Ridge are of "continental origin and belong to submarine elevations that are natural components of the continental margin under paragraph 6 of Article 76 of the Convention, which are not subject to the distance limit of 350 nautical miles from the baselines."[226]

From Canada's point of view, more scientific studies are required to sort out the origins of the igneous province, to understand how it formed in relation to the Canada Basin, and to provide further evidence that the Alpha Ridge is geologically continuous with Canada's land mass. Hence, there is still much geological work to be done.

Lomonosov Ridge

While much remains to be known about the Alpha Ridge, there is very little dispute about Lomonosov Ridge being a continental fragment and a submarine elevation. The Lomonosov Ridge was once attached to the Barents and Kara sea margin but became separated as the result of sea floor spreading over the past 55 million years.[227] The deep crustal velocity measurements collected on the 2006 LORITA mission showed that there is continuity between the coastal continental crust and that of the Lomonosov Ridge.[228] The Lomonosov Ridge is a continental fragment from the Barents Shelf, which has geological continuity with the continental margins of Ellesmere Island, Greenland, and Siberia.[229] This conclusion is supported by the gravity and magnetic signatures, which provide an idea of what is underneath the Alpha and Lomonosov Ridges and Amundsen Basin.[230] As a submarine elevation, the outer limit of Canada's claim will not be limited by the 350-nautical-mile constraint; however, as is discussed in chapter 6, Denmark and Russia included the Lomonosov Ridge in their submissions; thus, the outer limits of their respective claims on the Lomonosov Ridge will have to be resolved through bilateral and/or multilateral negotiations.

Amundsen Basin

Geologically, it is well established that the Amundsen Basin is an oceanic basin.[231] The Gakkel Ridge is the most northerly extension of the Atlantic spreading ridge, which continues to add new oceanic crust to the ocean floor, as the Nansen and Amundsen Basins drift apart. The Eurasian Basin is an extension of the North Atlantic spreading ridge. It has a very distinct geologic history from that of the Amerasian Basin of the Arctic Ocean.

Contributions to Science Generally

While Canada's Arctic ECS Program collected data with the express purposes of defining the parameters needed for Canada's submission to the Commission, it has had several spinoff benefits for science more generally. Canada's Arctic ECS Program injected millions of dollars into Arctic research, which would not otherwise have been available. The equipment purchased and developed remains to be used for future surveys in other scientific domains. Strategies and procedures as well as equipment were refined over the years and many lessons were learned that have broader applications. Canada's Arctic ECS Program has dramatically increased our understanding of the morphology and geology of the Arctic. Furthermore, it has fostered amazing collaboration between Canadian scientists and their Danish, American, Russian, German, and Swedish colleagues. Both the information gained and the networks of cooperation are fabulous legacies.

The information derived from bathymetry about water depths and the shape of the seabed is not only vital to determining the foot of the slope and the 2,500-metre isobath but is essential for safe navigation, identifying shallow waters, shoals, reefs, and rocks that pose serious hazards to ocean going vessels. Prior to the UNCLOS surveys, there was a dearth of bathymetric information about the High Arctic north of Canada as it was so inaccessible. Furthermore, it is hard to justify expensive surveys for navigational safety in deep waters, such as those found in the Canada Basin. Yet the bathymetry needed for Canada's submission has also produced information relevant to navigation for the region. The data collected have been used to update the International Bathymetric Chart of the Arctic Ocean, which is part of a larger database called the General Bathymetric Chart of the Oceans. These charts depict the large-scale morphology of the ocean floor. They have multiple users, including governments and shipping companies. They are used to build the Google Earth maps, which are utilized by the general public around the world. Of course, water depth and profiles of the seabed are also important to Canada's navigational charts. The multibeam sonar provides the data needed to create a three-dimensional picture of the ocean floor, and shows the morphology and features, which may be relevant to science generally. It was thanks to the UNCLOS bathymetry done in collaboration with the United States that the Savaqatigiik Seamount was discovered in 2009. During CCGS *Louis S. St-Laurent's* transits to Norway en route to the final ECS surveys, scientists from the Canadian Hydrographic Service did mapping for other programs, thereby maximizing usage of the icebreaker time. In 2016 they discovered a chain of uncharted undersea volcanoes (as many as thirty) south of Greenland. This discovery would not have been made at that point without this voyage, which was financed by Canada's ECS Program. In shallow water, bathymetry can even show a shipwreck or a large school of fish, which may be of interest to those concerned with fish stocks in Canada's Department of Fisheries and Oceans and Department of the Environment.[232]

The AUVs designed and built for Canada's Arctic ECS Program can be used not only in future Arctic scientific studies but also for other types of research. For example, they were used in 2014 to search for Sir John Franklin's ill-fated ships HMS *Erebus* and HMS *Terror*, which were lost in 1846. In short, the UNCLOS bathymetric surveys have had important benefits, both for Canada and for the international scientific community.

The UNCLOS seismic surveys produced very important information about the geological history and composition of the seabed, which will be used for decades to come. While determining sediment thickness was the primary seismic objective in the Amundsen Basin and Canada Basin, the results show very different geologic histories. The age of rocks was not a primary interest of the UNCLOS Program, but this information is vital to a scientific understanding of the Arctic.

In the Canada Basin, we collected reflection and refraction seismic data so we could get sediment thickness in metres but the stratigraphic interpretation of seismic reflection data has implications on the depositional history of the Arctic Ocean. Did the sediment always come in from the Beaufort Sea and Mackenzie Delta or did they come in from Alaska or the Lincoln Sea? Did the sources of the sediments that fill the basin change over time? When did change occur and how do we tie the stratigraphy in with the large tectonic framework of the whole oceanic basin?[233]

The data from Canada's Arctic ECS Program provides some answers to these questions.

Geological Survey of Canada has a mandate to manage natural resources, which requires knowledge of the resource potential. How much exists? What is its quality? What is its value? How much could be extracted? What environmental regulations will be needed to ensure safe development of the resource? Then if a company asks to buy a big block of real estate off Canada's Arctic coast, the value of the property can be determined and appropriate conditions can be decided. Geological Survey of Canada is incorporating the UNCLOS data into its assessments for the Canada Basin, so they have practical applications beyond Canada's Arctic submission.

The CTD rosette casts resulted in a wealth of water samples, all labelled with their respective date, location, and depth, that can be used for a wide array of testing. The Department of Fisheries and Oceans uses such samples to test for biological diversity. The CTD casts also provide information about ocean currents. In areas of the Arctic Ocean that had rarely, if ever, been accessed, drifter bottles were launched to observe circulation patterns, and many measurements of salinity and temperature profiles were taken.

Now the UNCLOS research is completed, there will likely to be far fewer resources allocated to scientific studies in the Arctic. The ECS provisions in UNCLOS required the Canadian government, as well as those of other Arctic coastal states, to allocate large resources to Arctic research. What will be the incentive to continue to fund maritime scientific research in the High Arctic after the submission research is completed?

CONCLUSION

In spite of all the challenges resulting from remoteness, harsh weather conditions, impenetrable ice, and many logistical nightmares, Canadian scientists and technicians, alone and in fruitful collaboration with their colleagues from other countries, have done a remarkable job of collecting and analyzing large quantities of high-quality data. As a result of their work, Canada will likely be able to define a large Arctic ECS in its submission to the Commission. Furthermore, Canada's Arctic ECS Program has greatly enhanced our understanding of the Arctic, and the data will be used for decades to come.

Over the years, the UNCLOS equipment was redesigned and rebuilt. While the most serious problems occurred on the first UNCLOS voyage, and hence the most elaborate redesigning took place between the 2007 and 2008 cruises, they continued to improve the operating systems over the subsequent years. For instance, prior to the 2014 mission, CCGS *Louis S. St-Laurent* underwent some major refurbishing including the installation of a multibeam sonar as well as new air vents for the compressors to ensure the better airflow needed to prevent overheating.

While the process of delineating Canada's ECS gives us much to celebrate, the case also raises some concerns. Questions are raised about the efficacy of the procurement process within the federal government. Many of the scientists' recommendations were not followed and some questionable decisions were made. Why was the fifty-five-year-old CCGS *Louis S. St-Laurent* not retrofitted before the ECS surveys began rather than toward the end of the program? In 2007 the Harper government committed to procuring a new polar icebreaker, *John G. Diefenbaker*, for the Canadian Coast Guard. The ship was originally expected in 2017, but the date for commissioning was pushed back and it is unlikely to arrive before 2022. Why did the government not purchase the new icebreaker in time for the UNCLOS missions rather than spending money on refurbishing one scheduled for decommissioning in 2017? Recommended equipment was often not purchased on the grounds that it was too expensive, as exemplified by all the compressor problems on the 2007 voyage. Such choices ended up costing the program dearly in terms of lost productivity. Why was a new sub-bottom profiler not installed to provide better quality data instead of leaving the science team to struggle along with an old, small one that had to sound through the six centimetres of steel of the hull of the vessel? High-quality equipment is expensive but choosing cheaper options is not always the best use of scarce resources. Using retired members of staff to serve on the missions capitalized on their wealth of experience, but why was greater effort not made to train a new generation of Arctic experts? In short, the ECS team achieved an amazing amount but, with more foresight and longer-term planning on the part of senior levels of government, the program could have left an even bigger legacy in terms of equipment and expertise for future surveys.

6

CANADA'S SUBMISSION AND OTHER OUTSTANDING ISSUES

Until December 2013 Canada was expected to make a full and comprehensive submission pertaining to the ECSs off its Atlantic and Arctic coasts. It therefore came as a shock to the UNCLOS team, neighbouring Arctic countries, and the attentive public when, on December 4, 2013, Prime Minister Stephen Harper announced that Canada would only be making a partial submission to the Commission pertaining to the Atlantic ECS rather than to both its Atlantic and Arctic ECSs — and that more research was required so Canada's Arctic ECS could be expanded to include the North Pole. Two days after the announcement, Canada filed its partial submission, pertaining only to the Atlantic Ocean, and preliminary information for a future submission regarding the Arctic Ocean, with the Commission.[1] Further Arctic research missions were conducted in 2014, 2015, and 2016. As a result the data collected will need to be processed, analyzed, and related to the legal provisions in UNCLOS before the submission pertaining to Canada's Arctic ECSs can be presented to the Commission; meaning, it will be several years before Canada files its Arctic submission. Yet there are issues that warrant consideration now in order to ensure effective future planning. Will the submission receive an expeditious review or will the commissioners take years to provide their recommendations? How will Canada keep its Arctic databases updated in the period between its submission and the receipt of the Commission's recommendations? How will overlapping claims be handled? What are the implications of the revenue sharing provisions in Article 82 for Canada and the development of its

ECS? The chapter begins by examining the implications of the prime minister's December 2013 announcement. Thereafter it considers the above questions pertaining to the work of the Commission, overlapping claims, and revenue sharing.

THE DECEMBER 2013 ANNOUNCEMENT

Prior to Harper's announcement, Canada's actual physical submission pertaining to both the Atlantic and Arctic ECSs was in Ottawa — printed, bound, indexed and catalogued as required under UNCLOS and ready to go to the U.N. In numerous documents, the Canadian government had stated its commitment to mapping the ECS in both the Arctic and the Atlantic, and its intention to make a comprehensive submission in December 2013.[2] No references were made to partial submissions. It came as a big surprise, then, on December 4, just two days before the submission was due, to read the *Globe and Mail*'s front-page story announcing that Prime Minister Harper had "ordered government bureaucrats back to the drawing board to craft a more expansive international claim for seabed riches in the Arctic after the proposed submission they showed him failed to include the geographic North Pole."[3] The report was subsequently corroborated in a speech given by the minister of foreign affairs.[4] The team working on the ECS (including Minister of Foreign Affairs John Baird as well as the public servants who had worked so long and hard on the project) were reported to be "stunned by the PM's sudden rejection of their findings."[5] The announcement implicitly criticized Canadian public servants for not having included the North Pole in the submission. It is impossible to document the full story of what transpired behind the scenes as the Harper government was careful to keep it out of the public domain. In an attempt to unearth the truth, Bob Weber of the Canadian Press requested documents pertaining to the decision under the Access to Information Act. After waiting eight months, Weber finally received five hundred pages of briefing notes, emails, transcripts, and other documents; however, of the material not already in the public domain (e.g., press releases), most was heavily redacted to the point where often only the names of the sender and the recipient were visible.[6] What was evident was that there had been a flurry of correspondence just prior to the December 4 announcement and that the decision to include the North Pole in Canada's Arctic submission was made at the last minute.[7]

The prime minister's announcement raises several important questions. First, did the partial submission fulfill Canada's legal obligations? Second, what were the consequences of Prime Minister Harper's announcement?

Did the Partial Submission Fulfill Canada's Legal Obligations?

The answer to the first question is a somewhat qualified "yes." By 2008 it was clear that many developing countries lacked the scientific expertise and resources to meet their submission deadlines, so the states parties to UNCLOS agreed that states could fulfill their obligations under the Convention by filing preliminary information indicating that they intended to make a submission, the status of the preparatory work, and when they expected to submit.[8] The question is answered in the affirmative because when Canada filed its submission pertaining to the Atlantic Ocean, it also stated its intention to make a future submission regarding the Arctic. The "yes" is qualified because the information provided about the status of preparatory work and the intended submission date was vague: "Canada intends to make a partial submission in respect of areas in the Arctic Ocean at an appropriate date that may depend, among other things, on the acquisition of additional data. Canada will keep the Commission informed of progress in this respect."[9] Of the forty-six notices of preliminary information filed with the Commission as of November 2015, only four countries (Comoros, Cuba, Mexico and Vanuatu — all developing states) supplied less information than did Canada. Canada's preliminary information was two pages long, whereas those of Angola, the Bahamas, France, Nicaragua, South Korea and Spain were ten, seven, fourteen, thirty-two, eight, and fifty-two pages, respectively; all included maps of the area to be surveyed.[10]

What Were the Consequences of Prime Minister Harper's Announcement?

Prime Minister Harper's decision to include the North Pole in Canada's Arctic submission had one positive outcome: the collection and analysis of considerably more High Arctic data than would have been possible without the authorization of funds for the 2014, 2015, and 2016 missions. Although it was not a zero-sum situation, as the Treasury Board had already allocated some money to allow the Canadian Hydrographic Service and Natural Resources to continue their Arctic surveying after the 2011 ECS mission, the prime minister's 2013 decision resulted in significantly more resources being allocated. CCGS *Louis S. St-Laurent* would not have been refurbished with a multibeam sonar device without further UNCLOS missions being mandated. There is of course the question raised at the end of chapter 5: Was refurbishing an icebreaker scheduled to be decommissioned in 2022 or 2023 (when Canada's new polar icebreaker is commissioned) the best use of resources? Nonetheless, the 2014, 2015, and 2016 surveys contributed new information, understandings, and insights to the existing body of scientific knowledge.

At the same time, Harper's announcement was problematic in at least five respects: it unjustly disparaged the work done by Canadian public servants; it raised questions about ministerial responsibility; it deviated from the equidistance principle previously used to establish maritime boundaries between Greenland and Canada; it undermined relations with our Arctic neighbours, especially Denmark; and it resulted in a missed opportunity for Canada to present its data and analysis to the Commission before Denmark/Greenland made their submission pertaining to the area north of Greenland in 2014 and the Russian Federation presented its submission regarding the Arctic Ocean in 2015.

1. Cast Aspersions

The prime minister's announcement cast aspersions on the excellent work done by science staffs from the Departments of Natural Resources, and Fisheries and Oceans, under extraordinarily challenging conditions, and on the legal experts in the Department of Foreign Affairs, Trade and Development who compiled the submission. As seen in chapters 3, 4, and 5, through their dedication, ingenuity, and sheer hard work, Canadian scientists and technical staff overcame a myriad of obstacles to collect and analyze large quantities of high-quality data in the Arctic. Likewise, officials in the Department of Foreign Affairs, Trade and Development worked hard compiling the submission document, relating the scientific findings to the legal provisions in the Convention. The goal of the public servants involved with the ECS was always to maximize their country's ECS; however, to be credible, Canada's submission needed to be both based on scientific data and analysis *and* consistent with international law (UNCLOS and the Commission's rules and regulations).

There is no doubt that the Conservative government's treatment of scientists, in general, negatively affected morale among them and caused many to leave the public service.[11] According to Steven Campana, former director of the Canadian Shark Research Laboratory at the Bedford Institute of Oceanography, "We're at the point where the vast majority of our senior scientists are in the process of leaving now disgusted as I am with the way things have gone."[12] The Harper government was accused of waging a "war on science" because of its cuts to scientific jobs and funding for scientific research, muzzling of scientists, and tendency to let ideology trump scientific evidence.[13] In June 2013 the Professional Institute of the Public Service of Canada surveyed members who were federal scientists and concluded that there was a "big chill" within the scientific community. Of the 4,069 respondents, 71 percent believed that political interference had compromised "Canada's ability to develop policy, law and programs based on scientific evidence" and "nearly one-quarter (24 percent) report[ed] being directly asked to exclude or alter information for non-scientific reasons."[14] As noted in an editorial in the *Chronicle Herald*, "it's no laughing matter when government scientists, through their union, feel they must seek clauses in a new collective agreement to protect themselves from being coerced to alter data and to prohibit policy-makers from knowingly misrepresenting their work."[15] In 2015, 815 scientists from thirty-two countries signed a letter to Harper criticizing his government for placing "excessive and burdensome restrictions and barriers to scientific communication and collaboration."[16] Several scientists from the Departments of Fisheries and Oceans, and Natural Resources, who were not involved with the ECS, spoke publicly about their disgust at the "toxic" work environment facing government scientists under the Harper administration, which compromised the integrity of their research and prompted them to take early retirement.[17]

The prime minister's rejection of the Arctic submission was a bitter pill for those who had worked so long and hard on it. As a scientist with Natural Resources Canada confided off the record, "when you work at the Bedford Institute of Oceanography, you are part of a club. It does not really matter if you come from Fisheries and Oceans or NRCan. There is a huge sense of pride that goes along with the work. That is why it was so shattering when the team was told that more data was required and that what they had produced was not sufficient." Internationally respected marine geophysicist Ron Macnab pointed out, "If you work on something for 10 years and it finally gets to the top, and you discover it's been thrown in the garbage, it's a bit hard to take for professionals who have put everything they had into it."[18]

Some months after the December 2013 announcement, Jacob Verhoef, head of the UNCLOS Program, and Stephen Forbes, lead hydrographer and director, Law of the Sea Project, retired; Louis Simard, the senior UNCLOS official in the Department of Foreign Affairs, Trade and Development, left his portfolio. In 2015 David Mosher, who had continued as manager of the UNCLOS Program when Verhoef retired, left the country to become a full professor at the University of New Hampshire, where he is now contributing to the U.S. ECS Program. As they are bound by confidentiality agreements that prevent them from discussing such matters, outsiders cannot know for sure what prompted them to leave; however, in light of the timing of their departures and the views expressed above by scientists not involved with the ECS Program but who nonetheless worked on maritime issues for the Departments of Fisheries and Oceans, and Natural Resources, it is reasonable to think that the disrespectful treatment they endured played a significant role in the decisions to leave the government. Retired Geological Survey of Canada scientist Ron Macnab supports this conclusion in arguing that the former prime minister's rejection of the scientists' findings prompted several key members of the UNCLOS team to leave.[19] The departure of scientists of their international stature, with their wealth of Arctic experience and expertise, is a sad loss for Canada! Furthermore, the depth and breadth of their knowledge is no longer available for the drafting of Canada's new Arctic ECS submission. It is ironic that in 2015 key public servants involved with Canada's Arctic submission received government awards for their excellent work for Canada's ECS. Verhoef and others from Natural Resources Canada directly connected with the UNCLOS Program were each presented with their department's Excellence in Science Award. Stephen Forbes and the Canadian Hydrographic Service team each received the Distinction Award from the Department of Fisheries and Oceans. Allison Saunders, deputy director of the Continental Shelf Division in the Department of Foreign Affairs, Trade and Development, won the Canadian Foreign Service Officer Award.

2. Raised Questions About Ministerial Responsibility

The Canadian democracy functions under a Westminster system of government, for which a key doctrine is ministerial responsibility. According to this doctrine, public servants are accountable to their minister and ministers are responsible to Parliament, which was elected by the people, for the actions of their respective departments and all those who work under them.[20] The Arctic and the Arctic continental shelf had been key priorities for the Harper government. Former minister of Natural Resources Gary Lunn described surveying Canada's continental shelf as "a top priority."[21] Public servants kept the ministers of the three key departments involved with the submission (Natural Resources, Fisheries and Oceans, and Foreign Affairs, Trade and Development) apprised of developments throughout the UNCLOS process, and the ministers authorized over one hundred million dollars for research expenses. John Baird, then minister of foreign affairs, is said to have been as surprised by the prime minister's response as was the rest of the UNCLOS team; thus it seems reasonable to assume that the three ministers did report back to the prime minister or at least to the prime minister's office.[22] Furthermore, Baird did not dispute "published reports that Prime Minister Stephen Harper stepped in at the last minute to insist that the North Pole be included."[23] Why did the prime minister react so late in the process? What was his motivation for insisting that Canada's claim include the North Pole? Was it seen as a politically expedient opportunity to present himself as the champion of Canadian sovereignty in the Arctic? To what extent was timing a factor? The announcement was made three weeks before Christmas when thoughts of Santa Claus and his workshop at the North Pole were in the thoughts of many. Was there concern about being seen to abandon Santa just before Christmas? Clearly the communication failure occurred at the political level. Why were the public servants publicly criticized and humiliated for conducting surveys approved by their ministers? What does this turn of events say about ministerial responsibility, which holds ministers — not the public servants who work under them — publicly responsible for activities carried out in their departments?

3. Deviated from the Equidistance Principle Previously Used to Establish Maritime Boundaries Between Greenland and Canada

The equidistance principle is frequently used to establish maritime boundaries between neighbouring countries with overlapping maritime zones. As Ted McDorman, an expert in international law, points out, a two-step approach has become customary law as the result of numerous international adjudications of maritime boundary disputes.[24] First, a provisional equidistant line is drawn. Second, the provisional line is examined in light of relevant case-specific circumstances to determine if the line needs to be adjusted to ensure an equitable outcome. The special circumstances are largely limited to geographic factors. Canada and Denmark used equidistance lines in their 1973 treaty outlining the boundary between their respective exclusive economic zones between Greenland and Canada in the Labrador Sea, Davis Strait, Baffin Bay, and Nares Strait, and again in the 2012 agreement among the ministers regarding the Lincoln Sea north of Ellesmere Island and Greenland.[25]

Based on past practice, one would have expected Canada and Denmark to again use the equidistance principle in delimiting their respective ECSs. Unfortunately for Canada, the North Pole is significantly closer to Greenland than to Canada. While philosophical debates about whether Santa Claus can belong to any one country or whether he belongs to humanity as a whole are beyond the scope of this book, suffice it to say that the North Pole is not within Canadian jurisdiction. It may be a blow to our sense of national pride, but Santa is not Canadian.

4. Undermined Collaborative UNCLOS Process

The prime minister's announcement "caught Canada's polar neighbours totally by surprise" and "triggered the immediate termination of co-operation with Russia and Denmark."[26]

Prior to the December 2013 announcement, Canada had enjoyed highly cooperative relations with its Arctic neighbours throughout the delineation process. Its scientists had run numerous joint surveys in the Arctic with their Danish and American counterparts, and their joint findings had been presented orally and in joint publications to the international community. Beginning in 2007 Canadian, Danish, and Russian scientists held annual meetings to discuss scientific and technical matters pertaining to the Arctic ECSs. In 2008 U.S. scientists were invited to participate as observers. In 2009 representatives of the Canadian, Danish, and Russian foreign ministries also began to attend the meetings. In 2010, participation was further widened to include Norwegian officials. Thereafter the meetings involved scientists and diplomats from all five Arctic coastal countries. Thus the meetings not only served as venues in which to share scientific findings but also provided opportunities for the international legal experts to discuss other issues relevant to submission preparation. It is inconceivable that they never addressed the issue of maritime boundary delimitation.

The commitment to peaceful cooperation was formalized in the 2008 Ilulissat Declaration, in which Canada, Denmark, Norway, the Russian Federation, and the United States recalled the extensive legal framework that applies to the Arctic Ocean, pledged to cooperate closely and in accordance with international law in the delineation of their respective Arctic ECSs, and committed themselves to the orderly settlement of any possible overlapping claims.[27] The commitment to maintain peace, stability and cooperative relations was reaffirmed in the 2015 Iqaluit Declaration.[28] Unilateral action that will inevitably result in more difficult and extensive maritime boundary disputes is not consistent with either declaration.

Denmark and Canada had an agreement that Canada would not claim the North Pole.[29] Scientific data would allow Canada's ECS to stretch east of the Lomonosov Ridge and Denmark's ECS to extend west of the Lomonosov Ridge; however, the two countries agreed that Canada's submission would not extend east of the Lomonosov Ridge and Denmark's ECS would not extend west of the Lomonosov Ridge. The agreement was consistent with the pledges made by the two countries in the 2008 Ilulissat Declaration. Potential overlaps in their respective ECS submissions had been resolved.

While the agreement is not in the public domain, four factors support its existence. First, prior to December 2013, Denmark had collected the data in the North Pole area needed for its submission. Canada had not. Why would Canadian scientists, who had been so conscientious in their decade-long research program, fail to collect adequate data in an area their country planned to include in its claim? Second, as discussed above, Canada and Denmark had used equidistance lines to establish maritime boundaries in their overlapping exclusive economic zones. Why would they not continue to use these accepted international norms to establish a maritime boundary beyond two hundred nautical miles from shore? Third, the years of meetings involving legal experts and scientists from all five Arctic coastal states had provided significant opportunities to discuss boundary delineation. Settling such matters amicably in advance was clearly in everyone's best interest. Fourth, Canada's Arctic neighbours were surprised by the prime minister's announcement. If they had expected Canada to include the North Pole in its Arctic submission, they would not have been surprised by the prime minister's announcement. Well before December 2013, Denmark had publicly declared its intention to include the North Pole in its submission.[30] Canada had not!

There is no doubt that the prime minister's decision to include the North Pole in Canada's ECS claim alienated the Danes. Once the prime minister had decided that the North Pole was to be included in Canada's Arctic submission, Ottawa sought to buy mapping data pertaining to the area from Denmark; however, the Danes made clear that "the data were not for sale."[31] As such, Canada had to mount its own missions to survey the area. The Danes were invited to participate in Canada's 2014 mission; however, they declined. Was their decision the result of the tight timeline, limited personnel resources, or displeasure over Prime Minister Harper's decision to claim the North Pole? In response to Canada's invitation, Denmark did send a senior Arctic expert, Thomas Funck, on Canada's 2015 mission.

When Denmark made its own submission pertaining to the area north of Greenland, it included the North Pole, as expected; however, its claim was over 150,000 square kilometres larger than originally anticipated.[32] The claim was expected to stop at the equidistant line; however, the 895,541-square-kilometre area includes the Lomonosov Ridge from the two-hundred-nautical-mile exclusive economic zones north of Greenland and Ellesmere Island all the way to Russia's exclusive economic zone and westward almost to the Alpha Ridge.[33] Would Denmark have made such an extensive claim if Canada had not violated its agreement with Denmark? To what extent was the much larger claim in retaliation for Canada's actions? Overlaps in the ECS claims of Canada, Denmark, and Russia were expected; however, the Danish submission ensured that they were much larger than anticipated.[34]

Although the December 2013 announcement caused the biggest upset in relations between Denmark and Canada, it was also not well viewed in Moscow. [35] It was probably not well regarded in Washington D.C., either. John B. Belinger III, an international law expert who had advised the Bush administration on matters pertaining to UNCLOS, commented, "If Canada tries to take the North Pole just before Christmas, I think the United States would be very opposed to that."[36] The prime minister's announcement further undermined the already strained relations with Russia. "Instructions were issued to members of Canada's ECS Program to have no contact with their Russian counterparts, notwithstanding the positive working relationships that had existed between the two teams up until then."[37] Of course, Harper's unilateral action was not the only — or even the most important — issue to soured relations with the Russian Federation. Russia's involvement in the Ukraine and Harper's public denunciations of Russian president Vladimir Putin were major sources of discord. The Russian Federation is the pre-eminent Arctic power. As Andrea Charron, Joël Plouffe, and Stéphane Roussel point out, "Russia not only has the longest Arctic coastline and the most populated Arctic region, it has the largest ice-breaking fleet in the world (nuclear or diesel propelled), the biggest year-round ice-free port/ city in the entire Arctic zone (Murmansk), and it has conducted the most Arctic sorties and has made command of its Arctic a top domestic and foreign policy goal."[38] Thus, it is not in Canada's best interest either to exclude Russian officials from Arctic negotiations or to alienate them. Furthermore, Russia can be an important ally. Unlike most states, the Russian Federation is sympathetic to Canada's claim that the Northwest Passage is internal waters and, unlike other Arctic countries, it shares Canada's reluctance to grant Observer status in the Arctic Council to more non-Arctic states.[39]

It is worth noting that in spite of Canada's contravention of its bilateral agreement with Denmark (and probably a multilateral understanding with its other Arctic neighbours), in spite of Denmark's expansive submission, and in spite of tensions between the Russian Federation and the West over the Ukraine, Russia was remarkably restrained when it made its 2015 submission regarding the Arctic Ocean. The ECS area of the Arctic Ocean included in the 2015 document is similar to that delineated in 2001.[40] The Russian Federation continues to reiterate the commitments made in the Ilulissat Declaration, the salience of international law in governing relations among states in the Arctic, and the need to use peaceful, diplomatic channels to resolve maritime boundary disputes.[41] Some scholars speculated that Canada's relations with its Arctic neighbours would improve following the October 2015 federal election and that the government of Prime Minister Justin Trudeau would "be less bullish than the previous government on claiming the North Pole."[42] One year later, the *National Post* reported "the Trudeau government has moved away from the more-confrontational approach that dominated Conservative policy, with Foreign Affairs Minister Stéphane Dion putting Russia at the centre of Canada's northern policy."[43]

5. A Missed Opportunity and Its Consequences

Being first to present data and analysis offers distinct advantages. Scientists from the coastal state(s) that has/have mapped an area are the only ones with in-depth knowledge of its geology, geophysics, and hydrography. Although the commissioners are required to evaluate each submission on its own merits, their first in-depth exposure to the scientific findings pertaining to a specific ECS comes from the oral presentation that the coastal state's officials make to the full Commission when the latter first meets to decide how it will proceed with the submission.[44]

On December 20, 2001, the Russian Federation became the first country in the world to present its submission to the Commission. Because the Commission found the Russian information pertaining to the Arctic Ocean insufficient to support its proposed outer limit of its continental shelf, Russian scientists conducted "a wide range of geological and geophysical studies" in the area between 2005 and 2014 and presented a revised submission on August 3, 2015.[45] Submissions are generally reviewed in the order in which they are received.[46] As Russia's 2015 submission was a revised version of part of its 2001 submission, the former goes to the head of the queue.[47] In August 2016 at the Commission's forty-first session, a subcommission began its review of Russia's 2015 submission. Given the backlog at the Commission, even if Canada had presented its Arctic submission in 2013, Russia's submission would have been reviewed first; however, had Canada presented its Arctic ECS submission in 2013, Canadian officials would have had the opportunity to present their findings and conclusions orally and *before* Denmark/Greenland and the Russian Federation made their presentations in 2014 and 2015, respectively. The commissioners have now heard the Danish and Russian interpretations of the data pertaining to features, such as the Lomonosov Ridge, that will be central to establishing Canada's Arctic ECS. Furthermore, their submissions will be examined before Canada's. Their interpretations of the origins, morphology, and composition of these features may differ from Canada's and the positions taken by them may not necessarily enhance Canada's case.

Not being first means that the commissioners' current knowledge of the Arctic Ocean north of Canada's land territory is based primarily on what they have heard from Russia and Denmark. Of course, the commissioners also have access to data and analysis published in refereed scientific journals and books, so the presentations and submissions are not the only source of information. Nonetheless, not being the first to present their Arctic data and analysis will result in more work and less flexibility for Canadian officials drafting Canada's Arctic submission; it will be necessary to take into consideration details from the Russian and Danish submissions and to reframe Canada's arguments in light of the information already before the Commission.

Third, the later Canada makes its submission, the lower it will be in the queue and hence the longer it will be before Canada receives the Commission's recommendations, on the basis of which it will establish its Arctic ECS. If the Commission continues working at its current pace, Canada's submission will not be reviewed for at least a decade after it is submitted, by which time the software and surveying techniques may well have changed and most of the government officials involved with the ECS Program will have retired. The original plan was to keep the ECS team together until April 2014 to answer any questions that the Commission had following the December 2013 submission and thereafter to have a smaller team in place for at least four years — again to ensure continuity until the earliest point at which the submission was expected to be reviewed. This smaller team would include the senior person from each of the three lead departments as well as a computer software expert to keep the submission documents updated as the software evolved. Of course, these plans changed when Prime Minister Harper decided not to present the Arctic submission to the Commission in December 2013, the senior ECS officials from Natural Resources and Fisheries and Oceans announced their retirements, and the senior official from Foreign Affairs, Trade and Development left the ECS Program to take up a new assignment. By the summer of 2015, David Mosher, manager of the UNCLOS Program, was gone, too. Computer software expert Walli Rainey joined the ECS Program in 2010 to work on the production of the maps, documentation, and a database for the 2013 submission. The initial plan was that only 20 percent of her time would be devoted to maintaining the database after the 2013 submission was made and the remaining 80 percent would be spent on other projects; however, these plans have been revised as there continues to be fresh data to process and maps and documents to create. Once the submission is finally made, she will continue to spend 20 percent of her time maintaining the data base until the Commission has conducted its review; however, other scientific endeavours will benefit from having the lion's share of her time.

In addition to continuing work on the Arctic submission, the Canadian government must give further thought to two other outstanding issues: Article 82 of UNCLOS, and the ultimate delimitation of its Arctic ECS. These issues are discussed sequentially below.

ARTICLE 82

As mentioned in chapter 2, the ECS provisions in UNCLOS represent a compromise between wide-margin states and countries, particularly the members of the Group of 77, that wanted the international seabed to be as large as possible because its resources are to be developed to benefit humanity as a whole, giving special consideration to the needs and interests of Southern countries (countries of the Global South). In recognition of the fact that ECSs reduce the area otherwise considered the common heritage of humanity, Article 82 requires coastal states to make monetary payments or contributions in kind related to the exploitation of non-living seabed resources beyond two hundred nautical miles. The obligation to make payments or contributions in kind begins in the sixth year of production at a rate of 1 percent of the value or volume of production from a site. From the seventh to the twelfth year, the rate increases by 1 percent annually and, thereafter, it remains at 7 percent. The monetary payments or contributions in kind are made through the International Seabed Authority, which distributes them "on the basis of equitable sharing criteria, taking into account the interests and needs of developing States, particularly the least developed and the land-locked among them."[48] Consistent with the desire to assist developing countries, a Southern country is exempt from making payments or contributions in kind regarding a mineral produced on its ECS when it is a net importer of that particular commodity. Although Canada was first to propose revenue sharing in return for rights to an ECS, its delegation expressed reservations about Article 82 on the grounds that the suggested rates could render exploitation of the seabed resources beyond two hundred nautical miles uneconomical.[49]

The provisions in Article 82 are imprecise, leaving many important questions unanswered.[50] How will payments and contributions in kind be calculated? The coastal state must make payments or contributions of 1 to 7 percent after the sixth year of production, but 1 to 7 percent of what? How is value to be assessed, especially for mining operations? Does the term refer to the gross or the net value of production? How is volume of production to be measured? Who will determine the value or volume of production? Both value and volume fluctuate according to market conditions, economies of scale in production, and technological innovation. Will the payments be recalculated each year to take account of price fluctuations and changes in other relevant factors? If a coastal state chooses to base the payments on value, must it continue to use this basis of assessment or can it switch in subsequent years to calculations predicated on volume? Can an ECS state select the type of payments to be paid (i.e., monetary payments or contributions in kind) on an annual basis, or must it choose one form and stick with it? Payments are due annually, but does this mean on the basis of a calendar year or a government's budgetary year? What currencies may be used to make payments? What period of time may elapse between setting the amount of the payment or contribution in kind and its delivery?

The provision to allow contributions in kind was included to provide state beneficiaries with access to resources; however, it is fraught with uncertainties.[51] At what point will the share of resources be transferred to the recipient? Will the payments in kind be given directly to the recipient country or will the non-living resources first be sold and the cash generated passed on to the beneficiary? Who will handle the logistics and pay the costs of transporting, storing, and marketing the resources being transferred? Who will set the market price, which can vary from region to region? In light of all the complexity and problems associated with contributions in kind, experts at an international workshop on the subject recommended that ECS states fulfill their legal obligations by making monetary payments rather than transferring natural resources.[52]

Article 82 not only imposes obligations on ECS states but also puts demands on the International Seabed Authority and adds yet another level of complexity to their relationship. What administrative procedures are needed to ensure consistency, efficiency, transparency, predictability, and convenience? How are states to notify the International Seabed Authority that production has been started, suspended, or terminated? What rules and procedures are necessary to ensure that the distribution is indeed equitable? How will disputes between the International Seabed Authority and ECS states be handled? Are there also security considerations? What balance should be struck between the International Seabed Authority's need for details about a production site and the coastal state's need to protect politically, economically, and commercially sensitive information? How will the International Seabed Authority treat confidential information?

While extracting resources from the seabed is always challenging and potentially hazardous, as was all too apparent in the 2010 oil spill in the Gulf of Mexico, the difficulties and risks are much greater in the Arctic as a result of harsh climatic conditions; short seasons; geographic remoteness; huge exploration, exploitation, transportation, and insurance costs; inadequate infrastructures; and the fragility of the environment. As a general rule the deeper the water the more difficult and expensive the extraction, and Arctic waters can be very deep as exemplified by the eastern Canada Basin (depth around 3,800 metres).[53] Drilling in deep water is time-consuming; the rigs are expensive to hire (e.g., in 2008 the cost was six hundred thousand dollars per day); and, on average, only one in eight holes results in the discovery of resources.[54] In the Arctic, the success rate may be significantly less. Will Article 82's one-size-fits-all approach to ECS development work in the Arctic? Will the initial five-year period of grace, during which no payments or contributions are made, be sufficient to allow operators to recover exploration and start-up costs? As Wylie Spicer points out, when the grace period was negotiated, wells were expected to be "in much shallower water and closer to shore than is the case in 2015."[55] Moreover, the drafters of UNCLOS were thinking of exploitation in open waters rather than in ice-covered regions.

Canada's federated political system adds yet another set of questions to an already complicated scenario. Arctic governance involves diverse sets of actors, including the national government, territorial governments, and Indigenous land claims bodies, all of which have rights and responsibilities pertaining to natural resources. Furthermore, their respective sets of responsibilities are evolving. A process of devolution, whereby the control and administration of lands and resources is being transferred from the federal government to territorial and Indigenous governments, has been under way for decades in Canada. The degree to which devolution has taken place and the specific forms it takes vary from territory to territory, as each negotiates separately with the federal government.[56] At present, Arctic offshore resources remain largely under federal jurisdiction. The question is: where will Canada be in the devolution process by the time commercial production is into its sixth year of operation? Who will benefit from this production and who will make the payments or contributions? Will the federal government, which is responsible for upholding the country's obligations under international law, pay or will it pass the costs on to other entities such as the territorial government(s), Indigenous governance bodies, private corporations engaged in resource extraction on the ECS, or some combination of these other actors? Canada has no legislative structure "to establish the meaning of 'total production,' or any mechanism in existing licenses by which Canada can recover payments from licensees."[57] The 1987 Canada-Newfoundland and Labrador Atlantic Accord Implementation Act provides for joint federal-provincial management of the offshore but gives the government of Newfoundland and Labrador responsibility for negotiating and implementing royalty agreements. Royalties go to the province as part of the national equalization program, rather than to the federal government, although the latter bears the legal responsibility for implementing Article 82.[58] What agreements will the federal government, territorial governments, and Indigenous governance bodies negotiate to govern exploration and exploitation on the Arctic ECS and revenue sharing from the resulting production? Are decisions about who pays irreversible or can they be altered as circumstances pertaining to a site change?

The issue of consistency arises in the context of production from areas governed by different regimes. Should Canada seek to ensure that the payment and contribution arrangements it makes through the International

Seabed Authority pertaining to the ECS are consistent with those it has established in its exclusive economic zone so that commercial production within two hundred nautical miles is not privileged over that from the ECS? What happens when a Canadian resource project straddles the exclusive economic zone and ECS? Canadian ECS sites that overlap with the exclusive economic zones or ECSs of other countries or the international seabed raise further challenging questions. Should Canada and its Arctic neighbours adopt common methods for calculating the payments and contributions?

In short, it is unclear what exactly Article 82 will mean for a coastal state like Canada, both because the provisions in UNCLOS are ambiguous and because developing resources on Canada's Arctic ECS is not going to be economically viable in the foreseeable future. Canada faces a Catch-22 dilemma. On one hand, Arctic production beyond two hundred nautical miles will not occur for decades, which makes it extremely difficult if not impossible to address questions whose answers depend on having precise, detailed information about exploration and exploitation. This situation encourages the deferral of decision-making until commercial production actually begins. On the other hand, Canadian officials cannot afford to delay in establishing positions apropos Article 82 for two reasons: first, the Commission has now reviewed twenty-six submissions, and as the number of established ECSs increases, so will the international pressure to resolve the ambiguities arising from Article 82 before commercial production begins; second, while resource development on the Arctic ECS is decades away, such is not the case for the Atlantic ECS. Canada may be the first country legally required to make payments worth millions of dollars to the International Seabed Authority, and it is ill-prepared to fulfill its obligation.[59] While current production licences off the East Coast pertain to sites within the exclusive economic zone, Canada has granted licences to explore for hydrocarbons on the Atlantic ECS since the early 1960s.[60] Not only has exploration taken place but there have been some very substantial finds:

Exploration continues to take place well beyond 200 nautical miles (NM) from the east coast of Newfoundland & Labrador (NL). Recently Statoil and its co-venturer Husky Energy announced a significant hydrocarbon discovery in the Flemish Pass area approximately 300 miles from the coast in an area regulated by the

Canada-Newfoundland and Labrador Offshore Petroleum Board (CNLOPB). Statoil estimated that this discovery is between 300 and 600 million barrels of recoverable oil.[61]

Until 2013, the Canadian government did not provide official notice of the Article 82 obligations to companies applying for licences to explore beyond two hundred nautical miles.[62]

Offshore drilling, especially on the ECS, will be extremely expensive and logistically difficult. In addition, oil and gas prices are currently depressed. Nonetheless, there may come a time in the not-too-distant future when Statoil applies for a licence to develop its sizable discovery. Having not established a domestic legal regime consistent with its obligations under Article 82, the Canadian government is ill-equipped to deal with this eventuality. Even the United States, which is not a party to UNCLOS, has been more proactive than Canada in addressing Article 82 issues. Its lease agreements pertaining to areas beyond two hundred nautical miles from shore outline the ways in which the obligations arising from Article 82 will be calculated, should the United States eventually accede to the Convention.[63]

In short, there is increasing pressure on the federal government, both at home and abroad, to establish a domestic regime for the implementation of Article 82. The task cannot be left for some distant time when resource exploitation on the Arctic ECS is contemplated; it must be done now! As is so often the case with implementing international treaty obligations, the devil is in the details, and how the UNCLOS provisions are interpreted domestically and in international venues will have serious implications for the development of Canada's resources beyond two hundred nautical miles.

DELIMITATION OF ARCTIC EXTENDED CONTINENTAL SHELVES

Just as there may be overlaps in the exclusive economic zones between adjacent or opposing states, as exemplified by the ongoing maritime boundary dispute between Canada and the United States in the Beaufort Sea, there will be overlaps in the ECSs of Canada and its neighbours. Canada, Denmark, and the Russian Federation either have or are expected to include sections of the Lomonosov Ridge in their respective submissions, although, until Canada actually makes its submission, the extent to which they are claiming the same seabed will not be fully known. Likewise, there are likely to be overlaps between the United States and Canadian ECSs in the Canada Basin.

The Commission is a technical body responsible for making recommendations pertaining to the outer limits of the continental shelf. It was never intended to be a court of law and it has no mandate to resolve overlapping maritime boundaries.[64] Submissions to the Commission "are without prejudice to the question of delimitation of the continental shelf between States with opposite or adjacent coasts."[65] When making a submission, the coastal state is required to inform the Commission of any outstanding maritime boundary disputes pertaining to the ECS area it has delineated.[66]

Along with its submission, the coastal state must provide the "charts and relevant information, including geodetic data, permanently describing the outer limits of its continental shelf" to the U.N. secretary-general, who makes this information public.[67] Thus, while the details of the submission are confidential, others may know the extent of the area delineated. Furthermore, at least three months must elapse between the date the submission is received and the start of its review,[68] which gives other states time to examine the executive summary to determine if the area included in it overlaps with what they consider to be their own ECSs.

The Commission is not authorized to review a submission involving one or more boundary disputes unless all the states directly involved in the dispute give their prior consent.[69] When making their submissions in 2014 and 2015, respectively, Denmark and Russia secured bilateral assurances from their neighbours, in which the latter acknowledged the existence of an overlap and stated that they did not object to the reviews going ahead, while, at the same time, insisting that the Commission's recommendations would not prejudice either the delineation or the delimitation of their own ECSs. Canada, Norway, the Russian Federation, and the United States sent diplomatic notes regarding Denmark/Greenland's submission pertaining to the area north of Greenland.[70] In the case of the Russian Federation's submission pertaining to the Arctic Ocean, diplomatic notes were sent by Canada, Denmark, and the United States.[71] Canada received similar bilateral assurances regarding its submission pertaining to its Atlantic ECS from Denmark (pertaining to the Labrador Sea) and the United States (regarding the Nova Scotia region). These diplomatic notes are consistent with the cooperation pledged by the Arctic coastal states in the Ilulissat and Iqaluit Declarations and allow the Commission to proceed with the reviews. When the full Commission first meets to consider a submission, it not only hears the oral presentation by officials from the submitting state but it also considers information pertaining to any maritime boundary disputes, including notes verbales received from neighbouring coastal states.[72] This information is a key determinant of whether the review goes ahead.[73]

Responsibility for resolving overlapping claims rests with the states involved, which can use a variety of mechanisms, including bilateral negotiations, multilateral negotiations, arbitration, mediation, and the taking of a case to the International Tribunal for the Law of the Sea or International Court of Justice.[74] Past experience has shown that resolving maritime boundary disputes can be difficult and protracted. In the 1970s, Canadian and U.S. negotiators worked for years to reach an agreement on fishing rights in the Gulf of Maine, only to have the settlement rejected in the U.S. Senate. The maritime boundary dispute was then referred to the International Court of Justice, which issued its judgment in 1984.[75] The Canada–United States boundary dispute in the Beaufort Sea has dragged on for years and it is definitely an irritant in bilateral relations.[76] These examples indicate that resolving disputes over maritime boundaries can be difficult and time-consuming; however, political and legal channels have been used in the past and they will be used in the future, as evidenced by the 2010 agreement between the Russian Federation and Norway, ending their bitter maritime boundary dispute of some forty years in the Barents Sea.

Having an orderly process is also in the best interests of private corporations wishing to develop resources. No company wants to invest millions of dollars in exploration and drilling costs without being certain of the rules under which it will operate and be able to reap the benefits of its long-term investment. This fact is evident in the Beaufort Sea, where the exclusive economic zones of Canada and the United States overlap and where rich resources are known to exist; yet, until the two countries agree on a maritime boundary, the uncertainties are too great to warrant resource exploitation. For example, would corporations have to operate under U.S. laws or Canadian laws? Few, if any, creditors in the world would finance exploitation before titles were agreed on. There will be no exploitation without certainty. No oil or gas company will undertake resource exploitation without the concerned countries having resolved overlaps in their jurisdictions.

CONCLUSION

Prime Minister Harper's December 2013 announcement has left several unfortunate legacies. It resulted in the loss of senior Arctic experts, who were never in large supply. It raised concerns about ministerial responsibility. It undermined the highly cooperative relations that Canada had previously enjoyed with its neighbours, especially Denmark. It will take years to rebuild the trust and the collegiality previously enjoyed. It ensured that Canada, Denmark, and Russia eventually will have to engage in negotiations to resolve their overlapping claims that are more time-consuming, more onerous, and more costly than might otherwise have been the case.[77] Failing to meet the 2013 deadline has lost Canada the advantage of being first to present its findings, created more work for government officials both in terms of the extra surveys and in terms of the drafting process, reduced their flexibility in framing arguments, and delayed the process of establishing Canada's Arctic ECS.

As the December 2013 deadline is now passed, there is no rush to make Canada's Arctic submission and, after the bad experience of the past, efforts are sure to be made to ensure that all senior officials, including the prime minister, have signed off well in advance. The final survey took place in summer of 2016. Thereafter it will take at least two years to complete the submission. By that point, Canada's Arctic submission will be further down the queue and, with the Commission's ongoing backlog problem, the prospects of a speedy review are negligible.

Nonetheless, there are other pressing issues in need of attention. In particular, the Canadian government needs to establish rules, regulations, and procedures for the implementation of Article 82, as resource exploitation beyond two hundred nautical miles off the East Coast is not a distant prospect. Clarity and transparency are essential to ensure fairness, efficiency, and stability. Clarity at home will also mean that Canada's positions on the various aspects of the topic can be well defined, which will facilitate more effective participation in international workshops and negotiations devoted to the implementation of Article 82. What is agreed to internationally will, in turn, set parameters within which Canadian stakeholders have to act, so the better prepared Canadians are when they engage in such discussion, the greater their chances of exerting influence and advancing Canada's interests.

7

CONCLUSION

SUMMARY OF FINDINGS

Although media stories may foster pessimism about Canada's prospects in the Arctic and make assumptions that Canada's rights are under serious threat, the delineation of Canada's Arctic ECS has been a good news story in most respects. The United Nations responded to the need to codify the rules and regulations governing the world's oceans by convening a series of law-making conferences. Its Third Conference on the Law of the Sea produced UNCLOS, which came into force in 1994. Not only is there an international regime in place, but its norms are guiding state behaviour. The regime's rules are being observed by all five Arctic coastal states: Canada, Denmark, Norway, the Russian Federation, and the United States. These countries have no need to stake claims as their sovereign rights over the non-living and sedimentary resources of the continental shelf beyond two hundred nautical miles do not depend on occupation or proclamation. Furthermore, twelve non-Arctic states have pledged to respect the sovereign rights of Arctic countries, including those outlined in UNCLOS, as a condition of being granted observer status at the Arctic Council. As such, the countries with greatest interest in the Arctic are formally committed to observing the rule of law in the region. The existence of UNCLOS (and compliance with its norms) has contributed to international peace and stability and it continues to serve Canada and its Arctic neighbours well.

Another positive aspect of the case is the high degree of cooperation and collaboration. The delineation process has been characterized by cooperation among federal departments and, for the most part, in dealings with other Arctic states. Canadian scientists have conducted numerous joint surveys with their Danish and American counterparts. In both cases, their joint findings have been presented to the international scientific community in refereed journal articles and conference presentations. The prior vetting of conclusions through the peer-review process should enhance the legitimacy of each country's findings in the eyes of the commissioners who ultimately review the submissions.

The scientific achievements are indeed good news. In conducting their research, Canadian scientists grappled with formidable challenges: the size and remoteness of the survey area, physical oceanography, weather, ice conditions, short seasons, the logistics of ensuring that all the necessary equipment was on hand, and the limited pool of scientists and technical support with Arctic expertise. Yet in spite of all the challenges, they managed to collect large quantities of high-quality data. The acquisition and subsequent analysis of the data is a remarkable accomplishment. Furthermore, Canada's ECS Program not only has provided data and analysis to support an Arctic ECS submission but has also done much to advance humankind's scientific knowledge and understanding of the geomorphology and the geological history and composition of the Arctic seabed.

Of course, it has not been all good news. The exemplary level of bilateral and multilateral cooperation suffered a setback in December 2013 when former prime minister Stephen Harper announced his plans to claim the North Pole. This unilateral action contravened customary international legal practice and the use of the equidistance principle. Furthermore, it undermined the highly cooperative relations that Canada had previously enjoyed with its neighbours, especially Denmark. The latter responded the following year with a highly expansive submission pertaining to the ECS north of Greenland. Fortunately the Russian Federation showed considerable restraint when it made its submission in 2015. Nonetheless, as a result of the unilateral actions by Canada and then Denmark, the overlaps in the ECS of the three Arctic neighbours are expected to be much larger than originally anticipated.

Consequently, Canada, Denmark, and Russia will eventually have to engage in negotiations to delimit their Arctic ECS that are more difficult, more time-consuming, and more costly than might otherwise have been the case. In not meeting the 2013 submission deadline, Canada lost the advantage of being first to present its findings, which created more work for government officials both in terms of the extra surveys and in terms of the drafting process, reduced their flexibility in framing arguments, and delayed the process of establishing Canada's Arctic ECS. Former prime minister Harper's announcement also raised concerns about ministerial responsibility, seriously demoralized the public servants involved with Canada's ECS Program, and resulted in the loss of several senior, highly experienced public servants with Arctic expertise, which is a scarce commodity.

Yet not all the problems have been of the former government's own making. Certain developments at the international level have also spawned negative repercussions and caused difficulties. The obligations enshrined in Article 82 place Canadian policy-makers in the unenviable position of having to make decisions now without having the full information necessary to predict their implications for Arctic resource development that may take place at some distant future date. When Canada's Arctic ECS submission is finally made, it is unlikely to receive a timely review because of the backlog in the workload of the Commission. In the meantime, Canadian officials need to continue to work with other states parties to ensure that the implementation of UNCLOS proceeds in ways that further Canada's interests as well as those of the international community more generally.

While UNCLOS's ECS provisions are highly beneficial for coastal states with wide continental shelves, their gains have been at the expense of the common heritage of humanity. The ECSs outlined in the Danish, Norwegian, and Russian submissions, along with those expected from Canada and the United States, leave little Area beyond national jurisdiction to benefit humanity, generally, and to address the needs of less developed countries, in particular.[1]

LINKS TO THE LITERATURE

The book's findings confirm key tenets found in much of the Canadian foreign policy literature: that the international environment sets the parameters within which Canadian policy-makers must function; that multilateralism is frequently the preferred tool to achieve objectives; that Canadian policy-makers often used a "functionalist" approach to achieve policy objectives; and that domestic interests — particularly those bene-fiting the economic elite — are key determinants of specific foreign policy choices, while those of ordinary people tend to be relegated to the side-lines. Contrary to the findings of some prominent scholars, the case does not substantiate the idea that states resort to military strategies in a scram-ble for scarce resources; nor does it exemplify the interdepartmental com-petition predicted by the bureaucratic politics model.

International Sets Parameters

Conventional wisdom regarding Canadian foreign policy tells us that the external environment constitutes a major determinant of Canada's international relations; it sets the parameters within which Canadian decision-makers have to operate.[2] These assertions are borne out in this case. The actions of other states and developments outside Canada's bor-ders, such as the Truman Declaration, Ambassador Pardo's speech to the U.N. General Assembly, and fluctuations in the prices and demand for offshore resources, played pivotal roles in determining the agendas at international negotiations and the issues to which Canadian officials had to respond. Of course, Canada is not merely a passive pawn; in some instances Canadian actions affected developments abroad. For example, Canada was first to present a detailed proposal to the U.N. Third Conference on the Law of the Sea regarding the mandate and member-ship of the Commission, and its proposals were subsequently incorpor-ated into UNCLOS and now comprise part of the legal regime by which all states parties are bound. Former prime minister Stephen Harper's decision to claim the North Pole soured relations with the Danes and upset previous multilateral understandings about maritime boundary delimitation in the area. Thus the case provides examples of Canada exerting influence on the world stage; however, overall the international environment has had far more impact on Canadian foreign policy than the latter has had on the development of the ECS regime.

Multilateralism

Tom Keating describes multilateralism as the defining characteristic of Canadian foreign policy,[3] and its importance is widely recognized in the literature.[4] According to Keating, "Multilateral diplomacy involves working with coalitions of states, primarily but not exclusively within formal associations or institutions, to achieve foreign policy objectives. It also implies a willingness to maintain solidarity with these coalitions and to maintain support for these institutions."[5] Thus, multilateral diplomacy is not just about policy coordination among three or more countries; it also connotes objectives: coalition solidarity and institutional support. Most scholars see multilateralism as a constructive approach to Canadian foreign policy; however, it is not without its critics. David Black and Claire Turenne Sjolander urge us to probe more deeply and to ask the question: Whose interests are best upheld by multilateralism?[6] Their response is that multilateral diplomacy serves the interests of elites at home and abroad, especially those of "American-centred (state and corporate) hegemony."[7]

The importance accorded to multilateralism varies with the issue at hand and the particular government in power. For example, Andrew Cooper finds that bilateralism — rather than multilateralism — has dominated Canada-U.S. trade relations.[8] Many scholars as well as some former senior Canadian diplomats have criticized the Harper government for abandoning the multilateralism that guided much of Canadian foreign policy over the preceding six decades.[9] While the Harper government was not the first to be censured for giving insufficient priority to multilateralism,[10] the former's general disregard for the concept was considered particularly egregious.

For most of the period covered by this book, multilateralism was the defining characteristic of Canada's strategy for pursuing its interests regarding its Arctic ECS. Instead of taking unilateral actions, as did many coastal states, Canada generally used multilateral channels to advance its interests. At the First and Second Conferences on the Law of the Sea, in the Seabed Committee, and at the Third Conference on the Law of the Sea, which produced UNCLOS, Canada was a strong and effective advocate of coastal state rights over the continental shelf. At the same time, it also gave high priority to securing international agreements, as exemplified by its willingness at the First Conference to relinquish its original preferences, and instead to accept the two-hundred-metre isobath and exploitability criteria in order to facilitate agreement on the Convention on the Continental Shelf. At the Third Conference, Canada proposed revenue sharing in exchange for the coastal state jurisdiction over the seabed resources of the continental shelf beyond two hundred nautical miles. It would have preferred weaker wording pertaining to the Commission's role in the delineation process (i.e., having the coastal state take account of the Commission's recommendations rather than basing its limits on them); however, it acquiesced in order to secure the extension and general acceptance of the Convention. In this case, multilateral diplomacy facilitated the creation of a legal regime highly beneficial to Canadian interests. Its rules and regulations privilege coastal states, especially those with wide continental shelves, whether they be developed or developing countries. While multilateralism may be portrayed as the morally correct path to follow, there is no doubt that Canada's pursuit of the strategy has been guided most of all by self-interest.

The multilateral process has not, however, done much to advance the common heritage of humanity principle in two respects: the original convention provisions for the Area were seriously watered down in the secretary-general's 1994 agreement; and, the delineation process has left little of the Arctic seabed outside coastal state control. Former prime minister Harper's unilateral decision to claim the North Pole stands in stark contrast to the country's multilateral approach to defining the regime and delineating its Arctic ECS. It remains to be seen whether the Liberal Party's 2015 election promise to return to a foreign policy promoting multilateral diplomacy[11] will translate into concrete actions to rebuild cooperative relations with Canada's Arctic neighbours in the final delineation phase and in the subsequent delimitation of Arctic ECS boundaries.

Functionalism

Canadian functionalism was initially conceived as a strategy by which Canada could argue for greater representation in international organizations so as to enhance its influence and status on an international stage. According to the doctrine, representation in international organizations should be based on a country's stake in the issues being considered and its willingness to contribute to the work of the body. With time, the concept of functionalism broadened from a strategy aimed at securing membership on international bodies to one that also sought to realize other foreign policy objectives in international negotiations. The strategy was issue-oriented and flexible so it could evolve as circumstances changed to maximize Canada's bargaining position. As Andrew Cooper explained,

> Functionalism legitimized the application of issue-specific strengths and skills possessed by individual countries. On the basis of this criteria, Canada could marshal its time and energy in the compartmentalized way. Instead of pointing Canada in the direction of diffuseness, where Canada tried to 'do everything' and 'be everywhere,' functionalism underscored the logic of Canada defining its priorities, identifying its areas of comparative advantage, and calculating how best its resources could be applied to maximum advantage.[12]

Doctrinaire positions and rigid alignments with a particular negotiating bloc were to be avoided, so as to facilitate cooperating with different states at various points on the basis of shared interests.

Throughout the Third Conference, Canada "pursued a functionalist approach whereby no more jurisdiction would be exercised than would be required to protect its specific interests."[13] Instead of claiming full sovereignty over the entire continental margin, Canada agreed that the coastal state would have limited rights. In the exclusive economic zone, the coastal state has sovereign rights to explore, exploit, conserve, and manage the living and non-living resources in the water column and seabed; however, it cannot impede the freedoms of navigation or overflight. On the ECS, coastal state jurisdiction is limited to exploring and exploiting the non-living resources and sedentary species of the seabed. Freedom of the high seas prevails in the superjacent water column. Rather than adhering to rigid, doctrinaire policies, Canada's positions evolved as the negotiations progressed and compromises were accepted in the interest of protecting its top priorities and getting agreement on the overall treaty package. Likewise, alignments varied with the issue under negotiation. It worked with the margineers (wide-margin countries) to secure the ECS provisions, with the coastal states more broadly to maximize coastal state jurisdiction in maritime zones, and with the Group of 77 to protect the interests of land-based mining countries, like itself, from the threat of unregulated production from the international seabed.

Foreign Policy for Whom?

Much scholarly attention has been given to the motivation behind Canada's foreign policies.[14] In these discussions, economic considerations are often considered to be of primary importance. For example, Cranford Pratt identified a systemic bias to promoting capitalism within Canadian foreign policy.[15] The main motivation for Canada's policies regarding the continental shelf since 1945 has been economic interests: the desire to maximize its jurisdiction so as to secure the right to exploit as many resources as possible.

If economic interests, in general, and resource development, in particular, were the primary motivations behind Canada's ECS policies and positions, whose interests were relegated to the sidelines? Feminist theory raises important questions that need to be applied to all levels of policy-making. Who makes which decisions and why? Who has access to resources and who controls resources? Whom is a policy or program targeted toward? Who will benefit? Who will lose? Who is consulted when solutions to a problem are being sought? Internationalism, which has been a dominant idea in Canadian foreign policy for much of the past seven decades, has been defined in terms of five characteristics.

> First, internationalism puts a premium on the idea of each state taking *responsibility for playing* a constructive role in the management of conflicts that will inevitably arise in global politics. Second, an internationalist policy suggests that *multilateralism* is essential for defusing conflicts in international affairs and that therefore states should not act unilaterally in international politics. Third, internationalism places emphasis on involvement with, and support for, *international institutions*, for it is believed that institutionalization promotes multilateralism and dampens the unilateral impulse. Fourth, support of international institutions must be given concrete expression by a willingness to use national resources for the system as a whole. Finally, internationalism suggests an emphasis on international law, which is assumed to enhance the stability of the international system.[16]

Yet internationalism has been criticized for being state centric, assuming gender and race neutrality, reflecting a colonial bias, and ignoring the experiences of ordinary people.[17]

The people most likely to be affected by resource development on Canada's Arctic ECS are its Arctic inhabitants:

> Any resource extraction that occurs in the extended continental shelf has the potential to impact the marine wildlife in the Arctic Ocean, not only in the immediate area but throughout the Arctic ocean [sic] due to the migration of various species though the Arctic Ocean and also due to ocean currents and hydrological cycles that would spread any oil spill, or other environmental contaminants beyond the immediate area of the resource extraction.[18]

Damage to the Arctic environment and its wildlife could do irreparable harm to the economic, social, and cultural well-being of Indigenous peoples. Yet the process of defining and implementing the ECS regime has been state centric. At the international level, states negotiated the Convention on the Continental Shelf and UNCLOS. The multilateral cooperation and collaboration involved government officials from the Arctic states. Domestically, the delineation process is the domain of the federal government. UNCLOS is premised on state sovereignty rather than on the Inuit concept of pan-Arctic sovereignty. In traditional legal terms, sovereignty is the right of a state to determine its own domestic and foreign policies without foreign interference. This state-centric approach contrasts with the Inuit concept of sovereignty, which focuses on cooperation that transcends national boundaries and whose objective is to advance the economic, social, and cultural interests of Arctic inhabitants and to safeguard their environment. While Arctic countries cooperated and collaborated in the delineation process, they never seriously considered the Indigenous concept of pan-Arctic sovereignty or any kind of joint management of their Arctic ECSs, let alone joint management focused on the well-being of Arctic inhabitants.

Prior to each survey, an assessment of its environmental impact was done. Meetings were held with five Indigenous coastal communities in the western Arctic as well as in Grise Fjord, to inform them of the process and to explain the need for the surveys and their objectives. In consultations with the local communities, it was agreed that Indigenous mammal observers would travel on the icebreakers and that the seismic airguns would not be fired within one kilometre of a mammal. Indigenous wildlife monitors were also employed in the ice camps, where they were not only important to the safety of humans and other mammals but also contributed valuable knowledge about how to live and work in the Arctic. Nonetheless the involvement of Indigenous peoples in Canada's ECS should not be overstated. No survey mission had more than four mammal observers and no Indigenous women participated in the missions. Neither the Indigenous communities nor federal government officials appeared to consider the ECS delineation a priority for Indigenous peoples for three reasons. First, the ECS surveys were conducted a long way north of any settlements or traditional hunting grounds. Second, for the most part, the ECS surveys took place far beyond the jurisdiction of Indigenous governance bodies, and little of the area covered by treaty agreements extends into Canada's Arctic ECS. The exception is the Inuvialuit settlement region that extends beyond Canada's exclusive economic zone and "overlaps with a portion of the extended continental shelf."[19] Third, Arctic resource development beyond two hundred nautical miles from shore is decades away and there are so many pressing issues affecting the well-being of Indigenous peoples that need immediate attention.

Canada has obligations under domestic and international law to protect the Indigenous peoples' traditional ways of life and right to sustainable development; to secure their free, prior, and informed consent before proceeding with resource development on the ECS; to ensure that they benefit from the development of natural resources in their region; and to safeguard the environment.[20] If and when resource exploitation on Canada's Arctic ECS is contemplated, it will be important to ensure that Indigenous peoples participate fully in the decision-making process.

Military Response to Resource Scarcity

The delineation of the Arctic ECS stands in contrast to the findings of scholars, such as Michael Klare, who have examined state responses to the scarcity of oil, natural gas, minerals, and water in other parts of the world. In *Resource Wars: The New Landscape of Global Conflict*, Klare concludes that states are increasingly resorting to military policies in their global scramble for natural resources.[21] While there has been military rhetoric to back claims of sovereignty in the Arctic generally, the process of delineating the ECSs has been characterized primarily by bilateral and multilateral cooperation. Why the difference? Several factors help answer the question. First, scientists have a long history of cooperating in the Arctic, and delineating the continental shelf has been largely a scientific enterprise. Second, Arctic countries have a mutual interest in cooperating, and the need to do so is well recognized. Collecting the data required for the submissions is expensive and time-consuming — factors militating in favour of cooperative ventures. Third, there is little immediate pressure to develop resources on the ECS. While the long-term potential for exploiting natural resources beyond two hundred nautical miles may be considerable, expectations of great riches need to be tempered for several reasons. The greatest potential is on land and within the exclusive economic zones. Developing seabed resources beyond two hundred nautical miles will be fraught with difficulties, including the enormous costs and environmental risks of extracting and transporting the resources to markets, the short seasons, the challenging climatic conditions, and the high insurance premiums. There are still many resources to develop on land, where the risks and logistical problems are far less daunting. While Arctic coastal states are eager to establish their ECSs, there is relatively little pressure to begin mining and oil and gas extraction beyond two hundred nautical miles. Having clear norms, an orderly process, and well-defined areas of national jurisdiction are also in the best interests of private corporations wishing to develop resources. No company wants to invest millions of dollars in both exploration and drilling costs without being certain of the rules under which it will operate; a company also wants assurances it will be able to reap the benefits of its long-term investment. This fact is evident in the Beaufort Sea, where the exclusive economic zones of Canada and the United States overlap and where rich resources are known to exist; yet, until the two countries agree on a maritime boundary, the uncertainties are too great to warrant resource exploitation. At present many questions remain unanswered and unanswerable. For example, would corporations have to operate under U.S. laws or Canadian laws? Few, if any, creditors in the world would finance exploitation before titles were agreed on. The lack of immediate pressure for resources development, the strong incentives for bilateral and multilateral collaboration, and the well-established patterns of scientific cooperation have all contributed to making the delineation of Arctic ECSs peaceful, orderly, and notable for the high levels of cooperation engendered. The fears about violent conflicts over Arctic resources that are frequently perpetuated in the media are unfounded. In the delineation of Arctic ECSs, there has been no need to resort to military solutions as there is a regime in place and its rules are being respected. As such, this study supports the findings of scholars arguing that the circumpolar politics have been marked by a high degree of cooperation.[22]

Governmental Politics

Contrary to the governmental politics model of government, the process of preparing Canada's submission for the Commission has been marked by interdepartmental cooperation and collaboration rather than conflict and competition. The governmental politics model sees public policy resulting from a bargaining process in which diverse government actors, each with their own particular set of priorities to advance, compete to determine outcomes. The approach was developed and popularized by Graham Allison, who used the term "bureaucratic politics." In Canadian context, the term "governmental" rather than "bureaucratic" politics is often used to reflect the close relationship that exists between cabinet ministers and those who work under them.[23] The model challenges the traditional concept of public policies emanating from a rational monolithic entity: the government. According to the approach, it is necessary to identify the relevant government actors and their respective goals, to assess their relative bargaining resources and skills, and to understand the nature of the bargaining process and the influence it exerts over policy outcomes.

Although Allison was writing about American foreign policy, he claimed the model could also be applied to the study of other national governments. Kim Richard Nossal took up the challenge, and he concluded that the model is "both useful and applicable" in the Canadian context, although the Canadian process is less conflict ridden and more prone to "friendly competition" than the American system.[24]

Competition among government actors has featured prominently in many cases involving Canadian foreign policy. During Canada's so-called Turbot War with Spain (1994–1996), tensions arose between the Department of Fisheries and Oceans and the Department of Foreign

Affairs and International Trade over which department would assume the lead and over what approach should be used: the "quiet diplomacy" advocated by Foreign Affairs and International Trade or the more aggressive style taken by Fisheries and Oceans.[25] Interdepartmental wranglings — this time primarily involving the Department of the Environment and National Resources Canada — were also very much in evidence when positions for 1997 Kyoto Accord negotiations for a legally binding protocol to reduce greenhouse gas emissions were being determined.[26] A similar spat over control erupted between the departments of national defence and international trade during the campaign to ban anti-personnel land mines.[27] After examining the implementation of Canada's "whole of government" approach to interventions in failed and fragile states, Marie-Eve Desrosiers and Philippe Lagassé concluded that the two departments "embraced the idea of failed and fragile states to reinforce their organisational essences and recycle their existing missions, roles, and capabilities. In addition, the departments used a 'whole of government' approach to secure their autonomy, fence their respective functions, and enlarge their unique capabilities, under the guise of greater efficiency."[28]

Governmental politics in the Canadian foreign policy-making process are generally viewed as being less competitive and to involve less "pulling and hauling" than is thought to be characteristic of the American system. Yet even taking this difference into consideration, there has been little intragovernmental competition to determine policies and strategies during Canada's ECS Program. Three federal departments play central roles in the delineation of Canada's Arctic ECS: Natural Resources, Fisheries and Oceans, and Global Affairs. The first two provide the scientific team. Their collaboration is necessary for financial reasons, as the cost of the Arctic missions is exorbitant, but it is also vital because their research is symbiotic and their close collaboration is essential in conducting the research and analysis needed to produce cohesive, comprehensive data sets and sound scientific explanations. Occasionally, there has been minor friction over the relative priority given to the different types of testing and over who should get credit for what; but overall they have functioned as a highly effective, collegial team. The third departmental member of Canada's ECS team, Global Affairs Canada, is responsible for the legal aspects and is coordinating the preparation, presentation, and ultimate defence of the submission. All three departments share the same macro-level objective: to maximize Canada's Arctic ECS in accordance with scientific evidence and the legal requirements specified in UNCLOS. Other government departments provide expertise and equipment as required but they have not competed with the lead departments to determine Canada's policies and positions regarding the ECS.

According to the governmental politics paradigm, the policy-making process involves players with different interests; hence trade-off must be made. The method of reconciling differences among various government bodies depends on the relative status and influence of the participants.[29] When they are fairly evenly matched, compromises must be negotiated. In contrast, when the process involves sets of actors with disparate status and influence, the interests of the stronger tend to take precedence. Such was the case in the fall of 2013 when former prime minister Harper suddenly became directly involved. His decision to reject the Arctic submission prepared by the Canadian public servants with the support of their respective ministers exemplifies the bureaucratic politics model's arguments about the importance of bargaining resources in determining policy outcomes. In the policy-making process, the prime minister is pre-eminent.[30] As "the head of the government, its chief spokesperson, in and outside Parliament; the chair of cabinet; and head of the parliamentary caucus and the extra-parliamentary party," as well as the person best positioned to dispense patronage, the prime minister occupies "a central and commanding position in Canadian politics."[31] Furthermore, the prime minister's influence in the foreign policy process increased during the Harper administration.[32] As Kim Nossal observed, There can be no denying the powerful impact of Stephen Harper's own views — institutionally backed by both the Prime Minister's Office and the Privy Council Office — on the foreign policy process."[33] According to Paul Gecelovsky, "The level of control exercised by Stephen Harper far surpasses that of any other previous prime minister."[34] Thus it is not surprising that former prime minister Harper's preference to claim the North Pole took precedence over the views of his cabinet ministers and the public servants.

A FINAL WORD

Several years before the U.N. Third Conference on the Law of the Sea ended its sessions and adopted UNCLOS, it was already clear that Canada was to be a major beneficiary of the Convention. As then secretary of state for external affairs Mark MacGuigan said, the "coastal states have obviously done well at the Conference — and none better than Canada."[35] One could add, of all the many UNCLOS provisions advantageous to Canada, none is more important than those pertaining to the continental shelf. It continues to be a high priority, as evidenced by the time, energy, and money that the government has devoted to defining its limits, to securing coastal states' rights over it, to incorporating these rights into its own legislation, to mapping the seabed, and to preparing its submission to the Commission.

As Stephen Forbes pointed out, the ECS work does not end with the submission.[36] The commissioners may ask for clarification and additional information. After the whole submission process is completed, the coastal state is responsible for delineating its ECS and for resolving any overlaps with the ECS of neighbouring states. Responding to the Commission and completing the delineation and delimitation of its ECS will necessitate keeping the databases current and keeping abreast of new technologies and new data processing applications. Thus the Arctic ECS will continue to be salient on political, legal, scientific, and economic grounds for decades to come.

INTERVIEWEES

Hans Böggild

Member of the Canadian High Arctic Seismic Expedition as "Artist at Sea" and writer of the daily blog for the 2011 voyage aboard CCGS *Louis S. St-Laurent*; Halifax, Nova Scotia, May 28, 2015.

Kai Böggild

Research assistant (student), 2014, 2015, and 2016 expeditions on CCGS *Louis S. St-Laurent*; Halifax, Nova Scotia, May 26, 2015.

Borden Chapman

Chief technologist for the 2007, 2008, 2009, 2010, 2011, and 2015 ECS surveys using CCGS *Louis S. St-Laurent* and consulting engineer for the 2014, 2015, and 2016 voyages; Halifax, Nova Scotia, May 27, 2015.

Sonya Dehler (Dr.)

Chief scientist for the 2015 ECS Mission and Subdivision Head, Geological Survey of Canada, Natural Resources Canada; Halifax, Nova Scotia, May 27, 2015.

Kevin DesRoches

Physical scientist, UNCLOS, Geological Survey of Canada, Natural Resources Canada; Halifax, Nova Scotia, May 26, 2015.

Mary-Lynn Dickson (Dr.)

Chief scientist for the 2016 survey and director of the UNCLOS Program (2015–), Geological Survey of Canada, Natural Resources Canada; Halifax, Nova Scotia, October 4, 2016.

Stephen Forbes

Director, Law of the Sea Project (2009–2014), Canadian Hydrographic Service, Department of Fisheries and Oceans; Halifax, Nova Scotia, September 30, 2011.

Michel Goguen

Director, Hydrography (Central and Arctic), Canadian Hydrographic Service Department of Fisheries and Oceans; Burlington, Ontario, October 16, 2015.

Mike Gorveatt

Arctic Logistics, Natural Resources Canada; Halifax, Nova Scotia, May 27, 2015.

Ruth Jackson (Dr.)

Research scientist and chief scientist for the 2007 LORITA and 2008 ARTA ice camps and the 2007 and 2008 missions on CCGS *Louis S. St-Laurent*, Geological Survey of Canada, Natural Resources Canada; Halifax, Nova Scotia, May 26, 2015.

Tim Janzen

Hydrographer in charge of the 2010 Camp Borden and engineering project supervisor, data acquisition, Canadian Hydrographic Service, Department of Fisheries and Oceans; Burlington, Ontario, October 16, 2015, and November 27, 2015.

Richard (Dick) MacDougall

Director, Law of the Sea Project, Canadian Hydrographic Service, Department of Fisheries and Oceans; Halifax, Nova Scotia, December 21, 2007; February 8, 2008; August 21, 2008; December 7, 2009; and March 7, 2011.

Desmond Manning

Marine geoscience technologist for the 2014, 2015, and 2016 expeditions on CCGS *Louis S. St-Laurent*, Geological Survey of Canada, Natural Resources Canada; Halifax, Nova Scotia, May 27, 2015.

David Mosher (Dr.)

Research scientist, manager of the UNCLOS Program and chief scientist for the 2009, 2010, 2011, and 2014 surveys on CCGS *Louis S. St-Laurent*, Geological Survey of Canada, Natural Resources Canada; Halifax, Nova Scotia, May 26, 2015.

Gordon Oakey (Dr.)

Research scientist and participant on the 2016 survey on *Oden*, Geological Survey of Canada, Natural Resources Canada; Halifax, Nova Scotia, May 28, 2015.

Patrick Potter

Geophysicist, Geological Survey of Canada, Natural Resources Canada; Halifax, Nova Scotia, May 26, 2015.

Walta-Anne (Walli) Rainey

Marine geoscience technologist, Geological Survey of Canada, Natural Resources Canada; Halifax, Nova Scotia, May 26, 2015.

John Shimeld

Geophysicist during the 2007 LORITA and 2008 ARTA ice camps, second scientist for the 2007, 2008, 2009, 2010, and 2014 ECS surveys using CCGS *Louis S. St-Laurent*, and seismic lead for the 2016 Canada-Sweden Polar Expedition using CCGS *Louis S. St-Laurent* and the icebreaker Oden, Geological Survey of Canada, Natural Resources Canada; personal correspondence.

Paola Travaglini

Chief hydrographer, 2014 Canadian Polar Expedition; Halifax, Nova Scotia, May 27, 2015.

Jacob Verhoef (Dr.)

Director of the Geological Survey of Canada and director of the UNCLOS Program, Department of Natural Resources; Halifax, Nova Scotia, February 8, 2008; December 7, 2009; and March 7, 2011.

Scott Youngblut

Engineering project supervisor, data acquisition, Canadian Hydrographic Service, Department of Fisheries and Oceans; Burlington, Ontario, October 16, 2015.

NOTES

PREFACE

1. For example, Anthony Browne, "Melting Ice Starts Rush for Arctic Resources," *London Times*, January 28, 2006; Scott Borgerson, "Averting a Cold War on Ice: Arctic Ambitions," *International Herald Tribune*, August 9, 2007; Owen Bowcott, "World Battle for Seabed," *Mail and Guardian*, January 9, 2008; Paul Reynolds, "The Arctic's New Gold Rush," *BBC News*, October 25, 2005; Ed Struzik, "'Who's Guarding Our Back Door?': The Arctic Has Immense Oil Resources and Mineral Wealth, but Canada Has Been Slow to Protect Its Northern Sovereignty," *Toronto Star*, November 18, 2007; Fred Weir, "As Icecaps Melt, Russia Races for Arctic's Resources," *Christian Science Monitor*, July 31, 2007; and Barbara Yaffe, "Arctic Politics Means a Tussle over Who Owns the North," *Vancouver Sun*, November 17, 2005; Richard Sale and Eugene Potapov, *The Scramble for the Arctic: Ownership, Exploitation and Conflict in the Far North* (London: Frances Lincoln, 2010).

CHAPTER 1: INTRODUCTION

1. The book draws together and expands upon my previous publications, including Elizabeth Riddell-Dixon, "The Seven Decade Quest to Maximize Canada's Continental Shelf," *International Journal* 69, No. 3 (2014): 422–443; *Multilateral Code to Govern Arctic Offshore Resource Development* (Toronto:

Bill Graham Centre for Contemporary International History, Trinity College, University of Toronto, 2014); "Neither Conflict nor 'Use It or Lose It': Delineating Extended Continental Shelves in the Arctic," *OpenCanada.org*, September 19, 2013, www.opencanada.org/features/neither-conflict-nor-use-it-or-lose-it; *Canada's Arctic Policy* (London, ON: Canada-U.S. Institute, Western University, 2012); "Meeting the Deadline: Canada's Arctic Submission to the Commission on the Limits of the Continental Shelf," *Ocean Development and International Law* 42, No. 4 (2011): 368–382; "Seismic Testing in Lancaster Sound: Lessons Learned," *Policy Options* 32, No. 9 (2011): 72–75; *Arctic Research Program of the Canada-U.S. Institute* (London, ON: CUSI, Western University, 2010); "Not for the Faint-Hearted: Mapping Canada's Arctic Continental Shelf Beyond 200 Nautical Miles," *Policy Options* 30, No. 4 (2009): 60–64; "Canada and Arctic Politics: The Continental Shelf Delimitation," *Ocean Development and International Law* 39, No. 4 (2008): 343–359; "Canada's Arctic Continental Shelf Extension: Debunking Myths," *Policy Options* 29, No. 8 (2008): 39–43; "Individual Leadership and Structural Power," *Canadian Journal of Political Science* 30, No. 2 (1997): 257–283; "The Preparatory Commission on the International Seabed Authority: New Realism?," *International Journal of Estuarine and Coastal Law* 7, No. 3 (1992): 195–216; "Winners and Losers: Formulating Canada's Policies on International Technology Transfers," *International Journal* 47, No. 1 (1991/1992): 159–183; "To Sign or Not to Sign the Law of the Sea Convention: Governmental Politics in the United Kingdom and Canada," *Journal of Commonwealth and Comparative Politics* 29, No. 2 (1991): 212–233; *Canada and the International Seabed: Domestic Determinants and External Constraints* (Montreal: McGill-Queen's University Press, 1989); "Canada at the Preparatory Commission: Policies and Challenges," in *Canadian Oceans Policy: National Strategies and the New Law of the Sea*, eds. Donald McRae and Gordon Munro (Vancouver: University of British Columbia Press, 1989), 69–91; "State Autonomy and Canadian Foreign Policy: The Case of Deep Seabed Mining," *Canadian Journal of Political Science* 21, No. 2 (1988): 297–317; "Deep Seabed Mining: A Hotbed for

Governmental Politics?," *International Journal* 41, No. 1 (1985/1986): 72–94; and "Canadian Foreign Policy and the United Nations Third Conference on the Law of the Sea," in *Mackenzie King to Philosopher King: Canadian Foreign Policy in the Modern Age*, ed. O.P. St. John (Winnipeg: University of Manitoba Press, 1984), 173–180.

2.   See PEW Charitable Trusts, "Exclusive Economic Zones," *Sea Around Us*, 2014, www.seaaroundus.org.

3.   Canada, House of Commons, *Debates*, 2nd session, 20th Parliament, August 28, 1946, 5524.

4.   Canada, House of Commons, *Debates*, 1st session, 24th Parliament, July 7, 1958, 1879.

5.   Lawrence Cannon, "Address by Minister Cannon at News Conference Following Arctic Visit," speech, April 9, 2010, http://news.gc.ca/web/article-en.do?m=/index&nid=524529.

6.   Department of Foreign Affairs and International Trade, "Canada to Assume Chairmanship of Arctic Council," news release, May 12, 2013, http://news.gc.ca/web/article-en.do?nid=741239.

7.   *United Nations Convention on the Law of the Sea*, November 16, 1994, 1833 U.N.T.S. 397. Its provisions are legally binding on its 167 parties.

8.   See Shelagh Grant, *Polar Imperative: A History of Arctic Sovereignty in North America* (Vancouver: Douglas and McIntyre, 2010), 6.

9.   Jacob Verhoef, Interview with the author, February 8, 2008.

10.   Government of Canada, "Backgrounder — 2016 Arctic Survey, July 21, 2016, http://news.gc.ca/web/article-en.do?nid=1102489.

11.   Ted L. McDorman, "The Continental Shelf," *The Oxford Handbook of the Law of the Sea*, eds. Donald R. Rothwell, Alex G. Oude Elferink, Karen N. Scott, and Tim Stephens (Oxford: Oxford University Press, 2015), 182.

12.   Harald Brekke, "Defining and Recognizing the Outer Limits of the Continental Shelf in the Polar Regions," in *Polar Geopolitics?: Knowledge, Resources and Legal Regimes*, eds. Richard C. Powell and Klaus Dodds (Cheltenham, UK: Edward Elgar, 2014), 39.

13.   BBC News, "Canada Launches Mission to Map Arctic Seabed," *BBC News*, August 9, 2014, www.bbc.com/news/world-us-canada-28718806; Vladimir Isachenkov, "Russia Submits Claim for Vast Arctic Seabed Territories at UN," *CBC News*, August 4, 2015,

www.cbc.ca/news/canada/north/russia-submits-claim-for-vast-arctic-seabed-territories-at-un-1.3178447; Andre Mayer, "Race to Claim High Arctic's Oil Resources May be a Fool's Mission," *CBC News*, December 12, 2013, www.cbc.ca/news/canada/race-to-claim-high-arctic-s-oil-resources-may-be-a-fool-s-mission-1.2461910; Max Paris, "Arctic Resources Claim Deadline Today for Canada," *CBC News*, December 6, 2013, www.cbc.ca/news/politics/arctic-resources-claim-deadline-today-for-canada-1.2452794; Max Paris, "Canada's Claim to Arctic Riches Includes the North Pole," *CBC News*, December 9, 2013, www.cbc.ca/news/politics/canada-s-claim-to-arctic-riches-includes-the-north-pole-1.2456773; Asaf Shalev, "Russia Just Claimed a Broad Swath of the Arctic Shelf; Why Isn't the US Doing the Same," *Alaska Dispatch News*, August 8, 2015, www.adn.com/article/20150808/russia-just-claimed-broad-swath-arctic-shelf-why-isnt-us-doing-same; Asaf Shalev, "Russia Submits Application for Stake of $30 Trillion Arctic Shelf Oil and Gas Rights," *Siberian Times*, August 4, 2015, http://siberiantimes.com/other/others/news/n0341-russia-submits-application-for-stake-of-30-trillion-arctic-shelf-oil-and-gas-rights; and Fred Weir, "As Icecaps Melt, Russia Races for Arctic Resources," *Christian Science Monitor*, July 31, 2007.

14. Kenneth J. Bird, et al., *Circum-Arctic Resource Appraisal: Estimates of Undiscovered Oil and Gas North of the Arctic Circle* (Reston, VA: U.S. Geological Survey, 2008), http://pubs.usgs.gov/fs/2008/3049/fs2008-3049.pdf.

15. Jessica Robinson, "90 Billion Barrels of Oil and 1,670 Trillion Feet of Natural Gas Assessed in the Arctic," *USGS*, July 23, 2008, www.usgs.gov/media/audio/90-billion-barrels-oil-and-1670-trillion-cubic-feet-natural-gas-assessed-arctic.

16. Osman Askin Bak, *The High North: Emerging Challenges and Opportunities; Special Draft Report* (Brussels: NATO Parliamentary Assembly, Science and Technology Committee, 2015), www.nato-pa.int/default.asp?SHORTCUT=3788.

17. Publications citing the USGS figures include Gisele M. Arruda, "Arctic Governance Regime: The Last Frontier for Hydrocarbons Exploitation," *International Journal of Law and Management* 57, No. 5 (2015): 501; Committee on Responding to Oil Spills in the

U.S. Arctic Marine Environment, *Responding to Oil Spills in the U.S. Arctic Marine Environment* (Washington, DC: National Academic Press, 2014), 16–17; Heather A. Conley, *Arctic Economics in the 21st Century: The Benefits and Costs of Cold* (New York: Center for Strategic and International Studies, 2013), 2; Charles K. Ebinger and Evie Zambetakis, "The Geopolitics of Arctic Melt," *International Affairs* 85, No. 5 (2009): 1216; Grace Xingxin Gao, Liang Heng, Todd Walter, and Per Enge, "Breaking the Ice: Navigation in the Arctic," in *Global Navigation Satellite Systems: Report of a Joint Workshop of the National Academy of Engineering and the Chinese Academy of Engineering*, eds. Lance A. Davis, Per Enge, and Grace Xingxin Gao (Washington, DC: National Academic Press, 2012), 229; Anne Merrild Hansen, Julia Adamson, Hans-Peder Barlach Christensen, Eimund Garpestad, and Hugo Le Breton, "Corporate Collaboration: Drivers Behind a Joint Industry Social Baseline Study Related to Hydrocarbon Exploration in Greenland," *Impact Assessment and Project Appraisal* 33, No. 4 (2015): 284; Oistein Harsem, Arne Eide, and Knut Heen, "Factors Influencing Future Oil and Gas Prospects in the Arctic," *Energy Policy* 39, No. 12 (2011): 8038; Peter Kaznacheev and Regina Bazaleva, "A Comparison of the Roles of Privately and State-Owned Oil Companies in Developing the Arctic Shelf," *Energy Exploration and Exploitation* 34, No. 1 (2016): 2; Hyun Jung Kim, "Success in Heading North?: South Korea's Master Plan for Arctic Policy," *Marine* 61 (2015): 266; Mead Treadwell, "Witnessing an Arctic Renaissance," *The Fast-Changing Arctic: Rethinking Arctic Security for a Warmer World*, ed. Barry Scott Zellen (Calgary: University of Calgary Press, 2013), ix; Wentao Wang and Yanhua Liu, "Geopolitics of Global Climate Change and Energy Security," *Chinese Journal of Population Resources and Environment* 13, No. 2 (2015): 123.

18. Jacob Verhoef and Richard MacDougall, Interview with the author, February 8, 2008.

19. Rig Zone, "Offshore Rig Day Rates," *Rig Data*, May 13, 2014, www.rigzone.com/data/dayrates.

20. Carrie Holba, *Exxon Valdez Oil Spill: FAQs, Links and Unique Resources at ARLIS* (Anchorage: Alaska Resources Library and Information Services, 2014), www.arlis.org/docs/vol2/a/EVOS_FAQs.pdf.

21. Paul Koring, "Proposed Arctic Council Treaty on Oil Spills 'Useless,' Greenpeace Says," *Globe and Mail*, February 4, 2013, www.theglobeandmail.com/news/politics/proposed-arctic-council-treaty-on-oil-spills-useless-greenpeace-says/article8158237.

22. *Northern Oil and Gas Annual Report 2012* (Ottawa: Department of Aboriginal Affairs and Northern Development, 2012), 23, www.aadnc-aandc.gc.ca/DAM/DAM-INTER-HQ-NOG/STAGING/texte-text/pubs_ann_ann2012_1367342987466_eng.pdf.

23. See BBC News, "Shell Stops Arctic Activity After 'Disappointing' Tests," and Sean Davidson, "Oil Companies Give Arctic the Cold Shoulder," *CBC News*, September 29, 2015, www.cbc.ca/news/business/oil-arctic-drilling-shell-1.3248233.

24. See Guy Quenneville and David Thurston, "Chevron Puts Arctic Drilling Plans on Hold Indefinitely," *CBC News*, December 18, 2014, www.cbc.ca/news/canada/north/chevron-puts-arctic-drilling-plans-on-hold-indefinitely-1.2877713. See also Steven Kopits, "Regional Report: The Arctic," *World Oil* 234, No. 11 (2013), www.worldoil.com/magazine/2013/november-2013/features/regional-report-the-arctic; and Chris Plecash, "Arctic Hydrocarbon Boom a Long Way Off," *Hill Times*, November 2, 2012, www.hilltimes.com/policy-briefing/2012/11/05/arctic-hydrocarbon-boom-a-long-way-off/22672.

25. Quoted in "Opportunities and Challenges for Arctic Oil and Gas Development," *Eurasia Group Report* (Washington, DC: Wilson Center, 2013), 6, www.wilsoncenter.org/sites/default/files/Artic%20Report_F2.pdf.

26. Canadian Polar Commission, *The State of Northern Knowledge in Canada* (Ottawa: Canadian Polar Commission, 2014), 9.

27. Richard MacDougall, Interview with the author, December 21, 2007.

28. Verhoef and MacDougall, Interview, February 8, 2008.

29. Greg Flakus, "Arctic Draws International Competition for Oil," *VOA News*, August 26, 2015, www.voanews.com/content/arctic-draws-international-competition-for-oil/2933283.html.

30. Tristin Hopper, "A New Cold War: Denmark Gets Aggressive, Stakes Huge Claim in Race for Arctic," *National Post*, December 15, 2014, http://news.nationalpost.com/news/a-new-cold-war-denmark-gets-aggressive-stakes-huge-claim-in-race-for-the-arctic.

31. Dominic Hinde, "Iceland Summit Aims to Avert Tensions as Race for Arctic Resources Heats Up," *Washington Times*, October 19, 2015, www.washingtontimes.com/news/2015/oct/19/arctic-circle-assembly-aims-to-avert-tensions-as-r.

32. Andrey Gubin, "International Competition over Arctic Resources Imminent," *Russia and India Report*, April, 25, 2014, http://in.rbth.com/opinion/2014/04/25/international_competition_over_arctic_resources_imminent_34803.

33. RT, "Arctic Resources: The Fight for the Coldest Place on Earth Heats up," *RT*, April 15, 2014, www.rt.com/news/arctic-reclamation-resources-race-524.

34. Paul Watson, "Canada Well Behind Russia in Race to Claim Arctic Seaways and Territory," *Toronto Star*, December 22, 2011, www.thestar.com/news/world/2011/12/22/canada_well_behind_russia_in_race_to_claim_arctic_seaways_and_territory.html.

35. Mike Blanchfield, "Canada-Russia Arctic War Up for Renewal; Both Countries Talking Aggressively in Battle for Sovereignty," *Toronto Sun*, March 18, 2010.

36. Mark Galeotti, *Jane's Intelligence Review*, October 2008, 8–15.

37. Chris Windeyer, "Resource Grab Risks Arctic Arms Race, Study Says," *Nunatsiaq News*, April 5, 2010, www.nunatsiaqonline.ca/stories/article/050410_resource_grab_risks_arctic_arms_race_study_says.

38. Vesna Guzina, Rodney Neufeld, and Caterina Ventura, Interview with the author, quoted in Elizabeth Riddell-Dixon, "Canada and Arctic Politics: The Continental Shelf Delimitation," *Ocean Development and International Law* 39, No. 4 (2008): 350. Vesna Guzina served as Legal Officer, Oceans and Environmental Law Division; Rodney Neufeld served as Legal Officer, Oceans Law Section; and Caterina Ventura served as Deputy Director, Oceans Law Section, Department of Foreign Affairs and International Trade.

39. Verhoef and MacDougall, Interview, February 8, 2008.

40. Department of Foreign Affairs and International Trade Canada, *Joint Statement on Canada-Russia Economic Cooperation* (Ottawa: Department of Foreign Affairs and International Trade, 2007), 2.

41. Arctic Ocean Conference, *Ilulissat Declaration* (Ilulissat, Greenland: Arctic Ocean Conference, 2008), www.oceanlaw.org/downloads/arctic/Ilulissat_Declaration.pdf.
42. Ibid., 2.
43. Arctic Council, *Iqaluit Declaration* 2015, April 24, 2015, https://oaarchive.arctic-council.org/handle/11374/662.

CHAPTER 2: THE EXTENDED CONTINENTAL SHELF REGIME

1. Suzette V. Suarez, *The Outer Limits of the Continental Shelf: Legal Aspects of Their Establishment* (Berlin: Springer-Verlag, 2008), 22.
2. Ibid.
3. For an in-depth examination of international efforts to define coastal states' rights pertaining to the continental shelf from 1945 to 1976, see Barry G. Buzan and Danford W. Middlemiss, "Canadian Foreign Policy and the Exploitation of the Seabed," in *Canadian Foreign Policy and the Law of the Sea,* eds. Barbara Johnson and Mark W. Zacher (Vancouver: University of British Columbia Press, 1977), 1–51. See also M.L. Jewett, "The Evolution of the Legal Regime of the Continental Shelf, Part I," *Canadian Yearbook of International Law 22* (1984): 153–193, and "The Evolution of the Legal Regime of the Continental Shelf, Part II," *Canadian Yearbook of International Law* 23 (1985): 201–225; and Ted L. McDorman, "Canadian Offshore Oil and Gas: Jurisdiction and Management Issues in the 1980s and Beyond," *Canadian Oceans Policy: National Strategies and the New Law of the Sea,* eds. by Donald McRae and Gordon Munro (Vancouver: University of British Columbia Press, 1989), 39–68.
4. McDorman, "The Continental Shelf," 183.
5. Proclamation No. 2667, 10 Fed. Reg. 12303 (September 28, 1945).
6. Thomas H. Heidar, "Legal Aspects of Continental Shelf Limits," in *Legal and Scientific Aspects of Continental Shelf Limits,* eds. Myron H. Nordquist, John Norton Moore, and Thomas H. Heidar (Leiden: Martinus Nijhoff, 2004), 21.
7. Suarez, *The Outer Limits of the Continental Shelf,* 25.
8. See UN General Assembly, "Convention on the Continental Shelf," Treaty Series 499, No. 7302, June 10, 1964, 311, https://treaties.un.org/doc/publication/UNTS/Volume%20499/v499.pdf.

9. Buzan and Middlemiss, "Canadian Foreign Policy and the Exploitation of the Seabed," 11.

10. McDorman, "The Continental Shelf," 183–184.

11. United Nations, *United Nations Convention on the Law of the Sea* (New York: United Nations, 1983), Article 311(1), 106.

12. D.P. O'Connell, *The International Law of the Sea* (Oxford: Oxford University Press, 1982), 475–476, quoted in Ted L. McDorman, "The Continental Shelf Beyond 200 NM: Law and Politics in the Arctic Ocean," *Journal of Transnational Law and Policy* 18, No. 2 (2009): 164.

13. UN General Assembly, "Convention on the Continental Shelf," Articles 2(1)–2(3), 1; and UN, *Convention on the Law of the Sea*, Article 77(3), 28.

14. J. Alan Beesley, "The Law of the Sea Conference: Factors Behind Canada's Stance," *Canada and the Law of the Sea: Resource Information* (Ottawa: Department of External Affairs, 1977), 39–40.

15. Ibid., 40.

16. Buzan and Middlemiss, "Canadian Foreign Policy and the Exploitation of the Seabed," 17.

17. Department of External Affairs of Canada, "A Note Verbale from the Department of External Affairs of Canada, Dated September 10, 1957," in *United Nations Conference on the Law of the Sea: Official Records, Vol. I, Preparatory Documents, A/CONF.13/5 and Addendas 1–4, February 24–April 27, 1958*, ed. United Nations Conference on the Law of the Sea (Geneva: United Nations, 1958), 76.

18. For a detailed discussion of the Third Conference on the Law of the Sea and its origins, see Elizabeth Riddell-Dixon, *Canada and the International Seabed: Domestic Determinants and External Constraints* (Montreal & Kingston: McGill-Queen's University Press, 1989); Barbara Johnson and Mark W. Zacher, *Canadian Foreign Policy and the Law of the Sea* (Vancouver: University of British Columbia Press, 1977); R. Logan, *Canada, the United States, and the Third Law of the Sea Conference* (Washington: Canadian-American Committee, 1974); and Clyde Sanger, *Ordering the Oceans: The Making of the Law of the Sea* (Toronto: University of Toronto Press, 1987).

19. UN General Assembly, *Declaration and Treaty Concerning the Reservation Exclusively for Peaceful Purposes of the Sea-Bed and of the*

Ocean Floor Underlying the Seas Beyond the Limits of Present National Jurisdiction, and the Use of Their Resources in the Interest of Mankind, 22nd Session, August 18, 1967, A/6695.

20. Buzan and Middlemiss, "Canadian Foreign Policy and the Exploitation of the Seabed," 15.

21. Ibid., 16.

22. Canada, House of Commons, *Minutes of Proceedings and Evidence of the Standing Committee on External Affairs and National Defence,* 1st session, 29th Parliament, November 6, 1973, 22:21.

23. United Nations, *Seventh Session (First Part) of Third United Nations Conference on Law of Sea, Geneva, 28 March–19 May: Tackles "Hard-core" Issues for Law of Sea Convention,* BR/78/21 (London: Information Centre, 1978), 4–5.

24. Donald Crosby (director general of the Resource Management and Conservation Branch), Interview with the author, September 17, 1987, quoted in Riddell-Dixon, *Canada and the International Seabed,* 68.

25. Department of External Affairs, *Third United Nations Conference on the Law of the Sea* (Ottawa: Department of External Affairs, 1973), 14.

26. UN, *Convention on the Law of the Sea,* Article 1(1), 2, and Article 140(1), 43.

27. Ibid., Article 57, 18.

28. Ibid., Article 56(1)(a), 18.

29. Ibid., Article 58(1), 19, and Article 87(1), 31.

30. Department of External Affairs, *Third United Nations Conference,* 14 and 15.

31. UN, *Convention on the Law of the Sea,* Article 76(1), 27.

32. McDorman, "The Continental Shelf," 4.

33. UN, *Convention on the Law of the Sea,* Article 76(5), 27.

34. Ibid., Article 77(1 and 4), 28.

35. "Canada's Extended Continental Shelf: Canada's Program," *Department of Foreign Affairs, Trade and Development,* August 15, 2012, www.international.gc.ca/arctic-arctique/continental/program-canada-programme.aspx?lang=eng.

36. Verhoef and MacDougall, Interview, February 8, 2008.

37. Oceans Act, S.C. 1996, c. 31.

38. See Elizabeth Riddell-Dixon, "Canada at the Preparatory Commission: Policies and Challenges," *Canadian Oceans Policy: National Strategies and the New Law of the Sea*, eds. Donald McRae and Gordon Munro (Vancouver: University of British Columbia Press, 1989), 69–91; and "The Preparatory Commission on the International Sea-bed Authority: 'New Realism'?," *International Journal of Estuarine and Coastal Law* 7, No. 33 (1992): 195–216.

39. UN General Assembly, *Agreement Relating to the Implementation of Part XI of the United Nations Convention on the Law of the Sea of December 10, 1982, A/RES/48/263* (New York: United Nations, 1983).

40. The importance of UNCLOS to Canadian interests is discussed in Ted L. McDorman, "Canada Ratifies the 1982 United Nations Convention on the Law of the Sea: At Last," *Ocean Development and International Law* 35, No. 2 (2004): 103–114; and Rob Huebert, "Canada and the Law of the Sea Convention," *International Journal* 52, No. 1 (1996–1997): 69–88.

41. "Senate Confirmation Hearing: Hillary Clinton," *New York Times*, January 13, 2009, www.nytimes.com/2009/01/13/us/politics/13text-clinton.html. See also *The UN Convention on the Law of the Sea: Hearings of the United States Senate Foreign Relations Committee, September 27*, 110th Congress (2007) (testimony by John Negroponte, Deputy Secretary of State), 3; U.S., Department of Commerce, National Oceanic and Atmospheric Administration, *U.S. Ocean Action Plan: The Bush Administration's Response to the U.S. Commission on Ocean Policy* (Washington, DC: National Oceanic and Atmospheric Administration 2004), 5; and United States Geological Survey, *Law of the Sea — Outer Limits of the U.S. Continental Margins* (Woods Hole, MA: Woods Hole Science Center, 2008), 1.

42. U.S. Department of State, Bureau of Oceans and International Environmental and Scientific Affairs, "Defining the Limits of the U.S. Continental Shelf," *Diplomacy in Action*, 2010, www.state.gov/e/oes/continentalshelf.

43. Allan J. MacEachen, *Notes for Remarks by the Honourable, Deputy Prime Minister and Secretary of State for External Affairs, at the Final Session of the Third United Nations Conference on the Law of the Sea, Montego Bay, Jamaica, December 6, 1982* (Ottawa: Bureau of Information, Department of External Affairs, 1982), 3.

44. UN, *Convention on the Law of the Sea*, Annex II, Article 4, 112.

45. States Parties to UNCLOS, *Decision Regarding the Date of Commencement of the Ten-Year Period for Making Submissions to the Commission on the Limits of the Continental Shelf set out in Article 4 of Annex II to the United Nations Convention on the Law of the Sea*, 11th Meeting, May 29, 2001, SPLOS/72, www.un.org/Depts/los/index.html.

46. States Parties to UNCLOS, *Decision Regarding the Workload of the Commission on the Limits of the Continental Shelf and the Ability of States, Particularly Developing States, to Fulfil the Requirements of Article 4 of Annex II to the United Nations Convention on the Law of the Sea, As Well as the Decision Contained in SPLOS/72, Paragraph (A)*, 11th Meeting, June 20, 2008, SPLOS/183, www.un.org/Depts/los/index.html.

47. Commission on the Limits of the Continental Shelf: CLCS/3, September 12, 1997; CLCS/3/Corr. 1, April 27, 1998; CLCS/3/Rev. 1, May 14, 1998; CLCS/3/Rev. 2, September 4, 1998; CLCS/3/Rev. 2/Corr. 1, March 28, 2000; CLCS/3/Rev. 3, February 6, 2001; and, CLSC/3/Rev. 3/Corr. 1, May 22, 2001. The current set of rules can be found at CLCS/40/Rev. 1, April 17, 2008.

48. Commission, *Scientific and Technical Guidelines of the Commission on the Limits of the Continental Shelf*, 5th Session, May 13, 1999, CLCS/11.

49. Commission, *Scientific and Technical Guidelines*, 6th Session, September 3, 1999, CLCS/11/Add., specifically "Annex II: Flowcharts and Illustrations Summarizing the Procedure for Establishing the Outer Limits of the Continental Shelf."

50. Commission, *Training Manual for Delineation of the Outer Limits of the Continental Shelf Beyond 200 Nautical Miles and for Preparation of Submissions to the Commission on the Limits of the Continental Shelf* (New York: Division for Ocean Affairs and the Law of the Sea, 2006). Other resource material compiled by the Commission to assist coastal states in preparing their submissions include *Practical Suggestions Concerning the Final Preparation And Deposit of Submissions to the CLCS Through the Secretary-General of the United Nations*, CLCS/61 (New York: Division for Ocean Affairs and the Law of the Sea, 2009); *Outline for a Five-Day Training Course for Delineation of the Outer Limits of the Continental Shelf Beyond 200 Nautical Miles and for*

Preparation of a Submission of a Coastal State to the Commission on the Limits of the Continental Shelf, CLCS/24 (New York: Division for Ocean Affairs and the Law of the Sea, 2000). See www.un.org/depts/los/clcs_new/practicalsuggestions.pdf and www.un.org/depts/los/clcs_new/commission_documents.htm.

51. Ron Macnab, "Submarine Elevations and Ridges: Wild Cards in the Poker Game of UNCLOS Article 76," *Ocean Development and International Law* 39, No. 2 (2008): 225.

52. These documents are available at www.un.org/Depts/los/clcs_new/commission_submissions.html.

53. See Australia, "Executive Summary, Submission to the Commission," Submissions, November 15, 2004; and Australia, "Summary of Recommendations," Submissions, April 9, 2008, www.un.org/Depts/los/clcs_new/commission_submissions.html.

54. UN General Assembly, *Oceans and the Law of the Sea,* 57th Session, February 21, 2003, A/Res 57/141, par. 40, http://documents-dds-ny.un.org/doc/UNDOC/GEN/N02/547/54/Doc/N0254754.Doc.

55. UN, *Directory of National Sources of Training, Advice and Expertise and Technological Services* (New York: Division for Ocean Affairs and the Law of the Sea, 2011), http://www.un.org/Depts/los/clcs_new/sources/sources_of_expertise.html.

56. See, for example, Harald Brekke and Philip Symonds, "Submarine Ridges and Elevation of Article 76 in Light of Published Summaries of Recommendations of the Commission on the Limits of the Continental Shelf," *Ocean Development and International Law* 42, No. 4 (2011): 289–306.

57. International Tribunal for the Law of the Sea, *North Sea Continental Shelf (Federal Republic of Germany v Denmark; Federal Republic of Germany v The Netherlands) (Judgment) International Court of Justice,* Report 3, 1969, par. 19, 23; and International Tribunal for the Law of the Sea, *Delimitation of the Maritime Boundary in the Bay of Bengal (Bangladesh/Myanmar) (Judgment),* Report 4, March 14, 2012, par. 409, quoted in McDorman, "The Continental Shelf," 184.

58. McDorman, "The Continental Shelf," 186.

59. For in-depth discussions of the ECS regime provisions, see Bjarni Már Magnusson, *The Continental Shelf Beyond 200 Nautical Miles:*

Delineation, Delimitation and Dispute Settlement (Leiden: Brill Nijhoff, 2015); Nordquist, Moore, and Heidar, eds., *Legal and Scientific Aspects of Continental Shelf Limits*; and Suarez, *The Outer Limits of the Continental Shelf.*

60. UN, *Convention on the Law of the Sea*, Article 76(1), 27.

61. Heidar, "Legal Aspects of Continental Shelf Limits," 24.

62. UN, *Convention on the Law of the Sea*, Article 77, 28.

63. Ibid., Article 87(1), 30–31.

64. Ibid., Article 76(4)(b), 27.

65. Commission, *Scientific and Technical Guidelines*, par. 6.1.1–6.1.2, 29.

66. Ibid., par. 6.4.1(iv), 34.

67. MacDougall, Personal Correspondence, May 11, 2011.

68. Ruth Jackson in Patrick Potter, *UNCLOS Storyboard* (Halifax: NP, 2011), 2.

69. Commission, *Scientific and Technical Guidelines*, par. 6.1.3, 29, par. 2.1.13, 8.

70. UN, *Convention on the Law of the Sea*, Article 76(4)(a)(i), 27.

71. Jackson in Potter, *UNCLOS Storyboard*, 3.

72. UN, *Convention on the Law of the Sea*, Article 76(4)(a)(ii), 27.

73. See McDorman, "The Continental Shelf," 193.

74. UN, *Convention on the Law of the Sea*, Article 76(5), 27.

75. Ibid., Article 76(8), 28.

76. Canada, "Proposal by Canada on the Continental Shelf Boundary Commission," *Revised Single Negotiating Text II*, April 29, 1976, 321–322, quoted in Suarez, *The Outer Limits of the Continental Shelf*, 77–78.

77. UN, *Convention on the Law of the Sea*, Annex II, Article 3(1), 112.

78. See Suzette V. Suarez, "The Commission on the Limits of the Continental Shelf and its Function to Provide Scientific and Technical Advice," *Chinese Journal of International Law* 12, No. 2 (2013): 343, 346. Neither the Commission nor its subcommissions are bound by the advice provided by an individual commissioner. See ibid., 351. For more detailed examinations of the Commission, see Anna Cavnar, "Accountability and the Commission on the Limits of the Continental Shelf: Deciding Who Owns the Ocean Floor," *Cornell International Law Journal* 42, No. 3 (2009): 387–440;

Vladimir Jares, "The Continental Shelf Beyond 200 Nautical Miles: The Work of the Commission on the Limits of the Continental Shelf and the Arctic," *Vanderbilt Journal of Transnational Law* 42, No. 4 (2009): 1265–1306; Oystein Jensen, "The Commission on the Limits of the Continental Shelf: An Administrative, Scientific or Judicial Institution?," *Ocean Development and International Law* 45, No. 2 (2014): 171–185; Magnusson, *The Continental Shelf Beyond 200 Nautical Miles*, especially chapters 3–5; Ted McDorman, "The Role of the Commission on the Limits of the Continental Shelf: A Technical Body in a Political World," *International Journal of Marine and Coastal Law* 17, No. 3 (2002): 301–324; and Suarez, *The Outer Limits of the Continental Shelf*, 75–117.

79. UN, *Convention on the Law of the Sea*, Article 76(8), 28.
80. Department of External Affairs, *Law of the Sea conference — New York portion of the Ninth Session, March 3–April 4, 1980: Assessment by the Canadian Delegation*, 2.
81. UN, *Convention on the Law of the Sea*, Annex II, Article 2(1), 111.
82. Ibid., Annex II, Article 2(3), 112.
83. See States Parties to UNCLOS, *Report of the Twenty-Second Meeting of States Parties*, 22nd Meeting, July 11, 2012, SPLOS/251, par. 83, 14.
84. See, for example, Commission on the Limits of the Continental Shelf, *Progress of Work in the Commission on the Limits of the Continental Shelf: Statement by the Chair*, 32nd Session, September 24, 2013, CLCS/80, par. 77, 16.
85. Commission on the Limits of the Continental Shelf, *Progress of Work in the Commission on the Limits of the Continental Shelf: Statement by the Chair*, 39th Session, December 21, 2015, CLCS/91, par. 44, 7.
86. UN, *Convention on the Law of the Sea*, Article 76(8), 28.
87. Ibid., Annex II, Article 5, 112.
88. Commission on the Limits of the Continental Shelf, Rules of Procedure of the Commission on the Limits of the Continental Shelf, 21st Session, April 17, 2008, CLCS/40/Rev.1, Rule 35(2), 13.
89. UN, *Convention on the Law of the Sea*, Annex II, Article 6(2), 113.
90. Ibid., Annex II, Article 8, 113.
91. Piers R.R. Gardiner, "The Limits of the Area Beyond National Jurisdiction — Some Problems with Particular Reference to the

Role of the Commission on the Limits of the Continental Shelf," in *Maritime Boundaries and Ocean Resources,* ed. G. Blake (London: Croom Helm, 1987), 69.

92. Jares, "The Continental Shelf Beyond 200 Nautical Miles," 169.

93. Cavnar, "Accountability and the Commission on the Limits," 407.

94. Sara Cockburn, Sue Nichols, Dave Monahan, and Ted McDorman, "Intertwined Uncertainties: Policy and Technology on the Juridical Continental Shelf," paper presented at the 2001 Advisory Board on the Law of the Sea (ABLOS) Conference: Accuracies and Uncertainties in Maritime Boundaries and Outer Limits, Monaco, October 15–17, 2001, 7. See also McDorman, "The Role of the Commission on the Limits of the Continental Shelf," 301–324; and McDorman, "The Continental Shelf," 192.

95. Ted L. McDorman, "The Continental Shelf Beyond 200 NM: Law and Politics in the Arctic Ocean," *Journal of Transnational Law and Policy* 18, No. 2 (2009): 155–193.

96. UN, *Convention on the Law of the Sea,* Article 77(3), 28.

97. Ibid., Article 77(2), 28.

98. Office of the Prime Minister, "Prime Minister Stephen Harper Announces New Arctic Offshore Patrol Ships," news release, July 9, 2007, http://news.gc.ca/web/article-en.do?crtr. sj1D=&mthd=advSrch&crtr.mnthndVl=&nid=335789&crtr. dpt1D=&crtr.tp1D=&crtr.lc1D=&crtr.yrStrtVl=2008&crtr. kw=&crtr.dyStrtVl=26&crtr.aud1D=&crtr.mnthStrtVl=2&crtr. yrndVl=&crtr.dyndVl=.

99. *Delimitation of the Maritime Boundary in the Bay of Bengal* (Bangladesh/Myanmar), par. 408, quoted in McDorman, "The Continental Shelf," 192.

100. UN, *Convention on the Law of the Sea,* Article 82(3), 29.

101. See Alexei A. Zinchenko, "Emerging Issues in the Work of the Commission on the Limits of the Continental Shelf," in *Legal and Scientific Aspects of Continental Shelf Limits,* eds. Myron H. Nordquist, John Norton Moore, and Thomas H. Heidar (Leiden: Martinus Nijhoff, 2004), 234–240; and Heidar, "Legal Aspects of Continental Shelf Limits," 31.

102. For a discussion of the challenges facing the Commission, see Ted McDorman, "The Role of the Commission the Limits of the

Continental Shelf," 301–324. See also Cavnar, "Accountability and the Commission on the Limits of the Continental Shelf," 387–440; Ron Macnab, "The Case for Transparency in the Delimitation of the Outer Continental Shelf in Accordance with UNCLOS Article 76," *Ocean Development and International Law* 35, No. 11 (2004): 1–17; and Surya P. Subedi, "Problems and Prospects for the Commission on the Limits of the Continental Shelf in Dealing with Submissions by Coastal States in Relation to the Ocean Territory Beyond 200 Nautical Miles," *International Journal of Marine and Coastal Law* 26, No. 13 (2011): 413–431.

103. A list of the submissions received, subcommissions struck and recommendations provided can be found at UN, Division for Ocean Affairs and the Law of the Sea, "Submissions, Through the Secretary-General of the United Nations To the Commission on the Limits of the Continental Shelf, pursuant to article 76, paragraph 8, of the United Nations Convention on the Law of the Sea of 10 December 1982," www.un.org/depts/los/clcs_new/commission_submissions.htm.

104. Clive Schofield and Robert van de Poll, "Exploring the Outer Continental Shelf: Working Paper," paper prepared for the International Workshop on Further Consideration of the Implementation of Article 82 of the United Nations Convention on the Law of the Sea, Beijing, China, November 2012, 26–30. See International Seabed Authority, "Annex 5," *Implementation of Article 82 of the United Nations Convention on the Law of the Sea: Report of an International Workshop Convened by the International Seabed Authority in Collaboration with the China Institute for Marine Affairs in Beijing the People's Republic of China, November 26–30, 2012*, ISA Technical Study, No. 12 (Kingston, Jamaica: ISA, 2012), 69–81.

105. Magnusson, *The Continental Shelf Beyond 200 Nautical Miles*, 44.

106. States Parties to UNCLOS, "Report of the Seventeenth Meeting of States Parties," 17th Meeting, July 16, 2007, SPLOS/164, par. 56, 12.

107. Commission on the Limits of the Continental Shelf, *Progress of Work in the Commission on the Limits of the Continental Shelf: Statement by the Chair*, 13th Session, September 5, 2012, CLCS/76; Commission, *Decision Regarding the Conditions of Service of the Members of the Commission on the Limits of the Continental Shelf*, 24th Meeting, June 1, 2014, 1.

108. Commission, *Progress of Work*, 37th Session, April 20, 2015, CLCS/85, Item 4(12), 4.

109. Ibid.

110. Commission, *Progress of Work*, 13th Session, CLCS/76, par. 13, 4.

111. Commission, *Rules of Procedure of the Commission on the Limits of the Continental Shelf*, 31st Session, April 17, 2008, CLCS/40/Rev. 1, Rule 51(4bis), 18.

112. Commission, *Progress of Work*, 37th Session, 4.

113. UN General Assembly, *Oceans and the Law of the Sea*, 62nd Session, December 4, 2007, A/62/L.27, especially pars. 39 and 41, 6.

114. For examples, see States Parties to the UNCLOS, *Decision on Issues Related to the Workload of the Commission on the Limits of the Continental Shelf*, 17th Meeting, June 26, 2007, SPLOS/162; Commission, *Decision Regarding the Workload of the Commission on the Limits of the Continental Shelf*, 21st Meeting, June 16, 2011, SPLOS/229; Commission, *Decision Regarding the Conditions of Service*, 24th Meeting, SPLOS/276.

115. UN, *Convention on the Law of the Sea*, Article 208(1), 74.

116. Ibid., Article 79, 28–29.

117. See Wylie Spicer, "Canada, the Law of the Sea and International Payments: Where Will the Money Come From," *SPP Research Papers* 8, No. 31 (2015): 7.

CHAPTER 3: SCIENTIFIC RESEARCH AND THE LAW OF THE SEA CONVENTION

1. The principal source of information for this chapter was David Mosher, who not only gave generously of his time in interviews but also reviewed the penultimate draft of the chapter and kindly agreed to allow his detailed and extensive comments to be incorporated into the text. I would also like to thank Michel Goguen, Tim Janzen, and Scott Youngblut for meeting with me to explain techniques used to gather bathymetric data. Thanks to Tim and Scott for their written comments. Thanks are also due to Jacob Verhoef, and Richard MacDougall for all the times they discussed bathymetric and seismic surveys with me and for their valuable oral and written comments that were incorporated into earlier publications. Other sources of information are indicated in the endnotes.

2. Ron Macnab, "The Case for Transparency in the Delimitation of the Outer Continental Shelf in Accordance with UNCLOS Article 76," *Ocean Development and International Law* 35, No. 1 (2004): 3.

3. Canadian Hydrographic Service, *Arctic Ice Camp Field Manual, 2009* (Ottawa: Department of Fisheries and Oceans, 2009), 20.

4. Ibid., 20.

5. Tim Janzen, Interview with the author, October 16, 2015.

6. Canadian Hydrographic Service, *Arctic Ice Camp Field Manual, 2009*, 20.

7. Canadian Hydrographic Service, *Final Field Report: United Nations Convention on the Law of the Sea (UNCLOS): Borden Island* (Ottawa: Department of Fisheries and Oceans), 5.

8. Patrick Potter, Interview with the author, May 26, 2015.

9. Ibid.

10. Ron Verrall, *Alpha Ridge Test of Appurtenance (ARTA): Newsletter #5*, March 27, 2008, www.arcticnewsletters.com/Newsletters_2008/Introduction08.html.

11. Ron Verrall and Trine Dahl-Jensen, *The Continental Shelf Project: 9. Field Report (Alert)*, ed. Henrik Hojmark Thomsen, April 18, 2006, http://a76.dk/greenland_uk/north_uk/gr_n_expeditions_uk/lorita-1_uk/9_fieldreport.html.

12. Potter, Interview, May 26, 2015.

13. Ibid.

14. Ibid.

15. Ron Verrall and Trine Dahl-Jensen, *The Continental Shelf Project: 3. Field Report (Alert)*, ed. Henrik Hojmark Thomsen, April 3, 2006, http://a76.dk/greenland_uk/north_uk/gr_n_expeditions_uk/lorita-1_uk/2_fieldreport.html.

16. Potter, Interview, May 26, 2015.

17. Ibid.

18. Ibid.

19. Ibid.

20. H. Ruth Jackson and Patrick Potter, eds., *Expedition Report for the Alpha Ridge Test of Appurtenance (ARTA) 2008*, Open File 6842 (Halifax: Geological Survey of Canada, 2011), 17.

21. Ron Verrall, *Alpha Ridge Test of Appurtenance (ARTA): Newsletter*

#10, April 3, 2008, www.arcticnewsletters.com/Newsletters_2008/Introduction08.html.

22. I am indebted to Mike Gorveatt for explaining the methodology for conducting reflection seismology from a remote ice camp. Interview with the author, May 27, 2015.

23. Ron Verrall, *Alpha Ridge Test of Appurtenance (ARTA): Newsletter #18*, April 17–18, 2008, www.arcticnewsletters.com/Newsletters_2008/Introduction08.html.

24. Thanks to Desmond Manning, Marine Geoscience Technologist, Geological Survey of Canada, Natural Resources Canada, for providing this paragraph's description of the airgun. Interview with the author, May 27, 2015.

25. Borden Chapman, Interview with the author, May 27, 2015.

26. Kai Böggild, Interview with the author, May 26, 2015.

27. Ibid.

28. UN Commission on the Limits of the Continental Shelf, 5th Session, May 13, 1999, CLCS/11, par. 8.2.19, 42.

29. As David Mosher explained, "If the earth were completely round and completely homogenous, then the gravitational field (the pull of gravity) would be the same everywhere; however, the earth is neither round nor homogenous, so there exists a gravitation field that varies with latitude and with perturbations in its shape as well as with rock types. Perturbations occur at all scales. In general, the earth's field consists of very long wavelength features and we're looking for smaller changes on top of these long wavelength. These shorter wavelength changes that tell us about the underlying rock types." Personal Correspondence, March 1, 2016.

30. Walta-Anne Rainey, "Meet the People Video Gallery: Walta-Anne Rainey," Government of Canada, http://www.science.gc.ca/eic/site/063.nsf/eng/h_EE4C9599.html.

31. Ibid.

32. Paola Travaglini, Interview with the author, May 27, 2015.

33. Ibid.

34. UN, Commission on the Limits of the Continental Shelf, 5th Session, May 13, 1999, CLCS/11, par. 5.4.7, 28.

35. Walli Rainey, Interview with author, May 26, 2015.

36. Commission on the Limits of the Continental Shelf, *Scientific and Technical Guidelines of the Commission on the Limits of the Continental Shelf*, 5th Session, May 13, 1999, CLCS/11, par. 1.3, 5.

37. Harald Brekke and Philip A. Symonds, "The Ridge Provisions of Article 76 of the UN Convention on the Law of the Sea," *Legal and Scientific Aspects of Continental Shelf Limits*, eds. M.H. Nordquist, J.N. Moore, and T.H. Heidar (Leiden: Martinus Nijhoff, 2004), 175.

38. UN, *Convention on the Law of the Sea*, Article 76(4)(a)(i–ii), 27.

39. Commission on the Limits of the Continental Shelf, *Scientific and Technical Guidelines*, CLCS/11, par. 5.4.5, 28.

40. UN, *Convention on the Law of the Sea*, Article 76(5), 27.

41. Commission on the Limits of the Continental Shelf, *Scientific and Technical Guidelines*, CLCS/11, par. 4.2.2–4.2.3, 22.

42. For more detailed examinations of sea floor highs, see Harald Brekke and Philip Symonds, "Submarine Ridges and Elevation of Article 76 in Light of Published Summaries of Recommendations of the Commission on the Limits of the Continental Shelf," *Ocean Development and International Law* 42, No. 4 (2011): 289–306; and "The Ridge Provisions of Article 76," 169–197; Jianjun Gao, "The Seafloor High Issue in Article 76 of UNCLOS: Some Views from the Perspective of Legal Interpretation," *Ocean Development and International Law* 43, No. 2 (2012): 119–145; and Ron Macnab, "Submarine Elevations and Ridges: Wild Cards in the Poker Game of UNCLOS Article 76," *Ocean Development and International Law* 39, No. 2 (2008): 223–234.

43. Macnab, "Submarine Elevations and Ridges," 224.

44. Commission, *Scientific and Technical*, par. 7.2.11, 37.

45. "The Outer Limit of the Continental Shelf in the Arctic Ocean," *Legal and Scientific Aspects of Continental Shelf Limits*, eds. M.H. Nordquist, J.N. Moore, and T.H. Heidar (Leiden: Martinus Nijhoff, 2004), 303.

46. Macnab, "Submarine Elevations and Ridges," 224.

47. Commission, *United Nations Convention on the Law of the Sea*, Article 76(3), 27.

48. Ibid., Article 76(6), 27.

49. Commission, *Scientific and Technical Guidelines*, par. 2.1.11, 8.

50. Thomas H. Heidar, "Legal Aspects of Continental Shelf Limits" in *Legal and Scientific Aspects of Continental Shelf Limits*, eds. M.H.

Nordquist, J.N. Moore, and T.H. Heidar (Leiden: Martinus Nijhoff, 2004), 28.

51. UN, Commission on the Limits of the Continental Shelf, *Scientific and Technical Guidelines of the Commission on the Limits of the Continental Shelf*, par. 7.3.1 (a) and (b), 37.

CHAPTER 4: ICE CAMPS AND ICEBREAKERS

1. J. Richard MacDougall, Jacob Verhoef, Wendell Sanford and Christian Marcussen, "Challenges of Collecting Data for Article 76 in Ice Covered Waters of the Arctic," paper presented to the Advisory Board on the Law of the Sea, Monaco, 2008, 8, http://a76.dk/greenland_uk/north_uk/index.html.
2. Marie-Danielle Smith, "Liberals Continue Conservative Quest for North Pole: Third Multi-Million-Dollar Data-Gathering Mission to Go Ahead This Summer, Says Global Affairs Canada," *Embassy*, February 17, 2016.
3. The distances were calculated using http://timeanddate.com.
4. Tim Janzen, Interview with the author, October 16, 2015.
5. Ibid.
6. David Mosher, Personal Correspondence, February 16, 2016.
7. Ibid.
8. Ruth Jackson, Interview with the author, May 26, 2015.
9. Mosher, Personal Correspondence, February 16, 2016.
10. Patrick Potter, Interview with the author, May 26, 2015.
11. Ibid.
12. Mike Gorveatt, Interview with the author, May 27, 2015.
13. Ronald Verrall, *A Guide to Arctic Field Trips 2001*, www.arcticnewsletters.com/Field_guide/Guide.pdf, 36.
14. Janzen, Interview, November 27, 2015.
15. Ibid.
16. UNCLOS Continental Shelf Project, *UNCLOS Continental Shelf Project — Arctic Ocean — Update #1*, March 2, 2009, http://a76.dk/xpdf/arctic_field_trip_2009_newsletter_01.pdf, 3.

17. Ron Verrall and Trine Dahl-Jensen, *The Continental Shelf Project: 8. Field Report (Alert)*, ed. Henrik Hojmark Thomsen, April 17, 2006, http://a76.dk/greenland_uk/north_uk/gr_n_expeditions_uk/lorita-1_uk/8_fieldreport.html, 1; and Verrall and Dahl-Jensen, *The Continental Shelf Project: 13. Field Report (Alert)*, May 2, 2006, http://a76.dk/greenland_uk/north_uk/gr_n_expeditions_uk/lorita-1_uk/x13_fieldreport.html, 2.

18. Mosher, Personal Correspondence, February 16, 2016.

19. These experiences of erratic climatic conditions and their consequences for achieving research goals were drawn from interviews with Richard MacDougall and Jacob Verhoef, February 8, 2008, and August 21, 2008.

20. Travaglini, Interview, May 27, 2015.

21. MacDougall, Interview, December 21, 2007.

22. Jackson, Interview, May 26, 2015.

23. Ibid.

24. Ibid.

25. Ibid.

26. Ibid.

27. Ibid.

28. Ibid.

29. MacDougall, Interview, December 21, 2007.

30. Jackson, Interview, May 26, 2015.

31. Mosher, Personal Correspondence, February 16, 2016.

32. Ibid.

33. MacDougall, Verhoef, Sanford, and Marcussen, "Challenges of Collecting Data for Article 76 in Ice Covered Waters of the Arctic," 6.

34. UNCLOS Continental Shelf Project, *UNCLOS Continental Shelf Project — Arctic Ocean — Update #0*, March 2009, http://a76.dk/xpdf/arctic_field_trip_2009_newsletter_00.pdf, 1–2.

35. Ron Verrall, *A Guide to Arctic Field*, 17–18.

36. Ron Verrall and Trine Dahl-Jensen, *The Continental Shelf Project: 3. Field Report (Alert)*, ed. Henrik Hojmark Thomsen, April 3, 2006, http://a76.dk/greenland_uk/north_uk/gr_n_expeditions_uk/lorita-1_uk/3_fieldreport.html, 1.

37. Ron Verrall, *Alpha Ridge Test of Appurtenance (ARTA): Newsletter #2*, March 24, 2008, www.arcticnewsletters.com/Newsletters_2008/Introduction08.html, 1.

38. UNCLOS Continental Shelf Project, *UNCLOS Continental Shelf Project — Arctic Ocean — Update #11*, March 27–28, 2009, http://a76.dk/xpdf/arctic_field_trip_2009_newsletter_11.pdf, 2.

39. Janzen, Interview, October 16, 2015.

40. Canadian Hydrographic Service, *Arctic Ice Camp Field Manual, 2009* (Ottawa: Department of Fisheries and Oceans, 2009), 24.

41. I am indebted to Dick MacDougall and Jacob Verhoef for explaining this problem from a historical perspective. Interview with the author, August 21, 2008.

42. Verrall, *A Guide to Arctic Field Trips.*

43. Jackson, Interview, May 26, 2015.

44. Criminal Code, S.C., ch. C-21 (2003).

45. Jackson, Interview, May 26, 2015.

46. Ibid.

47. Potter, Interview, May 26, 2015.

48. UNCLOS Continental Shelf Project, *UNCLOS Continental Shelf Project — Arctic Ocean — Update #9*, March 22–23, 2009, http://a76.dk/xpdf/arctic_field _trip_2009_ncwsletter_09.pdf, 2.

49. Jackson, Interview, May 26, 2015.

50. ArcticNet, "CCGS Amundsen Helicopter Crash," *ArcticNet*, 2013, www.arcticnet.ulaval.ca/news/helicopter.php; and CBC News, "Helicopter Crash Victims' Bodies Arrive in Nunavut," *CBC News*, September 11, 2013, www.cbc.ca/news/canada/north/helicopter-crash-victims-bodies-arrive-in-nunavut-1.1699434.

51. Mosher, Personal Correspondence, February 16, 2016.

52. Jackson, Interview, May 26, 2015.

53. Mosher, Personal Correspondence, February 16, 2016.

54. Mosher, Interview, May 26, 2015.

55. Sonya Dehler, Interview with the author, May 27, 2015.

56. Ibid.

57. Desmond Manning, Interview with the author, May 27, 2015.

58. Ibid.

59. Ibid.

60. Borden Chapman, Interview with the author, May 27, 2015.

61. Ibid.

62. Verhoef, Interview, August 21, 2008.

63. Walli Rainey, Interview with the author, May 26, 2015.

64. Canadian Hydrographic Service, *Arctic Ice Camp Field Manual 2009*, 34.

65. Ibid.

66. Mosher, Personal Correspondence, February 16, 2016.

67. Rainey, Interview, May 26, 2015.

68. Ibid.

69. Ibid.

70. Canadian Hydrographic Service, *Arctic Ice Camp Field Manual 2009*, 37.

71. Ibid., 17, 21.

72. Gorveatt, Interview, May 27, 2015.

73. Ron Verrall, *Project Cornerstone: Newsletter #12*, March 22, 2009, www.arcticnewsletters.com/Newsletters_2009/Newsletter09-12.pdf, 3.

74. Gorveatt, Interview, May 27, 2015.

75. Ibid.

76. Ibid.

77. Thanks to Mike Gorveatt and Ruth Jackson for sharing the experience with me. Interviews with the author, May 27 and May 26, 2015, respectively.

78. UNCLOS Continental Shelf Project, *Update #16: UNCLOS Continental Shelf Project: Ward Hunt Island Ice Camp,* April 7–11, 2009, http://a76.dk/xpdf/arctic_field_trip_2009_newsletter_16.pdf, 2.

79. Ibid.

80. Ron Verrall, *Project Cornerstone: Newsletter #15*, April 6, 2009, www.arcticnewsletters.com/Newsletters_2009/Newsletter09-15.pdf, 1.

81. Gorveatt, Interview, May 27, 2015.

82. Dehler, Interview, May 27, 2015.

83. Ibid.

84. Gorveatt, Interview, May 27, 2015.

85. Manning, Interview, May 27, 2015.

86. Gorveatt, Interview, May 27, 2015.

87. Rainey, Interview, May 26, 2015.

88. Gorveatt, Interview, May 27, 2015.

89. Ibid.

90. David Mosher, "Meeting the Ship 2," *Third Canada-U.S. Extended Continental Shelf Survey in the Arctic (2010), Government of Canada*, www.science.gc.ca/eic/site/063.nsf/eng/h_C571F860.html# wsF18EA089.

91. Jackson, Interview, May 26, 2015.

92. Dehler, Interview, May 27, 2015.

93. Ron Verrall, *Alpha Ridge Test of Appurtenance (ARTA): Newsletter #1*, March 23, 2008, www.arcticnewsletters.com/Newsletters_2008/ Introduction08.html.

94. Ibid., 2.

95. Ron Verrall and Trine Dahl-Jensen, *The Continental Shelf Project: 7. Field Report (Alert)*, ed. Henrik Hojmark Thomsen, April 12, 2006, http://a76.dk/greenland_uk/north_uk/gr_n_expeditions_uk/ lorita-1_uk/7_fieldreport.html, 1.

96. Verrall, *A Guide to Arctic Field Trips*, 11–12.

97. Verhoef and MacDougall, Interviews, August 21, 2008.

98. Janzen, Interview, November 27, 2015.

99. Ibid.

100. UNCLOS Continental Shelf Project, *UNCLOS Continental Shelf Project — Arctic Ocean — Update #0*, March 2009, http://a76.dk/ xpdf/arctic_field_trip_2009_newsletter_00.pdf, 2.

101. Ibid.

102. Verrall, *Alpha Ridge Test of Appurtenance (ARTA): Newsletter #2*, 1.

103. Ibid.

104. Ron Verrall, *Alpha Ridge Test of Appurtenance (ARTA): Newsletter #6*, March 29, 2008, www.arcticnewsletters.com/Newsletters_2008/ Introduction08.html, 2.

105. UNCLOS Continental Shelf Project, *UNCLOS Continental Shelf Project — Arctic Ocean — Update #7*, March 9–20, 2009, http://a76. dk/xpdf/arctic_field_trip_2009_newsletter_07.pdf, 2

106. UNCLOS Continental Shelf Project, *UNCLOS Continental Shelf Project — Arctic Ocean — Update #10*, March 24–26, 2009, http:// a76.dk/xpdf/arctic_field_trip_2009_newsletter_10.pdf, 1.

107. I am indebted to Tim Janzen for explaining these procedures. Interview, November 27, 2015.

108. The detailed planning of an ice camp is described in Verrall, *A Guide to Arctic Field Trips,* 61–62.

109. Thanks to Tim Janzen for explaining these sanitation arrangements. Interview, November 27, 2015.

110. Ibid.

111. Mosher, Personal Correspondence, February 16, 2016.

112. Ibid.

113. Janzen, Interview, November 27, 2015.

114. Mosher, Personal Correspondence, February 16, 2016.

115. I am indebted to Mike Gorveatt for describing life in a remote camp. Interview, May 27, 2015.

116. Ibid.

117. H. Ruth Jackson and Patrick Potter, eds., *Expedition Report for the Alpha Ridge Test of Appurtenance (ARTA) 2008,* Open File 6842 (Ottawa: Geological Survey of Canada, 2011).

118. Ron Verrall and Trine Dahl-Jensen, *The Continental Shelf Project: 2. Field Report (Alert),* ed. Henrik Hojmark Thomsen, April 2, 2006, http://a76.dk/greenland_uk/north_uk/gr_n_expeditions_uk/lorita-1_uk/2_fieldreport.html.

119. Verrall, *A Guide to Arctic Field Trips,* 55.

120. UNCLOS Continental Shelf Project, *UNCLOS Continental Shelf Project — Arctic Ocean — Update #1,* March 2, 2009, http://a76.dk/xpdf/arctic_field_trip_2009_newsletter_01.pdf, 1.

121. Ron Verrall, *Alpha Ridge Test of Appurtenance (ARTA): Newsletter #16,* April 14, 2008, www.arcticnewsletters.com/Newsletters_2008/Introduction08.html, 1.

122. UNCLOS Continental Shelf Project. *Update #16,* 2.

123. Mosher, Interview, May 26, 2015. Ruth Jackson concurred.

124. Ibid.

125. Mosher and Jackson, Interviews, May 26, 2015.

126. Ibid.

127. Rainey, Interview, May 26, 2015.

128. Mosher, Interview, May 26, 2015.

129. Rainey, Interview, May 26, 2015.

130. Ibid.

131. Ibid.

132. Mosher and Rainey, Interviews. May 26, 2015.

133. Rainey, Interview. May 26, 2015.

134. Hans Böggild, Interview with the author, May 28, 2015.

135. Kai Böggild, *Arctic Survey Expedition (2014)* (Halifax: Natural Resources Canada, 2014), 23, www.science.gc.ca/default.asp?lang= En&n=80F7E17E-1.

136. Ibid., 24.

137. Ibid.

138. Mosher, Interview, May 26, 2015.

139. Rainey, Interview, May 26, 2015.

140. Kevin DesRoches, Interview with the author, May 26, 2015.

141. Hans Böggild, Interview, May 28, 2015.

142. Rainey, Interview. May 26, 2015.

143. Mosher, Personal Correspondence, February 16, 2016.

144. Scott Youngblut, Interview with the author, October 16, 2015.

145. Hans Böggild, Interview, May 28, 2015.

146. Walta Ann Rainey, "Living On Board a Ship in the Arctic," *Third Canada-U.S. Extended Continental Shelf Survey in the Arctic (2010)*, *Government of Canada*, www.science.gc.ca/eic/site/063.nsf/eng/h_ C571F860.html#wsF18EA089.

147. Mosher, Personal Correspondence, February 16, 2016.

148. Hans Böggild, Interview, May 28, 2015.

149. Jackson, Interview, May 26, 2015.

150. John Shimeld, "Meet the People Video Gallery: John Shimeld," Government of Canada, http://www.science.gc.ca/eic/site/063.nsf/ eng/h_000D448A.html.

151. Manning, Interview, May 27, 2015.

152. Kai Böggild, Interview with the author, May 26, 2015.

153. Travaglini, Interview, May 27, 2015.

154. Hans Böggild, Interview, May 28, 2015.

155. Patrick Potter, "Meet the People Video Gallery: Patrick Potter," Government of Canada, http://www.science.gc.ca/eic/site/063.nsf/ eng/h_DA483C56.html.

156. Rainey, Interview, May 26, 2015.

157. Rainey, "Meet the People Video Gallery: Walta-Anne Rainey."

158. Hans Böggild, Interview, May 28, 2015.

159. Dehler, Interview, May 27, 2015.

160. Hans Böggild, Interview, May 28, 2015.

161. Gorveatt, Interview, May 27, 2015.

162. Rainey, Interview, May 26, 2015.

163. Gorveatt, Interview, May 27, 2015.

CHAPTER 5: THE ARCTIC EXTENDED CONTINENTAL SHELF SURVEYS

1. A large debt of gratitude is due to David Mosher, who not only gave generously of his time in interviews but also reviewed the penultimate draft of this chapter and kindly allowed his comments to be incorporated into the text.

2. Jacob Verhoef, David C. Mosher, and Stephen R. Forbes, "Defining Canada's Extended Continental Shelves," in *Voyage of Discovery: Fifty Years of Marine Research at Canada's Bedford Institute of Oceanography*, eds. David N. Nettleship, Donald C. Gordon, C.F. Michael Lewis, and Michel P. Latremouille (Dartmouth: Bedford Institute of Oceanography, 2014), 408.

3. "Canada's Extended Continental Shelf: Canada's Program," *Department of Foreign Affairs, Trade and Development*, August 15, 2012.

4. Jacob Verhoef and Dick MacDougall, "Delineating Canada's Continental Shelf According to the United Nations Convention on the Law of the Sea," *Ocean Sovereignty* 3, No. 1 (2008): 1–2.

5. Natural Resources Canada, "A Catalyst for Canada's Arctic Research," Polar Continental Shelf Program, 2010, http://publications.gc.ca/collections/collection_2011/rncan-nrcan/M78-4-1-1-2010.pdf.

6. The discussion of Hobson's Choice Ice Island is drawn from the interview with Mike Gorveatt, May 27, 2015.

7. See Franz Tessensohn, H. Ruth Jackson and Ian D. Reid, "The Tectonic Evolution of Nares Strait: Implications of New Data," *Polarforschung* 74, No. 1–3 (2006): 191–198.

8. Chapman, Interview, May 27, 2015.

9. I am indebted to Gordon Oakey for explaining this survey. Interview with the author, May 28, 2015.

10. Mosher, Interview, May 26, 2015.

11. Ibid.

12. DesRoches, Interview, May 26, 2015.

13. Ibid.

14. Ibid.

15. Ibid.

16. Ibid.

17. Ibid.

18. Ruth Jackson, Interview with the author, May 26, 2015.

19. Ibid.

20. Nelson Ruben, John Ruben, and Jonah Nakimayak, "Marine Mammals Monitor Report," *Field Report for 2007 the CCGS Louis S. St-Laurent Seismic Cruise to the Canada Basin,* ed. H. Ruth Jackson, Open File 5818 (Ottawa: Geological Survey of Canada, 2008), 139.

21. Ibid.

22. Ibid.

23. Potter, Interview, May 26, 2015.

24. Potter, Personal Correspondence, May 10, 2016.

25. Kai Böggild, *Arctic Survey Expedition (2014)* (Halifax: Natural Resources Canada, 2014), 23, www.science.gc.ca/default.asp?lang=En &n=80F7E17E-1.

26. Ibid.

27. Thanks to Patrick Potter for sharing this memory. Interview, May 26, 2015.

28. Verhoef, Mosher, and Forbes, "Defining Canada's Extended Continental Shelves," 411.

29. J. Richard MacDougall, Jacob Verhoef, Wendell Sanford, and Christian Marcussen, "Challenges of Collecting Data for Article 76 in Ice Covered Waters of the Arctic," paper presented to the Advisory Board on the Law of the Sea, Monaco, 2008, 8, http://a76. dk/greenland_uk/north_uk/index.html.

30. Verhoef, Mosher, and Forbes, "Defining Canada's Extended Continental Shelves," 409.

31. See Treasury Board of Canada Secretariat, *Supplementary Estimates (B) 2014–2015* (Ottawa: Department of Finance, 2014).

32. For further details of the mission, see H. Ruth Jackson and Trine Dahl-Jensen, "Sedimentary and Crustal Structure from the Ellesmere Island and Greenland Continental Shelves onto the Lomonosov Ridge, Arctic

Ocean," *Geophysical Journal International* 182, No. 1 (2010): 11–35.

33. J. Richard, MacDougall, Wendell Sanford, and Jacob Verhoef, "Ice and No Ice: The Canadian UNCLOS Bathymetric Mapping Program," paper presented to the Canadian Hydrographic Conference and National Surveyors Conference, Canada, 2008.

34. Ron Verrall and Trine Dahl-Jensen, *The Continental Shelf Project: 9. Field Report (Alert)*, ed. Henrik Hojmark Thomsen, April 18, 2006, http://a76.dk/greenland_uk/north_uk/gr_n_expeditions_uk/lorita-1_uk/9_fieldreport.html, 1.

35. Ibid.

36. Ron Verrall and Trine Dahl-Jensen, *The Continental Shelf Project: 1. Field Report (Alert)*, ed. Henrik Hojmark Thomsen, March 30, 2006, http://a76.dk/greenland_uk/north_uk/gr_n_expeditions_uk/lorita-1_uk/1_fieldreport.html.

37. John Shimeld, Personal Correspondence, May 17, 2016.

38. Ibid.

39. Ibid.

40. Ron Verrall and Trine Dahl-Jensen, *The Continental Shelf Project: 2. Field Report (Alert)*, ed. Henrik Hojmark Thomsen, April 2, 2006, http://a76.dk/greenland_uk/north_uk/gr_n_expeditions_uk/lorita-1_uk/2_fieldreport.html.

41. Ron Verrall and Trine Dahl-Jensen, *The Continental Shelf Project: 14. Field Report (Alert)*, ed. Henrik Hojmark Thomsen, May 9, 2006, 2, http://a76.dk/greenland_uk/north_uk/gr_n_expeditions_uk/lorita-1_uk/x14_fieldreport.html.

42. Verhoef, Jacob, David C. Mosher, and Stephen R. Forbes, "Defining Canada's Extended Continental Shelves," in *Voyage of Discovery: Fifty Years of Marine Research at Canada's Bedford Institute of Oceanography: A Commemorative Volume in Celebration of the 50th Anniversary of the Bedford Institute of Oceanography, Dartmouth, Nova Scotia, Canada, 1962-2012*, eds. David N. Nettleship, Donald C. Gordon, C.F. Michael Lewis, and Michel P. Latremouille (Dartmouth: Bedford Institute of Oceanography, 2014), 411.

43. Ibid.

44. Verhoef and MacDougall, "Delineating Canada's Continental Shelf," 4.

45. Potter, Interview, May 26, 2015.

46. MacDougall, Sanford, and Verhoef, "Ice and No Ice," 6.

47. MacDougall, Verhoef, Sanford, and Marcussen, "Challenges of Collecting Data for Article 76," 14.

48. MacDougall, Sanford, and Verhoef, "Ice and No Ice," 7.

49. Ibid.

50. Unless otherwise indicated, the details of the mission are drawn from Richard MacDougall, former Director, Law of the Sea Project, Canadian Hydrographic Service, Department of Fisheries and Oceans, Interview, Halifax, Nova Scotia, December 21, 2007, and Personal Correspondence, March 16, 2008.

51. For details of the survey, see T. Funck, R. Jackson and J. Shimeld, "The Crustal Structure of the Alpha Ridge, Arctic Ocean," paper presented at the 2010 Fall Meeting, American Geophysical Union, San Francisco, California December 13–17, 2010.

52. Ron Verrall, *Alpha Ridge Test of Appurtenance (ARTA): Newsletter #2*, March 24, 2008, www.arcticnewsletters.com/Newsletters_2008/Introduction08.html, 1.

53. Verrall, *Alpha Ridge Test of Appurtenance (ARTA): Newsletter #1*.

54. Ibid., 4; Verrall, *Alpha Ridge Test of Appurtenance (ARTA): Newsletter #2*, 1; and "Newsletters from the High Arctic: Field Work and Newsletters: Field Trial 2008," 2. All three documents can be accessed from www.arcticnewsletters.com/index.htm#Field Work.

55. Ron Verrall, *Alpha Ridge Test of Appurtenance (ARTA): Newsletter #16*. April 14, 2008, www.arcticnewsletters.com/Newsletters_2008/Introduction08.html, 1.

56. Gorveatt, Interview, May 27, 2015.

57. Potter, Interview, May 26, 2015.

58. Ibid.

59. H. Ruth Jackson and Patrick Potter, eds., *Expedition Report for the Alpha Ridge Test of Appurtenance (ARTA) 2008*, Open File 6842 (Halifax: Geological Survey of Canada, 2011), 6.

60. Ibid.

61. Ibid., 24, 37.

62. Ibid., 20, 21.

63. Ibid., 4.

64. Ibid., 36.

65. Ron Verrall, *Alpha Ridge Test of Appurtenance (ARTA): Newsletter #18,* April 17–18, 2008, www.arcticnewsletters.com/Newsletters_2008/ Introduction08.html, 4.

66. Ibid.

67. Jackson and Potter, "Expedition Report for the Alpha Ridge Test of Appurtenance," 4.

68. Verrall, *Alpha Ridge Test of Appurtenance (ARTA): Newsletter #18,* 1.

69. Verrall, *Alpha Ridge Test of Appurtenance (ARTA): Newsletter #19,* April 26, 2008, www.arcticnewsletters.com/Newsletters_2008/ Introduction08.html, 1–2.

70. Ibid.

71. MacDougall, Personal Correspondence, May 1, 2011.

72. Verhoef, Interview, March 7, 2011.

73. UNCLOS Continental Shelf Project, *UNCLOS Continental Shelf Project — Arctic Ocean — Update #0,* March 2009, http://a76.dk/ xpdf/arctic_field_trip_2009_newsletter_00.pdf, 1.

74. UNCLOS Continental Shelf Project, *Update #14: UNCLOS Continental Shelf Project: Ward Hunt Island Ice Camp,* March 31–April 1, 2009, http://a76.dk/xpdf/arctic_field_trip_2009_newsletter_14.pdf, 1.

75. UNCLOS Continental Shelf Project, *UNCLOS Continental Shelf Project — Arctic Ocean — Update #10,* March 24–26, 2009, http://a76.dk/xpdf/ arctic_field_trip_2009_newsletter_10.pdf, 1, and *Update #14,* 1.

76. UNCLOS Continental Shelf Project, *Update #14,* 1.

77. Verhoef, Mosher, and Forbes, "Defining Canada's Extended Continental Shelves," 5.

78. Jon Biggar, *Final Field Report: UNCLOS 2009 — Ward Hunt Island Project CHSDIR Project Number: 4012989* (Dartmouth: Canadian Hydrographic Service, 2009), 4, 12.

79. Oakey, Interview, May 28, 2015.

80. Ibid.

81. Mosher and Oakey. For further details of the survey see Jurgen Matzka, Thorkild M. Rasmussen, Arne V. Olesen, Jens Emil Nielsen, Rene Forsberg, Nils Olsen, John Halpenny, and Jacob Verhoef, "A New Aeromagnetic Survey of the North Pole and the Arctic Ocean North of Greenland and Ellesmere Island," *Earth Planets Space* 62 (2010): 829–832.

82. Mosher, Interview, May 26, 2015.

83. Oakey, Interview, May 28, 2015.

84. Christian Marcussen and the LOMROG II Scientific Party, *Lomonosov Ridge off Greenland 2009 (LOMROG II) — Cruise Report* (Copenhagen, Geological Survey of Denmark and Greenland, 2011), 9, http://a76.dk/greenland_uk/north_uk/gr_n_expeditions_uk/lomrog_2009_uk/index.html.

85. Ibid., 7.

86. Ibid.

87. Ibid.

88. Ibid.

89. Ron Verrall, *Project Cornerstone: Newsletter #2*, March 22, 2009, www.arcticnewsletters.com/Newsletters_2009/Newsletter09-02.pdf, 3.

90. The Scope, "In Our Yellow Explorer AUV," May 1, 2012, http://thescope.ca/science/in-our-yellow-explorer-auv. The Explorer AUV was built by the same Vancouver-based company, International Submarine Engineering Ltd., that subsequently built the AUVs for Canada's Arctic Extended Continental Shelf Program.

91. Ron Verrall, *Project Cornerstone: Newsletter #7*, March 29, 2009, www.arcticnewsletters.com/Newsletters_2009/Newsletter09-07.pdf., 2.

92. Ron Verrall, *Project Cornerstone: Newsletter #18*, April 10, 2009, www.arcticnewsletters.com/Newsletters_2009/Newsletter09-18.pdf, 2.

93. Ron Verrall, *Project Cornerstone: Newsletter #4*, March 24, 2009, www.arcticnewsletters.com/Newsletters_2009/Newsletter09-4.pdf, 1.

94. Ibid.

95. Ibid.

96. David C. Mosher, J. Shimeld, D. Hutchinson, N. Lebedeva-Ivanova, and C.B. Chapman, "Source Submarine Mass Movements and their Consequences," *Advances in Natural and Technological Hazards Research* 31 (2012), 147.

97. For a detailed discussion of the mission see H. Ruth Jackson, ed., *Field Report for 2007 the CCGS Louis S. St-Laurent Seismic Cruise to the Canada Basin*, Open File 5818 (Ottawa: Geological Survey of Canada, 2008).

98. Thanks to Borden Chapman for explaining the necessary adaptations. Interview, May 27, 2015.

99. Chapman, Personal Correspondence, May 28, 2016.

100. Chapman, Interview, May 27, 2015.

101. Chapman, Personal Correspondence, May 28, 2016.

102. MacDougall, Personal Correspondence, March 8, 2008.

103. Chapman, Personal Correspondence, May 28, 2016.

104. Ibid.

105. Chapman, Interview, May 27, 2015.

106. Ibid.

107. Jackson, Interview, May 26, 2015.

108. Chapman, Personal Correspondence, May 28, 2016.

109. Ibid.

110. Ibid.

111. Jackson, ed., *Field Report for 2007*, 3, 4.

112. Ibid., 4.

113. Ibid., 5.

114. My thanks to Borden Chapman who read the section below describing the acquisitions and alterations made to the equipment on CCGS *Louis S. St-Laurent* between its 2007 and 2008 ECS surveys and kindly allowed his comments to be incorporated into the text. Personal Correspondence, May 28, 2016.

115. Details of the mission are contained in H.R. Jackson and K.J. DesRoches, eds., *2008 Louis S. St-Laurent Field Report August 22 — October 3, 2008,* Open File 6275 (Ottawa: Geological Survey of Canada, 2010). See also Jon Biggar, *UNCLOS Project — Canada Basin 2008* (Dartmouth: Canadian Hydrographic Service, 2008).

116. Jackson and DesRoches, eds., *2008 Louis S. St-Laurent Field Report.*

117. D.R. Hutchinson, H.R. Jackson, J.W. Shimeld, C.B. Chapman, J.R. Childs, T. Funck, and R.W. Rowland, "Acquiring Marine Data in the Canada Basin, Arctic Ocean," *EOS* 90, No. 23 (2009): 197.

118. See Ibid., 197–198.

119. Mosher, Interview, May 26, 2015.

120. Ibid.

121. Ibid.

122. Hutchinson, Jackson, Shimeld, Chapman, Childs, Funck, and Rowland, "Acquiring Marine Data in the Canada Basin, Arctic Ocean," 197.

123. Jon Biggar, *UNCLOS Project — Canada Basin 2008* (Dartmouth: Canadian Hydrographic Service, 2008), 2.

124. For a detailed account of the mission, see D.C. Mosher, J.W. Shimeld and D.R. Hutchinson, *2009 Canada Basin Seismic Reflection and Refraction Survey, Western Arctic Ocean: CCGS Louis S. St-Laurent Expedition Report*, Open File 6343 (Ottawa: Geological Survey of Canada, 2009).

125. Ibid., iv.

126. Verhoef and MacDougall, Interviews, December 7, 2009.

127. Mosher, Shimeld, and Hutchinson, *2009 Canada Basin Seismic Reflection and Refraction Survey*, iv.

128. Verhoef and MacDougall, Interview, December 7, 2009.

129. Lawrence Taylor, "September 16, 2009 — Seamount," Second Canada-U.S. Extended Continental Shelf Survey in the Arctic: Expedition Blogs, 2009, www.science.gc.ca/default.asp?lang=En&n=9293A4FA-1, 25.

130. David Mosher, "Meet the People Video Gallery: David Mosher," Government of Canada, http://www.science.gc.ca/eic/site/063.nsf/eng/h_80703280.html.

131. Verhoef, Mosher, and Forbes, "Defining Canada's Extended Continental Shelves," Figure B, 412. For a discussion of the 2010 AUV deployment, see Tristan Crees, Chris D. Kaminski, and James Ferguson, "UNCLOS Under-Ice Survey: A Historic AUV Deployment in the High Arctic," *Sea Technology* 51, No. 12 (2010), 39–44.

132. Jacob Verhoef and Julian Goodyear, "Defining Canada's Extended Continental Shelf in the Arctic," *Meridian*, Spring/Summer 2011, 6.

133. Ibid.

134. Ibid. For more detailed information about the mission, see Crees, Kaminski, and Ferguson, "UNCLOS Under-Ice Survey," 6.

135. Janzen, Interview, November 27, 2015.

136. MacDougall, Personal Correspondence, May 1, 2011.

137. D.C. Mosher, J. Verhoef; P. Travaglini; and R. Pederson, "A Deep Water, Under-Ice AUV: Extended Continental Shelf Mapping in the Arctic," paper presented to the Arctic Technology Conference, Copenhagen, Denmark, March 23–25, 2015, 3.

138. Verhoef, Interview, March 7, 2011.

139. Janzen, Interview, November 27, 2015.

140. MacDougall, Personal Correspondence, May 1, 2011.

141. Paul Watson, "Explorer Sub Embarks on Maiden Mission," *Toronto Star*, April 13, 2010.

142. Mosher, Verhoef, Travaglini and Pederson, "A Deep Water, Under-Ice AUV," 1.

143. Verhoef, Mosher, and Forbes, "Defining Canada's Extended Continental Shelves," 412.

144. Mosher, Verhoef, Travaglini, and Pederson, "A Deep Water, Under-Ice AUV," 1.

145. Ibid.

146. Janzen, Interview, November 27, 2015.

147. Verhoef, Interview, March 7, 2011.

148. D.C. Mosher, J.W. Shimeld, and C.B. Chapman, *2010 Canada Basin Seismic Reflection and Refraction Survey, Western Arctic Ocean: CCGS Louis S. St-Laurent Expedition Report August 4–September 15, 2010 Kugluktuk, NWT to Kugluktuk, NWT,* Open File 6343 (Ottawa: Geological Survey of Canada, 2011).

149. David Mosher, "Communication is Critical" and "Goodbye," *Third Canada-U.S. Extended Continental Shelf Survey in the Arctic (2010),* Government of Canada, http://www.science.gc.ca/eic/site/063.nsf/eng/h_C571F860.html#wsF18EA089.

150. Mosher, "Communication is Critical."

151. Mosher, Shimeld, and Chapman, *2010 Canada Basin Seismic Reflection and Refraction Survey,* iv.

152. David Mosher, "The End," *Third Canada-U.S. Extended Continental Shelf Survey in the Arctic (2010),* Government of Canada, http://www.science.gc.ca/eic/site/063.nsf/eng/h_C571F860.html#wsF18EA089.

153. D.C. Mosher, *2011 Canadian High Arctic Seismic Expedition: CCGS Louis S. St-Laurent Expedition Report,* Open File 7053 (Ottawa: Geological Survey of Canada, 2012), iv.

154. Stephen Forbes, Interview with the author, September 30, 2011.

155. Chapman, Interview, May 27, 2015.

156. Mosher, Verhoef, Travaglini, and Pederson, "A Deep Water, Under-Ice AUV," 3.

157. Chapman, Interview, May 27, 2015.

158. Forbes, Interview, September 30, 2011.

159. Mosher, Verhoef, Travaglini, and Pederson, "A Deep Water, Under-Ice AUV," 1.

160. Chapman, Interview, May 27, 2015.

161. Chapman, Personal Correspondence, May 28, 2016.

162. Mosher, *2011 Canadian High Arctic Seismic Expedition*, iv.

163. Mosher, Verhoef, Travaglini, and Pederson, "A Deep Water, Under-Ice AUV," 4.

164. G.N. Oakey, R.W. Saltus, and J.W. Shimeld, "A Crustal Structure Model of the Beaufort-Mackenzie Margin, Southern Canada Basin." Paper presented to the Arctic Technology Conference, Copenhagen, Denmark, March 23–25, 2015, 1.

165. Forbes, Interview, September 30, 2011. For a discussion of how much was accomplished prior to the 2011 survey vis-a-vis the original survey plans, see Verhoef and Goodyear, "Defining Canada's Extended Continental Shelf in the Arctic," 108.

166. See Treasury Board of Canada Secretariat, *Supplementary Estimates (B) 2014–2015* (Ottawa: 2014).

167. See Foreign Affairs, Trade and Development Foreign Affairs, Trade and Development Canada, "Backgrounder — Canada's Continental Shelf Submission," Canada's Continental Shelf Submission, December 6, 2013, www.international.gc.ca/media/aff/news-communiques/2013/12/09a_bg1.aspx?lang=eng.

168. Alex Boutilier, "Canada Scrambled for Data to Back North Pole Claims, Documents Show," *Toronto Star*, August 13, 2014.

169. Janzen, Interview, November 27, 2015.

170. Foreign Affairs, Trade and Development Canada, "Harper Government Launches First of Two Scientific Surveys to Complete Canada's Arctic Continental Shelf Submission," news release, August 8, 2014.

171. Thanks go to Tracey Clarke, Senior Naval Architect, Canadian Coast Guard, who led the project to purchase, engineer, and install the multibeam sounder on CCGS *Louis S. St-Laurent*, for providing details of the installation.

172. Youngblut, Interview, October 16, 2015.

173. Ibid.

174. Ibid.

175. Travaglini, Interview, May 27, 2015.

176. Ibid.

177. Youngblut, Interview, October 16, 2015.

178. Travaglini, Interview, May 27, 2015.

179. D.C. Mosher, *Canadian Polar Expedition, 2014 Canada Basin, Arctic Ocean, August 9-September 17, 2014: St. John's, NL to Kugluktuk, NWT: CCGS Louis S. St-Laurent and Terry Fox* (Halifax: Natural Resources Canada, 2014), 2.

180. Ibid., 86.

181. Thanks to Borden Chapman for explaining the transit problems resulting from the heavy ice conditions and relative sizes of the icebreakers, for reading my description of it and for allowing his comments to be incorporated into this paragraph. Interview, May 27, 2015.

182. Mosher, *Canadian Polar Expedition, 2014*, 14.

183. Ibid., 14, 85.

184. Ibid., 14.

185. Ibid., 85–86.

186. Ibid., 86.

187. Quoted in Fred McCague, "The North Pole and Beyond," *Western Ports and Terminals*, November 2014, 50–51.

188. Mosher, *Canadian Polar Expedition, 2014*, 87.

189. Ibid., 87–88.

190. Ibid., 88; and Kai Böggild, *Arctic Survey Expedition*, 44.

191. Mosher, *Canadian Polar Expedition, 2014*, 2.

192. Ibid.

193. Scott Youngblut, *Final Field Report: Amundsen Basin Survey: UNCLOS 2015*, CHSDIR Project Number 4013733 (Dartmouth: Canadian Hydrographic Service, 2014), 4.

194. Walli Rainey, Interview with the author, May 26, 2015.

195. S.A. Dehler, ed., *Canadian Polar Expedition 2015, Amundsen Basin, Arctic Ocean; August 6–September 17, 2015; Tromsø, Norway to Kugluktuk, NWT; CCGS Louis S. St-Laurent and CCGS Terry Fox*, (Ottawa: Geological Survey of Canada), 2016, 2.

196. Unless otherwise indicated, the details of this voyage are drawn from the interview with Scott Youngblut, October 16, 2015.

197. The discussion of the AUV in this paragraph is drawn from Scott Youngblut, Interview, October 16, 2015.

198. Dehler, *Canadian Polar Expedition 2015*, 2.

199. Ibid.

200. Ibid.

201. Ibid.

202. Ibid.

203. Dehler, Personal Correspondence, August 31, 2016.

204. I am indebted to Mary-Lynn Dickson (chief scientist for the 2016 survey and director of the UNCLOS Program, Geological Survey of Canada, Natural Resources Canada) for providing details of the mission and for allowing her written description of the survey to be incorporated into the text. Personal Correspondence, October 1, 2016, and Interview, October 4, 2016.

205. D.C. Mosher, J. Shimeld, D. Hutchinson, D. Chian, N. Lebedeva-Ivanova, and R. Jackson, "Canada Basin Revealed," paper presented to the Arctic Technology Conference, Houston, Texas, December 3–5, 2012, 1.

206. Mosher, Verhoef, Travaglini, and Pederson, "A Deep Water, Under-Ice AUV," 1.

207. D.C. Mosher, C.B. Chapman, J. Shimeld, H. R. Jackson, D. Chian, J. Verhoef, D. Hutchinson, N. Lebedeva-Ivanova, and R. Pederson, "High Arctic Marine Geophysical Data Acquisition." *Leading Edge* 32, No. 5 (2013): 524.

208. Jacob Verhoef, "Meet the People Video Gallery: Jacob Verhoef," Government of Canada, http://www.science.gc.ca/eic/site/063.nsf/eng/h_3F700A30.html.

209. Oakey, Interview, May 28, 2015.

210. Jackson, Interview, May 26, 2015.

211. Ibid.

212. Ibid.

213. This conclusion is confirmed in Verhoef, Mosher, and Forbes, "Defining Canada's Extended Continental Shelves," 413.

214. Oakey, Interview, May 28, 2015. For detailed discussions of the scientific findings see Mosher, Shimeld, Hutchinson, Chian, Lebedeva-Ivanova, and Jackson, "Canada Basin Revealed"; and Oakey, Saltus, and Shimeld, "A Crustal Structure Model of the Beaufort-Mackenzie Margin, Southern Canada Basin."

215. Oakey, Interview, May 28, 2015.

216. Jackson, Interview, May 26, 2015.

217. In essence, it is a mega-volcano. Shimeld, "Meet the People Video Gallery: John Shimeld."

218. Oakey, Interview, May 28, 2015. For a more detailed discussion of the findings see Funck, Jackson, and Shimeld, "The Crustal Structure of the Alpha Ridge at the Transition to the Canadian Polar Margin: Results from a Seismic Refraction Experiment," 1–26.

219. Oakey, Interview, May 28, 2015.

220. Harald Brekke and Philip Symonds, "Submarine Ridges and Elevation of Article 76 in Light of Published Summaries of Recommendations of the Commission on the Limits of the Continental Shelf," *Ocean Development and International Law* 42, No. 4 (2011): 304.

221. Oakey, Interview, May 28, 2015.

222. Ibid.

223. Jackson, Interview, May 26, 2015.

224. Ibid.

225. Government of Demark, *Partial Submission of the Government of the Kingdom of Denmark together with the Government of Greenland to the Commission on the Limits of the Continental Shelf: the Northern Continental Shelf of Greenland: Executive Summary* (Copenhagen: Geological Survey of Denmark and Greenland, 2014), 14.

226. Government of Russia, *Partial Revised Submission of the Russian Federation to the Commission on the Limits of the Continental Shelf in Respect of the Russian Federation in the Arctic Ocean: Executive Summary* (Moscow: Government of Russia, 2015), 6.

227. Jackson, Interview, May 26, 2015.

228. Verhoef, Mosher, and Forbes, "Defining Canada's Extended Continental Shelves," 411. For a more detailed discussion of the findings, see Jackson and Dahl-Jensen, "Sedimentary and Crustal Structure from the Ellesmere Island and Greenland Continental Shelves onto the Lomonosov Ridge, Arctic Ocean," 11–35.

229. Mosher, Interview, May 26, 2015.

230. Ibid.

231. Thanks to Gordon Oakey for sharing these findings pertaining to the Amundsen Basin. Interview with the author, May 28, 2015.

232. Travaglini, Interview, May 27, 2015.

233. Oakey, Interview, May 28, 2015.

CHAPTER 6: CANADA'S SUBMISSION AND OTHER OUTSTANDING ISSUES

1. The full submission is confidential and not publicly available; however, the executive summary of the *Partial Submission of Canada to the Commission on the Limits of the Continental Shelf regarding its continental shelf in the Atlantic Ocean* is found at www. international.gc.ca/arctic-arctique/assets/pdfs/continental_shelf_ summary-plateau_continental_resume-eng.pdf. Geological and geomorphological evidence indicates that Canada's continental margin in the Atlantic Ocean "extends continuously from offshore Nova Scotia in the south, along the Grand Banks to the northern tip of Labrador." See Government of Canada, *Partial Submission of Canada to the Commission on the Limits of the Continental Shelf Regarding Its Continental Shelf in the Atlantic Ocean: Executive Summary* (Ottawa: Government of Canada, 2013), 2. The area included in Canada's partial submission comprises some 1.2 million square kilometres, which is "roughly the size of Alberta and Saskatchewan, combined." See John Baird, "Address by Minister Baird to Media Concerning Canada's Continental Shelf Submissions," *Global Affairs Canada*, December 9, 2013, www.international.gc.ca/media/aff/speeches-discours/2013/12/09a.aspx?lang=eng.

2. Consider, for example, the following government news release: "Canadian scientists are conducting mapping surveys to establish with certainty where the country's continental shelf begins and ends. Particulars of the outer limits of these continental shelves will be submitted to the UN Commission on the Limits of the Continental Shelf by the end of 2013 — 10 years after Canada ratified the Convention." See also Government of Canada, "Government Commemorates 25th Anniversary of UN Convention on the Law of the Sea," news release, December 10, 2007, http://news. gc.ca/web/article-en.do?mthd=advSrch&crtr.mnthndVl=4&crtr. mnthStrtVl=1&crtr.page=3&nid=366839&crtr.yrndVl=2014&crtr. kw=continental+shelf&crtr.yrStrtVl=2002&crtr.dyStrtVl=1&crtr. dyndVl=11. See also Government of Canada, "Northern Strategy — Backgrounder," news release, March 10, 2008, http://news. gc.ca/web/article-en.do?mthd=advSrch&crtr.mnthndVl=4&crtr.

mnthStrtVl=1&crtr.page=4&nid=384529&crtr.yrndVl=2014&crtr.
kw=continental+shelf&crtr.yrStrtVl=2002&crtr.dyStrtVl=1&crtr.
dyndVl=1; Government of Canada, "Minister Cannon Concludes Arctic
Visit and Holds Media Availability," news release, 7 April 2010, http://
news.gc.ca/web/article-en.do?mthd=advSrch&crtr.mnthndVl=4&crtr.
mnthStrtVl=1&crtr.page=2&nid=523209&crtr.yrndVl=2014&crtr.
kw=continental+shelf&crtr.yrStrtVl=2002&crtr.dyStrtVl=1&crtr.
dyndVl=11; Lawrence Cannon, "Address by Minister Cannon at Launch
of Statement on Canada's Arctic Foreign Policy," news release, August
20, 2010, http://news.gc.ca/web/article-en.do?mthd=advSrch&crtr.
mnthndVl=4&crtr.mnthStrtVl=1&crtr.page=6&nid=554739&crtr.
yrndVl=2014&crtr.kw=continental+shelf&crtr.yrStrtVl=2002&crtr.
dyStrtVl=1&crtr.dyndVl=11; Government of Canada, "Canada
Holds Bilateral Talks with Russia," news release, September 16, 2010,
http://news.gc.ca/web/article-en.do?mthd=advSrch&crtr.mnthnd
Vl=4&crtr.mnthStrtVl=1&crtr.page=4&nid=560449&crtr.
yrndVl=2014&crtr.kw=continental+shelf&crtr.yrStrtVl=2002&crtr.
dyStrtVl=1&crtr.dyndVl=11; Government of Canada, "Canadian
Coast Guard Ship Louis S. St-Laurent Departs for Arctic Support
Science and Northern Shipping," news release, July 2011, http://news.
gc.ca/web/articleen.do?mthd=advSrch&crtr.mnthndVl=4&crtr.
mnthStrtVl=1&crtr.page=2&nid=610769&crtr.yrndVl=2014&crtr.
kw=continental+shelf&crtr.yrStrtVl=2002&crtr.dyStrtVl=1&crtr.
dyndVl=11.

3.   Steven Chase, "Harper Orders New Draft of Arctic Seabed Claim to
Include North Pole," *Globe and Mail*, December 4, 2013.

4.   John Baird, Minister of Foreign Affairs, "Address by Minister Baird to
Media Concerning Canada's Continental Shelf Submissions."

5.   Ron Macnab, "How Harper Froze out Scientists and Triggered an
Arctic Debacle," *Chronicle Herald*, June 17, 2015.

6.   Bob Weber, "Stephen Harper's North Pole Bid Caught Bureaucrats by
Surprise," *Canadian Press*, November 9, 2014.

7.   Ibid.

8.   See Eighteenth Meeting of the States Parties, *Decision Regarding the
Workload of the Commission on the Limits of the Continental Shelf
and the Ability of States, Particularly Developing States, to Fulfil the*

Requirements of Article 4 of Annex II to the United Nations Convention on the Law of the Sea, as well as the Decision Contained in SPLOS/72, Paragraph (A), 18th Meeting, June 20, 2008, SPLOS/183, www.un.org/depts/los/clcs_new/issues_ten_years.htm.

9. Government of Canada, *Preliminary Information Concerning the Outer Limits of the Continental Shelf of Canada in the Arctic Ocean* (New York: Commission on the Limits of the Continental Shelf, 2013), 2, www.un.org/Depts/los/clcs_new/submissions_files/preliminary/can_pi_en.pdf.

10. Their preliminary information is available at www.un.org/Depts/los/clcs_new/commission_preliminary.html.

11. Mary Ellen MacIntyre, "Scientist Speaks Out On Muzzling by Ottawa," *Chronicle Herald,* May 19, 2015; and Dick Pickrill, "Canada Scuttles its Ocean Science Capability," *Chronicle Herald,* May 27, 2015.

12. Steven Campana, Interview on CBC News, May 19, 2015, www.cbc.ca/player/Featured/News/ID/2667449500/.

13. Chris Turner, *The War on Science: Muzzled Scientists and Willful Blindness in Stephen Harper's Canada* (Vancouver: Greystone Books, 2013); and Carol Linnitt, "Canada's War on Science Brings Us International Shame," *Huffington Post,* November 9, 2015, www.huffingtonpost.ca/carol-linnitt/war-on-science-canada_b_5775054.html.

14. Professional Institute of the Public Service of Canada, *The Big Chill: Silencing Public Interest Science, A Survey* (Ottawa: Professional Institute of the Public Service of Canada, 2013), 3–4, www.pipsc.ca/portal/page/portal/website/issues/science/pdfs/bigchill.en.pdf.

15. Chronicle Herald, "Ottawa Obsessed with Control in Muzzling Scientists," Editorial, *Chronicle Herald,* May 21, 2015.

16. *An Open Letter on Science to Canadian Prime Minister Stephen Harper,* October 21, 2014, https://s3.amazonaws.com/ucs-documents/science-and-democracy/canada-letter-word-by-country.pdf.

17. MacIntyre, "Scientist Speaks out on Muzzling by Ottawa."

18. Ron Macnab, quoted in Marie-Danielle Smith, "Canada Spent $20 million on North Pole Claim Mission," *Embassy,* September 30, 2015. Since his retirement from the Geological Survey of Canada, Macnab has worked as a private consultant advising other countries on law of sea matters.

19. See Ron Macnab, "How Harper Froze Out Scientists and Triggered an

Arctic Debacle," June 17, 2015. See also Macnab, quoted in Danielle Smith, "Canada Spent $20 million on North Pole Claim Mission."

20. See Parliament of Canada, *Governance in the Public Service of Canada: Ministerial and Deputy Ministerial Accountability*, 1st Session, 38th Parliament, 2004–2005, www.parl.gc.ca/housepublications/publication.aspx?docid=1812721&file=33; and Canada, Privy Council Office, "Governing Responsibly — A Guide for Ministers and Ministers of State," Information Resources, 2003, www.pco-bcp.gc.ca/index.asp?lang=eng&page=information&sub=publications&doc=aarchives/ag-gr/2003/guide-eng.htm#I, 1.

21. Government of Canada, "Government of Canada Welcomes New Mapping Data on Canada's North," news release, August 8, 2008, http://news.gc.ca/web/article-en.do?mthd=advSrch&crtr.mnthndVl= 4&crtr.mnthStrtVl=1&crtr.page=1&nid=413799&crtr. yrndVl=2014&crtr.kw=continental+shelf&crtr.yrStrtVl=2002&crtr. dyStrtVl=1&crtr.dyndVl=11.

22. Macnab, "How Harper Froze Out Scientists."

23. Weber, "Stephen Harper's North Pole Bid Caught Bureaucrats by Surprise."

24. See Ted McDorman, *Salt Water Neighbors: International Ocean Law Relations between the United States and Canada* (New York: Oxford University Press, 2009), especially 155–163 and 197–206. See also Michael Byers, *Who Owns the Arctic? Understanding Sovereignty Disputes in the North* (Vancouver: Douglas and McIntyre, 2009); and Michael Byers and James S. Baker, "Crossed Lines: The Curious Case of the Beaufort Sea Maritime Boundary Dispute," *Ocean Development and International Law* 43, No. 11 (2012), 70–95.

25. UN General Assembly, "Denmark and Canada: Agreement Relating to the Delimitation of the Continental Shelf Between Greenland and Canada," Treaty Series, No. 13550, December 17, 1973, https://treaties.un.org/doc/Publication/UNTS/Volume%20950/volume-950-I-13550-English.pdf. The sovereignty of Hans Island was not addressed in the treaty. The 2012 referendum agreement has yet to be translated into a legally binding treaty.

26. Macnab, "How Harper Froze Out Scientists." As a consultant, Macnab continues to have extensive contact with both Danish and Russian

scientists on continental shelf matters.

27. Arctic Ocean Conference, *Ilulissat Declaration*.

28. Arctic Council, *Iqaluit Declaration*.

29. Sources in the public domain indicating the existence of an agreement include Martin Breum, "Is Harper's Pole Claim an Arctic Deal-Breaker?" *Arctic Journal Opinion*, December 19, 2013; and Mikå Mered, "Editor's Briefing: A Polar Play," *Arctic Journal*, December 16, 2014.

30. See Kingdom of Denmark, *Strategy for the Arctic 2011-2020* (Copenhagen: Kingdom of Denmark, 2011), http://um.dk/en/~/media/UM/English-site/Documents/Politics-and-diplomacy/Greenland-and-The-Faroe-Islands/Arctic%20strategy.pdf.

31. Alex Boutilier, "Canada Scrambled for Data to Back North Pole Claims, Documents Show," *Toronto Star*, August 13, 2014, www.thestar.com/news/canada/2014/08/13/canada_scrambled_for_data_to_back_north_pole_claims_documents_show.html.

32. See Marc Lanteigne, "Arctic Sovereignty: More Lines on the Ice," *Arctic Journal*, December 16, 2014. See also Macnab, "How Harper Froze out Scientists"; and Mered, "Editor's Briefing," 2.

33. Kingdom of Denmark, *Partial Submission of the Government of the Kingdom of Denmark together with the Government of Greenland to the Commission on the Limits of the Continental Shelf: The Northern Continental Shelf of Greenland* (Copenhagen: Kingdom of Denmark, 2015).

34. Martin Breum, "The Claim Game," *Arctic Journal*, December 19, 2014, http://arcticjournal.com/opinion/1206/claim-game.

35. Macnab, "How Harper Froze out Scientists," quoted in Max Paris, "Arctic Resources Claim Deadline Today for Canada." *CBC News*, December 6, 2013, www.cbc.ca/news/politics/arctic-resources-claim-deadline-today-for-canada-1.2452794.

36. Quoted in Max Paris, "Arctic Resources Claim Deadline Today for Canada."

37. Macnab, "How Harper Froze out Scientists."

38. Andrea Charron, Joël Plouffe, and Stéphane Roussel, "The Russian Arctic Hegemon: Foreign Policy Implications for Canada." *Canadian Foreign Policy Journal* 18, No. 1 (2012): 38.

39. Ibid., 47.

40. Compare the area delineated in Map 2 of Russia's 2001 submission (www.un.org/depts/los/clcs_new/submissions_files/submission_rus.htm) with that outlined in Figure 1, 7, of its *Partial Revised Submission of the Russian Federation to the Commission on the Limits of the Continental Shelf in Respect of the Continental Shelf of the Russian Federation in the Arctic Ocean: Executive Summary,* April 2015, (www.un.org/depts/los/clcs_new/submissions_files/submission_rus_rev1.html).

41. See Sergey Lavrov, Russian Minister of Foreign Affairs, "International Cooperation for Arctic Prosperity" *Embassy,* January 27, 2016; Alexander Darchiev, "Arctic Co-operation Must Continue." *Embassy,* June 3, 2015; and Kari Roberts, "Why Russia will Play by the Rules in the Arctic." *Canadian Foreign Policy Journal* 21, No. 2 (2015): 112–128.

42. Greg Poelzer, Executive Chair of the International Centre for Northern Governance and Development, University of Saskatchewan, quoted in Marie-Danielle Smith, "Liberals Continue Conservative Quest for North Pole," *Embassy,* February 17, 2016.

43. Marie-Danielle Smith, "Trudeau Government Announces 'Rational' Shift in Arctic Policy, Will Seek to Work with Russia," *National Post,* October 1, 2016, http://news.nationalpost.com/news/canada/canadian-politics/trudeau-government-announces-rational-shift-in-arctic-policy-will-seek-to-work-with-russia.

44. Commission, *Rules of Procedure of the Commission on the Limits of the Continental Shelf,* 21st Session, April 17, 2008, CLCS/40/Rev. 1, Annex III, Part II, par. 2, 27.

45. Government of Russia, *Partial Revised Submission of the Russian Federation to the Commission on the Limits of the Continental Shelf in Respect of the Russian Federation in the Arctic Ocean: Executive Summary* (Moscow: Government of Russia, 2015), 13.

46. Commission, *Rules of Procedure,* 21st Session, CLCS/40/Rev. 1, Rule 51(4ter), 18.

47. Commission, *Statement by the Chairperson of the Commission on the Limits of the Continental Shelf on the Progress of Work in the Commission,* 26th Session, September 17, 2010, CLCS/68, par. 57, 13–14.

48. United Nations Convention on the Law of the Sea, November 16, 1994, 1833 U.N.T.S. 397, Article 82(4), 29.

49. Canada, Department of External Affairs, *Law of the Sea Conference — New York Portion of the Ninth Session, March 3–April 4, 1980: Assessment by the Canadian Delegation* (Ottawa: Government of Canada, 1980), 2.

50. The discussion of these questions draws on insights from Jacob Verhoef, Richard MacDougall, and Ted McDorman, as well as from a detailed examination of reports of the International Seabed Authority and scholarly papers assessing the challenges posed by Article 82 for both ECS states and the International Seabed. See *Implementation of Article 82 of the United Nations Convention on the Law of the Sea*, ISA Technical Study, No. 12; *Non-living Resources of the Continental Shelf Beyond 200 Nautical Miles: Speculations on the Implementation of Article 82 of the United Nations Convention on the Law of the Sea*, ISA Technical Study, No. 5 (Kingston, Jamaica: International Seabed Authority, 2010); and *Issues Associated with the Implementation of Article 82 of the United Nations Convention on the Law of the Sea*, ISA Technical Study, No. 4 (Kingston, Jamaica: International Seabed Authority, 2009). See also Aldo Chircop, "International Royalty and Continental Shelf Limits: Emerging Issues for the Canadian Offshore," *Dalhousie Law Journal* 26 (2003): 273–302; and "Operationalizing Article 82 of the United Nations Convention on the Law Sea: A New Role for the International Sea Bed Authority?," *Ocean Yearbook* 18, No. 1 (2004): 395–412. See also Michael W. Lodge, "The International Seabed Authority and Article 82 of the UN Convention on the Law of the Sea," *International Journal of Marine and Coastal Law* 21 (2006): 323–333; and "The International Seabed Authority — Its Future Direction," in *Legal and Scientific Aspects of Continental Shelf Limits*, eds. Myron H. Nordquist, John Norton Moore, and Thomas H. Heidar (Leiden: Martinus Nijhoff, 2004), 403–409. See also Cleo Paskal and Michael Lodge, *A Fair Deal on Seabed Wealth: The Promise and Pitfalls of Article 82 on the Outer Continental Shelf* (London: Royal Institute of International Affairs, 2009); and Wylie Spicer, "Canada, the Law of the Sea and International Payments: Where Will the Money Come From," *SPP Research Papers* 8, No. 31 (2015): 1–24.

51. International Seabed Authority, *Implementation of Article 82 of the United Nations Convention on the Law of the Sea,* 20.

52. International Seabed Authority, *Implementation of Article 82,* Annex 3, par. 4, 31.

53. MacDougall and Verhoef, Interviews, February 2008.

54. Ibid.

55. Spicer, "Canada, the Law of the Sea and International Payments," 12.

56. For a more in depth treatment of these issues, see Frances Abel, Thomas J. Courchene, F. Leslie Seidle, and France St-Hilaire, eds., *Northern Exposure: Peoples, Powers and Prospects in Canada's North* (Montreal: Institute for Research on Public Policy, 2009), 354–372.

57. Wylie Spicer, "Pacing off the Continental Shelf: UN Convention Governs Canadian Claims on Extending Oil and Gas Rights," *Lawyers Weekly,* January 17 2014, www.lawyersweekly.ca/articles/2054.

58. Spicer, "Canada, the Law of the Sea and International Payments," 13. See Government of Canada. *Canada-Newfoundland Atlantic Accord Implementation Act,* S.C. 1987, c. 3, http://laws-lois.justice.gc.ca/eng/acts/c-7.5/.

59. Spicer, "Canada, the Law of the Sea and International Payments," 1–24.

60. Ibid., 1, n2.

61. Ibid., 1.

62. Ibid., 16.

63. Ibid.

64. Alexei A. Zinchenko, "Emerging Issues in the Work of the Commission on the Limits of the Continental Shelf," in *Legal and Scientific Aspects of Continental Shelf Limits,* eds. Myron H. Nordquist, John Norton Moore, and Thomas H. Heidar (Leiden: Martinus Nijhoff, 2004), 225. For more detailed examinations of the delimitation of Arctic ECSs, see Monique Andree Allain, "Canada's Claim to the Arctic: A Study in Overlapping Claims to the Outer Continental Shelf," *Journal of Maritime Law and Commerce* 42, No. 1 (2011), 1–48; Byers and Baker, "Crossed Lines," 70–95; Alex G. Oude Elferink and Constance Johnson, "Outer Limits of the Continental Shelf and 'Disputed Areas': State Practice concerning Article 76(10) of the LOS Convention," *International Journal of*

Marine and Coastal Law 21, No. 4 (2006), 461–487; Magnusson, *The Continental Shelf Beyond 200 Nautical Miles*, chapter 5; and Suarez, *The Outer Limits of the Continental Shelf*, 223–238.

65. *United Nations Convention on the Law of the Sea*, Article 76(10), 28. See also Commission, *Rules of Procedure*, Annex 1, 22.

66. Ibid.

67. UN, *Convention on the Law of the Sea*, Article 76(9), 28.

68. Commission, *Rules of Procedure*, Rule 51(1), 18.

69. Ibid., Annex 1, par. 5(a), 22.

70. See Permanent Mission of Canada to the United Nations, Note No. 1361, New York, December 29, 2014; Permanent Mission of Norway to the United Nations, New York, December 17, 2014; Permanent Mission of the Russian Federation to the United Nations, No. 2764/N, New York, July 21, 2015; and United States Mission to the United Nations, Diplomatic Note, New York, October 30, 2015. All of these diplomatic notes are available at www.un.org/depts/los/clcs_new/commission_submissions.html.

71. See Permanent Mission of Canada to the United Nations, Note No. 2328, New York, November 30, 2015; Permanent Mission of Denmark to the United Nations, Ref. No. 2015-14962, New York, October 7, 2015; and United States Mission to the United Nations, Diplomatic Note, New York, October 30, 2015.

72. Commission on the Limits of the Continental Shelf, "Rules of Procedure of the Commission on the Limits of the Continental Shelf," 21st Session, April 17, 2008, CLCS/40/Rev. 1, Annex III, Part II, par. 2(a) (iv–v), 27.

73. Ibid.

74. UN, *Convention on the Law of the Sea*, Article 287(1), 98.

75. Gulf of Maine Case (Canada v. United States), International Court of Justice Report 246, 1984.

76. See Ted L. McDorman, *Salt Water Neighbors: International Ocean Law Relations Between the United States and Canada* (New York: Oxford, 2009), 181–190.

77. Macnab, "How Harper Froze out Scientists."

CHAPTER 7: CONCLUSION

1. "Maritime Jurisdiction and Boundaries in the Arctic Region," Research, 2015, www.dur.ac.uk/ibru/resources/arctic.

2. Kim Richard Nossal, Stéphane Roussel, and Stéphane Paquin, *International Policy and Politics in Canada* (Toronto: Pearson, 2011), 17–83; and Andrea Charron, Joël Plouffe, and Stéphane Roussel, "The Russian Arctic Hegemon: Foreign Policy Implications for Canada," *Canadian Foreign Policy Journal* 18, No. 1 (2012), 38–50.

3. See Tom Keating, *Canada and World Order: The Multilateralist Tradition in Canadian Foreign Policy*, 2nd ed. (Don Mills, ON: Oxford University Press, 2002).

4. See Greg Donaghy and Neil Carter, "'There Are No Half-Countries': Canada, La Francophonie, and the Projection of Canadian Biculturalism, 1960–2002," in *Handbook of Canadian Foreign Policy*, eds. Patrick James, Nelson Michaud, and Marc J. O'Reilly (Lanham, MD: Lexington Books, 2006), 133–164; and Tom Keating "Multilateralism Reconsidered," in *Readings in Canadian Foreign Policy: Classic Debates and New Ideas,* eds. Duane Bratt and Christopher J. Kukucha (Don Mills, ON: Oxford University Press, 2011), 44–51; Nossal, Roussel, and Paquin, *International Policy and Politics in Canada*, especially 37–48; and Heather A. Smith and Claire Turenne Sjolander, eds., *Canada in the World: Internationalism in Canadian Foreign Policy* (Don Mills, ON: Oxford University Press, 2013).

5. Keating, *Canada and World Order,* 4.

6. David Black and Claire Turenne Sjolander, "Multilateralism Reconstituted and the Discourse of Canadian Foreign Policy," *Studies in Political Economy* 49 (1996): 7–36.

7. Ibid., 11.

8. Andrew Cooper, *Canadian Foreign Policy: Old Habits and New Directions* (Scarborough, ON: Prentice Hall Canada, 1997), especially 97–100.

9. The Harper government's move away from multilateralism is well documented and critiqued in the collection edited by Heather A. Smith and Claire Turenne Sjolander, *Canada in the World: International in Canadian Foreign Policy*. See also Black and Turenne Sjolander,

"Multilateralism Re-Constituted and the Discourse of Canadian Foreign Policy," especially 13–14; Louise Frechette, "Canada at the United Nations: A Shadow of its Former Self" in *Canada Among Nations: 2009-2010: As Others See Us*, eds. Fen Osler Hampson and Paul Heinbecker (Montreal and Kingston: McGill-Queen's University Press, 2010), 265–274; Paul Heinbecker, *Getting Back in the Game: A Foreign Policy Playbook for Canada* (Toronto: Key Porter Books, 2010); Jeremy Kinsman, "A Betrayal of Canada's Multilateral Tradition," *National Post*, January 17, 2014; Linda McQuaig, *Holding the Bully's Coat: Canada and the U.S. Empire* (Toronto: Doubleday, 2007); Roland Paris, "Are Canadians Still Liberal Internationalists? Foreign Policy and Public Opinion in the Harper Era," *International Journal* 69, No. 3 (2014): 274–307; and Roland Paris, "A Decade of Diplomatic Darkness," *Globe and Mail*, September 24, 2014.

10. Examples include Andrew Cohen, *While Canada Slept: How We Lost Our Place in the World* (Toronto: McClelland and Stewart, 2003); Michael Ignatieff, "Canada in the Age of Terror: Multilateralism Meets a Moment of Truth," *Policy Options*, February 2003, 14–18; Maureen Appel Molot and Norman Hillmer, "The Diplomacy of Decline," in *Canada Among Nations 2002: A Fading Power*, eds. Maureen Appel Molot and Norman Hillmer (Don Mills, ON: Oxford, 2002), 1–33; Kim Richard Nossal, "Pinchpenny Diplomacy: the Decline of 'Good International Citizenship' in Canadian Foreign Policy," *International Journal* 54, No. 1 (1998/1999): 88–105; Jean-Francois Rioux and Robin Hay, "Canadian Foreign Policy: From Internationalism to Isolationism?," *International Journal* 54, No. 1 (1998/1999), 57–75; and Jennifer M. Welsh, "Reality and Canadian Foreign Policy" in *Canada Among Nations 2005: Split Images*, eds. Andrew F. Cooper and Dane Rowlands (Montreal: McGill-Queen's University Press, 2005), 23–46. Some authors argue that the Chrétien government started the decline that accelerated under Harper. See Justin Massie and Stéphane Roussel, "The Twilight of Internationalism? Neocontinentalism as an Emerging Dominant Idea in Canadian Foreign Policy," in *Canada in the World: Internationalism in Canadian Foreign Policy*, eds. Heather A. Smith and Claire Turenne Sjolander (Don Mills, ON: Oxford University Press, 2013), 36–52; and Kim Richard Nossal, "The Liberal

Past in the Conservative Present: Internationalism in the Harper Era," in *Canada in the World*, eds. Smith and Sjolander, 21–35.

11.   See Liberal Party of Canada, *A New Plan For A Strong Middle Class* (Ottawa: Liberal Party of Canada, 2015), 68.

12.   Cooper, *Canadian Foreign Policy*, 37.

13.   Canada, Department of External Affairs, *The Law of the Sea in Historical Perspective: Background Notes* (Ottawa: Government of Canada, 1977), 5.

14.   Duane Bratt and Christopher J. Kukucha, eds., *Readings in Canadian Foreign Policy: Classic Debates and New Ideas*, 2nd ed. (Don Mills, ON: Oxford University Press, 2011); Cooper, *Canadian Foreign Policy*; Keating, *Canada and World Order*; and Nossal, Roussel, and Paquin, *International Policy and Politics in Canada*.

15.   See "Competing Perspectives on Canadian Development Assistance Policies," *International Journal* 5, No. 2 (1996): 235–258. More recent examples of scholars discussing the importance of trade, finance and other economic considerations include Alex Bugailiskis and Andrés Rozental, eds., *Canada Among Nations, 2011–2012: Canada and Mexico's Unfinished Agenda* (Montreal: McGill-Queen's University Press, 2012); Linda McQuaig, *Holding the Bully's Coat*; Rohinton Medhora and Dane Rowlands, eds., *Canada Among Nations: 2014: Crisis and Reform: Canada and the International Financial System* (Waterloo, ON: Centre for International Governance Innovation, Norman Paterson School of International Affairs, 2014); Nossal, Roussel, and Paquin, *International Policy and Politics in Canada*, 32–37; and Heather Smith, "Forget the Fine Tuning: Internationalism, the Arctic and Climate Change," in *Canada in the World*, eds. Smith and Sjolander, 208.

16.   Kim Richard Nossal, "The Liberal Past in the Conservative Present: Internationalism in the Harper Era" in *Canada in the World*, eds. Smith and Sjolander, 23.

17.   Smith, "Forget the Fine Tuning," 200–216; and Claire Turenne Sjolander, "Canada and the Afghan 'Other': Identity Difference, and Foreign Policy," in *Canada in the World*, eds. Smith and Sjolander, 238–254.

18.   Peter W. Hutchins, Monique Caron, Biana Suciu and Robin Campbell, *Setting out Canada's Obligations to Inuit in Respect of the Extended*

Continental Shelf in the Arctic Ocean (Montreal: Paper Commissioned by Senator Charlie Watt 2015), 21.

19. Hutchins, Caron, Suciu, and Campbell, *Setting out Canada's Obligations to Inuit in Respect of the Extended Continental Shelf in the Arctic Ocean*, 18.

20. See Ibid.

21. Michael Klare, *Resource Wars: The New Landscape of Global Conflict* (New York: Henry Holt, 2002).

22. For example, see Whitney Lackenbauer, "From Polar Race to Polar Saga: An Integrated Strategy for Canada and the Circumpolar World" and "Sovereignty, Security, and Stewardship: An Update," in Franklyn Griffiths, Rob Huebert, and P. Whitney Lackenbauer, *Canada and the Changing Arctic: Sovereignty, Security and Stewardship* (Waterloo, ON: Wilfrid Laurier University Press, 2011), 69–179, 227–253.

23. See Graham Allison, *Essence of Decision: Explaining the Cuban Missile Crisis* (Boston: Little Brown, 1971), 144–184. The synopsis of the governmental politics model is drawn from the author's previous books, *Canada and the Beijing Conference on Women: Governmental Politics and NGO Participation* (Vancouver: University of British Columbia Press, 2001), chapter 8; and *Canada and the International Seabed*, chapter 8.

24. Kim Richard Nossal, "Allison Through the (Ottawa) Looking Glass: Bureaucratic Politics and Foreign Policy in a Parliamentary System," *Canadian Public Administration* 22 (1979): 610, 626. For other examinations of the model in the Canadian context, see Michael M. Atkinson and Kim Richard Nossal, "Bureaucratic Politics and the New Fighter Aircraft Decisions," *Canadian Public Administration* 24, No. 4 (1981): 531–562; Marie-Eve Desrosiers and Philippe Lagassé, "Canada and the Bureaucratic Politics of State Fragility," *Diplomacy and Statecraft* 20, No. 4 (2009): 659–678; Kim Richard Nossal, "Bureaucratic Politics and the Westminster Model" in *International Conflict and Conflict Management: Readings in World Politics,* eds. Robert O. Matthews, Arthur G. Rubinoff, and Janice Gross Stein (Scarborough, ON: Prentice Hall Canada, 1984), 120–127; and Elizabeth Riddell-Dixon, "Deep Seabed Mining: a Hotbed for Governmental Politics," *International Journal* 41, No. 1 (1985/1986): 72–94; as well as "Winners and Losers:

Formulating Canada's Policies on International Technology Transfers" *International Journal* 47, No. 1 (1991/1992): 159–183.

25. See Cooper, *Canadian Foreign Policy*, 157. See also 158–172.

26. See Douglas Macdonald and Heather A. Smith, "Promises Made, Promises Broken: Questioning Canada's Commitments to Climate Change," *International Journal* 55, No. 1 (1999–2000): 107–124.

27. Brian W. Tomlin, "On a Fast Track to the Ban: The Canadian Policy Process," *Canadian Foreign Policy* 5, No. 3 (1998): 3–23.

28. Marie-Eve Desrosiers and Philippe Lagassé, "Canada and the Bureaucratic Politics of State Fragility." *Diplomacy and Statecraft* 20, No. 4 (2009): 659.

29. Nossal, "Allison Through the (Ottawa) Looking Glass," 619–620.

30. Kim Richard Nossal, *The Politics of Canadian Foreign Policy*, 3rd ed. (Scarborough, ON: Prentice Hall Canada, 1997), 176.

31. Ibid.

32. Andrew F. Cooper, "Looking Back to and Forward from Kim Richard Nossal's The Politics of Canadian Foreign Policy," *International Journal* 69, No. 2 (2014): 250–251; and Richard Nossal, "Old Habits and New Directions Indeed" *International Journal* 69, No. 2 (2014): 254–255.

33. Kim Richard Nossal, "Old Habits," 254–255. See also Lawrence Martin, *Harperland: The Politics of Control* (Toronto: Viking, 2010).

34. Paul Gecelovsky, "The Prime Minister and the Parable: Stephen Harper and Personal Responsibility Internationalism," in *Canada in the World*, eds. Smith and Sjolander, 111.

35. Mark MacGuigan, "Beyond the Law of the Sea Conference: An Address by the Honourable Mark MacGuigan, Secretary of State for External Affairs, to the Ninth Annual Conference of the Canadian Council on International Law, Ottawa, October 24, 1980," *Statements and Speeches* 80, No. 24 (1980): 2.

36. Stephen Forbes, Interview with the author, September 30, 2011.

BIBLIOGRAPHY

DOCUMENTS
Canada

Baird, John. "Address by Minister Baird to Media Concerning
Canada's Continental Shelf Submissions." Global Affairs Canada,
December 9, 2013. www.international.gc.ca/media/aff/speeches-
discours/2013/12/09a.aspx?lang=eng.

Beesley, J. Alan. "The Law of the Sea Conference: Factors Behind Canada's
Stance." In *Canada and the Law of the Sea: Resource Information*,
edited by Department of External Affairs, 28–35. Ottawa: Department
of External Affairs, 1977.

Biggar, Jon. *Final Field Report: UNCLOS 2009 — Ward Hunt Island
Project, CHSDIR Project Number: 4012989*. Dartmouth: Canadian
Hydrographic Service, 2009.

———. *UNCLOS Project — Canada Basin 2008*. Dartmouth: Canadian
Hydrographic Service, 2008.

Böggild, Hans. *Fourth Joint Canada-US Extended Continental Shelf Survey
in the Arctic*. Halifax: Natural Resources Canada, 2011. www.science.
gc.ca/default.asp?lang=En&n=E1A86309-1.

Böggild, Kai. *Arctic Survey Expedition (2014)*. Halifax: Natural
Resources Canada, 2014. www.science.gc.ca/default.
asp?lang=En&n=80F7E17E-1.

Canadian Hydrographic Service. *Arctic Ice Camp Field Manual, 2009*.
Ottawa: Department of Fisheries and Oceans, 2009.

————. *Final Field Report: United Nations Convention on the Law of the Sea (UNCLOS): Borden Island.* Ottawa: Department of Fisheries and Oceans, 2010.

Cannon, Lawrence. "Address by Minister Cannon at Launch of Statement on Canada's Arctic Foreign Policy." News Release. August 20, 2010. http://news.gc.ca/web/article-en.do?mthd=advSrch&crtr. mnthndVl=4&crtr.mnthStrtVl=1&crtr.page=6&nid=554739&crtr. yrndVl=2014&crtr.kw=continental+shelf&crtr.yrStrtVl=2002&crtr. dyStrtVl=1&crtr.dyndVl=11.

————. "Address by Minister Cannon at News Conference Following Arctic Visit." Speech. April 9, 2010. http://news.gc.ca/web/article-en. do?mthd=advSrch&crtr.mnthndVl=4&crtr.mnthStrtVl=1&crtr. page=1&nid=524529&crtr.yrndVl=2014&crtr.kw=continental+shelf&crtr. yrStrtVl=2002&crtr.dyStrtVl=1&crtr.dyndVl=11.

Commission on the Limits of the Continental Shelf. *Preliminary Information Concerning the Outer Limits of the Continental Shelf of Canada in the Arctic Ocean.* New York: Commission on the Limits of the Continental Shelf, 2013.

Department of External Affairs. "A Note Verbale from the Department of External Affairs of Canada, Dated September 10, 1957." In *United Nations Conference on the Law of the Sea: Official Records, Vol. I, Preparatory Documents, A/CONF.13/5 and Addendas 1–4, February 24–April 27, 1958*, edited by United Nations Conference on the Law of the Sea, 76. Geneva: United Nations, 1958.

————. *Law of the Sea Conference — New York Portion of the Ninth Session, March 3–April 4, 1980: Assessment by the Canadian Delegation.* Ottawa: Government of Canada, 1980.

————. *The Law of the Sea in Historical Perspective: Background Notes.* Ottawa: Government of Canada, 1977.

————. *Third United Nations Conference on the Law of the Sea.* Ottawa: Department of External Affairs, 1973.

Department of Foreign Affairs and International Trade. "Canada to Assume Chairmanship of Arctic Council." News Release. May 12, 2013. http://news.gc.ca/web/article-en.do?nid=741239.

————. *Joint Statement on Canada-Russia Economic Cooperation.* Ottawa: Department of Foreign Affairs and International Trade, 2007.

Department of Foreign Affairs, Trade and Development. "Backgrounder
— Canada's Continental Shelf Submission." *Canada's Continental Shelf
Submission*. December 6, 2013. www.international.gc.ca/media/aff/
news-communiques/2013/12/09a_bg1.aspx?lang=eng.

———. "Canada's Extended Continental Shelf: Canada's Program."
Canada and the Arctic, August 15, 2012. www.international.
gc.ca/arctic-arctique/continental/program-canada-programme.
aspx?lang=eng.

———. "Harper Government Launches First of Two Scientific Surveys
to Complete Canada's Arctic Continental Shelf Submission." News
Release. August 8, 2014.

Fisheries and Oceans Canada. "Canada's Ocean Estate: A Description
of Canada's Maritime Zones." *Canada's Maritime Zones*. October 10,
2013. www.dfo-mpo.gc.ca/oceans/marinezones-zonesmarines/index-
eng.html.

———. "Canadian Coast Guard Ship *Louis S. St-Laurent* Departs for
Arctic Support Science and Northern Shipping." News Release. July
10, 2011. http://news.gc.ca/web/article-en.do?mthd=advSrch&crtr.
mnthndVl=4&crtr.mnthStrtVl=1&crtr.page=2&nid=610769&crtr.
yrndVl=2014&crtr.kw=continental+shelf&crtr.yrStrtVl=2002&crtr.
dyStrtVl=1&crtr.dyndVl=11.

Global Affairs Canada. "Canada Holds Bilateral Talks with
Russia." News Release. September 16, 2010. http://news.gc.ca/
web/article-en.do?mthd=advSrch&crtr.mnthndVl=4&crtr.
mnthStrtVl=1&crtr.page=4&nid=560449&crtr.yrndVl=2014&crtr.
kw=continental+shelf&crtr.yrStrtVl=2002&crtr.dyStrtVl=1&crtr.
dyndVl=11.

———. "Canada's Extended Continental Shelf." *Canada and the Arctic*.
2015. www.international.gc.ca/arctic-arctique/continental/index.
aspx?lang=eng.

———. "Government Commemorates 25th Anniversary of UN
Convention on the Law of the Sea." News Release. December 10,
2007. http://news.gc.ca/web/article-en.do?mthd=advSrch&crtr.
mnthndVl=4&crtr.mnthStrtVl=1&crtr.page=3&nid=366839&crtr.
yrndVl=2014&crtr.kw=continental+shelf&crtr.yrStrtVl=2002&crtr.
dyStrtVl=1&crtr.dyndVl=11.

————. "Minister Cannon Concludes Arctic Visit and Holds Media Availability." News Release. April 7, 2010. http://news.gc.ca/web/article-en.do?mthd=advSrch&crtr.mnthndVl=4&crtr.mnthStrtVl=1&crtr.page=2&nid=523209&crtr.yrndVl=2014&crtr.kw=continental+shelf&crtr.yrStrtVl=2002&crtr.dyStrtVl=1&crtr.dyndVl=11.

————. *Partial Submission of Canada to the Commission on the Limits of the Continental Shelf Regarding Its Continental Shelf in the Atlantic Ocean: Executive Summary.* Ottawa: Government of Canada, 2013.

Government of Canada. "Backgrounder — 2016 Arctic Survey," July 21, 2016. http://news.gc.ca/web/article-en.do?nid=1102489.

————. "2016 Arctic Survey." *Canada's Extended Continental Shelf Program.* April 2016. www.science.gc.ca/default.asp?lang=En&n=0DEBF752-1.

House of Commons. *Debates.* 2nd session, 20th Parliament, August 28, 1946, 5524.

————. *Debates.* 1st session, 24th Parliament, July 7, 1958, 1879.

————. *Minutes of Proceedings and Evidence of the Standing Committee on External Affairs and National Defence.* 1st session, 29th Parliament, November 6, 1973, 22:21.

Jackson, H. Ruth, ed. *Field Report for 2007: The CCGS Louis S. St-Laurent Seismic Cruiseto the Canada Basin.* Open File 5818. Halifax: Geological Survey of Canada, 2008.

Jackson, H. Ruth, and K.J. DesRoches, eds. *2008 Louis S. St-Laurent Field Report August 22–October 3, 2008.* Open File 6275. Halifax: Geological Survey of Canada, 2010.

Jackson, H. Ruth, and Patrick Potter, eds. *Expedition Report for the Alpha Ridge Test of Appurtenance (ARTA) 2008.* Open File 6842. Halifax: Geological Survey of Canada, 2011.

Janzen, Tim. *Final Field Report: United Nations Convention on the Law of the Sea (UNCLOS): Borden Island.* Burlington, Ontario: Canadian Hydrographic Service, 2010.

Liberal Party of Canada. *A New Plan for a Strong Middle Class.* Ottawa: Liberal Party of Canada, 2015.

MacEachen, Allan J. *Notes for Remarks by the Honourable, Deputy Prime Minister and Secretary of State for External Affairs, at the Final Session of the Third United Nations Conference on the Law of the Sea, Montego Bay, Jamaica, December 6, 1982.* Ottawa: Bureau of Information, Department of External Affairs, 1982.

"Meet the People Video Gallery." Government of Canada. http://www. science.gc.ca/eic/site/063.nsf/eng/h_726BE31B.html.

Mosher, David C. *2011 Canadian High Arctic Seismic Expedition: CCGS Louis S. St-Laurent Expedition Report.* Open File 7053. Halifax: Geological Survey of Canada, 2012.

———. *Canadian Polar Expedition, 2014 Canada Basin, Arctic Ocean, August 9–September 17, 2014: St. John's, NL, to Kugluktuk, NWT: CCGS Louis S. St-Laurent and Terry Fox.* Halifax: Natural Resources Canada, 2014.

Mosher, D.C., J. Shimeld, R. Jackson, D. Hutchinson, C.B. Chapman, D. Chian, J. Childs, L. Mayer, B. Edwards, and J. Verhoef. *Sedimentation in Canada Basin, Western Arctic.* Open File 6759. Halifax: Geological Survey of Canada, 2011.

Mosher, David, and Walta Ann Rainey. "Third Canada-US Extended Continental Shelf Survey in the Arctic (2010)." *Canada's Extended Continental Shelf Program, Past Surveys,* 2015. www.science.gc.ca/ default.asp?lang=En&n=C571F860-1.

Mosher, D.C., J.W. Shimeld, and D.R. Hutchinson. *2009 Canada Basin Seismic Reflection and Refraction Survey, Western Arctic Ocean: CCGS Louis S. St-Laurent Expedition Report.* Open File 6343. Ottawa: Natural Resources Canada, 2009.

Mosher, D.C., J.W. Shimeld, and B. Chapman. *2010 Canada Basin Seismic Reflection and Refraction Survey, Western Arctic Ocean: CCGS Louis S. St-Laurent Expedition Report August 4–September 15, 2010 Kugluktuk, NWT, to Kugluktuk, NWT.* Open File 6720. Ottawa: Geological Survey of Canada, 2011.

Natural Resources Canada. "A Catalyst for Canada's Arctic Research." *Polar Continental Shelf Program.* 2010. http://publications.gc.ca/ collections/collection_2011/rncan-nrcan/M78-4-1-1-2010.pdf.

———. "Government of Canada Welcomes New Mapping Data on Canada's North." News Release. August 8, 2008. http://news. gc.ca/web/article-en.do?mthd=advSrch&crtr.mnthndVl=4&crtr. mnthStrtVl=1&crtr.page=1&nid=413799&crtr.yrndVl=2014&crtr.

kw=continental+shelf&crtr.yrStrtVl=2002&crtr.dyStrtVl=1&crtr.
dyndVl=11.

Office of the Prime Minister. "Northern Strategy — Backgrounder."
News Release. March 10, 2008. http://news.gc.ca/web/
article-en.do?mthd=advSrch&crtr.mnthndVl=4&crtr.
mnthStrtVl=1&crtr.page=4&nid=384529&crtr.yrndVl=2014&crtr.
kw=continental+shelf&crtr.yrStrtVl=2002&crtr.dyStrtVl=1&crtr.
dyndVl=11.

————. "Prime Minister Stephen Harper Announces New Arctic
Offshore Patrol Ships." News Release. July 9, 2007. http://news.
gc.ca/web/article-en.do?crtr.sj1D=&mthd=advSrch&crtr.
mnthndVl=&nid=335789&crtr.dpt1D=&crtr.tp1D=&crtr.lc1D=&crtr.
yrStrtVl=2008&crtr.kw=&crtr.dyStrtVl=26&crtr.aud1D=&crtr.
mnthStrtVl=2&crtr.yrndVl=&crtr.dyndVl=.

Parliament of Canada. *Governance in the Public Service of Canada: Ministerial and Deputy Ministerial Accountability.* 1st Session, 38th Parliament, 2004–2005. www.parl.gc.ca/HousePublications/Publication.as-
px?Mode=1&Parl=38&Ses=1&Language=E&DocId=1988069&File=0.

Privy Council Office. "Governing Responsibly — A Guide for Ministers
and Ministers of State." Information Resources, 2003.
www.pcobcp.gc.ca/index.asp?lang=eng&page=information&sub=
publications&doc=aarchives/ag-gr/2003/guide-eng.htm#I.1.

"Proposal by Canada on the Continental Shelf Boundary Commission."
Revised Single Negotiating Text II, April 29, 1976, 321–322.

Ruben, Nelson, John Ruben, and Jonah Nakimayak. *Marine Mammals
Monitor Report Field Report for 2007: The CCGS Louis S. St-Laurent
Seismic Cruise to the Canada Basin,* ed. H. Ruth Jackson. Open File
5818. Ottawa: Geological Survey of Canada, 2008.

Shimeld, J., R. Jackson, K. DesRoches, and J. Verhoef. "2007 Deep-
Water Marine Seismic Acquisition to Define the Canadian Extended
Continental Shelf Under Article 76 of the United Nations Convention
on the Law of the Sea." Paper presented to the 34th Colloquium and
Annual General Meeting of the 2008 Atlantic Geoscience Society,
Dartmouth, Nova Scotia, February 1–2, 2008.

Taylor, Lawrence. "Second Canada-US Extended Continental Shelf
Survey in the Arctic: Expedition Blogs 2009." Canada's Extended

Continental Shelf Program, Past Surveys, 2015. www.science.gc.ca/
default.asp?lang=En&n=9293A4FA-1.

Treasury Board of Canada Secretariat. *Supplementary Estimates (B) 2014–2015*. Ottawa: Department of Finance, 2014.

Verrall, Ronald. *A Guide to Arctic Field Trips: Technical Report DREA TR 2000-094*. Halifax: Defence Research and Development Canada: Atlantic, 2001. http://cradpdf.drdc-rddc.gc.ca/PDFS/zbd93/p516835.pdf.

Youngblut, Scott. *Final Field Report: Amundsen Basin Survey: UNCLOS 2015*. CHSDIR Project Number: 4013733. Dartmouth: Canadian Hydrographic Service, 2014.

Commission on the Limits of the Continental Shelf

Australia. "Executive Summary, Submission to the Commission." Submissions, November 15, 2004. www.un.org/Depts/los/clcs_new/commission_submissions.htm.

———. "Summary of Recommendations." Submissions, April 9, 2008. www.un.org/Depts/los/clcs_new/commission_submissions.htm.

Commission on the Limits of the Continental Shelf. *Outline for a Five-Day Training Course for Delineation of the Outer Limits of the Continental Shelf Beyond 200 Nautical Miles and for Preparation of a Submission of a Coastal State to the Commission on the Limits of the Continental Shelf*. CLCS/24. New York: Division for Ocean Affairs and the Law of the Sea, 2000.

———. *Practical Suggestions Concerning the Final Preparation And Deposit of Submissions to the CLCS Through the Secretary-General of the United Nations*. CLCS/61. New York: Division for Ocean Affairs and the Law of the Sea, 2009.

———. *Progress of Work in the Commission on the Limits of the Continental Shelf: Statement by the Chair*. 13th Session, September 5, 2012, CLCS/76.

———. *Progress of Work in the Commission on the Limits of the Continental Shelf: Statement by the Chair.* 32nd Session, September 24, 2013. CLCS/80.

———. *Progress of Work in the Commission on the Limits of the Continental Shelf: Statement by the Chair*. 39th Session, December 21, 2015. CLCS/91.

————. *Rules of Procedure of the Commission on the Limits of the Continental Shelf.* 21st Session, April 17, 2008, CLCS/40/Rev. 1.

————. *Scientific and Technical Guidelines of the Commission on the Limits of the Continental Shelf.* 5th Session, May 13, 1999, CLCS/11.

————. *Scientific and Technical Guidelines of the Commission on the Limits of the Continental Shelf.* 6th Session, September 3, 1999, CLCS/11/Add.

————. *Scientific and Technical Guidelines of the Commission on the Limits of the Continental Shelf Annex II ("Flowcharts and Illustrations Summarizing the Procedure for Establishing the Outer Limits of the Continental Shelf").* 6th Session, September 3, 1999, CLCS/11/Add.

————. *Statement by the Chairperson of the Commission on the Limits of the Continental Shelf on the Progress of Work in the Commission.* 26th Session, September 17, 2010, CLCS/68.

————. *Training Manual for Delineation of the Outer Limits of the Continental Shelf Beyond 200 Nautical Miles and for Preparation of Submissions to the Commission on the Limits of the Continental Shelf.* New York: Division for Ocean Affairs and the Law of the Sea, 2006.

Government of Denmark. *Partial Submission of the Government of the Kingdom of Denmark Together With the Government of Greenland to the Commission on the Limits of the Continental Shelf: The Northern Continental Shelf of Greenland: Executive Summary.* Copenhagen: Geological Survey of Denmark and Greenland, 2014. www.un.org/depts/los/clcs_new/submissions_files/dnk76_14/dnk2014_es.pdf.

Government of Russia. *Partial Revised Submission of the Russian Federation to the Commission on the Limits of the Continental Shelf in Respect of the Russian Federation in the Arctic Ocean: Executive Summary.* Moscow: Government of Russia, 2015. www.un.org/depts/los/clcs_new/submissions_files/rus01_rev15/2015_08_03_Exec_Summary_English.pdf.

Denmark

Kingdom of Denmark. *Strategy for the Arctic 2011–2020.* Copenhagen: Kingdom of Denmark, 2011.

Marcussen, Christian, and the LOMROG II Scientific Party. *Lomonosov Ridge off Greenland 2009 (LOMROG II) — Cruise Report.* Copenhagen: Geological Survey of Denmark and Greenland, 2011.

International Seabed Authority

International Seabed Authority. *Implementation of Article 82 of the United Nations Convention on the Law of the Sea: Report of an International Workshop convened by the International Seabed Authority in Collaboration with the China Institute for Marine Affairs in Beijing the People's Republic of China, 26–30 November 2012*, ISA Technical Study No. 12. Kingston, Jamaica: International Seabed Authority, 2012.

———. *Issues Associated with the Implementation of Article 82 of the United Nations Convention on the Law of the Sea*. ISA Technical Study No. 4. Kingston, Jamaica: International Seabed Authority, 2009.

———. *Non-living Resources of the Continental Shelf beyond 200 Nautical Miles: Speculations on the Implementation of Article 82 of the United Nations Convention on the Law of the Sea*. ISA Technical Study No. 5. Kingston, Jamaica: International Seabed Authority, 2010.

United Nations

Directory of National Sources of Training, Advice and Expertise and Technological Services. New York: Division for Ocean Affairs and the Law of the Sea, October 20, 2011.

Division for Ocean Affairs and the Law of the Sea, Submissions, Through the Secretary-General of the United Nations To the Commission on the Limits of the Continental Shelf, Pursuant to Article 76, Paragraph 8, of the United Nations Convention on the Law of the Sea of December 10, 1982. www.un.org/depts/los/clcs_new/commission_submissions.htm.

Seventh Session (First Part) of Third United Nations Conference on Law of Sea, Geneva, 28 March–19 May: Tackles "Hard-core" Issues for Law of Sea Convention, BR/78/21. London: Information Centre, June 6, 1978.

States Parties to UNCLOS. *Decision Regarding the Date of Commencement of the Ten-Year Period for Making Submissions to the Commission on the Limits of the Continental Shelf Set Out in Article 4 of Annex II to the United Nations Convention on the Law of the Sea*. 11th Meeting, May 29, 2001, SPLOS/72.

———. *Decision on Issues Related to the Workload of the Commission on the Limits of the Continental Shelf*. 17th Meeting, June 26, 2007, SPLOS/162.

———. *Decision Regarding the Conditions of Service of the Members of the Commission on the Limits of the Continental Shelf.* 24th Meeting, June 1, 2014, SPLOS/276.

———. *Decision Regarding the Workload of the Commission on the Limits of the Continental Shelf.* 21st Meeting, June 16, 2011, SPLOS/229.

———. *Decision Regarding the Workload of the Commission on the Limits of the Continental Shelf and the Ability of States, Particularly Developing States, to Fulfil the Requirements of Article 4 of Annex II to the United Nations Convention on the Law of the Sea, As Well As The Decision Contained in SPLOS/72, Paragraph (A).* 18th Meeting, June 20, 2008, SPLOS/183.

United Nations Convention on the Continental Shelf. June 10, 1964, 499 U.N.T.S. 311.

United Nations Convention on the Law of the Sea. 1833 U.N.T.S. 397.

UN General Assembly. *Agreement Relating to the Implementation of Part XI of the United Nations Convention on the Law of the Sea of December 10, 1982, A/RES/48/263.* New York: United Nations, 1983.

———. *Declaration and Treaty Concerning the Reservation Exclusively for Peaceful Purposes of the Sea-Bed and of the Ocean Floor Underlying the Seas Beyond the Limits of Present National Jurisdiction, and the Use of Their Resources in the Interest of Mankind.* 22nd Session, August 18, 1967, A/6695.

———. "Denmark and Canada: Agreement Relating to the Delimitation of the Continental Shelf Between Greenland and Canada." Treaty Series, No. 13550, December 17, 1973. https://treaties.un.org/doc/Publication/UNTS/Volume%20950/volume-950-I-13550-English.pdf.

United States

Bird, Kenneth J., et al. *Circum-Arctic Resource Appraisal: Estimates of Undiscovered Oil and Gas North of the Arctic Circle.* Reston, VA: U.S. Geological Survey, 2008.

Childs, Jon R., and Deborah R. Hutchinson. "Joint U.S.-Canadian Icebreaker Surveys in the Arctic." *Ocean Sound Waves*, April 2009. http://soundwaves.usgs.gov/2009/04/index.html.

Department of Commerce, National Oceanic and Atmospheric Administration. *U.S. Ocean Action Plan: The Bush Administration's Response to the U.S. Commission on Ocean Policy.* Washington, DC: National Oceanic and Atmospheric Administration 2004.

Department of State, Bureau of Oceans and International Environmental and Scientific Affairs. "Defining the Limits of the U.S. Continental Shelf." *Diplomacy in Action,* 2010. www.state.gov/e/oes/continentalshelf/.

Geological Survey. "90 Billion Barrels of Oil and 1,670 Trillion Feet of Natural Gas Assessed in the Arctic." *USGS Newsroom,* July 23, 2008. www.usgs.gov/newsroom/article.asp?ID=1980.

———. *Law of the Sea: Outer Limits of the U.S. Continental Margins.* Woods Hole, MA: Woods Hole Science Center, January 15, 2008.

National Oceanic and Atmospheric Administration. "U.S.-Canada Arctic Ocean Survey Partnership Saved Costs, Increased Data: 2011 Mission Concludes Joint Seafloor Survey Operations." Washington, DC: United States Department of Commerce, December 15, 2011. www.noaanews.noaa.gov/stories2011/20111215_arctic.html.

The UN Convention on the Law of the Sea: Hearings of the United States Senate Foreign Relations Committee, September 27. 110th Congress (2007). Testimony by John Negroponte, deputy secretary of state.

United States Mission to the United Nations, Diplomatic Note, New York, October 30, 2015. www.un.org/depts/los/clcs_new/commission_submissions.htm.

Other

Arctic Council. *Iqaluit Declaration.* Iqaluit: Arctic Council Ninth Ministerial Meeting, 2015.

Arctic Ocean Conference. *Ilulissat Declaration.* Ilulissat, Greenland: Arctic Ocean Conference, 2008.

Bak, Osman Askin. *The High North: Emerging Challenges and Opportunities — Draft Report.* Brussels: NATO Parliamentary Assembly, Science and Technology Committee, 2015.

International Tribunal for the Law of the Sea. *Delimitation of the Maritime Boundary in the Bay of Bengal (Bangladesh/Myanmar) (Judgment).* Report 4, March 14, 2012.

———. *North Sea Continental Shelf (Federal Republic of Germany v. Denmark; Federal Republic of Germany v. The Netherlands) (Judgment)* International Court of Justice. Report 3, 1969.

BOOKS, CHAPTERS, ARTICLES, AND CONFERENCE PAPERS

Abel, Frances, Thomas J. Courchene, F. Leslie Seidle, and France St-Hilaire, eds. *Northern Exposure: Peoples, Power and Prospects in Canada's North*. Montreal: Institute for Research on Public Policy, 2009.

Allain, Monique Andree. "Canada's Claim to the Arctic: A Study in Overlapping Claims to the Outer Continental Shelf." *Journal of Maritime Law and Commerce* 42, No. 1 (2011): 38–82.

Allison, Graham. *Essence of Decision: Explaining the Cuban Missile Crisis*. Boston: Little Brown, 1971.

Armstrong, Andrew, Jon Biggar, Julian Goodyear, Larry Mayer, and Richard MacDougall. "Joint United States-Canada Arctic Extended Continental Shelf Bathymetry Program." Paper presented at the 36th Annual Conference of the Canadian Hydrographic Association, Québec City, June 2010.

Armstrong, A.A., L.A. Mayer, and D.C. Mosher. "Gathering Multibeam Bathymetry Data Aboard Icebreakers." *Sea Technology*, October 2012.

Arruda, Gisele M. "Arctic Governance Regime: The Last Frontier for Hydrocarbons Exploitation." *International Journal of Law and Management* 57, No. 5 (2015): 498–521.

Atkinson, Michael M., and Kim Richard Nossal. "Bureaucratic Politics and the New Fighter Aircraft Decisions." *Canadian Public Administration* 24, No. 4 (1981): 531–562.

Black, David, and Claire Turenne Sjolander. "Multilateralism Re-constituted and the Discourse of Canadian Foreign Policy." *Studies in Political Economy* 49 (1996): 7–36.

Brekke, Harald. "Defining and Recognizing the Outer Limits of the Continental Shelf in the Polar Regions." In *Polar Geopolitics? Knowledge, Resources and Legal Regimes*, eds. Richard C. Powell and Klaus Dodds, 38–54. Cheltenham, UK: Edward Elgar, 2014.

Brekke, Harald, and Philip Symonds. "Submarine Ridges and Elevation of Article 76 in Light of Published Summaries of Recommendations of the Commission on the Limits of the Continental Shelf." *Ocean Development and International Law* 42, No. 4 (2011): 289–306.

Bugailiskis, Alex, and Andrés Rozental, eds. *Canada Among Nations,*

2011–2012: Canada and Mexico's Unfinished Agenda. Montreal: McGill-Queen's University Press, 2012.

Buzan, Barry G., and Danford W. Middlemiss. "Canadian Foreign Policy and the Exploitation of the Seabed." In *Canadian Foreign Policy and the Law of the Sea*, eds. Barbara Johnson and Mark W. Zacher, 1–51. Vancouver: University of British Columbia Press, 1977.

Byers, Michael. *Who Owns the Arctic? Understanding Sovereignty Disputes in the North.* Vancouver: Douglas and McIntyre, 2009.

Byers, Michael, and James S. Baker. "Crossed Lines: The Curious Case of the Beaufort Sea Maritime Boundary Dispute." *Ocean Development and International Law* 43, No. 1 (2012): 70–95.

Cavnar, Anna. "Accountability and the Commission on the Limits of the Continental Shelf: Deciding Who Owns the Ocean Floor." *Cornell International Law Journal* 42, No. 3 (2009): 387–440.

Chircop, Aldo. "International Royalty and Continental Shelf Limits: Emerging Issues for the Canadian Offshore." *Dalhousie Law Journal* 26 (2003): 273–302.

———. "Operationalizing Article 82 of the United Nations Convention on the Law Sea: A New Role for the International Sea Bed Authority?" *Ocean Yearbook* 18, No. 1 (2004): 395–412.

Cockburn, Sara, Sue Nichols, Dave Monahan, and Ted McDorman. "Intertwined Uncertainties: Policy and Technology on the Juridical Continental Shelf." Paper presented at the 2001 Advisory Board on the Law of the Sea (ABLOS) Conference: Accuracies and Uncertainties in Maritime Boundaries and Outer Limits, Monaco, October 2001.

Cohen, Andrew. *While Canada Slept: How We Lost Our Place in the World.* Toronto: McClelland and Stewart, 2003.

Committee on Responding to Oil Spills in the U.S. Arctic Marine Environment. *Responding to Oil Spills in the U.S. Arctic Marine Environment.* Washington, DC: National Academic Press, 2014.

Conley, Heather A. *Arctic Economics in the 21st Century: The Benefits and Costs of Cold.* New York: Center for Strategic and International Studies, 2013.

Cooper, Andrew F. *Canadian Foreign Policy: Old Habits and New Directions.* Scarborough, ON: Prentice Hall Canada, 1997.

————. "Looking Back to and Forward from Kim Richard Nossal's *The Politics of Canadian Foreign Policy*." *International Journal* 69, No. 2 (2014): 246–252.

Crees, T., C.D. Kaminski, and J. Ferguson. "UNCLOS Under-Ice Survey: A Historic AUV Deployment in the High Arctic." *Sea Technology* 51, No. 12 (2010): 39–44.

Desrosiers, Marie-Eve, and Philippe Lagassé. "Canada and the Bureaucratic Politics of State Fragility." *Diplomacy and Statecraft* 20, No. 4 (2009): 659–678.

Donaghy, Greg, and Neil Carter. "'There Are No Half-Countries': Canada, La Francophonie, and the Projection of Canadian Biculturalism, 1960–2002." In *Handbook of Canadian Foreign Policy*, eds. Patrick James, Nelson Michaud, and Marc J. O'Reilly, 133–164. Lanham, MD: Lexington Books, 2006.

Døssing, Arne, H.R. Jackson, J. Matzka, I .Einarsson, T.M. Rasmussen, A.V. Olesen, and J.M. Brozena. "On the Origin of the Amerasia Basin and the High Arctic Large Igneous Province — Results of New Aeromagnetic Data." *Earth and Planetary Science Letters* 363 (2013): 219–230.

Ebinger Charles K., and Evie Zambetakis, "The Geopolitics of Arctic Melt." *International Affairs* 85, No. 5 (2009): 1215–1232.

Elferink, Alex G. Oude, and Constance Johnson. "Outer Limits of the Continental Shelf and 'Disputed Areas': State Practice concerning Article 76(10) of the LOS Convention." *International Journal of Marine and Coastal Law* 21, No. 4 (2006): 461–487.

Frechette, Louise. "Canada at the United Nations: A Shadow of its Former Self." In *Canada Among Nations: 2009–2010: As Others See Us*, eds. Fen Osler Hampson and Paul Heinbecker, 265–274. Montreal and Kingston: McGill Queen's University Press, 2010.

Funck, Thomas, H. Ruth Jackson, and John Shimeld. "The Crustal Structure of the Alpha Ridge at the Transition to the Canadian Polar Margin: Results From a Seismic Refraction Experiment." *Journal of Geophysical Research* 116 (2011): 1–26.

Funck, Thomas, H. Ruth Jackson, Keith E. Louden, and Frauke Klingelhöfer. "Seismic Study of the Transform-Rifted Margin in Davis Strait Between Baffin Island (Canada) and Greenland: What Happens

When a Plume Meets a Transform." *Journal of Geophysical Research* 112 (2007): 1–26.

Gao, Grace Xingxin, Liang Heng, Todd Walter, and Per Enge. "Breaking the Ice: Navigation in the Arctic." In *Global Navigation Satellite Systems: Report of a Joint Workshop of the National Academy of Engineering and the Chinese Academy of Engineering*, eds. Lance A. Davis, Per Enge, and Grace Xingxin Gao, 229–238. Washington, DC: National Academic Press, 2012.

Gao, Jianjun. "The Seafloor High Issue in Article 76 of the LOS Convention: Some Views from the Perspective of Legal Interpretation," *Ocean Development and International Law*, 43, No. 2 (2012): 119–145.

Gardiner, Piers R.R. "The Limits of the Area Beyond National Jurisdiction — Some Problems with Particular Reference to the Role of the Commission on the Limits of the Continental Shelf." In *Maritime Boundaries and Ocean Resources,* ed. G. Blake, 63–76. London: Croom Helm, 1987.

Grant, Shelagh. *Polar Imperative: A History of Arctic Sovereignty In North America.* Vancouver: Douglas and McIntyre, 2010.

Griffiths, Franklyn, Rob Huebert, and P. Whitney Lackenbauer. *Canada and the Changing Arctic: Sovereignty, Security and Stewardship.* Waterloo, ON: Wilfrid Laurier University Press, 2011.

Heinbecker, Paul. *Getting Back in the Game: A Foreign Policy Playbook for Canada.* Toronto: Key Porter Books, 2010.

Hopper, J.R., T. Funck, C. Marcussen, H.R. Jackson, and J. Shimeld "Arctic Tectonic Puzzles: The Makarov Basin, Marvin Spur, and the Lomonosov Ridge." Paper presented to the Fall Meeting of the American Geophysical Union, San Francisco, California, December, 2009.

Hopper, Tristin. "A New Cold War: Denmark Gets Aggressive, Stakes Huge Claim in Race for the Arctic." *National Post*, December 15, 2014. http://news.nationalpost.com/news/a-new-cold-war-denmark-gets-aggressive-stakes-huge-claim-in-race-for-the-arctic.

Huebert, Rob. "Canada and the Law of the Sea Convention." *International Journal* 52, No. 1 (1996–1997): 69–88.

Hutchins, Peter W., Monique Caron, Biana Suciu, and Robin Campbell. *Setting Out Canada's Obligations to Inuit in Respect of the Extended Continental Shelf in the Arctic Ocean.* Montreal: paper commissioned by Senator Charlie Watt, 2015.

Hutchinson, D.R., H.R. Jackson, J.W. Shimeld, C.B. Chapman, J.R. Childs, T. Funck, and R.W. Rowland. "Acquiring Marine Data in the Canada Basin, Arctic Ocean." *EOS* 90, No. 23 (2009): 197–204.

Ignatieff, Michael. "Canada in the Age of Terror: Multilateralism Meets a Moment of Truth." *Policy Options*, February 2003, 14–18.

International Boundaries Research Unit, Centre for Borders Research, Durham University. "Maritime Jurisdiction and Boundaries in the Arctic Region." Research. 2015.

Jackson, H. Ruth, and Trine Dahl-Jensen. "Sedimentary and Crustal Structure from the Ellesmere Island and Greenland Continental Shelves onto the Lomonosov Ridge, Arctic Ocean." *Geophysical Journal International* 182, No. 1 (2010): 11–35.

Jares, Vladimir. "The Continental Shelf Beyond 200 Nautical Miles: The Work of the Commission on the Limits of the Continental Shelf and the Arctic." *Vanderbilt Journal of Transnational Law* 42, No. 4 (2009): 1265–1306.

———. "Mounting Tension and Melting Ice: Exploring the Legal and Political Future of the Arctic: The Continental Shelf Beyond 200 Nautical Miles: The Work of the Commission on the Limits of the Continental Shelf and the Arctic." *Vanderbilt Journal of Transnational Law* 42, No. 4 (2009): 1265–1306.

Jensen, Oystein. "The Commission on the Limits of the Continental Shelf: An Administrative, Scientific, or Judicial Institution?" *Ocean Development and International Law* 45, No. 2 (2014): 171–185.

Jewett, M.L. "The Evolution of the Legal Regime of the Continental Shelf, Part I," *Canadian Yearbook of International Law* 22 (1984): 153–193.

———. "The Evolution of the Legal Regime of the Continental Shelf, Part II." *Canadian Yearbook of International Law* 23 (1985): 201–225.

Johnson, Barbara, and Mark W. Zacher. *Canadian Foreign Policy and the Law of the Sea.* Vancouver: University of British Columbia Press, 1977.

Keating, Tom. *Canada and World Order: The Multilateralist Tradition in Canadian Foreign Policy.* Second Edition. Don Mills, ON: Oxford University Press, 2002.

———. "Multilateralism Reconsidered." In *Readings in Canadian Foreign Policy: Classic Debates and New Ideas,* eds. Duane Bratt and Christopher J. Kukucha, 44–51. Don Mills, ON: Oxford University Press, 2011.

Kim, Hyun Jung. "Success in Heading North?: South Korea's Master Plan for Arctic Policy." *Marine Policy* 61 (2015): 264–272.

Kinsman, Jeremy. "A Betrayal of Canada's Multilateral Tradition." *National Post*, January 17, 2014.

Klare, Michael. *Resource Wars: The New Landscape of Global Conflict.* New York: Henry Holt, 2002.

Lodge, Michael W. "The International Seabed Authority and Article 82 of the UN Convention on the Law of the Sea." *International Journal of Marine and Coastal Law* 21 (2006): 323–333.

Logan, R. *Canada, the United States, and the Third Law of the Sea Conference.* Washington: Canadian-American Committee, 1974.

MacDonald, Douglas, and Heather A. Smith. "Promises Made, Promises Broken: Questioning Canada's Commitments to Climate Change." *International Journal* 55, No. 1 (1999–2000): 107–124.

MacDougall, J. Richard, Wendell Sanford, and Jacob Verhoef. "Ice and No Ice: The Canadian UNCLOS Batymetric Mapping Program." Paper presented to the Canadian Hydrographic Conference and National Surveyors Conference, Canada, 2008.

MacDougall, J. Richard, Jacob Verhoef, Wendell Sanford, and Christian Marcussen. "Challenges of Collecting Data for Article 76 in Ice-Covered Waters of the Arctic." Paper presented to the Advisory Board on the Law of the Sea, Monaco, 2008. http://a76.dk/greenland_uk/north_uk/index.html.

MacGuigan, Mark. "Beyond the Law of the Sea Conference: An Address by the Honourable Mark MacGuigan, Secretary of State for External Affairs, to the Ninth Annual Conference of the Canadian Council on International Law, Ottawa, 24 October 1980." *Statements and Speeches* 80, No. 24 (1980).

Macnab, Ron. "The Case for Transparency in the Delimitation of the Outer Continental Shelf in Accordance with UNCLOS Article 76." *Ocean Development and International Law* 35, No. 1 (2004): 1–17.

———. "Submarine Elevations and Ridges: Wild Cards in the Poker Game of UNCLOS Article 76." *Ocean Development and International Law* 39, No. 22 (2008): 223–234.

Magnusson, Bjarni Már. *The Continental Shelf Beyond 200 Nautical Miles: Delineation, Delimitation and Dispute Settlement.* Leiden: Brill Nijhoff, 2015.

Massie, Justin and Stéphane Roussel. "The Twilight of Internationalism? Neocontinentalism as an Emerging Dominant Idea in Canadian Foreign Policy." In *Canada in the World: Internationalism in Canadian Foreign Policy,* eds. Heather A. Smith and Claire Turenne Sjolander, 36–52. Don Mills, ON: Oxford University Press, 2013.

Martin, Lawrence. *Harperland: The Politics of Control.* Toronto: Viking, 2010.

Matzka, Jurgen, Thorkild M. Rasmussen, Arne V. Olesen, Jens Emil Nielsen, Rene Forsberg, Nils Olsen, John Halpenny, and Jacob Verhoef. "A New Aeromagnetic Survey of the North Pole and the Arctic Ocean North of Greenland and Ellesmere Island." *Earth Planets Space* 62 (2010): 829–832.

McDorman, Ted L. "Canada Ratifies the 1982 United Nations Convention on the Law of the Sea: At Last." *Ocean Development and International Law* 35, No. 2 (2004): 103–114.

———. "Canadian Offshore Oil and Gas: Jurisdiction and Management Issues in the 1980s and Beyond." In *Canadian Oceans Policy: National Strategies and the New Law of the Sea*, eds. Donald McRae and Gordon Munro, 39–68. Vancouver: University of British Columbia Press, 1989.

———. "The Continental Shelf." In *The Oxford Handbook of the Law of the Sea,* eds. Donald R. Rothwell, Alex G. Oude Elferink, Karen N. Scott, and Tim Stephens, 181–202. Oxford: Oxford University Press, 2015.

———. "The Continental Shelf Beyond 200 NM: Law and Politics in the Arctic Ocean." *Journal of Transnational Law and Policy* 18, No. 2 (2009): 155–193.

———. "The Role of the Commission on the Limits of the Continental Shelf: A Technical Body in a Political World." *International Journal of Marine and Coastal Law* 17, No. 301 (2002): 301–324.

———. *Salt Water Neighbors: International Ocean Law Relations Between the United States and Canada.* New York: Oxford University Press, 2009.

McQuaig, Linda. *Holding the Bully's Coat: Canada and the U.S. Empire.* Toronto: Doubleday, 2007.

Medhora, Rohinton, and Dane Rowlands, eds. *Canada Among Nations: 2014: Crisis and Reform: Canada and the International Financial System.* Waterloo, ON: Centre for International Governance Innovation, Norman Paterson School of International Affairs, 2014.

Molot, Maureen Appel, and Norman Hillmer. "The Diplomacy of Decline."
In *Canada Among Nations 2002: A Fading Power,* eds. Maureen Appel
Molot and Norman Hillmer, 1–33. Don Mills, ON: Oxford, 2002.

Mosher, D.C., C.B. Chapman, J. Shimeld, H.R. Jackson, D. Chian, J.
Verhoef, D. Hutchinson, N. Lebedeva-Ivanova, and R. Pederson.
"High Arctic Marine Geophysical Data Acquisition." *Leading Edge* 32,
No. 5 (2013): 524–536.

Mosher D.C., R.C. Courtney, M. Jakobsson, C. Gebhardt, and L. Mayer.
"Mapping the Surficial Geology of the Arctic Ocean: A Layer for
the IBCAO." Paper resented to the Arctic Technology Conference,
Copenhagen, Denmark, March 23–25, 2015.

Mosher, D.C., J.W. Shimeld, and D.R. Hutchinson. *2009 Canada Basin
Seismic Reflection and Refraction Survey, Western Arctic Ocean: CCGS
Louis S. St-Laurent Expedition Report.* Ottawa: Geological Survey of
Canada, Open File 6343, 2009.

Mosher, D.C., J. Shimeld, D. Hutchinson, D. Chian, N. Lebedeva-Ivanova,
and R. Jackson. "Canada Basin Revealed." Paper presented to the
Arctic Technology Conference, Houston, Texas, December 3–5, 2012.

Mosher, D.C., J. Shimeld, D. Hutchinson, N. Lebedeva-Ivanova, and
C.B. Chapman. "Submarine Landslides in Arctic Sedimentation:
Canada Basin" In *Advances in Natural and Technological Hazards
Research* 31 eds. Y. Yamada, K. Kawamura, K. Ikehara, Y. Ogawa,
R. Urgeles, D. Mosher, J. Chaytor, and M. Strasser, 147–157. Berlin:
Springer, 2012.

Mosher, D.C., J. Verhoef; P. Travaglini, and R. Pederson. "A Deep Water,
Under-Ice AUV: Extended Continental Shelf Mapping in the Arctic."
Paper presented to the Arctic Technology Conference, Copenhagen,
Denmark, March 23–25, 2015.

Nordquist, Myron H., John Norton Moore, and Thomas H. Heidar,
eds. *Legal and Scientific Aspects of Continental Shelf Limits.* Leiden:
Martinus Nijhoff, 2004.

Nossal, Kim Richard. "Allison Through the (Ottawa) Looking Glass:
Bureaucratic Politics and Foreign Policy in a Parliamentary System."
Canadian Public Administration 22 (1979): 610–626.

———. "Bureaucratic Politics and the Westminster Model." In
International Conflict and Conflict Management: Readings in World

Politics, eds. Robert O. Matthews, Arthur G. Rubinoff, and Janice Gross Stein, 120–127. Scarborough, ON: Prentice Hall Canada, 1984.

———. "The Liberal Past in the Conservative Present: Internationalism in the Harper Era." In *Canada In The World: Internationalism in Canadian Foreign Policy,* eds. Heather A. Smith and Claire Turenne Sjolander, 21–35. Don Mills, ON: Oxford University Press, 2013.

———. "Old Habits and New Directions Indeed." *International Journal* 69, No. 2 (2014): 254–255.

———. *The Politics of Canadian Foreign Policy.* Third edition. Scarborough, ON: Prentice Hall Canada, 1997.

———. "Pinchpenny Diplomacy: The Decline of 'Good International Citizenship' in Canadian Foreign Policy." *International Journal* 54, No. 1 (1998/1999): 88–105.

Nossal, Kim Richard, Stéphane Roussel, and Stéphane Paquin. *International Policy and Politics in Canada.* Toronto: Pearson, 2011.

O'Connell, D.P. *The International Law of the Sea.* Oxford: Oxford University Press, 1982.

Oakey, G.N., R.W. Saltus, and J.W. Shimeld. "A Crustal Structure Model of the Beaufort-Mackenzie Margin, Southern Canada Basin." Paper presented to the Arctic Technology Conference, Copenhagen, Denmark, March 23–25, 2015.

Paris, Roland. "Are Canadians Still Liberal Internationalists? Foreign Policy and Public Opinion in the Harper Era." *International Journal* 69, No. 3 (2014): 274–307.

Paskal, Cleo, and Michael Lodge. *A Fair Deal on Seabed Wealth: The Promise and Pitfalls of Article 82 on the Outer Continental Shelf.* London: Royal Institute of International Affairs, 2009.

Poselov, V.A., V. Butsenko, A. Chernykh, V. Glebovsky, H.R. Jackson, D.P. Potter, G. Oakey, J. Shimeld; and C. Marcussen. "The Structural Integrity of the Lomonosov Ridge with the North American and Siberian Continental Margins." Paper presented to the International Conference on Arctic Margins VI, Fairbanks, Alaska, May 2011.

Pratt, Cranford. "Competing Perspectives on Canadian Development Assistance Policies." *International Journal* 5, No. 2 (1996): 235–258.

Professional Institute of the Public Service of Canada. *The Big Chill: Silencing Public Interest Science, A Survey.* Ottawa: Professional Institute of the Public Service of Canada, 2013.

Riddell-Dixon, Elizabeth. *Arctic Research Program of the Canada-U.S. Institute.* London, ON: Canada and United States Institute, Western University, 2010.

———. "Canada and Arctic Politics: The Continental Shelf Delimitation." *Ocean Development and International Law* 39, No. 4 (2008): 343–359.

———. *Canada and the International Seabed: Domestic Determinants and External Constraints.* Montreal: McGill-Queen's University Press, 1989.

———. "Canada at the Preparatory Commission: Policies and Challenges." In *Canadian Oceans Policy: National Strategies and the New Law of the Sea,* eds. Donald McRae and Gordon Munro, 69–91. Vancouver: University of British Columbia Press, 1989.

———. "Canada's Arctic Continental Shelf Extension: Debunking Myths." *Policy Options* 29, No. 8 (2008): 39–43.

———. *Canada's Arctic Policy.* London, ON: Canada and United States Institute, Western University, 2012.

———. "Canadian Foreign Policy and the United Nations Third Conference on the Law of the Sea." In *Mackenzie King to Philosopher King: Canadian Foreign Policy in the Modern Age,* edited by O.P. St. John, 173–180. Winnipeg: University of Manitoba Press, 1984.

———. "Deep Seabed Mining: A Hotbed for Governmental Politics?" *International Journal* 41, No. 1 (1985/1986): 72–94.

———. "Individual Leadership and Structural Power." *Canadian Journal of Political Science* 30, No. 2 (1997): 257–283.

———. "Meeting the Deadline: Canada's Arctic Submission to the Commission on the Limits of the Continental Shelf." *Ocean Development and International Law* 42, No. 4 (2011): 368–382.

———. *Multilateral Code to Govern Arctic Offshore Resource Development.* Toronto: Bill Graham Centre for Contemporary International History, Trinity College, University of Toronto, 2014.

———. "Neither Conflict nor 'Use It or Lose It': Delineating Extended Continental Shelves in the Arctic." In *Cold Calculations: The Politics of Arctic Development,* September 19, 2013. www.opencanada.org/features/neither-conflict-nor-use-it-or-lose-it.

———. "Not for the Faint-Hearted: Mapping Canada's Arctic Continental Shelf Beyond 200 Nautical Miles." *Policy Options* 30, No. 4 (2009): 60–64.

———. "The Preparatory Commission on the International Seabed Authority: New Realism?" *International Journal of Estuarine and Coastal Law* 7, No. 3 (1992): 195–216.

———. "Seismic Testing in Lancaster Sound: Lessons Learned." *Policy Options* 32, No. 9 (2011): 72–75.

———. "The Seven Decade Quest to Maximize Canada's Continental Shelf." *International Journal* 69, No. 3 (2014): 422–443.

———. "State Autonomy and Canadian Foreign Policy: The Case of Deep Seabed Mining." *Canadian Journal of Political Science* 21, No. 2 (1988): 297–317.

———. "To Sign or Not to Sign the Law of the Sea Convention: Governmental Politics in the United Kingdom and Canada." *Journal of Commonwealth and Comparative Politics* 29, No. 2 (1991): 212–233.

———. "Winners and Losers: Formulating Canada's Policies on International Technology Transfers." *International Journal* 47, No. 1 (1991/1992), 159–183.

Rioux, Jean-Francois, and Robin Hay. "Canadian Foreign Policy: From Internationalism to Isolationism?" *International Journal* 54, No. 1 (1998/1999): 57–75.

Sale, Richard, and Eugene Potapov. *The Scramble for the Arctic: Ownership, Exploitation and Conflict in the Far North.* London: Frances Lincoln, 2010.

Sanger, Clyde. *Ordering the Oceans: The Making of the Law of the Sea.* Toronto: University of Toronto Press, 1987.

Schofield; Clive, and Robert van de Poll. "Exploring the Outer Continental Shelf: Working Paper." Paper prepared for the International Workshop on Further Consideration of the Implementation of Article 82 of the United Nations Convention on the Law of the Sea, Beijing, China, November 2012.

Shimeld, J., R. Jackson, K. DesRoches, and J. Verhoef. "2007 Deep-Water Marine Seismic Acquisition to Define the Canadian Extended Continental Shelf Under Article 76 of the United Nations Convention on the Law of the Sea." Atlantic Geoscience Society Abstracts: 2008 Colloquium & Annual General Meeting. *Atlantic Geology* 44 (2008): 40.

Smith, Heather A., and Claire Turenne Sjolander. *Canada in the World: Internationalism in Canadian Foreign Policy.* Don Mills, ON: Oxford University Press, 2013.

Spicer, Wylie. "Canada, the Law of the Sea and International Payments: Where Will The Money Come From?" *SPP Research Papers* 8, No. 31 (2015): 1–24.

Suarez, Suzette V. "The Commission on the Limits of the Continental Shelf and its Function to Provide Scientific and Technical Advice." *Chinese Journal of International Law* 12, No. 2 (2013): 339–362.

———. *The Outer Limits of the Continental Shelf: Legal Aspects of their Establishment.* Berlin: Springer-Verlag, 2008.

Subedi, Surya P. "Problems and Prospects for the Commission on the Limits of the Continental Shelf in Dealing with Submissions by Coastal States in Relation to the Ocean Territory Beyond 200 Nautical Miles." *International Journal of Marine and Coastal Law* 26, No. 13 (2011): 413–431.

Tan, Wei-en, and Yu-tai Tsai. "After the Ice Melts: Conflict Resolution and the International Scramble for Natural Resources in the Arctic Circle." *Journal of Politics and Law* 2, No. 1 (2010): 91–99.

Tessensohn, Franz, Ruth H. Jackson, and Ian D. Reid. "The Tectonic Evolution of Nares Strait: Implications of New Data." *Polarforschung* 74, No. 1–3 (2006): 191–198.

Tomlin, Brian W. "On a Fast Track to the Ban: The Canadian Policy Process." *Canadian Foreign Policy* 5, No. 3 (1998): 3–23.

Treadwell, Mead. "Witnessing an Arctic Renaissance." In *The Fast-Changing Arctic: Rethinking Arctic Security for a Warmer World*, ed. Barry Scott Zellen, ix–xi. Calgary: University of Calgary Press, 2013.

Turner, Chris. *The War on Science: Muzzled Scientists and Wilful Blindness in Stephen Harper's Canada.* Vancouver: Greystone Books, 2013.

Verhoef, Jacob, and Julian Goodyear. "Defining Canada's Extended Continental Shelf in the Arctic." *Meridian*, Spring/Summer 2011, 1–8.

Verhoef, Jacob, and Dick MacDougall. "Delineating Canada's Continental Shelf According to the United Nations Convention on the Law of the Sea." *Ocean Sovereignty* 3, No. 1 (2008): 1–6.

Verhoef, Jacob, David C. Mosher, and Stephen R. Forbes. "Defining Canada's Extended Continental Shelves." In *Voyage of Discovery: Fifty*

Years of Marine Research at Canada's Bedford Institute of Oceanography, eds. David N. Nettleship, Donald C. Gordon, C.F. Michael Lewis, and Michel P. Latremouille, 407–414. Dartmouth: Bedford Institute of Oceanography, 2014.

———. "Defining Canada's Extended Continental Shelves." *Geoscience Canada* 38, No. 2 (2011): 85–96.

Verrall, Ronald. *A Guide to Arctic Field Trips.* 2001. www. arcticnewsletters.com/Field_guide/Guide.pdf.

Wang, Wentao, and Yanhua Liu. "Geopolitics of Global Climate Change and Energy Security." *Chinese Journal of Population Resources and Environment* 13, No. 2 (2015): 119–126.

Welsh, Jennifer M. "Reality and Canadian Foreign Policy." In *Canada Among Nations 2005: Split Images,* eds. Andrew F. Cooper and Dane Rowlands, 23–46. Montreal: McGill-Queen's University Press, 2005.

BLOGS AND UNOFFICIAL NEWSLETTERS FROM THE FIELD

Informal blogs and newsletters, written by government employees to keep their family, friends, and other interested people apprised of developments and events occurring during the surveys, may be accessed at the following sites:

www.arcticnewsletters.com

http://a76.dk/greenland_uk/north_uk/gr_n_expeditions_uk/index.html

INDEX